Rethinking Securities in an Emergent Technoscientific New World Order:
Retracing the Contours for Africa's Hi-jacked Futures

Edited by

Munyaradzi Mawere & Artwell Nhemachena

Langaa Research & Publishing CIG
Mankon, Bamenda

Publisher:
Langaa RPCIG
Langaa Research & Publishing Common Initiative Group
P.O. Box 902 Mankon
Bamenda
North West Region
Cameroon
Langaagrp@gmail.com
www.langaa-rpcig.net

Distributed in and outside N. America by African Books Collective
orders@africanbookscollective.com
www.africanbookscollective.com

ISBN-10: 9956-764-11-6

ISBN-13: 978-9956-764-11-2

© Munyaradzi Mawere & Artwell Nhemachena 2018

List of Contributors

Munyaradzi Mawere is a Professor in the Simon Muzenda School of Arts, Culture and Heritage Studies at Great Zimbabwe University in Zimbabwe. He holds a PhD in Social Anthropology, three Masters Degrees – Social Anthropology, Development Studies, and Philosophy – and a BA (Hons) Degree in Philosophy. Before joining this university, Professor Mawere was a lecturer at the University of Zimbabwe and at Universidade Pedagogica, Mozambique, where he has also worked in different capacities as a senior lecturer, assistant research director, postgraduate co-ordinator, and professor. He is an author of more than 50 books and over 200 academic publications with a focus on Africa straddling the following areas: poverty and development, African philosophy, society and culture, democracy, politics of food production, humanitarianism and civil society organisations, urban anthropology, existential anthropology, cultural philosophy, environmental anthropology, society and politics, decoloniality and African studies. Some of his bestselling books are: *Humans, Other Beings and the Environment: Harurwa (Edible stinkbugs) and Environmental Conservation in South-eastern Zimbabwe* (2015); *Theory, Knowledge, Development and Politics: What Role for the Academy in the Sustainability of Africa?* (2016); *Democracy, Good Governance and Development in Africa: A Search for Sustainable Democracy and Development,* (2015); *Culture, Indigenous Knowledge and Development in Africa: Reviving Interconnections for Sustainable Development* (2014); *Myths of Peace and Democracy? Towards Building Pillars of Hope, Unity and Transformation in Africa* (2016); *Harnessing Cultural Capital for Sustainability: A Pan Africanist Perspective* (2015); *Divining the Future of Africa: Healing the Wounds, Restoring Dignity and Fostering Development,* (2014); *African Cultures, Memory and Space: Living the Past Presence in Zimbabwean Heritage* (2014); *Violence, Politics and Conflict Management in Africa: Envisioning Transformation, Peace and Unity in the Twenty-First Century* (2016); *African Philosophy and Thought Systems: A Search for a Culture and Philosophy of Belonging* (2016); *Africa at the Crossroads: Theorising Fundamentalisms in the 21st Century* (2017); *Colonial Heritage, Memory and Sustainability in Africa: Challenges, Opportunities and Prospects* (2016); *Underdevelopment, Development and the Future of Africa* (2017), and *Theorising Development in*

Africa: Towards Building an African Framework of Development (2017); *African Studies in the Academy: The Cornucopia of Theory, Praxis and Transformation in Africa?* (2017); *GMOs, Consumerism and the Global Politics of Biotechnology: Rethinking Food, Bodies and Identities in Africa's 21ˢᵗ Century* (2017); and *Human Trafficking and Trauma in the Digital Era: The Ongoing Tragedy of the Trade in Refugees from Eritrea* (2017).

Artwell Nhemachena holds a PhD in Social Anthropology; MSc in Sociology and Social Anthropology; BSc Honours Degree in Sociology and a Certificate in Law. He lectures in Sociology at the University of Namibia. His current areas of research interest are Knowledge Studies; Development Studies; Environment; Resilience; Food Security and Food Sovereignty; Industrial Sociology; Conflict and Peace; Transformation; Science and Technology Studies, Democracy and Governance; Relational Ontologies; Decoloniality and Anthropological Jurisprudence. He has published in the areas of social theory, research methods, democracy and governance; conflict and peace; relational ontologies; industrial sociology; development; science and technology studies; anthropological jurisprudence, environment, mining, biotechnology and knowledge studies; transformation and decoloniality.

Raymond Ogunade holds a PhD in Religious Studies. He is a Fulbright Fellow and Study of the United States Institute (SUSI), on Religious Pluralism and Public Presence, University of California, Santa Barbara, USA, 2011; a fellow of Association of Commonwealth Universities on Spirituality and Social work, Swansea University, Swansea, Wales, 2010-2011. He is an Award Winner; Science and Religion Course Program, Center for Theology and the Natural Sciences; and John Templeton Foundation, Berkeley, California, USA, 2001. He teaches Comparative Religious Studies and the Interface between Religion and Science at the University of Ilorin, Ilorin, Nigeria. He has two books and several publications to his credit locally and internationally. He plays chess and he is the university of Ilorin Chess coach. He is the University of Ilorin and the Kwara State Chess Coach in Nigeria. He has just been appointed on the Board of the Nigerian Chess Federation.

Fidelis Peter Thomas Duri is a Senior Lecturer of History in the Department of Archaeology, Culture and Heritage, History and Development Studies at Great Zimbabwe University. He is a holder of a PhD in History from the University of the Witwatersrand in Johannesburg, South Africa. He has published a number of books and articles which focus on environmental history, socio-cultural dynamics, subaltern struggles, African border studies, and Zimbabwe's socio-political landscape during the colonial and post-colonial periods. In addition to reviewing a number of scholarly articles, he has also edited books such as *Resilience Amid Adversity: Informal Coping Mechanisms to the Zimbabwean Crisis during the New Millennium* (2016) and *Contested Spaces, Restrictive Mechanisms and Corridors of Opportunity: A Social History of Zimbabwean Borderlands and Beyond since the Colonial Period* (2017). He is also a member of the editorial boards of international journals which include the *Zimbabwe Journal of Historical Studies* and the *International Journal of Developing Societies*. He is also a renowned political analyst for various Zimbabwean newspapers such as *The Mirror* and *TellZim*.

Last Alfandika is a Lecturer at Great Zimbabwe University in Media and Cultural Studies. He is currently doing a PhD in Media Studies with the University of Witwatersrand in South Africa.

Misheck P. Chingozha holds BMgt (HR), MBA, MSc. in Peace Leadership and Conflict Resolution from the Zimbabwe Open University, a MSc. in Development Studies from the Women's University in Africa (WUA). Mr Chingozha is also a holder of a Diploma in Adult Education from the University of Zimbabwe, Diploma in Business Studies (FBS), a National Diploma in Electrical Power Engineering, Certificate in Electrical Engineering (HEXCO), Certificate in Accountancy (ZAAT), and Skilled Worker Class One (manpower). Chingozha is also an incumbent part-time Lecturer in the Faculties of Commerce and Law, and Applied Social Sciences at the Zimbabwe Open University. Besides, Chingozha is an incumbent Senior Officer at the Rank of Chief Superintendent in the Police Force. Chingozha has written and published a Shona novel and co-authored 4 modules for the Zimbabwe Open University. His research interests lie in the areas of development, policing, gender, leadership, indigenous knowledge systems, and environmentally related issues.

Nancy Mazuru is a lecturer in the Department of History, Archaeology and Development studies at Great Zimbabwe University. She holds a Master of Science degree in Development Studies from Women's University in Africa. Currently, she is a Development studies PhD candidate at University of the Witwatersrand, Johannesburg.

Zaccheaus Gbenga holds a Masters degree in Comparative Religious Studies from the University of Ilorin, Ilorin, Nigeria. Being awarded as a "University Scholar", he graduated top of his first degree and postgraduate classes respectively. His research interests include; Christian ethics, Yoruba Religion and the interface between Science and Religion in the contemporary society. He is a co-author of the fast-spreading and award potential book *"Biblical Eschatology and American Biometrics: Obama's RFID vs the Mark of the Beast 666"* (Raymond Ogunade PhD and Gbenga Zaccheaus 2016). He has few publications to his credit locally and internationally.

Gift Gwindingwe is a part-time lecturer at Great Zimbabwe University in Media and Cultural Studies. He is currently studying for his PhD in Communication studies with Fort Hare University in South Africa.

Tom Tom is a Doctoral Research Fellow at the South African Research Chair Initiative- Chair in Social Policy, College of Graduate Studies at the University of South Africa (UNISA). He is also a Senior Lecturer in the Department of Development Studies, Faculty of Applied Social Sciences at the Zimbabwe Open University (ZOU). He holds a Bachelor of Science Honours in Sociology and Master of Science in Sociology and Social Anthropology, both attained at the University of Zimbabwe. His research, publication and teaching focuses on sociology, social policy, development and gender. He has also done several consultancies in these critical areas. His works have been published in various journals and books. The thrust of his work is to enhance wellbeing.

Edmore Dube holds a PhD in Christian-Muslim Dialogue (2003) from the University of Zimbabwe. His Masters of Arts (UZ 1995) was biased towards Islamic Studies, while his Honours dissertation (1993) was on the Remba of Mposi in Mberengwa. He has grappled with the Remba discourse since 1993, and has published three articles on the subject. He has published an equal number on Islam in Africa and continues to research in that area. His interest on justice and peace as pillars of dialogue has seen him working keenly on the Catholic Commission for Justice and Peace (CCJP) and the Zimbabwe Catholic Bishops' Conference (ZCBC) pastoral letters. He has made one publication in that area and two are still pending. He has also published one article on the injustices of 'Land Tenure in Zimbabwe' in a volume edited Munyaradzi Mawere and Tapuwa Raymond Mubaya, who have been very inspirational to upcoming scholars. He is currently lecturing in Biblical and Islamic Studies at Great Zimbabwe University.

ORJI Boniface Ifeanyi is a lecturer in the Department of History and Diplomatic Studies, Crown Hill University, Eiyenkorin, Ilorin, Kwara State Nigeria. He has BA and MA History from the University of Ilorin, and he is currently a PhD candidate at the same University of Ilorin, Kwara State. His areas of interest include History, Migration and Diaspora Studies, Gender Studies, Economic and Social History; Peace and Conflict Studies.

Tapuwa Raymond Mubaya is a Lecturer at Great Zimbabwe University's Simon Muzenda School of Arts, Culture and Heritage Studies and a PhD candidate at Tilburg University, Netherlands. He holds a Master of Arts Degree in Heritage Studies and a Bachelor of Arts Honours Degree in Philosophy both from the University of Zimbabwe. He is currently studying for a Post Graduate Diploma in Higher and Tertiary Education with the Great Zimbabwe University. Mr. Mubaya co-edited and co-authored five books and over 40 publications comprising book chapters and journal articles in internationally renowned journals and publishing houses. Besides, Mr. Mubaya played a pivotal role in co-authoring more than 25 books straddling various subjects and fields such as Heritage Studies, Guidance and Counselling and Visual and Performing Arts for the approved new primary and secondary curriculum. Before joining the Great Zimbabwe University, Mr. Mubaya worked for the National Museums and Monuments of Zimbabwe (NMMZ) for more than eight years as both the Curator in charge and the head of the Great Zimbabwe Monuments Conservation Department.

Prosper Hellen Tlou received her Master of Arts with Bachelor of Arts Honours at the University of Venda (UNIVEN), Bachelor Of Arts Degree at Great Zimbabwe University and is teaching Tshivenda language at Great Zimbabwe University. She currently serves as a Tshivenda coordinator in the department of African languages and literature. Her research interest focuses on linguistics, onomastic and Sociolinguistics.

Aleck Mapindani obtained both his Master of Arts (2014) and Bachelor of Arts Honours (2012) Degrees from the University of Venda. He also holds a Bachelor of Arts General degree from the Great Zimbabwe University (2011). In 2011, he joined the Department of African Languages and Literature as a Teaching Assistant at the Great Zimbabwe University. Currently, he is employed by the Great Zimbabwe University as a Xitsonga (Shangaan) lecturer. He is also coordinating the Xitsonga Section in same Department, under the Simon Muzenda School of Arts, Culture and Heritage Studies. He is interested in onomastic studies, sociolinguistics and literature.

Alice Makama is a Zimbabwean woman living with albinism. She is an undergraduate student at Great Zimbabwe University where she is studying for a Bachelor of Arts Honours Degree in History. As an upcoming historian, she has a passion for research on issues pertaining to disadvantaged sections of the population with particular focus on human rights, uneven development and subaltern livelihood dynamics in Zimbabwe since the pre-colonial period.

Clement Chipenda is a Doctoral Research Fellow at the South African Research Chair Initiative - Chair in Social Policy, College of Graduate Studies at the University of South Africa (UNISA). He holds a Master of Science in Development Studies and Bachelor of

Science Honours in Sociology, attained at the National University of Science and Technology (NUST) and University of Zimbabwe (UZ) respectively. Having worked for the Government of Zimbabwe and several NGOs, he has accumulated wide hands-on community practice and experience in research and publication in social policy, human rights and development. He is widely published in journals and books in pursuit of empirically-informed development practice.

Dolphin Mabale obtained her Master of Arts degree in Anthropology at the University of Venda. She also graduated with the Postgraduate Diploma in Arts specialising in Heritage Studies from the University of the Witwatersrand. Her specialist areas are Anthropology and Heritage Studies, with focal areas in Public Culture, Politics of Identity, and Sacred Landscape Heritage and Memory. Ms. Mabale is currently employed by her alma mater the University of Venda as a lecturer in Anthropology, Applied Anthropology, Archaeology, and African Studies at the E'skia Mphahlele Centre for African Studies since 2008. As an emerging researcher, Ms Mabale has presented papers at conferences, and has recently co-published a chapter with Dr Artwell Nhemachena titled "Conjugating Materialities and Symbols in Contemporary Africa? The Case of the Statue of King Nghunghunyani, South Africa" in Decolonisation of Materialities or Materialisation of (Re-)Colonisation? *Symbolisms, Languages, Ecocriticism and (Non) Representationalism in 21st Century Africa*", a volume that Dr Nhemachena co-edited in 2017.

Costain Tandi is a Graduate teacher for Advanced level History and Sociology as well as Head of Department (Humanities) at Rufaro High School in Chatsworth, Zimbabwe. He holds a Master of Arts Degree in Development Studies from Midlands State University; Bachelor of Arts 4th year Honours Degree in History from Great Zimbabwe University; Bachelor of Arts General Degree from the University of Zimbabwe; Graduate Certificate in Education from Great Zimbabwe University; An Executive Certificate in Project and Program Monitoring and Evaluation from the University of Zimbabwe; and An Executive Certificate in Project Management from the University of Zimbabwe. Tandi has six publications and his research interests include but not limited to Indigenous Knowledge Systems, Climate Change and Variability, Rural Poverty, Agriculture and Community Development.

Aluko Opeyemi Idowu is a lecturer in the Department of Political Science University of Ilorin. He is currently on his PhD Studies in Kwara State University Malete Kwara State Nigeria. His research interests include Comparative Politics; Urban Violence, Judicial Studies, Political Economy, Security Management, Democracy and Election, Police and Informal Security provisions. He has published a number of works on his research interest area and other areas.

Golden Maunganidze holds a Master of Arts Degree in Media and Society Studies from the Midlands State University (MSU) and several midcareer journalism courses from Germany. He is Edward R. Murrow fellow (2011) as well as 2016 Mandela Washington fellow and has won several awards in the past, which include The child reporter of the year from National Journalistic and Media Awards (NJAMA) in 2009 and National Integrity Award from Transparency International Zimbabwe (TIZ). He has over ten years' experience working in the Zimbabwean media industry. He currently lectures in the Department of English and Media Studies at Great Zimbabwe University (GZU), where he teaches practical journalism courses. Before joining GZU, Maunganidze worked as a journalist and editor for various community newspapers in Masvingo, Zimbabwe. He is currently pursuing his PhD with Tilburg University in the Netherlands.

Table of Contents

Chapter 1

The Development of (Neo-)Imperial Sacrifice, Global Atavism and African Insecurities: An Introduction

Artwell Nhemachena & Munyaradzi Mawere

The enormity of civilian population dislocation during armed conflicts, and the importance – yet difficulty – of reattaching people to lands and properties subsequent to conflict, presents large challenges for peacebuilding and recovery. Land and property restitution significantly influences the prospects for social, economic, livelihood, security and political recovery (Unruh, 2014: 111).

For many colonized peoples…decolonization is defined by the urgency of land struggle and by the restoration of traditional territories now separated by state borders…The mental, spiritual and emotional toll that colonization still exacts is neither fictive nor less important than the material; but without grounding land, water, and air as central, decolonization is a shell game. We cannot decolonize without recognizing the primacy of land and indigenous sovereignty over that land (Sium et al, 2012: 5).

No brutality, mistreatment, or torture has ever forced me to ask for grace, for I prefer to die with my head high, my faith steadfast, and my confidence profound in the destiny of my country, rather than to live in submission and scorn of sacred principles […] Do not weep for me my dear companion. I know that my country which suffers so much, will know how to defend its independence and its liberty. Long live the Congo! Long live Africa! (Patrice Lumumba 1961).

Introduction

In a world within which the global security of transnational capital is given more eminence than that of the security of [African] states and peoples of the global south, the states and peoples of the global south consequently become sacrificial lambs to create space for the

1

metaphysical and epistemological dances of the global capital. In this regard, while attenuated versions of terrorism would demonise Africa as harbouring terrorism, it is necessary to note ways in which transnational capital, institutions and foreign governments [especially Euro-American ones] terrorise Africa economically, politically, culturally, religiously, technologically, epistemically and socially. The dictation by Euro-American institutions, civil society and states in the realms of economics, politics as well as the cultural, social, political and religious spheres all constitute forms of terrorism on the African continent. In this sense, the parochial versions of terrorism in the so-called 'war on terror' neglect the broader forms of terrorism that date back to the enslavement and colonial eras. Unfortunately, the (neo-) colonial victims of Euro-American terrorism are still subjected to regimes of sanctions if they try to delink and free themselves from the resilient and predatory global matrices of power.

Contending that terrorism and broader insecurities were accentuated with the (neo-)enslavement era and the (neo-)colonial era, this chapter not only historicises insecurities but it also critically interrogates various forms of insecurities and terrorism that haunt Africa today, which is then sadly demonised as a haven of terrorists. We argue that contemporary attenuated versions of terrorism that simplistically demonise Africa and the global south more broadly, hide more than they reveal. They hide the terrorism and insecurities that are perpetrated on Africa by marauding Euro-American transnational corporations, institutions and states that continue to dictate to the continent which they have robbed for centuries. Furthermore, the (neo-)imperial technologies of global domination through the contemporary deployment of full-spectrum dominance, deployment of marauding drones, genetic modifications, the manufacture and deployment of humanoid robots [that are taking away humans' sexual partners as well as humans' jobs] and the deployment of contentious genetically modified organisms that are meant to decimate Africans, all speak to insecurities for Africans who have also been sadly denied restitution and compensation for (neo-)enslavement and for manifold Euro-American (neo-)colonial crimes on Africa. In this respect, we argue that the "global security" that is conventionally explained in terms of the deployment of drones, the deployment of militaries and security firms is not real security for Africans who would rather derive real and greater security through restoration and restitution of African resources that have been robbed from the continent for centuries. In other words, we argue that the problem with contemporary definitions of security is that it is the security of the beneficiaries of the colonial and enslavement era lootings of Africa that is given pre-eminence, and not the security of the victims of enslavement and colonisation that is accorded eminence in the contemporary definitions of security. In other words, contemporary global security depends on continued sacrificing of the real security of African victims of (neo-)colonial and (neo-)enslavement era lootings, who are forced to continue to depend on global criminal organisations, institutions and individuals that indiscriminately loot from Africa while paradoxically professing to be Africa's saviours. Notwithstanding (neo-)imperial pretences about the "responsibility to protect", "ethics of vulnerability", "ethics of care" and broader Euro-American anglings towards various forms of sham humanitarianisms, this chapter contends that it is the Euro-American and Asian dabbling on the continent of Africa that have generated profound insecurities for the bona fide inhabitants of the continent. So, the Euro-American privileging and monopolisation of global violence, be it structural or direct physical violence, visible or invisible violence, covert or overt forms of violence are understood herein as manifestations of forms of (neo-)imperial atavism that generate insecurities for Africans, some of whom in their paroxysms of resistance consequently brutalise and cannibalise their own kith and kin.

Some of the key questions that are of relevance in African security studies include why African security interests should be conflated with the security interests of rapacious global capital and elites, some of whom induce shocks (including the neoliberal shocks), that generate insecurities for Africans? If as is often assumed, the interests of African youths are at cross- purposes with the interests of African [elderly] leaders some of whom have recently faced postmodern revolutions led by youths on the continent, then how is it possible that the interests of African youths are assumed to resonate with the interests of global capital and elites, some of whom sponsor and use social media to incite the postmodern revolutions in which incited African youths are conveniently celebrated as YouTube Generations? If the security interests of African men are at cross-purposes with the security interests of African women then why must it be assumed that the security interests of African women can be harmonious with those of global elites and capital, some of whom sponsor divisive ideologies in Africa? Why must the security interests of global capital [that is ravaging the African continent] be deemed to be coterminous with the interests of Africans who are globally plundered and ravaged? If Africans are (neo-)colonised, why is it the case that they cannot effectively unite, across gender, age, class, 'ethnicity' and status to define and persuade the world to include (neo-)colonialism as one of the fundamental threats to the continent? Might it be possible that the term security, particularly global and international security, has been used equivocatively without precision about whose security interests are exactly given pre-eminence in the world and why so? Put another way, might it be possible that the security interests of a chameleon are coterminous with the security interests of the fly that it seeks to catch and swallow? Why must security questions not include or begin from foundational humanistic precolonial freedoms, liberties, autonomy, heritages and sovereignty to include securities of the formerly colonised and marginalised? All these are critical questions that warrant serious interrogation.

Cannibalism, Sacrifice and Insecurities within (Neo-)Imperial Logics and Praxis

Although allegations of cannibalism, sacrifice, barbarism and terrorism have historically and largely been levelled against Africans and other enslaved and colonised peoples, it is necessary to note that Euro-American and Asian slave traders, slave owners and colonisers were in fact the prototypical [barbaric] cannibalists and terrorists that embarked on sacrificing multitudes of people all over the world. These slave traders and colonisers enslaved, brutalised, butchered and ate their victims, sometimes alive. They [slave traders and colonisers], thus were cannibalists, barbarists and terrorists par excellence.

Africans were depicted as cannibalists characterised by confusion, inability to distinguish the fellow humans from animals, lacking morality, lacking humanity, lacking orderliness and lacking enlightenment (Independent, 4 August 2017; Independent, 10 May 1993). George Hegel (1956: 93) for instance provocatively and unashamedly wrote:

> In Negro life the characteristic point is the fact that consciousness had not yet attained to the realisation of any substantial existence [...] Thus distinction between himself as an individual and the universality of his essential being, the African in the uniform, undeveloped oneness of his existence has not yet attained.

In the same fashion, David Hume (repub.1978), in his: *The Treatise of Human Nature* and particularly his essay 'Of national characters', acerbically attacked the people of the global south [Africans included] when he notes:

> I am apt to suspect the Negroes, and in general all the other species of men (for there are four or five different kinds) to be naturally inferior to the whites. There never was a civilised nation of any other complexion than white, nor even any individual eminent either in action or speculation. I am apt to suspect the Negroes to be naturally inferior to the whites. There scarcely ever was a civilised nation of that complexion, or even any individual eminent either in action or speculation.

Hegel and Hume, together with many other Eurocentric scholars such as John Locke, Immanuel Kant, and Stuart Mill denied sovereignty to Africa arguing that Africans had no idea of a government or state, that they lacked morality, humanity and rationality (Mawere & Mubaya 2016). We however argue here that the profound insecurities, ontological and otherwise, of Africans emanated from (neo-)slave hunters and traders and from (neo-)colonisers who not only failed to distinguish African human beings from animals, but also stirred conflicts between the Africans who they targeted for enslavement and colonisation. In Euro-American history, there were general societal practices which involved consuming human body parts [including the blood of criminals], of which colonial era African corpses and skulls were shipped to Europe (Noble, 2011); and, in this regard, Africans and other people in the global south still suffer human organ trafficking that benefits the global north. On the other hand, in precolonial Africa, the consumption of human body parts was detested as prototypical witchcraft of which penalty was ostracisation and execution. At this point, we reiterate the question: "Who were cannibalists between Euro-American colonisers and the colonised Africans?"

Defined as territories over which Euro-American and Asian corporations, institutions and states forcibly exercise suzerainty, African territories have consequently had terror and insecurities consigned to them. Bearing not only their own insecurities but also the insecurities of Euro-America that were, since the enslavement and colonial era, consigned to them – African territories have become the proverbial sacrificial terrain wherein (neo-)liberal sacrifices have been forcibly extracted in addition to (neo-)enslavement and (neo-)colonial lootings. In this regard, while it is often simplistically held that Africa's security challenges include poverty, military coups, political assassinations, diseases, and other natural and man-made disasters which can [it is contended] be resolved via international aid (Forest *et al*, 2011); we contend that Africa's insecurity is principally a function of failure by the Euro-American colonisers to restitute and restore what is looted during the (neo-)colonial era, including the African dignity. In this vein, it is important to historicise insecurities in Africa so that we avoid parochialism.

As such, Africans are not insecure simply because of lack of aid, corruption, because of poverty, unemployment or natural disasters. Africa is in fact *a fortiori* insecure because Africans have had their resources and dignity looted and robbed for centuries. In this regard, the security of Euro-American economies that are based in Africa has not translated into the security of Africans who continue to be exploited and robbed by transnational corporations, which often work together with corrupted government officials. In other words, Africans continue to be cannibalised by marauding transnational corporations and Euro-American institutions and states, some of which have become Africa's *de facto* governors, whose failure to restitute and restore stolen resources and legacies to Africans is deliberately and conveniently foreshadowed by spurious discourses about African state failure. The significance of (neo-)colonial and (neo-)enslavement history in understanding African insecurities is underscored by Mohamed *et al* (2012: 14) thus:

> During the era of the slave trade, millions of Africans, particularly the young, women and children, were terrorised by the Westerners intentional acts of terrorism with millions perishing in the forests whilst running away from the slave abductors….Yet, millions more lost their lives from dehydration, dysentery and other diseases acquired during the journey. With no sanitary facilities in the lower deck, we do not know of any type of terrorism comparable to or worse than the one suffered by a human being shackled together with a dead body on his right leg and a diarrhoea patient on his left.

In the light of the insecurities embedded in the history of (neo-)enslavement and (neo-)colonisation, African insecurities cannot be simplistically understood in terms of poverty, absence of connections, the need for humanitarian aid or the necessity of fighting attenuated versions of terrorism. While some scholars and thinkers would privilege connections within the trope of open society (Ndulo, 2006), African security concerns should be understood not simplistically in terms of such tropes about connections and openness of societies. In fact the logic undergirds the enslavement and colonisation of Africa is that Euro-Americans, Arabs and Asians considered Africa to be open for them not only to extract resources but to loot, rob, rape, kill and exploit the Africans. As a new found site for the extraction of human bodies [body parts] and resources, Africa has been denied its security and worse still its dignity. Africa has been terrorised and worse still cannibalised and sacrificed by the global north for centuries. The continent has been parcelled out among countries of the global north in the same fashion African bodies are dismembered to extract body parts for shipment to the global north.

Similarly, today, African states while fractious and African unity is scuttled in ways that further the dismemberment of the continent. African identities are also rendered so fractious that Afrophobia has become rampant and indeed a talk of the day on the continent. Further to this, African leaders are preferred for trial and execution at such fora as the International criminal Court (ICC) where the crimes of the global north, that (neo-)enslaved and (neo-)colonised Africans, are paradoxically not part of the ICC's jurisdictional competence. Like in the historical Roman gladiators, Africans are incited to fight one another, and to steal or "collect" [livestock] from one another in the interests of (neo-)colonists' loot committees (Clarke *et al*, 2010). While the West incites African citizens against their states, African leaders are summarily condemned when they discipline the recalcitrant. In this regard, Africans are enjoined to reserve the rights of chastisation to the (neo-)imperial masters who currently control the transnational institutions that retain the prerogative to discipline Africans including their leaders in the emergent New World Order. Thus, describing colonial era theft of livestock in Africa where African leaders were forced to steal from their kith and kin, Clarke *et al* (2010: 128) note that:

These formerly very powerful men were supposed to show they had submitted to the new rulers by collecting cattle in their areas of jurisdiction. The animals would then be handed over to the "loot kraals" at Bulawayo. Regular levies on the national herd continued to be made throughout the first nine months of 1895, and the loot committee eventually accounted for 362 000 cattle....The British South Africa Company encouraged the transfer of what had been communal cattle from amabutho to individuals, especially men who collaborated with the Europeans.

Much as (neo-)imperial corporations and institutions are recidivists in continuing to rob Africans, some African leaders are recidivists in continuing to loot from their vulnerable kin and subjects, often on behalf of (neo-)imperial capital with whom the proceeds of corruption are subsequently shared or invested abroad. The eventuality is that not many leaders could be really genuinely caring for the generality of Africans. Though the global north pretends to offer humanitarian aid which, in a context where Africans

8

are generally denied human essence and rather considered as indistinct from animals, should in fact be understood as animal aid. In other words, humanitarian assistance presupposes the existence of human beings as contrasted to animals yet some scholars and civil society organisations postulate the absence of distinction between human beings and nonhumans (see Nhemachena, 2016). The point here is that such postulations of absence of distinctions have got security implications – they challenge the entire edifice of humanitarianism as well as the edifice of human security, especially Africans' security in particular. For there to be human security and humanitarian aid there should, in the first instance, be human beings who are clearly different from animals or from nonhumans. The risk of claims about absence of distinctions between human beings and animals is that human beings in Africa, as they already allege (Nhemachena, 2017), are given donations in the form of animal feeds. In this regard, to fail to distinguish between humans and nonhuman animals poses the risk of feeding [African] humans with animal feeds, which to humans are best described as toxins. Also, while human security is often used to challenge the pre-eminence of state security, the irony is that human security itself is also challenged by scholars, as will be explained in this chapter, who postulate absence of distinction between humans and animals – postmodernist scholars that seek to decentre and deconstruct the [African] human subject in effect also decentre and deconstruct human security. The net effect is not only that there is confusion in the terrain of security studies but that possession of clear human identities is necessary for human security, including social, political and economic security, to be feasible and plausible. Where, as in the (neo-)colonial era in Africa, human beings are not considered to possess human essence and clear human identities, it would not make sense to talk or write about human security – whether social, political, religious, cultural or economic security.

If Africans are, as is argued by some scholars like Deleuze and Guattari (1987), becoming animals, then what is the place of human security and humanitarian aid in Africa? In fact, becoming animal entails becoming insecure. It entails losing sovereignty, society, culture, economy, morality, ethics, autonomy, territory and state. If loss of sovereignty and autonomy, morality, ethics, culture, economy and territory was a product of colonisation, then loss of these same aspects in the contemporary era entail similar kinds of insecurities that marked the colonial era. It is as good as noting that Africans are still under the Euro-American colonial yoke. Security comes with sovereignty and autonomy, it comes with ownership and control over one's economy, resources, culture, society, institutions including marriage and the family –yet Africans are increasingly being divested of these institutions including sovereignty and autonomy and ownership and control of their resources that guarantee security and their humanity. In fact, African lives are not considered to matter as is evident in the recent "Black Lives Matter Movement" that recently protested against the blatant disregard of the lives of African-Americans who were killed by the police in America. Much as Africans and their leaders are often summarily regarded as terrorists particularly when they seek to free themselves from the global matrices of power, the African Americans involved in the Black Lives Matter Movement have been labelled as terrorists (Flynn *et al*, 2017; The Washington Post, 19 October 2017; Maharawi, 2017; The Guardian, 7 October 2017). Even as academies in the global north are popularising the idea that state security has been superseded by human security concerns, in the Black Lives Matter the American state assumed pre-eminence over the human security of the African-Americans who [in the interests of American state security] have been silenced and repressed by the police. Thus, while African state security concerns are often dismissed by some states and civil society organisations and institutions of the global north, the states in the global north do not suffer the same condemnations even when they suppress the human security of movements such as Black Lives Matter. This was the same scenario during the colonial era – where despite the untold sufferings, material loses and loses of [African] human lives the Western colonists caused on Africa, the colonists never suffered condemnation from the global south. African leaders are summarily condemned and indicted in the ICC for allegedly infringing the human security of their subjects, yet when the lives of African Americans are trampled upon, the American state is never called to account in the ICC or anywhere else. In fact, the same USA would proceed to claim via the United Nations Security Council, the prerogative to protect the entire world, through the famous 'Responsibility to Protect', even as it tramples on the human security of African Americans at home! Much as African people are spuriously and summarily deemed to constitute security threats in the world that has conveniently come to be preponderated over by the ICC, Black people generally are so much viewed as insecurities that the edifices of courts including the ICC are set up principally to catch and indict Africans – Black people are disproportionately represented and systematically over imprisoned in America giving the false impression that "Blacks" constitute greater security threats than "Whites" (Osman, 10 December 2017; Keenanga-Yamahtta, 2016).

Even if the (neo-)imperialists incite violence including revolutions in the peripheries where, via the military-industrial complex, they arm one group of people against others or incite the citizens against their governments (Blair, 2010), they remain immune to punishment. In fact, they arrogate the prerogatives to punish leaders and citizens of the global south, who constitute victims of (neo-)enslavement and (neo-)colonial dispossession and exploitation. Enrolled into the service of transnational capital (Zagami, 2016), some African leaders have come to constitute insecurity to their subjects who detest neo-colonialism and the attendant privations. Via the prison-industrial complex wherein private transnational businesses are linked up with governments' prison services (Goldberg *et al*, 2001), security for transnational capital is ensured by vesting the prerogative to punish in the hands of governments and institutions that are underwritten by the transnational [finance] capital. In this sense, when international or transnational peacekeepers rape African girls or force them to have sex with dogs (Independent, 31 March 2016), they are not held accountable. Neither are they taken to the International Criminal Court, or any court conveniently within the jurisdiction of the victims for that matter! Much like during the enslavement period when only the masters could chastise their slaves (Southey, 1827), the transnational security systems and institutions allow only for the international chastisement of Africans and other peoples of the global south – the masters remain unaccountable to the people of the global south that remain enslaved by an insecure, unaccountable and opaque global matrix of power. As Southey (1827: 27) notes, the practice was that:

> As masters and stewards can alone chastise slaves with that moderation which is required, no other person who is not their master, or his steward, shall injure, chastise, wound or kill them, without incurring the punishment enacted by the laws against those who commit the like excesses towards free people; and the master of the slave who has been injured, chastised, or killed, shall commence a lawsuit against the criminal…

The above quotation underscores the skewed nature of global security concerns, which enable the (neo-)imperial masters to punish the (neo-)imperial slaves without the existence of equality of power to punish the (neo-)imperial masters in turn. In the contemporary era, the masters can, under the guise of promoting democracy and human rights, incite revolutions in the peripheries where youths who are regarded as You Tube Generations (News24, 27 February 2013) are incited against their impecunious and dependency ravaged governments and states. But in a world marked by global master and servant relationships, when the masters appear to defend their slaves, what is effectively being defended are the human rights of the masters over their servants. Like in the enslavement era, the servants remain subhuman [although protected by the masters] at that global level. When a [global] master protects a servant or slave, the human rights being protected are not necessarily those of the slave or servant but those of the global master. If the [global] servants or slaves have real rights, it would be expected that they are really equal, not merely among themselves as slaves but, with their [global] masters. On this note, we advance that global masters constitute insecurities in so far as they seek to covertly and overtly foreground their own interests in the world. In this regard, some scholars have noted that the emergent New World Order is led by the illuminati who intend to establish a "One World Government" led by Euro-America. In such a New World Order, the illuminati seeks to establish one family for the human race [even as Africans are being depicted as indistinct from animals], they seek to erase states and leaders of the global south

(Wheen, 2004) and in this way they create for themselves an open world wherein they are free to exploit all [planetary] resources and peoples in the different parts or places.

In this regard, the Euro-American project of creating an open world with a One World Government is happening through the incitement of revolutions against African states and others in the global south, which are conveniently portrayed as failed or weak or rogue or corrupt states. The uprisings such as in the Middle East were not merely a result of new social media's [which assumes openness in the world] ability to pass on information within a country (Blair, 2010), but they were also a result of covert plans by global elite families that are noted to constitute the illuminati (Wheen, 2004; Zagami, 2016). Youths in the global south are not only incited against their governments and states but they are also incited against their elders, against their parents, against their families, against their cultures, against their languages, and against their religions that are deemed to be impediments to the establishment of the New World Order and the One World Government. The youths such as in the Arab digital generation are argued to be seeking to change their identities from those of their elders, they are noted as transforming their families, friends, political spheres, religions and so on, often for purposes of forcing more transparency and accountability on their governments [but not on the (neo-)imperial system] (Sabbagh *et al*, 2012). The point here is that youths are constituted as vehicles, and not necessarily as human beings, for the achievement of the project of the New World Order with a One World Government. They are made to fight their governments for accountability and transparency yet they are not allowed to fight the (neo-)imperial system for purposes of restitution and restoration of what is (neo-)colonially looted and robbed from them. If transparency and accountability are necessary, they are more so for struggles against (neo-)empire that still has to restore and restitute for the enslavement and colonisation of Africans and the global south more generally. In this regard, there is something missing in observations that cell phones, Facebook, Twitter and so on, embolden youths to use instantaneous transmission of messages and images to mobilise locally around issues like improved economic standards of life, freedom of expression and press, access to high quality education and employment opportunities (Laremont, 2013). Their [the youths] attention is diverted to local issues as they are blinkered by the (neo)imperial system not to see beyond the local. The missing aspect is that youths also have to organise to fight for restitution and restoration for enslavement and colonial lootings and exploitation. They cannot simply mobilise against their states or for local improvements of economic standards or freedoms of expression or access to education and employment while ignoring the historical and ongoing insecurities that are constituted by the presence of dispossessive and exploitative transnational corporations and institutions which dwarf African states and governments in matters of corruption and insecurity. So, while it is argued that the participatory, web-inspired social and political movements have forced youths to realise an intolerable wide gap that exists between their standards of living and those enjoyed by their peers in the rest of the world, for these youths (Laremont, 2013), it is necessary to note that the point of focus need not be the wide gap in standards of living. Instead, the focus must be on the fact that the so-called rich countries have looted and robbed the global south – and this explains the wide gaps in standards of living between and amongst peoples of the world. Instead of paying reparations and restoration to the global south, (neo-)imperial countries of the global north are choosing instead to use the poverty which they generated in the south to incite revolutions that are hoped to help them pull down states of the global south in readiness for the New World Order and One World Government. Thus, Al Jazeera (21 February 2011) notes that:

> Much has already been written about the plethora of social media networks that both helped engineer protests and, crucially, amplified them across cyber-space. Online – activists, sitting behind fibre optic cables and flat screens, collated and disseminated updates, photographs and video and played the role of subversive hero from the comfort of their homes.

In terms of security, the new social media is rendering Africa open to manipulations by the (neo-)imperial organisations, institutions and states aiming at the constitution of a New World Order and (neo-)imperial One World Government. The new social media is creating open societies in Africa but the openness does not translate to security for the continent whose youths – termed You Tube Generation – are exploited and incited against their cultures, states, governments, families, religions, and so on. Much as the neoliberal opening up of African economies has been ravaging and damaging to Africa, openness in terms of social media manipulation of African youths will turn out to be beneficial to (neo-)empire rather than to the Africans who are used as raw materials in the crucibles for the covert emergent One World Government. So, Pambazuka (3 November 2016) observes that: "These destabilisations of Africa are aided and abetted by empire building interests in the developed world, which see Africa as a soft target ripe for recolonisation".

As a presumed open society, Africa has been constituted, since the enslavement and colonial eras, into a field open for conflicts, violence, experimentation in various fields such as politics, science, social, cultural, biological, economic experimentation and other activities that compromise the security of the Africans. Presumed to be an open society, Africa is constituted into an open field for various experiments in political, social, cultural, economic, biological, and physical engineering. As an open society and field, the continent is used as a testing ground for drones –and some civil society organisations sadly promote this notion of Africa as an open society that should be readily accessed by outsiders, even those who quest to exploit the continent right into the bone. We argue here that this is because Africa and the global south are deemed to need more of global capital's surveillance [through the deployed drones and other modalities] than the global north which is deemed to be less criminal and less wayward than the global south. Globally, "Black people" are subjected to more surveillance – for instance, the recent Black Lives Matter Movement in America was subjected to surveillance through social media accounts in Facebook, Twitter and vine (Fynn *et al*, 2017). The future of global surveillance will increasingly include the deployment of drones, use of DNA profiling, facial recognition and body scanners that are getting normalised via spurious discourses that associate or connect Africa with terrorism when in fact the continent is itself paradoxically a victim of resilient Western terrorism. Deemed to be an open society (Bond, 2013; Global Research, 4 July 2003) where the West also takes the liberty to incite conflicts and postmodern revolutions in various institutions [like the family, marriage, culture, religion, politics and education], Africa is also sadly a victim of the dumping of drugs, spiritually loaded hair products, second hand clothes from the dead people in the West and the dumping of toxic e-waste from the West (Ajib, 2016; Hicks, 2016; Mawere and Nhemachena, 2017). The generation and international movement of hazardous waste including their disposal in the global south remains a topical issue in environmental justice and security debate. Most of these hazardous wastes and "second hand" materials – including used motor vehicles – are shipped to and dumped in African countries even though the Basel convention [which other countries like America have refused to sign] regulates the dumping (Ajib, 2016; Hicks, 2016). Just as it is immune in the International Criminal Court, the global north enjoys immunity for polluting the African environment, as evident in their refusal to sign the Kyoto Protocol to protect the environment (The Guardian, 26 November 2012).

In the light of all these observations, we argue here that what is understood as environmental insecurity is often on a deeper analysis in fact insecurities emanating from the global north's dumping of toxic waste in Africa – environmental insecurity originates also from the global north manipulation and weaponisation of the weather, for example, through the American High Frequency Active Auroral Research Program (HAARP) which is responsible for climate insecurities in the contemporary world (Global Research, 9 November 2017; Nhemachena *et al*, 2017; Mawere and Nhemachena, 2017). In the contemporary world where the USA army is understood to be gunning for full spectrum dominance including via the use of electronic magnetic warfare that helps it to remotely generate earthquakes, weather changes and tsunamis, to disrupt global communication, blast enemy missiles in the skies, blind enemy soldiers in the battlefield and control unruly world crowds by burning their skin (Global Research 9 November 2017), the weather and climate are being deliberately weaponised. It has been sadly noted that many universities, particularly in the global north, participate in the HAARP wherein radio waves especially the microwave band can be used to put words into people's heads and those words can be used to drive a person crazy or to hypnotize them in a world where the military and intelligence have insatiable desire to win the battles for the humans, even if these manipulations of the minds turn the targeted people into zombies (Smith, 1998). In such a contemporary world where there is increasing remote manipulation of conditions in distant regions, the global north's response to the exposure of its projects of manipulating others has been to allege conspiracy theories on the part of those that expose them. Allegations that those that expose the global north's manipulation of the world are conspiracy theorists are in fact a strategy to generate and maintain ignorance about the nefarious covert global north manipulations – it is a global north strategy to ensure manipulations of others, distant and near, with impunity. We argue here that in a world where there is both the implicate-order-metaphysics and the explicate-order-metaphysics and the manipulations of microphysics, the logics of manipulation of others by manipulating physics are plausible.

While some scholars (see Nhemachena, 2016; Nhemachena, 2017) contend that it is Cartesian binaries including separations, disconnections and dissociations that generated insecurities in the world, it is necessary to note that in so far as Africa is concerned, the problem is not separation or disconnections, but rather the fact that colonialists implanted themselves onto Africa shamelessly dispossessing and exploiting Africans who they portrayed as indistinct to animals (Nhemachena, 2016; Hughes, 2010). Since the eras of enslavement and (neo-)colonisation, the problems of insecurity in Africa have resulted from connections, associations and relations with the exploitative and dispossessive West – the problem for Africa has not been simplistically that of separation, disconnection or alienation (Nhemachena et al, 2017). For Hughes (2010), Euro-Americans implanted and bonded themselves onto African land by pretending that they were nature lovers; they integrated themselves through the environment rather than engaging with "Black society" and they assumed symbolic kinship with plants and animals as ways to naturalise themselves into Africa. In the

17

contemporary era, Euro-American academies are still popularising notions of 'relationships' with nature, 'relationships' and 'associations' with animals, 'relationships' with soil and land and mountains (Nhemachena, 2017; Hoffman, 2016) as ways by which to implant themselves into Africa and of hopefully 'becoming' indigenous. In fact, 'associating' human beings with nature or assuming that there are 'relationships' between human beings and nature, carries the implication that it is natural to colonise Africans. Logically, if, as is assumed, there is no difference between human beings and nature and if both human beings and nature can be understood as "colonising others", then this implies that it is natural to colonise others. Therefore, to argue that there is no distinction between nature and humans, by extension, naturalises colonisation and the attendant insecurities. Thus, Hoffman (2016: 3) states:

> Ecologists now accept that people are not disconnected from the environment, and thus scientific understanding of our own spread across the globe cannot be isolated from that of all other species...yet certainly in prehistoric times our survival and further spread was fully compliant with, and restricted to, the rules of nature, or were we a biological invasion?

Insecurities in Africa have also originated from erroneous colonial presuppositions that Africans were animists and indistinct from animals (Nhemachena, 2016; Temples, 1959; Nhemachena, 2017). Whereas in African indigenous knowledges, it is the errant witches that are deemed not only to go about naked, but also to use owls, crocodiles, hyenas, fish otters, baboons, snakes to commit adultery, bestiality and incest, to transform themselves into snakes and other animals (Posselt, 1935; Lan, 1987; Gelfand, 1959), scholars that postulate animism and animatism seek to generalise and normalise the nefarious logics of witchcraft by assuming that there are no distinctions between humans and nonhuman animals. In fact, other scholars sadly argue for the erosion of distinctions between good and evil (Pledger, 2013), yet this effectively normalises witchcraft (as it normalises the colonists' wicked activities) by effacing the distinctions between good and bad. Niehaus' (2012) observation that witches can progressively take hold of victims' body parts and even deceive victims' kin by leaving an image of the victim aptly underscores the insecurities (see Ashforth, 2005) that emanate from witchcraft. Witches not only generate insecurities by disregarding precepts of Ubuntu and the attendant humanism – they also generate insecurities by digging up and exhuming corpses in the same way some colonial 'fortune seekers' exhumed African burial mounds, stripped skeletal remains of jewellery on the arms, necks and legs (Ellert, 1984). Whereas in African societies the dead were secure once interred, colonialist disregarded the security of both the dead and living Africans – living Africans were forced, by colonial loot committees, to exhume in the false name of archaeology, and loot corpses of their interred kin. This generated metaphysical insecurities for Africans who were made to become witches by exhuming and robbing corpses of their kin. (Neo-)colonialists have caused African insecurities by the disintegration of discipline, institutions which supported family life, communal organisation and African self-respect. Because the global north generated insecurities by disintegrating discipline in the lives of Africans, indigenous people associate the global north with evil, illness, magic, misfortune and death par excellence – the country of the dead is considered to be in the West while the east is identified with life, health and wealth (Posselt, 1935).

To posit, as scholars on animism do, that there is no distinction between humans and nonhuman animals amounts to legitimisation of ontological, metaphysical, moral, and epistemological insecurities among Africans. In so far as they generate ontological insecurity, identity crises entail loss of self-integrity, lack of sense of human presence in the world, it entails lack of wholeness, lack of temporal continuity (Du Plock, 1999; Croft, 2012). As Boswell (2008) argues, the loss of identity and rootedness means that memories of the past cannot be retrieved, it means that there is loss of self-affirmation – it entails [ontological] violence. Assumptions of erosion of distinctions between human beings and animals entail loss of ontological security – this kind of security requires stable relationships – actions which unsettle established narratives and routines result in ontological insecurity (Rumelili, 2015). In other words, (neo-)colonial portrayals of Africans as monstrous, queer, grotesque, posthuman, nomadic, animistic, beastly and savages created ontological insecurities (Wijnants, 2016; Nhemachena, 2016). We argue that it is not necessarily a human right to become queer, monstrous, grotesque or beastly – in fact to become beastly, queer or animal amounts to losing humanity and the attendant human rights as well as the security implied in African humanness of Ubuntu. Whereas some scholars as noted by Nhemachena (2016) argue in favour of becoming animals, becoming queer, becoming grotesque, becoming posthuman and becoming monstrous, we contend that, logically, to become other than human or to become indistinct from the nonhuman effectively amounts to losing human security as well as state security and sovereignty.

To contend that African bodies are monstrous and queer is to replicate colonial insecurities and portrayals of Africans as monstrous cannibals without control over their bodies, without the ability to distinguish human flesh and the meat from other animals, it is in fact to deny Africans their cultural humanely identities – it is to deny them humanely authenticity (Jacobs, 2012; Partridge, 2010; Bielawski, 2013). The queer and monstrous body is one that cannot be contained, it refuses to be incorporated into the political body, it is an inimical body, it is a savage body which is anthropophagic and cannibalistic, it is a body that must be exterminated, swallowed up and masticated through violence (Bielawski, 2013). In this sense, the bodies of the colonised who were considered to be queer, savage and monstrous were obliterated and their properties and resources were looted (Partridge, 2010). For (neo-)colonialists, describing the African body as queer, monstrous, grotesque, posthuman, transhuman and as indistinct from animals helped them bypass possible charges of genocide as to kill a queer, grotesque, monstrous, posthuman, transhuman would not constitute genocide or even a crime. It would be as good as killing a beast in the forest. To the extent that Euro-America is immune to the ICC for (neo-)enslavement and (neo-)colonial crimes it committed against [African] humanity and for abusing human rights of Africa, its immunity can be understood as legitimised by mischievous discourses that depict Africans as queer, grotesque, monstrous and savage and therefore nonhuman. In this sense, to become queer, posthuman, grotesque, and monstrous is to lose security – it is to become insecure.

Such monstrous, queer, grotesque bodies and the attendant insecurities also originate from contemporary genetic engineering propagated by the global north. Genetic engineering partly uses animal DNA rather than human DNA to produce human beings that are transgenic –carrying DNA from other species (Brey, 2008). Thus, although enhancements are said to improve human capacities, lifespan, intellectual capacity, body functionality or sensory functions, mood, emotions, and energy (Podrouzkova, 2015), the biggest problem for humanity is that they erode [African] human identity in ways that result in ontological insecurity. Efforts to displace, decentre and deconstruct the human subjects whose human essence is increasingly demonised by some scholars (Sharon, 2013), create not only ontological insecurity. Deconstruction of the human subjects also results in human beings losing not only their identities but also their employment, cultures, marriages and families – human subjects are sadly being decentred and deconstructed in an age where humanoid robots are being manufactured to replace the human beings in various spheres. Apart from the contemporary productions of robodocs, robolawyers, animated doctors and robotic lawyers, robotic teachers, robotic drivers, robotic pharmacists that are already replacing human beings in the employment sector (The New York Times, 28 November, 2013), and robotic wives (and husbands) who are also replacing sexual partners and human spouses with humanoid sex robots and virtual sexualities that generate insecurities for the [African] family and marriage institutions (Mireault, 2014; Inkinen, 1998). Teledildonics virtual togetherness promotes promiscuity in cyberspace with distant partners at the click of a mouse (Inkinen, 1998). Whereas such teledildonics are celebrated by some scholars, other scholars have noted that it is only witches that use and have sex with familiars some of which are invisible (Nyakupfuka, 2012; Makoti, 2012) – witches are known not only to associate with certain animals like cats, dogs, frogs, mice, lizards, horses, but also to prefer nudity, pacts with [invisible] demons, to engage in sexual orgies including copulating with demons (Makoti, 2012).

All these observations, notwithstanding contemporary transnational corporations are producing sex robots that are ravaging human marriages, snatching human couples away from one another and they are becoming predominant in the sex industry within which Africans whose marriages and families have been conveniently destroyed are directed by the profiteering global corporate capital (Mail Online, 30 June 2016; Nhemachena, 2016; My Zimbabwe News 13 February 2018). Depicting ways in which humanoid robots are replacing humans, Veriggio *et al* (2008: 1513) note that: "Servant robots can clean and housekeep; they are fast and accurate, and never bored. They can babysit, because they are patient, talkative, and able to play many games, both intellectual and physical. They can assist patients, the elderly, and the handicapped in clinics or at home, being always available, reliable, and taught to provide physical support". Although the [life-size] sex robots are argued to constitute sexual therapy as companions for lonely, disabled or older people (The Telegraph, 5 July 2017), it would be important to notice that some Africans are becoming lonely and insecure precisely because of some transnational corporations, civil society organisations and NGOs that fund studies which meanly and summarily condemn natural African families and marriages. We argue that the condemnations of African marriages and families is nothing new given the history of slavery wherein African slaves were not allowed to marry and establish families – in some instances African women who were enslaved had sex partners chosen for them as a matter of the slave masters' imperatives of breeding for future slaves. In the contemporary era, global corporations that constitute the masters of Africans are also keen to deconstruct African marriages and families and then replace spouses and partners with profitable humanoid sex robots that are currently being advertised as patient, kind, protective, loving, trusting, persevering, respectful, uncompromising, complimentary, pleasant to talk to and sharing your sense of humour (Levy, 2017).

In efforts to market humanoid [sex] robots, the security risk downside of using them is rarely explored. The fact that the technologies emit electromagnetic radiation, into the human brain, which causes cancer – including brain tumours is rarely mentioned (Mail Online, 30 April 2012; Hossmann, 2003; Dangers, 2014;

Naeem, 2014). Other health security risks of the technologies include effects on neural activity, energy metabolism, genomic responses, neurotransmitter balance, cognitive functions, sleep and various brain diseases, damage to immune systems, malfunctioning and break of DNA strands, sleep disorders, loss of fertility and sperm quality (Hossmann, 2003; Dangers, 2014; Naeem, 2014; Goldworthy, 2012; Express, 25 August 2017). Thus, Global Research (16 December 2017) notes that: "Because cell phones could not exist without their towers and grids to help them connect, we also live within that grid of microwave radiation. Still, we do not seem concerned about it, or about its effects on our health and the health of our children…the electromagnetic energy they use can radiate and penetrate deep into the human body causing damage".

The fact that these technologies cause abnormalities, genetic mutations, cancer and so on, is hardly mentioned by the scholars that celebrate [African] queerness, monstrosity and beastliness and "untamed" becomings – including becoming animal. The security risks of marrying and living within proximity to the technologies including humanoid [sex] robots are not taken into cognisance by those that celebrate the emergent humanoid [sex] robots. Understood in the context of some scholars' celebrations of effacement of distinctions between nature and culture, between the natural and artificial genetic mutational effects of the technologies – that are set to transform the natural humans into global corporate capital's artifices – should serve as a warning about the downside of postmodernist discourses that celebrate such erosion of distinctions between natural humans and artifices, between culture and nature. The manipulations of natural [African] human genetic material, the inducement of microchips into human bodies and the transitioning of natural humans into artifices generate insecurities in so far as they entail the vulnerability of natural humans to global corporate capital that is bent on scientifically and technologically manipulating the world in its own interests. African security requires different sets of transformations. It requires "radical decolonisation" (Mawere 2018), including restitution and restoration – and they cannot be achieved by rendering African citizens vulnerable to global capital's scientific and technological experiments with transforming African human identities [including technologically and scientifically turning human Africans into queers or animals]. As posthumanists scholars postulate, the future is set by global corporate capital to deconstruct the human subject so as to render the [African] human subjects imperceptible by technologically and scientifically transforming them into queers, grotesque, monstrous beings – it is a process that generates profound ontological insecurity. It is a process that deconstructs human social welfare and social protection mechanism because with grotesque, queer, monstrous beings populating the continent, the [African] human subject will have vanished together with human society and [African] human nations that have hitherto anchored social welfare and social security.

Although humanoid robots and other pieces of technology including digital telehealth are being celebrated as assisting in addressing matters of health, it is necessary to take note of the security risk that emanate from use of such technologies. For instance, some writers argue that biohybrids or microbots [tiny microscopic robots –about the size of a blood cell- that are part machine and part –living thing] which are remotely controlled should be injected into human bodies to fight diseases including cancer (The Sun, 23 November 2017; Business News Daily, 2 January 2018; Daily Star, 26 November 2017). However, it has been noted on the contrary that too much radiation from medical testing and other sources such as body scanners is dangerous to human health including to DNA and the attendant genetic expression (Natural Society, 16 May 2012). Apart from the fact that some substances emit alpha particles that are hazardous to genetic material if they are ingested or inhaled (Richards et al, 2010), the injection of remotely controlled microbots or biohybrids into human bodies implies that the [African] human bodies themselves become remotely controlled by the global hegemons who are in charge of these remotely controlled technologies. For Africans to become remotely controlled via chips and microbots that are inserted or injected into their bodies would mean becoming intensely vulnerable to the global elite who control the technologies – it would be a remotely controlled world without freedom, without privacy, without human dignity. In other words, it will be an insecure posthuman world.

While some argue that robotic remedy will be available for insecure sexless marriages wherein men and women will have sex with robots and fall in love with them – in similar ways they have internet sex, sex with vibrators and sex dolls (Rubenstein, 2009), others argue that artificial companions [including sex robots, vibrators and sex dolls] are the mainstay of Satanism that would allow Satanists to mimic God and create partners for sex magic without the baggage and obnoxious habits of humans – and the added benefit would be the ability to produce the most vile, blasphemous, and shocking rituals imaginable without any human concern (Johnson, n.d; Johnson, 1996). It is argued by Johnson (1996: 60-1) thus:

> Satan cannot create organic life…In the meantime, Satan with his vastly superior knowledge can produce wonderful "make believe" or synthetic "humanoids" for his own deceptive purposes…To bring the world to such a state of social and spiritual anarchy Satan must first capture the minds of our thought leaders within the scientific, intellectual, government and religious communities. It will take the most innovative, overwhelming and seductive form of spiritualism to do so. In the process appearing as miracle-working world saviour, he will victimise nations, including their most brilliant minds.

The sex robots are anticipated to become a reality within decades. Some people are projected to use some form of sex using virtual headsets with many sex toys directly linked to human central nervous system or even tap into dreams and even body sharing, people are projected to start having sex wearing VR contact lenses and could be seeing a totally different person (Mail Online, 30 June 2016; The Telegraph, 5 July 2017). Human beings are projected to inhabit other people's bodies and even lock partners in place or control them in place electronically – it is projected that the sex robots will have customisable personality, silicon structure, can blink, smile, regurgitate facts about life – currently the sex dolls cost $9995 for females and males (Mail Online, 30 June 2016; The Telegraph, 5 July 2017). In addition to these developments, global corporations are producing technology that allows people to have sex at a distance (Daily Nation, 23 December 2016), yet these pieces of technology bring up intractable moral and ethical questions (Mireault, 2014) particularly for Africa where sex at a distance, sex with invisible entities, bestiality, incest and other kinds of lewdness are understood to be manifestations of witchcraft, sorcery and the attendant insecurities.

Human ontological and epistemological security is also threatened by the development of super-human robot soldiers; the development of human robotic augmentation in which human capabilities are extended through wearable robot exoskeletons meant to create superhuman strength, speed and endurance (Veriggio *et al*, 2008). Apart from the developments of remotely controlled android humanoid robot soldiers that threaten human security, there is also the development of cybernetic insects and bees (Kosek 2010; Mawere 2015) that can be controlled by a remote control and used in surveillance, and there is also the uploading of human minds into technological substrates (Estulin, 2014). Such developments in genetic modification and in human enhancements have attracted the attention of ethicists and legislators in the global north but less so in the global south (Knoppers, 1991; Marks, 2002). Thus, to be subjected to scanning in an age where human minds are being scanned and increasingly transferred to technological substrates is risky – yet from airports to border posts, scanning machines are being mounted and migrants are being forcibly subjected to scanning with little if any information about the attendant risks.

Besides these developments that generate insecurity for the global south, the USA is noted as developing weapons – weaponising space for full spectrum dominance. Tungstein rods that are also called '**rods from God**' [which can be fired from space] are installed in space as part of the planetary weaponisation project (The New York Magazine, 10 December 2006; Business Insider, 7 September 2017; Nhemachena *et al*, 2017). With their surveillance, drones are nevertheless being deployed and tested in Africa despite the security risks in testing the drones including mechanical failure, infringements of territorial and privacy spaces (Sandvic, 2015). It is sadly African airspace which is considered attractive for testing the drones and USA and European airspaces are considered inaccessible despite the fact that the drones are manufactured in the American and European states. Couched as a game changer in fighting terrorism in Africa, that purportedly needs international protection (Liden *et al*, 2016), drones are being donated to some African states by intelligence agents from the global north (Africa News, 26 May 2017). The drones have been used by the USA in the American-led invasions of Iraq and Afghanistan as well as in Pakistan (Institute for Security Studies, 3 February 2016). Thus, Satia (2014: 7) in Sandvic (2015) observes that: "In an increasingly anti-imperial and democratic world, air control allows covert pursuit of empire: drones 'offer a means of surmounting the awkward problem of engaging in military action over an ostensibly sovereign country".

Concurring with Satia (2014), the Institute for Security Studies (3 February 2016) states that: "As Western interests, led by the United States (US), increase their role in counter-terrorism efforts from Libya to Nigeria, leaders across Africa must question the wisdom of allowing weaponised drones on their sovereign territory". In fact, it is noted that Victorian Britain initially maintained a military presence in Africa as a step to full colonisation (Thomas, 1 Feb 2016) of the African continent.

While insecurity in Africa has been linked to terrorism on the continent, to poverty, environmental degradation and inadequate management of health related threats to survival (Attuquayetio, 2014), little regard is paid to insecurities emanating from the weaponisation of space by states in the global north. For instance, the USA accounts for over 90% of total global military space expenditures and maintains approximately 135 operational military-related satellites, Russia has about 60 % in orbit and the Chinese are beginning to use military satellites (Granoff *et al*, 2005). The map below shows military bases of the United States of America in Africa.

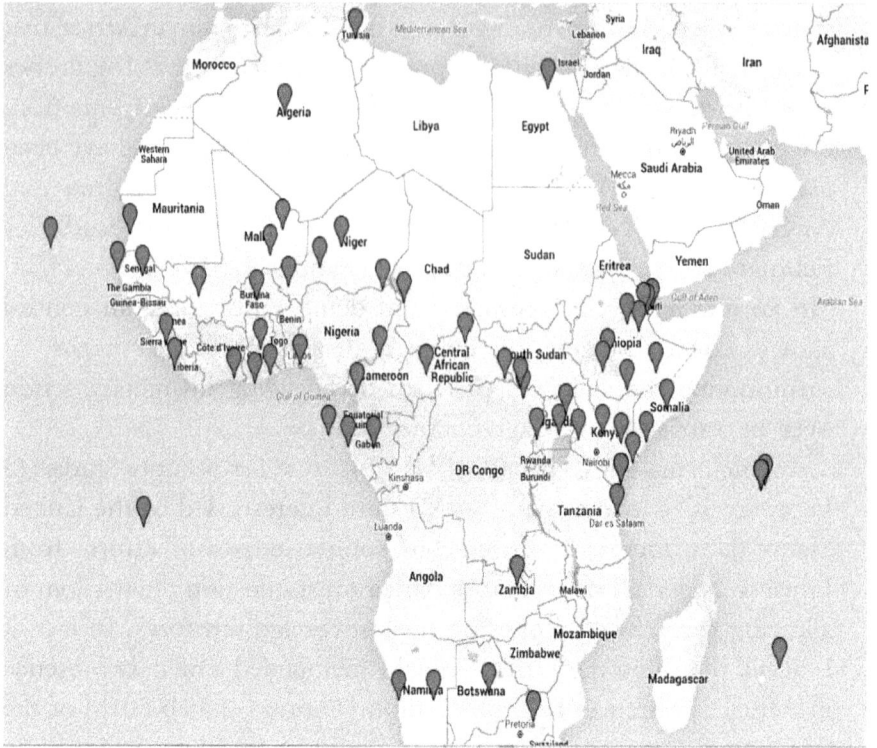

Map 2: US Military Bases in Africa
Source: africapublication.com

In fact, countries of the global north including Canada and USA
are increasing their military expenditures with Canada running a 25
billion military programme which was supported by every political
party within the country. For the reasons here explicated, Global
Research (August 2014) notes that: "The entire US military empire is
tied together using space technology. With military satellites in space
the US can see virtually everything on the Earth, can intercept all
communications on the planet, and can target virtually any place at
any time. Russia and China understand that the US military goal is to
achieve "full-spectrum dominance" on behalf of corporate capital".

Africa has for centuries made strenuous efforts to free itself from coloniality including the hegemony of the global north after realising that the efforts by countries of the global north to have full spectrum dominance in the world replicate coloniality and the attendant insecurities. Perhaps the African desperation to be free from global coloniality is well captured by Emmanuel Levinas' discussion of evasion - which is characterised as an imprisonment from which one must break free (Wyschogrod, 2012). Africa is rendered vulnerable and insecure paradoxically in a world where ethics of vulnerability and ethics of care are being postulated (Domrzalaski, 2010; Davis, 2000; Gilson, 2014; Butler, 2012; Held, 2005; Cortina *et al*, 2016). The paradoxical issue is that the global processes of change and transformation have historically involved rendering the [African] other vulnerable. Subjecting the [African] other to violence and insecurity is a mechanism that Euro-America has used to foist change and transformation in its interests. In this respect, Braidotti (2006: 14-15) argues that:

> Paradoxically, it is those who have already cracked up a bit, those who have suffered pain and injury, who are better placed to take the lead in the process of ethical transformation…They know about endurance, adequate forces, and the importance of relations…Ethics include the acknowledgement of and compassion for pain, as well as the activity of working through it. Any process of change must do some sort of violence to deeply engrained habits and dispositions which got consolidated overtime. Overcoming these engrained habits is a nec essary disruption, without which there is no ethical awakening.

In the light of our observations here underscored, it can be argued that the global north's inflictions of sanctions on states of the global south, the incitement of conflicts including revolutions in the global south, the vulnerability and exposure of people of the global south to various forms of afflictions, including colonial dispossession, exploitation and lootings of African properties were all means to render the African other vulnerable – to inflict pain so as to force Africans to the submission and transformation that the colonialists desired. The (neo-)imperial subjection of Africans to violence is a means to force them to the operating table – prostrate and ready for the West's surgical operations for the 'transformation' of the world into the New World Order with a dictatorial One World Government. The pain of suffering is preceded by the disappearance of everything in a Levinasian (2003) sense – disappearance of looted African property and resources, the disappearance of African cultures that are already suffering cultural genocide, the disappearance of African mores and ethics that formed the foundation of Ubuntu, the disappearance of African humanity and humanness within Ubuntu, the disappearance of African polities and societies, the disappearance of African marriages and families and kinship groupings, the disappearance of African identities and African social security, and the disappearance of African economies and religions are all precedent to the ethics of vulnerability and ethics of exposure that are constitutive of (neo-)imperial machinations. Such exposure and vulnerability to afflictions then constitute an insecure and impossible condition for Africans – it delivers them to the tutelage of the outside – of (neo-)empire. In Levinasian (2003: 66-7) explication of evasion:

There is in nausea a refusal to remain there, an effort to get out. Yet this effort is always already characterised as desperate: in any case, it is so for any attempt to act or think. And this despair, this fact of being riveted, constitutes all the anxiety of nausea. In nausea – which amounts to an impossibility of being what one is – we are at the same time riveted to ourselves, enclosed in a tight circle that smothers. We are there, and there is nothing more to be done, or anything to add to this fact that we have been entirely delivered up, that everything is consumed: this is the very experience of pure being, which we have promised from the beginning of this work. However, this "nothing-more-to-be-done" is the mark of a limit – situation in which the uselessness of any action is precisely the sign of the supreme instant from which we can only depart. The experience of pure being is at the same time experience of its internal antagonism and of the escape that foist itself on us.

Chapter Outlines

As a follow-up of the present chapter (Chapter 1), Artwell Nhemachena and Dolphin Mabale's Chapter 2 grapples with issues of [African] identities, particularly on how they are affected by coloniality persistent in Africa as a result of the continued quest of the global north to dominate African spaces, cultures and peoples. Using the case study of the Tsonga people of Southern Africa, the duo traces the colonial processes of changing African identities, 'including the attendant displacements, disruptions and destabilisations' that created not only ontological insecurity but epistemological insecurity on the continent. Nhemachena and Mabale, thus advance the argument that 'the ontologically insecure colonial processes of destabilising, displacing and disruption of African identities underpinned the colonial transformation of Africans into the zones of nonbeing or nothingness or into the wretched of the earth'. The duo concludes therefore that the various African insecurities originate largely from the colonial and apartheid era destabilisation and displacement of African identities and subjectivities.

In Chapter 3, Fidelis P. T. Duri and Alice Makama primarily pre-occupy themselves with the manner in which myths usually contribute to the instigation of various insecurities on women living with albinism and those who give birth to children with the same condition. While Duri and Makama are fully cognisant of the scholarly literature that seeks to address the various challenges encountered by albino children in the fields of health and education, their chapter focuses on the gender dynamics of albinism in post-colonial Zimbabwe. The chapter examines women –both albino and non-albino – in terms of their experiences with albinism, but paying particular attention to their victimisation and agency. Basing on the findings of this study, the chapter concludes that 'while the condition of albinism subjects the generality of the albino population to various insecurities in many aspects of life, women living with the condition and those who give birth to albino children, are the worst affected.

Interrogating technological oddity in view of religion, Raymond Ogunade and Gbenga Zaccheaus's Chapter 4 provides a survey of humanoid robots, exploring the spirituality of the same in Yoruba Religion and Christianity. The duo portray the two religions – Yoruba and Christianity – as monitors towards technological oddities in the African society in general and the Yoruba society in particular. They argue that 'the moral implications of unmonitored technologies especially the humanoids have greater defects than the benefits they are intended to offer'. This is true, according to Ogunande and Zaccheaus, simply because technology is not value free as it developed through scientific choices which by virtue of that imply value judgments of the society that developed it. As such, Ogunande and Zaccheaus are of the view that religion, being the bedrock of all morality, has responsibility towards technological oddities. It has to act as a watchdog for society to ensure that values are respected.

In Chapter 5, Clement Chipenda and Tom Tom explore social policy in sub-Saharan Africa with specific focus on Zimbabwe. The duo observes that social policy in the global north is generally framed in a manner that aims at enhancing the productive capacities of citizens, protecting citizens from the vagaries of the market, reconciling the burden of reproduction with that of other social tasks, and redistributing from the economy, this approach is different in contexts of the Global South. To confirm their observation, Chipenda and Tom 'explore the social policy architecture that has been dominant in countries in sub-Saharan Africa', by making special reference to Zimbabwe. From the explorations they make, Chipenda and Tom reveal that in Zimbabwe, as in other African countries, 'the acceptance and implementation of the social policies exhibit vacuity and non-recognition of the states' responsibility to protect their citizens'. The duo commendably manages to make this critical revelation by making a comparative analysis between social policy in Africa and that in many countries of the Global North such as Germany, Finland, Taiwan, and Japan, among others, where [social] policy has been used as a vehicle of development. and Singapore; social policy, with its multiple functions has not been used as a vehicle for development without being dominated by Bretton Woods Institutions, United Nations Agencies, and international non-governmental organisations (INGO's) and used as a conduit for insecurity as is in the case with Africa.

In his thought provoking Chapter 6, Aluko Opeyemi Idowu uses the game theory to explain how most African countries have been shortchanged in the global politics. The chapter takes an audacious stance to clarify the sequential and simultaneous games in the international relations, such as those on how African countries are entangled into debt crises due to the status of their political-economy as a result of neo-colonialism and existing colonial structures. Using six African states namely, Botswana, Ghana, Côte d'Ivoire, Kenya, Nigeria and Zimbabwe, Idowu demonstrates the degree to which African countries are entangled in global political matrices to argue for the need for Africa to craft development policies that emphasise sustainable development and shake off (neo)colonialism. This is critical, for Idowu, for Africa to effectively break-off from the global politics entanglements and insecurities and become a power broker in the current world politics'.

Chapter 7 by Munyaradzi Mawere and Costain Tandi tussles head on the causes of human insecurity in Africa. It argues that 'pressures unleashed by global forces in the form of liberalisation, privatisation, debt entanglements, and globalisation, among many others, undermine Africa's development in general and human security in particular'. To prop this argument, Mawere and Tandi interrogate conventional assumptions surrounding human security before arguing that in a heavily dependent region like Africa, fortunes are intricately tied to development in the wider global economy. Having argued as such, Mawere and Tandi contend that human insecurity in Africa cannot be fundamentally divorced from development in the international system such that whenever problematising human security, there is need to consider external factors.

Orji Boniface Ifeanyi's insightful Chapter 8 focuses on the United Nations Agencies and Management of Humanitarian Crisis of Internally Displaced Persons' (IDPs) in Nigeria's Abuja Camps, particularly Durumi Area one camp, New Kuchnigoro, Waru, Wassu, Nyanya/Karu/Orozo/Marraba axis, Kuje and Gwagwalada/Kwali axis camp at Dobi, in view of the security of Igbo migrants in the North between 2010 and 2016). For Ifeanyi, there are still various forms of insecurities hovering over the Igbo migrants in the North despite some of the efforts made by the international community to do away with the insecurities. Ifeanyi observes that the 'efforts have been jeopardised *and exacerbated* by Nigerian officials who divert the relief materials for their personal aggrandizements'. Ifeanyi, therefore, calls for transparency, accountability and responsibility among government officials and the agencies of the United Nations to avoid or lessen insecurities and plights of the Internally Displaced Persons' (IDPs) in the Nigerian Camps.

In Chapter 9, Edmore Dube tackles head on the heritage contestations (or conflicts) and religious praxis in African contexts such as those of Mberengwa and Masvingo of Zimbabwe. In so doing, Dube starts by critically examining the various [possible] sources of the Jewish-Arab acrimony from both Biblical and narratives throughout history. Dube thus, contextualises the Jewish-Arab conflict and the insecurities it poses on the Remba people of Zimbabwe, who in fact are of the Jewish-Arab genealogy. He argues that 'fears of insecurity are further exacerbated by Zionist Israel's deployment of missiles, missile defence systems and satellites to defend Jewish religious positions against those of their Arab cousins in Israel'. On this note, Dube blames politics and science which he argues, have been abused and cornered to become servants of religion. Dube thus, concludes that to avoid the revival and invocation of bitter memories of the 'cold war' fought on foreign soil as the United States of America and the Soviet Union in the past, the Jewish-Arab people should find means to cultivate long-lasting peace and avoid war.

Costain Tandi and Munyaradzi Mawere's Chapter 10 cross-examines electoral politics and complexities that come along with insecurities in Africa. To successfully rip through the electoral politics' discourse, Tandi and Mawere start by interrogating factors that 'promote human insecurity during elections, consequences of electoral violence as well as ways of combating electoral violence in Africa'. From their thoroughgoing interrogation, Tandi and Mawere conclude that elections in Africa, if not well monitored, can be flashpoints and hotspots for violence and human insecurity, which in turn will retard developmental efforts in the continent.

In Chapter 11, Prosper Hellen Tlou and Aleck Mapindani lay bare the linguistic vulnerability and techno-paranoia among the

Tshivenda and Xitsonga speakers in Zimbabwe. The duo deploy Sapir-Whorf hypothesis of 1929, which states that language determines thought and culture and that language influences thought and culture, to deliberate on the impacts that results from using English language as a medium of communication on social media in indigenous African contexts. As such, Tlou and Mapindani problematise the use of English, as embedded in contemporary technological gadgets, by the Tshivenda and Xitsonga speakers – speakers of indigenous African languages – in 'informal' settings to argue that such deployment of foreign languages – English in this case –poses threats and insecurities to indigenous languages and cultures. Tlou and Mapindani conclude that the non-usage of indigenous languages in 'formal' domains leads to their underdevelopment, cultural erosion and many other forms of insecurities on the African heritages.

Chapter 12 by Nancy Mazuru disentangles securities surrounding youths in Zimbabwe who abuse drugs in general and 'bronco' in particular. The chapter makes an effort to determine the degree to which the availability of over-the-counter drugs, particularly Broncleer (popularly known as 'Bronco') has [negatively] affected the lives of the youths in Zimbabwe. From the findings obtained during research, the chapter argues that 'although drug abuse is not a new phenomenon in Zimbabwe, the advent of Bronco and other over-the-counter drugs' has amplified the insecurities for youths. On that note, the chapter further argues that the smuggling of Broncleer into Zimbabwe, through its porous national boarders, has led to its availability and accessibility thereby exacerbating insecurities – political, social, religious, physical, psychological, and economic – to the country. Basing on its findings, the chapter recommends that strict measures should be put in place to curb the abuse of Broncleer and other [intoxicating] substances in the country.

Misheck P. Chingozha and Munyaradzi Mawere's luminous Chapter 13 explores the realism of democracy – particularly material and political democracy –in Africa as well as the threats of indoctrination imposed on the so-called Third World Countries and the possibilities for growth and survival in the Emergent New World Order in which Africa has lost all its sovereignty, autonomy, ownership and control, possession and human essence. The chapter is both empirical and theoretical in that it provokes efforts and stimulates creative discussions on the genuineness of democracy preached to Africa by the North. From this provocation and the discussion that ensues, the chapter concludes that democracy preached to the South by the Global North has never been genuine as the majority of African states had to endure and grapple with wars of liberation that left many of their people maimed, dead or deprived and denied of their property followed by spates of (neo)colonialism which remain visible even today.

In Chapter 14, Chioma Elizabeth Abuba dissects through the role of corporate social responsibility in Nigeria's quest to address issues of security in the country's oil rich but largely volatile Niger Delta Region. In this whole attempt, Abuba reveals serious contradictions inherent in corporate social responsibility (CSR) initiatives and engagements by oil multinational companies (MNCs) in host oil bearing communities in Africa and the Niger Delta Region in particular, which result in underdevelopment and various forms of insecurity. Abuba thus argues that although the Niger Delta Region has attracted a number of researches over the years due to volatility of issues and underdevelopment in the region, discourses on the role of CSR in curbing insecurity and promoting peace and development in the region 'is only just emerging with more emphasis on micro-CSR measures which border on provision of physical infrastructure and a minimum level of social infrastructure such as schools and hospitals'. For Abuba, there is need for CSR to come up with lasting results if the three major stakeholders and actors – oil MNCs, host communities and the state – cooperate to promote and sustain macro-CSR measures which address the issues of poverty and insecurity.

In Chapter 15, Tapuwa Raymond Mubaya grapples with the topical issue of genetic engineering, particularly the bio-technological insecurities and the implications it poses for Africa. In his critical engagement, Mubaya examines and interrogates the bio-technological dilemmas and [implicit] insecurities hidden within the Global North's ploy to clone human beings, which for him is akin to playing God. In advancing his argument, Mubaya poses serious questions: 'What could be the future of the planet earth in a world dominated by bio-technology that is largely instigated and engineered from the Global North? What is the role of God in a world where human beings are zealous in assuming responsibilities characteristic of the Creator? What are the unforeseeable social insecurity consequences associated with human cloning, particularly from an African perspective? How far will humanity go in using technology to (re) produce human life? Which ethical dilemmas does human cloning present?' The conclusion that Mubaya draws from this whole questioning is that the North is playing God through its [nefarious] activities such as cloning which it carries out in the name of genetic engineering and bio-technology.

The last chapter (Chapter 16) by Last Alfandika, Gift Gwindingwe and Golden Maunganidze examines vulnerabilities that emanate from the emergent digital media in Zimbabwe. Using Habermas' theoretical lenses, the trio clearly explain the rationale behind the celebration of social media after a long struggle against media oppression, yet they are quick to show the dark side of media. To show the dark side of media, Alfandika, Gwindingwe and Maunganidze deploy the French intellectual Jean Baudrillard's theorisation of social media in the post-modern era as epistemological lenses to forge an understanding of emergent insecurities and threats embedded within the social media revolution. Having shown both the struggles for media freedom and the downside of information revolution, the trio argues that emergent insecurities reproduced by social media have become a cardinal threat to social fibre, leading to 'tribal' wars and 'ethnic' divisions, which ultimately culminates into national insecurity.

References

African News, (26 May 2017) Somali Police Get Surveillance Drones to Combat al Shabaab Insecurity
http://www.africanews.com/2017/05/26/somali-police-get-surveillance-drones-to-combat-al-shabaab-insecurity/

Ajibo, K. I. (2016) Transboundary Hazardous Waste and Environmental Justice: Implications for Economically Developing Countries, in *Environmental Law Review* vol. 18 (4): 267-283.

Al Jazeera, 21 February 2011, In Search of an African Revolution http://www.aljazeera.com/indepth/features/2011/02/2011221 64254698620.html.

Ashforth, A. (2005 *Witchcraft: Violence, and Democracy in South Africa.* The University of Chicago Press. Chicago and London.

Attuquayetio, P. (2014) Drone, the US and The New Wars in Africa, in *Journal of Terrorism Research* vol. 5 (3): 3-13.

BBC History, (17 February 2011) Gladiators: heroes of the Roman Amphitheatre, www.bbc.co.uk/history/ancient/romans/gladiator_01.shtml.

Bielawski, T. M. (2013) States of Savagery: Cannibalism and the Political in Postwar Fiction PhD Thesis, Michigan States

Blair, T. (2010) *Tony Blair: A Journey.* Arrow Books: London.

Bond, P. (2013) *Looting Africa: The Economics of Exploitation.* Zed Books Ltd.

Boswell, R. (2008) *Challenges to Identifying and Managing Intangible Cultural Heritage in Mauritius, Zanzibar and Seychelles.* CODESRIA.

Braidotti, R. (2006) Affirmation Versus Vulnerability: On Contemporary Ethical Debates in Symbolism: *Canadian Journal of Continental Philosophy* vol.10 (1): 235-254.

Braidotti, R. (2006) The Ethics of Becoming Imperceptible, in Boundas, C., (ed) *Deleuze and Philosophy.* Edinburgh University Press: Edinburgh.

Brey, P. (2008) Human Enhancement and Personal Identity, in Berg, O. J. *et al* (eds) *New Waves in Philosophy of Technology. New Waves in Philosophy Series.* New York. Palgrave MacMillan.

Brey, P. (2009) Human Enhancement and Person Identity in Olsen, J. K. B. *et al* (eds) *New Waves in Philosophy of Technology.* Springer.

Business Insider, (7 September 2017) The Airforce's 'Rods from God' Could Hit with the Force a Nuclear Weapon but with no Fallout. www.businessinsider.com/air-force-rods-from-god-kinetics-weapon-hit-with-nuclear.

Business News Daily, (2 January 2018) How to Decrease Exposure to Your Smartphone's Radiation https://www.businessnewsdaily.com/10493-cellphone-radiation-tips.html.

Butler, T. (2012) Precarious Life, Vulnerability, and the Ethics of Cohabitation, in *The Journal of Speculative Philosophy* vol. 26 (2): 134-151.

Chaliand, G. *et al.* (2007) *The History of Terrorism from Antiquity to Al Qaeda.* University of California Press Berkeley, Los Angeles. London.

Cherubini, L. (2008) Aboriginal Identity, Misrepresentation, and Dependency: A Survey of the Literature, *The Canadian Journal of Native Studies* XXVIII (2): 221-239.

Cortina, A. *et al.* (2016) *Ethics of Vulnerability.* Springer.

Croft, S. (2012) Constructing Ontological Insecurity: The Insecuritisation of Britain's Muslims, in *Contemporary Security Policy* vol. 33 (2): 219- 235.

Daily Nation, (23 December 2016) Sex and Marriage with Robots: Science Fiction or New Reality? http://www.nation.co.ke/lifestyle/sex-and-marriage-with-robots-science-fiction-or-new-reality/1190-3496474-forrmation-xhtm/-coan2m/index.html.

Daily Star, (26 November 2017) Swarms of Tiny 'Bio – Hybrids' Cancer – Killing Robots Now Ready for Human Tests https://www.dailystart.co.uk/news/world-news/662787/nanotechnology-science-doctors-medical-robots-injections-testing-cancer-human.

Dangers, E. M. F. (2014) Don't Get Fooled by Cell Phone SAR Ratings in Earthcalm http://www.earthcalm.com/don't-get-fooled-sar-ratings.

Davis, C. (2000) *Hermeneutic and Ethical Encounters: Gadamer and Levinas, in Ethical Issues in Twentieth Century French Fiction.* Palgrave MacMillan: London.

Deleuze, G. and Guattari, F. (1987) *A Thousand Plateaus: capitalism and Schizophrenia.* Minneapolis: University of Minnesota Press.

Domrzalaski, R. (2010) *Suffering, Relatedness and Transformation: Levinas and Relational Psychodynamic Theory.* University of Chicago.

Du Plock, S. (1999) Ontological Insecurity, Existential Self-Analysis and Literature, in Tymieniecka, A. T., (ed) *The Outburst of Life in the Human Sphere. Analecta Husserliana*, vol. 60. Springer: Dordrecht

Ellert, H. (1984) *The Material Culture of Zimbabwe.* Longman Zimbabwe Pvt Ltd: Harare.

Estulin, D. (2014) *TransEvolution: The Coming Age of Human Deconstruction.* Trine Day

Express, (25 August 2017) Cancer Risk: Should You be Worried about Wi-Fi Radiation? https://www.express.co.uk/life-style/health/845494/cancer-risk-radiation-wifi-internet.

Flynn, S. *et al.* (2017) Introduction, in Flynn, S. *et al.* (eds) *Spaces of Surveillance: States and Selves.* Palgrave Macmillan: Oxford.

Forest, J. F. J. *et al.* (2011) Terrorism and Political Violence in Africa: Contemporary Trends in a Shifting Terrain, in *Perspectives on Terrorism* vol. 5 (3-4).

Gelfand, M. (1959) *Shona Ritual with Special Reference to the Chaminuka Cult.* Juta and Co: Cape Town.

Gilson, E. (2014) *The Ethics of Vulnerability: A Feminists Analysis of Social Life and Practice.* Routledge.

Global Research, (4 July 2003) George Soros: Prophet of an "Open Society" https://globalresearch.ca/article/TAL307A.html.

Global Research, (16 December 2017) Cell Phone Radiation: Health Impacts, What Ca We Do to Increase Safety https://www.globalresearch.ca/cell-phone-radiation-health-impacts-what-can-we-do-to-increase-safety/5622941.

Global Research, (9 November 2017) HAARP: Secret Weapon Used for Weather Modification, Electromagnetic warfare https://www.globalresearch.ca/haarp-secret-weapon-used-for-weather-modification-electromagnetic-warfare/20407.

Global Research, (August 2014) The Pentagon's Strategy for World Domination, Full Spectrum Dominance from Asia to Africa https://www.globalresearch.ca/the-pentagons-strategy-for-world-domination-full-spectrum-dominance-from-asia-to-africa/5397514.

Goldberg, E. *et al.* (2001) The Prison-Industrial Complex and the Global Economy. Centre for Research on Globalisation http://www.globalresearch.ca/articles/EVA 110A. html.

Goldsworthy, A. (2012) The Biological Effects of Weak Electromagnetic Fields https://www.bibliotecapleyades.net/scalar_tech/esp_scalartech _cellphonesmicrowave44.htm.

Granoff, J. *et al.* (2005) United States Masters of Space? The US Space Command's "Vision for 2020", in Global Security Institute https://gsinstitute.org/wp-content/uploads/s3/assets/docs/vision2020_Analysis.pdf.

Hegel, G. 1956. *The philosophy of history (adopted from Hegel's Lectures* of 1830-1831), Dover: New York. http://wssbd.com/wx/201503/a_Does_Africa_really_exist_.html.

Held, V. (2005) *The Ethics of Care: Personal, Political and Global.* University Press.

Hicks, M. A. (2016) E-Waste in Relation to Geopolitical Forces: A Case Study of the United States – Mexico Border Region http://academicworks.cuny.edu/hc-sas-etds??iii MA Thesis Hunter College The City University of New York.

Hoffman, B. D. (2016) Biological Invasions and Natural Colonisations: Are they that Different, in *NeoBiota* 29: 1-14 http://neobiota.penssoft.net.

Hossmann, K. A. (2003) Effects of Electromagnetic Radiation of Mobile Phones on the Central Nervous System in *Bioelectromagnetics* 24 (1): 49-62.

Hughes, D. M. (2010) *Whiteness in Zimbabwe: Race, Landscape, and the Problem of Belonging.* Palgrave MacMillan.

Hume, H. 1978. *A treatise* of *human nature,* edited by L.A. Selby-Bigge, (2nd Ed). revised by P.H. Nidditch (Oxford: Clarendon), I 3 iii, 146-147.

Independent, (31 March 2016) French Troops Accused of Forcing Girls into Bestiality in CAR as Rape Claims Mount against UN Peacekeepers http://www.independent.co.uk/news/world/africa/french-troops-accused-of-forcing-gi.

Independent, (4 August 2017) Even Cannibals Observed Manner and Etiquette When Eating Human Flesh hhtp://www.independent.co.uk/life-style/food-and-drink/even-cannibals-observed-table-manners-when-eating-human-flesh-a7852406.html.

Independent, (10 May 1993) History of the Common Cannibal: Its Not Everyone's Idea http://independent.co.uk/lifestyle/health-and-families/health-news/history-of-the-common-cannibal-its-not-everyones'-iea-of-a-wholesome.

Inknen, S. (1998) *Mediapolis: Aspects of Text, Hypertext and Multimedia Communication.* Walter de Gruyter and Co.

Institute for Security Studies, (3 February 2016) Should African Leaders Reconsider Drone Strikes? https://issafrica.org/iss-today/should-african-leaders-reconsider-drone-strike.

Jacobs, M. C. (2012) Assimilation through Incarceration: The Geographic Imposition of Canadian Law over Indigenous Peoples. PhD Thesis, Queens University. Ontario.

Johnson, J. D. (1996) *Signs of the Saucers: A Revealing study of the Flying Saucer-UFO Phenomenon.* Teach Service, Inc.

Johnson, R. (n.d) *The Satanic Warlock.* Lulu.com.

Keenanga – Yamahtta, T. (2016) *From Black Lives Matter to Black Liberation.* Chicago. Haymarket Books.

Kosek, J. (2010) "Ecologies of Empire: On the New uses of the Honey Bee." *Cultural Anthropology* 25 (4): 650–78.

Knoppers, B. M. (1991) *Human Dignity and Genetic Heritage: Protection of Life Series, A Study Paper Prepared for the Law Reform Commission of Canada.* Canada Cataloguing in Publication Data: Ottawa.

Lan, D. (1987) Guns and Rain: Guerrillas and Spirit Mediums in Zimbabwe. Berkeley and Los Angeles: University of California Press.

Laremont, R. R. (2013) Demographics, Economics and Technology: Background to the North African Revolution, in Laremont, R. R. (ed) *Revolution, Revolt and Reform in North Africa: The Arab Spring and Beyond.* Routledge.

Levinas, E. (2003) *On Escape De l'evasion.* Stanford University Press. California.

Levinas, E. (2003) *On Escape.* Stanford University Press.

Levy, D. (2017) Why Not Marry a Robot? In Cheok, A. D. et al (eds) *Love and Sex with Robots*, Lecture Notes in Computer Science 10237 Springer International Publishing AG https://reader.paper.com/books/love-and-sex-with-robots/1707857/A438322_1_EN.

Liden, K. *et al.* (2016) Poison Pill or ure-all Drone and the Protection of Civilians, in Bergtora, K. *et al* (eds) The Good Drone. Taylor and Francis.

Lindenbaum, S. (2004) Thinking about Cannibalism, in *Annu. Rev. Anthropol* vol. 33: 475-498.

Maharawai, M. M. (2017) Black Lives Matter, gentrification and the Security State in the San Franscisco Bay Area, in *Anthropological Theory* vol. 17 (3): 338-364.

Mail Online, (30 April 2012) Feeling Fried? Android App Warns How Much Radiation Your Phone is Blasting into You (But Apple Won't Allow it for iPhone) http://www.daily-mail.co.uk/sciencetech/article-2137442/feeling-fried-Android-app-warns-phone-blasts-brain-radiation-Apple-won't-allow-iphone.html.

Mail Online, (30 June 2016) Become a Robophile? Sex with Robots Could Replace Intimate Human Relationships within 30 Years Http://www.dailymail.co.uk/sciencetech/article-3668305/would-robophile-sex-robots-replace-human-relationships-30-years-women-sex-droids-me.

Makoti, J. (2012) Methodist Approaches to Power Evangelism Among the Shona People of Rural Zimbabwe. Mphil Thesis University of Manchester.

Marks, S. P. (2002) Tying Prometheus Down: The International Law of Human Genetic Manipulation, in *Chicago Journal of International Law* vol. 3 (1): 115 – 136.

Mawere, M. & Mubaya, T. (2016) African Philosophy and Thought Systems: A Search for a Culture and Philosophy of Belonging, Bamenda: Langaa RPCIG.

Mawere, M. and Nhemachena, A. (2017) *GMOs, Consumerism and the Global Politics of Biotechnology: Rethinking Food, Bodies and Identities in Africa's 21ˢᵗ Century*. Bamenda: Langaa RPCIG.

Mireault, A. (2014) *Virtual Sexuality: The Psychological Implications of Digital Age: The Truth about Virtual Sex.* Amy Mireault.

Mohamed, A. E. *et al.* (2012) Slavery and Colonialism: The Worst Terrorism on Africa, in *African Renaissance* vol. 9 (1): 9-26.

Morris, M. J. (2015) Material Entanglements with the Nonhuman World: Theorising Ecosexualities in Performance PhD Thesis the Ohio State University.

Naeem, Z. (2014) Health Risk Associated with Mobile Phones Use, in *Int J Health Sci* 8 (4): 5 – 6.

Nash, C. (2017) Genealogical Relatedness: Geographies of Shared Descent and Difference, in *Genealogy* 1 (7): 1-9.

Natural Society, (16 May 2012) Report Shows How Radiation Can Destroy DNA http://naturalsociety.com/report-shows-how-radiation-can-destroy-dna/.

Ndulo, M. (2006) *Democratic Reform in Africa: Its Impact on Governance and Poverty.* James Currency Publishers.

New York Post, (16 August 2015) Man Who Ate 5 People: Demonic or Desperate https://nypost.com/2015/08/16/was-this-traveling-cannibalism-driven-by-demons-or-desperate/.

News24, 27 February 2013) What we Can Learn from the Illuminati and Other Conspiracy Theories
https://m.news24.com/mynews.

Nhemachena, A *et al.* (2017) Transnational Corporations' Land Grabs and the Ongoing Second mad Scramble for Africa: An Introduction, in Warikandwa T. V. *et al.* (eds) *Transnational Land Grabs and Restitution in an Age of the (De-)Militarised New Scramble for Africa: A Pan African Socio-Legal Perspective.* Bamenda: Langaa RPCIG.

Nhemachena, A. (2016) Animism, Coloniality and Humanism: Reversing the Empire's Framing of Africa, in Mawere, M. and Nhemachena, A. (ed) *Theory, Knowledge, Development and Politics: What Role for Academy in the Sustainability of Africa?* Bamenda: Langaa RPCIG.

Nhemachena, A. (2017) *Relationality and Resilience in a Not So Relational World? Knowledge, Chivanhu and (De-)Coloniality in 21ˢᵗ Century Conflict-Torn Zimbabwe.* Bamenda: Langaa RPCIG.

Nhemachena, A. *et al.* (2017) Materialities and the Resilient Global Frontierisation of Africa: An Introduction, in Nhemachena, A. *et al* (eds) *Decolonisation of Materialities or Materialisation of (Re-)Colonisation? Symbolisms, Languages, Ecocriticism and (Non)Representationalism in 21ˢᵗ Century Africa.* Bamenda: Langaa RPCIG.

Niehaus, I. (2012) Witchcraft and the South African Bantustans: Evidence from Bushbuckridge, in *South African Historical Journal* vol. 64 (1): 41-58.

Noble, L. C. (2011) *Medicinal Cannibalism in Early Modern English Literature and Culture: Early Modern Culture Studies 1500-1700.* New York: Palgrave Macmillan.

Nyakupfukwa, A. (2012) *Superstition Diversity: Superstition, Witchcraft, Taboos and Legends.* Balboa Press.

Osman, J. (10 December 2017) Do Black Lives Matter in the Immigrant Rights Movement, in Al Jazeera, http://www.aljazeera.com/indepth/opinion/black-lives-matter-immigrant-rights-movement-171210095207677.html.

Pambazuka News, (3 Nov 2016) Anti-Terrorism in Africa: Experiences and Lessons https://www.pambazuka.org/human-security/anti-terrorism-africa-experiences-and-lesson.

Partridge, C. (2010) Residential Schools: The Intergenerational Impacts on Aboriginal Peoples in *Native Social Work Journal* vol. 7: 33-62.

Pledger, J. (2013) Deconstructing the Binary of Good and Evil: An Exploration of in Cold Blood and Columbine. University of Colorado Boulder Thesis.

Podrouzkova, J. (2015) Personal Identity in Enhancement, in *Ostium*, roc 11 c3.

Posselt, F.W.T. (1935) *Fact and Fiction: A Short Account of the Natives of Southern Rhodesia.* Government of Southern Rhodesia.

Rheingold, H. (1998) Teledildonics and Beyond, in Berger, A A. (ed) *The Postmodern Presence: Readings on Postmodernism in American Culture.* Rowman Altamira.

Richards, J. E. *et al,* (2010) *The Human Genome.* Academic Press.

Rubenstein, C. (2009) *The Superior Wife Syndrome: Why Women Do Everything so Well and Why – for the Sake of Our Marriages – We've Got to Stop*. Simon and Schuster.

Rumelili, B. (2015) *Conflict Resolution and Ontological Security: Peace Anxieties*. Routledge: London and New York.

Sabbagh, K. *et al.*, (2012) *Understanding the Arab Digital Generation: Strategy and Formerly*. Booz & Co.

Sandvic, K. B. (2015) African Drone Stories, in Behemoth: A Journal on Civilisation Vol 8 (2): https://ojs.ub.um-freiburgide/behemoth/article/viewfile/870/832.

Sharon, T. (2013) *Human Nature in an Age of Biotechnology: The Case for Mediated Posthumanism*. Springer Science and Business Media.

Sium, A. *et al.* (2012) Towards the Tangible Unknown: Decolonization and the Indigenous Future in *Decolonization: Indigeneity, Education and Society* vol. 1(1): I-XIII.

Smith, J. E. (1998) *HAARP: The Ultimate Weapon of the Conspiracy*. Adventures Unlimited.

Southey, T. (1827) *Chronological History of the West, Indies*, vol. 3. Longman: Brown and Green.

Temples, P. (1959) *Bantu Philosophy*. Presence Africaine.

The Guardian, (26 November 2012) The Kyoto Protocol is Not Quite Dead https://www.theguardian.com/environment/2012/nov/26/kyoto-protocol-not-dead.

The Guardian, (6 June 2014) From Teledildonics to Interactive Porn: the Future of sex in a Digital Age https://www.theguardian.com/lifeandstyle/2014/jun/06/teledildonics-interactive-porn-5.

The Guardian, (7 October 2017) FBI Terrorism Unit Say 'Black Identity Extremists Pose a Violent Threat https://www.theguardian.com/us-news/2017/oct/061fbi-black-idenity-extremist-racial-profiling.

The New York Times, (28 November 2013) A Scientist Predicts the Future. www.nytimes.com/2013/11/28/opinion/kaku-a-scientist-predicts-the-future.html.

The Sun, (23 November 2017) Microbot Miracle: Tiny Cancer Fighting Robots Could be Injected into Humans to Fight Disease https://www.thesun.co.uk/tech/4986776/cancer-cure-robot-injected-humans-desease/

The Sun, (15 July 2016) Epicentre of Terror: Why is France the Target of so many Terrorist Atrocities
https://www.thesun.co.uk/news/1449033/why-is-france-the-target-of-so-many-terrorist-atrocities.

The Telegraph, (5 July 2017) Why Female Sex Robots are More Dangerous than You Think
http://www.telegraph.co.uk/wmen/life/female-robots-why-this-women/life/female-robots-why-this-scarlett-johansson-bot-is-more-dangerous.

The Washington Post, 19 October 2017) We Say Black Lives Matter: The FBI Says that Makes Us a Security Threat
https://www.washingtonpost.com.news/posteverything wp/2017/10/19/we-say-black-lives-matter.

Thomas, C. G. (1 Feb 2016) The U.S. Can't Fight Terrorists in Africa. So Guess What it Does Instead in The Washington Post
https://www.washingtonpost.com/news/monkey-case/wp/2016/02/01/the-u.s-can't -fight-terrorist.

Unrul, J. D. (2014) Evidencing Restitution Landscapes: Pre-emptive and Advance Technologies for War-Torn Land and Property Rights Acquisition in *Land Use Policy* vol. 38: 111-122.

Veruggio, G. *et al* (2008) Roboethics: Social and Ethical Implications of Robotics, in Siliciano, B *et al*. (eds) *Springer Handbook of Robotics*. Springer Science and Business Media.

Vidal, C. (2005) Private and State Violence Against African Slaves in Lower Louisiana During the French Period, 1699-1769 in Smolenski, J. *et al*, (eds) *New World Orders: Violence, Sanctions and Authority in the Colonial Americans*. University of Pennsylvania Press: Philadelphia.

Webb, S. (2015) *If the Universe is Teeming with Aliens…Where is Everybody? Seventy-five Solutions to the Femi Paradox and the Problem of Extra-terrestrial Life*. Springer.

Wheen, F. (2004) *How Mumbo-Jumbo Conquered the World: A Short History of Modern Delusions*. Harper Perennial.

Wijnants, R. (2016) Cons/Me: Posthumanist Cannibal Ethics and Subjectivity in the Literary Imagination. MA Thesis.

Wyschogrod, E. (2012) *Emmanuel Levinas: The Problem of Ethical Metaphysics*. Springer Science and Business Media.

Zagami, L. L. (2016) *Confessions of an Illuminati, vol. II: The Time of Revelation and Tribulation Leading Up to 2020*. CCC Publishing Com.

Chapter 2

"Ethnicity", "Nomadic" Identities and (In-) Securities in Africa: The Case of the Tsonga Speaking People in South Africa

Artwell Nhemachena & Dolphin Mabale

In Rwanda, RTLM introduced dehumanizing language, such as calling Tutsis "cockroaches", slowly so as not to shock or disgust their listeners. Jokes and comments were used to condition people to hearing derogatory terms and phrases. The use of the word "cockroach" to mean Tutsi seeped slowly into the public's consciousness, and by the time the genocide started, a majority of the population no longer saw the Tutsis as human and were prepared to eliminate them, or at the very least, not protest against those who took part in the killings (Jorgensen, 2016: 4).

All Tutsi men, women and children were no longer citizens of a nation but cockroaches…Equating Tutsis with cockroaches meant that few would think twice about killing and attempting to exterminate something so vile, dirty and sneaky…And, in the end, from politician to the ordinary farmer, Hutus united to get rid of 'cockroaches', working together to exterminate their Tutsi friends, neighbours, co-workers and family members…Inyenzi [cockroach] was only one of the names used to equate Tutsis with animals deserving of death. There was also inzoka (snakes) which again evoked the notion of vile, sneaky and dangerous (The New Times, 13 March 2014).

Introduction

Despite the fact that the derogatory word 'ethnos' and derivative terms like 'ethnicity' and 'tribe' [referring to large, undifferentiated groups of animals, to the 'heathen', the 'barbarian' and 'uncivilized'] originated from colonising Europeans (Lentz, 1995: 305), some Africans have gullibly adopted and adapted the terms against one another – often referring to one another as 'cockroaches', 'snakes', 'monkeys', and 'dogs' – to dehumanise others and then perpetrate genocide within the continent. The recent agreement by anthropologists and historians that precolonial Africa was not made up of 'tribes' and 'ethnic' groups but by mobile, overlapping networks with multiple flexible group membership (Lentz, 1995: 319), is not surprising given the atavistic insecurities that are visited on Africa by colonial labels such as 'tribes' and 'ethnicities'. However, much as, for instance, the apartheid era Bantu Authorities fragmented African people into insular 'tribal' units, isolated from the others and without the possibility of developing national consciousness, but ruled by chiefs animistically thrust with the burden of doing the dirty work for the apartheid system (Mandela, 2013), the contemporary insecurities cannot be resolved simply by positing and urging "nomadism" or fluidities and becomings of identities, as will be discussed in this chapter. In fact, apartheid era 'autonomous' chiefs were hybridised – and in this sense the problem for African identities is hybridisation rather than rigidification – via the intercalary positions they were forced to operate in. Intercalary positions, which chiefs and contemporary African leaders have been forced to occupy in the world (Mandela, 2013; Blair, 2010), replicate apartheid era hybridisation rather than rigidification of the [indigenous chiefly] identities. While scholars like Terrence Ranger (1993) contend that colonialism invented and rigidified African 'traditions', 'ethnicity' and 'tribalism', it is also important to note that in so far as colonialism involved changing or transforming African identities, it involved processes of destabilising, displacing, disrupting and thus rendering African identities nomadic and fluid. Any subsequent rigidification was an event that was preceded by processes of such colonial displacement, disruption and destabilisation of original African identities.

This chapter traces the colonial processes of changing African identities including the attendant displacements, disruptions and destabilisations that created ontological insecurity on the continent. The argument is that the ontologically insecure colonial processes of destabilising, displacing and disruption of African identities underpinned the colonial transformation of Africans into the zones of nonbeing or nothingness or into the wretched of the earth (Fanon, 1963; Gordon, 2007; Webber, 2012). Defined in terms of lack of biographical continuity, lack of relations of trust, the sense of unrealism about oneself, precariousness, loss of autonomy, feeling of loss of distinction between life and death, lack of temporal continuity, deprivation of human essence, lack of sense of presence in the world, loss of wholeness, feelings of anxiety, dread and loss of identity (Chernobrov, 2016; Valente *et al*, 2017; Rumelili, 2015; Du Plock, 1999; Croft, 2012), ontological insecurity has been a core aspect of colonially induced loss of identity. In addition to this, since social welfare and social security provisions require beneficiaries to have clear identities, proponents of fluidity, effluxion of identities, nomadology of identities, and becomings ignore this very important aspect of possessing clearly delineated human identities that are fairly stable. To be said to be becoming animals is dangerous particularly in a continent where citizens are not only at the risk of being globally sacrificed for the ends of capital but also facing the danger of being fed with donated animals feeds. This chapter argues that scholarly arguments in favour of fluidity, nomadology, becomings, flows and fluxes of identities ignore the problems of (neo-)colonially induced ontological insecurity that results from such fluidity, becomings, disruptions, displacements and destabilisations of African identities. In this regard, it is argued herein that colonial dispossession of Africans, the lootings of African land and livestock, the exploitation of African labour, the reduction of Africans to the level of animals and the categorisation of Africans as 'tribes' and 'ethnicities' all resulted in ontological insecurities.

Arguing against Ranger's (Ibid) thesis that colonialism rigidified African 'traditions', this chapter traces African insecurities not necessarily and simplistically to alleged rigidities or bounded identities that some scholars have imputed to colonialism and apartheid. The chapter argues instead that African insecurities originate partly from the colonial and apartheid era destabilisation, disruption and displacement of African identities and subjectivities. In other words, the chapter argues that colonisers and architects of apartheid destabilised African identities and subjectivities as part of processes of transforming and rendering them nomadic/fluid/becomings towards the goals of the immoral apartheid and colonial systems that conceived Africans as other than humans - as is being replicated in postcolonial 'ethnic' conflicts on the continent. In this case, the colonial transposition of African identities and subjectivities from the plane of African humanity [as enshrined in *Ubuntu* and *Chivanhu*] to the plane of animality did not simplistically involve rigidification of African traditions, subjectivities and identities – rather it involved processes of rendering them nomadic, of unhinging and unmooring African identities and subjectivities for purposes of 'disappearing' the African humanity and 'original' agency into the imperceptible. In view of these observations, this chapter submits that colonial categories of 'ethnicity' and 'tribalism' were in fact the sequel of processes in which Africans were [insecurely] made to become animals – to become subhuman or nonhuman for purposes of colonial and apartheid exploitation. In this regard, postcolonial African quests for security cannot be sought or realised on the basis of indiscriminate becomings or indiscriminate assumptions of nomadic subjectivities and identities – in fact the trope of the 'nomad' was part of the arsenal of colonisers who used it to denigrate, dispossess and colonise Africans.

"Ethnicities", "Tribes" and Insecurities

In spite of the security African unity would bring to the continent, the contemporary resistance to Pan Africanist movements is in fact traceable to resilient colonial and apartheid era conceptualisations of Africans as 'tribes' and 'ethnic' nomads deemed to be fluid, unmoored, unhinged, without political and economic, social, cultural and religious institutions and affiliations. Equally, the contemporary Euro-American antipathy to African families and marriages is indicative of the resilient colonial attitudes that presuppose that African subjectivities are unmoored, unhinged and nomadic, underserving of family and marriage institutions – and this is in spite of the security that families and marriages offer on the continent. Thus, while on one hand African unity, including Pan Africanism, (Murithi, 2009) is often vilified, on the other hand, Pax Americana and the union of Europe are lavishly glorified (Blair, 2010. Notwithstanding the condemnation of African states as exhausted and failed – and of Africans as unruly 'tribes' and 'ethnicities'-, Euro-

American states and institutions are glorified even as they behave, on a global scale, in much more ethnic and tribal fashions than Africans do. The unfortunate assumption has been that [unruly] 'tribes' and 'ethnicities' reside on the African continent and so even if the nomadic World Bank and the International Monetary Fund, like 'tribal' and 'ethnic' chiefs, take pleasure in dictating to Africans, they are hardly identified as gigantic 'tribal' and 'ethnic' entities *albeit* possessed by the Hegelian *Geist* or world spirit and thus masquerading as inclusive on a global scale. For this reason, when scholars explain African "tribal" and 'ethnic' conflicts on the basis of competition for scarce resources or trespassing in one another's territories on the continent, they forget to include the 'gigantic' tribes of Euro-American origin that are possessed by the Hegelian [tribal] world spirit or Geist. The erroneous assumptions that 'traditions', 'tribes' and 'ethnicities' reside mainly or only in Africa should be dispelled on the basis of contemporary celebrations of Queendoms and Kingdoms in Euro-American regions: for instance, the British Queendom has been celebrated by Blair (2010: 133-4) thus:

> Above all, the Queen knew the importance of the monarchy standing for history, tradition and duty. She knew also that while there was need for the monarchy to evolve with the people, and that its covenant with them, unwritten and unspoken, was based on a relationship that allowed for evolution, it should be steady, carefully calibrated and controlled.

If 'ethnicity' and 'tribalism' are characterised by savagery, barbarism, dictatorships and absence of democracy, transparency and accountability, on the contrary, one would expect institutions such as the World Bank and the International Monetary Fund to be accountable to Africans that suffer dictatorships not necessarily by their 'tribes' and 'ethnic' groups but by these international institutions and by some foreign governments. If 'ethnicity' and 'tribalism' are characterised by dictatorship, absence of democracy and absence of transparency and accountability, we would, on the contrary, expect Euro-American governments to stop dictating policies to Africa, particularly where such governments shy away from attendant international obligations for instance to the Kyoto Protocol, International Criminal Court, Land Mines Treaty (Wheen, 2004. While some scholars like Vail (1989 [1991]) contend that most African states are still driven by 'ethnic' particularism commonly known as 'tribalism', it is necessary to note the particularism and hence 'tribalism' and 'ethnicity' that inhere in so-called international institutions, like the nomadic World Bank, the International Monetary Fund and transnational corporations, that like 'tribal' chiefs nevertheless arrogate global rights to dictate to Africa. In fact, particularism [and the attendant insecurity] is as much the essence of Western [individualistic] capitalism as it is of 'tribalism' and 'ethnicity' that are sadly erroneously popularly attributed to Africa. Contrary to Ranger's (1993) contentions that colonialism rigidified African 'traditions', we would argue here that colonialism destabilised, displaced and disrupted African traditions – in this respect, while Euro-Americans have got their Queens and Kings that unify them around their traditions [disguised as modernity] (Nhemachena, 2016; Blair, 2010), Africans who have, since the colonial era, been converted into [subhumans] animals are made to reject their own Queens and Kings, in preference for nomadic, fluid, hybrid subjectivities that have been deprived of cultural moorings and the attendant securities.

Although it is African 'ethnicities' and 'tribes' that are often used to explain violence and insecurity on the continent, experiences of the colonial era should serve to underscore that African insecurities have not historically emanated [simplistically] from African institutions on the continent. Much as other contemporary Western institutions are generating insecurities on the African continent, the colonial British institutions including the British South African Company and the British traditional institutions also generated insecurities in colonial Zimbabwe. In the contemporary world, it is not only African 'tribes' and 'ethnic' groups that fight for resources in ways that generate insecurity – Western international institutions that are nonetheless premised on logics of 'tribalism' and 'ethnicity' also struggle for Africa's resources, particularly where some authors like Cleveland *et al* (1997: 477) contend that:

Our world system is rapidly becoming more interconnected, and no natural, cultural, or technological resources are only "local" resources any longer. The "globalisation" of resources and the problems caused by increasing rates of resources use and degradation have increased conflicts over the meaning of and rights to, resources that have previously enjoyed what separate existences in indigenous and industrial worlds.

In a world that is understood to be global and characterised by global competition for resources, it would be parochial to focus only on researching and condemning 'tribes' and "ethnic' groups that are resident on the African continent where some 'tribes' and 'ethnic' groups from outside the continent, in fact, have virtual presence on the competitive scenes that generate conflicts therein. Such virtually present 'tribes' and 'ethnic' groups capitalise not only on virtual identities but also on flexibility, multiplicity of identities, openness of identities and subjectivities. In short, they capitalise on nomadic identities and subjectivities for which they need an unbounded world. What is postulated in discourses about an open world is in fact a regime where the extraterritorial virtual subjectivities and identities can be globally nomadic and fluid enough to influence distant events and processes, but without attracting liability and accountability. This takes us to the point that nomadic subjectivities underlie Blair's (2010: 388) statement that:

> In the 1980s we had armed Saddam as we had the Mujahideen in Afghanistan, so as to thwart Iran in the one case and the Soviet Union in the other… This time, we would bring democracy and freedom. We would hand power to the people. We would help them build a better future. We would bring not a different set of masters, but the chance to be the masters…

The ways in which some nomadic 'tribes' and 'ethnicities' become 'virtually' present on the African continent are underscored by Gelfand (1959: 121-140) who writes about *mashavi* or wondering restless foreign spirits that afflict local African subjectivities thus:

Like the *Mazungu* and *Varungu mashave* [European foreign spirits] they eventually settle upon innocent, unsuspecting Mashona who were more or less forced to accept the restless spirits and come to terms with them…The shave [*varungu shave*] reveals himself by causing one of the family to become ill.…The father says his prayer of praise, clapping his hands, 'Baasa, we recognise you. Let the child [or person] get better. We shall buy you the clothes you require and then conduct a fine ceremony for you'…His wife praises the *shave*. She says 'Baasa, we have prepared this ceremony for you…' When the people have all had their beer, dancing begins, and the spirit host gradually become possessed. Each host, as he becomes possessed exclaims [in the foreign language – English], 'Yes, yes, yes, I have come'".

Thus, although other scholars have posited [as sustainable and modern] nomadic identities and subjectivities characterised by flux, by becomings, transformation, dynamism and multiplicity (Braidotti, 2012; Pashnova, 2017), it is necessary to notice that colonial wondering foreign spirits (*mashavi*) were used to transform African identities and subjectivities as part of the colonisation process. Such foreign spirits are deemed to be restless and unfixed. They defy African roots, categories and belonging. They also constituted a colonial tool by which to defy otherwise closed boundaries of belonging in Africa, that is, they served to render Africans permeable and partible at a virtual level. In this regard, arguments by some contemporary scholars that humans yearn to disappear by merging into eternal flows of becomings, that humans yearn to lose the self, to surrender the self, to dissolve the subject (Braidotti, 2006; Braidotti, 2012), are reminiscent of colonial wondering foreign spirit afflictions and transformations of African subjectivities.

The nomadic subject with nomadic identities is one marked by open ended becomings, one whose identity is not premised on authenticity but on continuous variation (Galgenbeld, 2016). In some contemporary scholarship, identities including "ethnicity" and authenticity are deemed to constitute barriers to open-endedness and becomings. Scholars like Galgenbeld (2016 argue against collective identities and authenticity as they are deemed to be forces for solidification which closes off variation and becomings. The point here is that some scholars are antithetical to authentic identities because they are deemed to demarcate and protect 'preconceived' "ethnic" boundaries. In a context where capital is keen to exploit every part of the globe, and where descendants of former colonisers are keen to develop roots and routes, however inauthentic, in the indigenous territories, it would be necessary to carefully interrogate discourses that challenge authenticity of identities. Colonisation was similarly about challenging the human authenticity of African identities. If identities become inauthentic, the question is about how possible it would be to apprehend criminals on the African continent? On a continent that is afflicted by crimes of violence including rape, assault, political violence, domestic violence, theft, robbery, arson, fraud and so on, what value would obtain from celebrating inauthenticity of identities? In other words, what are the consequences of promoting inauthentic identities to insecurity on the continent? While other scholars dismiss, in favour of flexible citizenship, the model that links citizenship to belonging to a territory, an "ethnicity", and a nation state (Braidotti, 2012), it is important to question the security and accountability implications in such a world where identities are also understood to be inauthentic and in constant flux.

Apart from the fact that the idea of nomadic subjectivities and identities pre-empts the dispossessed indigenous people's demands for restitution and restoration of their heritages (Branchesi, 2007; Fay *et al*, 2008; Tutchener, 2013), tropes of fluid identities also provide escape routes to those that criminally dispossess others. If identities are understood as in flux, in becomings, as nomadic and flexible, the net effect is that colonisers and their descendants can subsequently claim to have become indigenous – and therefore to have become heirs eligible to inherit indigenous territories, property including land and minerals. In fact with popularisation of the trope on flexible identities, they can conveniently claim heritages both from their colonial forebears and from the indigenous peoples. o, scholars argue that heritage is the necessary other of identity and that for people to claim heritage they need to remember some origins – restitution applies if the ['ethnic' and 'tribal'] identities of the dispossessed can be clearly delineated from history (Branchesi, 2007: 71; Fay *et al*,

2008). Tutchener (2013: 97-8) therefore argues that: "Without a sense of heritage, collective identity cannot be constructed, as there would be no past to base this identity on. Without a sense of collective identity, heritage cannot be constructed…"

Despite the vital connections between indigenous people's identities and their heritages, some scholars challenge indigenous identities not only on the basis of spurious allegations of 'essentialism' but also on allegations of 'excluding' other people from outside the indigenous territories (Nash, 2017). In spite of the fact that colonisation was precisely about Westerners forcibly 'including' themselves in the heritage-spaces of Africans, contemporary scholarship continues to harp about the necessity of Africans including others in their heritages. In fact, the descriptors like 'tribal' and 'ethnic' as applied to Africans are meant to continue to portray them as backward and incapable to manage and exploit their heritages without including the 'more able' Euro-Americans. Notwithstanding the fact that Westerners do not include Africans in land ownership regimes within the Western hemisphere, when Africans assert claim over their heritages, they are paradoxically alleged to be racialising and 'ethnically excluding' others in their models of nationhood (Nash, 2017). For this reason, it has been contended by some scholars that the West needs to deconstruct, discard and displace [African] genealogical models in favour of 'progressive' models of flexible, mobile and hybrid identities that not only challenge [African] rootedness and purity (Nash, 2017), but also open up spaces for Westerners to enjoy African heritages.

Underscoring the necessity for nomadic identities and subjectivities, Braidotti (2006: 24-27) argues:

> Indeed what we humans truly yearn for is to disappear by merging into this eternal flow of becomings, the precondition for which is the loss, disappearance and disruption of the self…What we most truly desire is to surrender the self, preferably in the agony of ecstasy, thus choosing our own way of disappearing, our way of dying to and as our self. This can be described also as the moment of dissolution of the subject – the moment of its merging with the web of non-human forces that frame him/her…the becoming-imperceptible opens up towards

the unexpected and unprogrammed…It is the absolute form of deterritorialization and its horizon is beyond the immediacy of life…Such is the paradox of nomadic subjectivity at the height of its process of becoming other-than-itself, suspended between the no longer and the not yet.

Efforts to displace, replace and disrupt genealogical models date back to the colonial era in Africa where, for instance, Native Commissioners and other colonists in colonial Zimbabwe became notorious for raping African girls and women, including married women, who would have been ordered to the Native Commissioners' residences (Clarke *et al*, 2010). Though the African girls and women resorted to burning sores in their skins to imitate contagious diseases to avoid the attention of the white men (Clarke *et al*, 2010, there are reports that rape and forced impregnation of women in Africa were core features of British colonial rule – and for this reason, no white men were punished for rape even though black men were hanged for raping white women (Gqola, 2016). We therefore contend that the creation of mixed races was a deliberate ploy to generate ontological insecurities, including loss of self-identity, among Africans – it was a way to ensure that African identities became nomadic and fluid for the benefit of the colonial project.

Apart from the above ways to disrupt, displace, and replace African genealogical models, there are contemporary theoretical postulations designed to have similar effects. Disruptions to African genealogical models would also appear in the form of tropes that normalise postanthropocentric sexuality with nonhumans, including sex with animals (Morris, 2015; Nhemachena, 2016). In this regard, discourses about ecosexuality do not only challenge 'human exceptionalism' in 'anthropocentric sexuality' (Morris, 2015), but they also disrupt, displace and destabilise African anthropocentric genealogies on the basis of which Africans are claiming restitution and restoration of their heritages. In essence, to have sex with nonhumans including animals is to roll back into the colonial era animalisation of Africans – it is to become again a nomadic 'tribe' indistinct from the animals with which the tropes are encouraging Africans to sex.

There are also emergent practices of cloning that are feared to undermine human senses of self and identity – individuality and uniqueness (Brock, 2002). A number of other practices including surrogate motherhood, gene therapies, eugenics, genetic engineering, reassignment surgery, the use of recombinant DNA technology and embryonic stem cells, transplantation of human organs and tissues and biotechnology (de Oliveira *et al*, 2012) also render human identity nomadic. In fact genetic manipulation has already generated controversies about reproduction in society. Although they are presented as extending the life span, increasing intellectual capacity, body functionality or sensory functions, human enhancements will also render human identities nomadic such that loss of personal identity and the attendant deprivation of ontological security will result (Podrouzkova, 2015).

Underscoring ways in which such modifications displace and disrupt identities, Morales (2009: 41) observes that:

> We have already started a transition – a transhuman stage, which we should consider a transition to a posthuman stage, where humans will transcend their inherited body, with all its physical, social, emotional, and cognitive limitations, and convert it to an enhanced body which will have more chance to deal with the continual pressures and demands of our rapidly developing human civilization

If genealogies and the attendant identities are premised on ancestry and kinship (Fenton, 2010; 1988; Jenkins, 1997; Hutchinson and Smith, 1996) with clear boundaries of belonging that constitute markers of different groups (Nash, 1989; Fenton, 2010; Nagel, 1994; Pebley *et al*, 2005), then cloning, ecosexuality, genetic modifications and enhancements disrupt, displace and destabilise such genealogical identities and boundaries in so far as they render identities and subjectivities nomadic. Although Africans who were mobile on the African continent have historically and colonially been described as nomadic, we would be inclined to also underscore the fact that, in so far as there is an overarching African identity among African people, African identities and subjectivities have not been as nomadic and mobile as has been popularly presumed in colonial literature. In this

60

sense, we would argue that Europeans who moved to the African continent have been more nomadic than the Africans who they paradoxically derisively described as nomadic and as without common stable institutions, such as cross-cutting ethics and morality of *Ubuntu*. In so far as Africans had cross-cutting *Ubuntu* institutions, we argue that 'ethnic' and 'tribal' conflicts and insecurities were, at least, not as pronounced as purported by colonial writers, but they were in fact catalysed by colonisation that animalised Africans by rendering subjectivities and identities nomadic thereby disrupting, destabilising and displacing standard African humanist *Ubuntu* practices that offered the necessary security and peace in Africa. A closer look at the Tsonga people supports the contentions.

The Tsonga Speaking Groups in South Africa

The people classified as Tsonga are believed to have entered the Transvaal in two major waves of migrations from Mozambique. The first wave occurred in the 1830s when groups fled the destructive intrusion of the Nguni led by Soshangana into southern Mozambique (Setumo, 2005). Of note were the Nkuna who moved into the Transvaal around 1838-9 and subsequently settled in the Bakgaga region (Jaques, 1984; Harries, 1981). Government archival history (1 March 1907) of the Mamitwa indicates that the Mamitwa people of the Baloyi family left Portuguese East Africa "to escape the rule of the Zulus" and settled near Modjadji and became vassals of the latter. Such destructive intrusions and movements underscore the fact that nomadism, becomings, fluxes and flows are not necessarily beneficial to Africans. Africans that had settled in the continent earlier suffered such destructive intrusions from those that had lost or were devoid of *Ubuntu* values. For instance, in an interview dated 6th October 1906, Chief Mawawa Mamitwa stated that his father arrived there before Albasini and his people (File GOV 1086 Ref PS 50/8/07).

The war of succession, of the 1850s, between Manukosi's sons, Muzila and Mawewe, marked the onset of the second wave of migrations of the people of southern Mozambique into the Transvaal. Harries (in Vail, 1989) indicates that the migrations were also caused by ecological insecurities including diseases. However,

61

there are oral accounts (Halala, 2012: 96) that the Levubu-Limpopo confluence has been home to some Tsonga speaking groups like the Makuleke for centuries.

The people who entered the Transvaal, were refugees and so they had no leaders of their own (Van Warmelo, 1935). They settled under any chief to whom they could offer services and paid tribute. Their only quest was finding a place to live. They had come from various cultural traditions and their roots could not be linked to any single "clan" or chief. Because the refugees did not seek to dispossess their hosts, Chiefs competed to attract them and the refugees' loyalty shifted from leader to leader. One of the leaders these people served under was the Portuguese Joao Albasini who controlled the Spelonken area in the Soutpansberg. Harries (in Vail, 1989: 84) asserts that Albasini was the favourite choice of chief as he "…allowed his followers to retain their clan names and material culture…". Some of the immigrants occupied land that had been uninhabitable due to ecological risks. Regardless of where they settled, these newcomers kept their cultural traditions and foods (Harries in Vail, 1989). They were a conglomeration of people from various coastal chiefdoms (Harries in Vail, 1989.

Apartheid and the Formation of the Gazankulu Homeland

The year 1957 saw the beginning of territorial governments or homelands that rigidified 'ethnic' and 'tribal' belongings to particular spaces in South Africa when the then Prime Minister, H. F. Verwoerd invited chiefs from around the then northern Transvaal-Venda, Tsonga, Shangana and Pedi. His intention was to discuss the beginning of apartheid territorial authorities. Although these rigidified territorial boundaries were against the interests of Africans who had previously enjoyed mobility across the continent, it would be presumptuous to suppose that Africans merely found security in mobility and nomadism. In fact, we note here that the colonial and apartheid insecurities arose not simplistically from colonial rigidifications, boundedness or freeze-framing territorial governments. Rather African insecurities arose from the flows and nomadism of 'Ubuntu-less' European colonialists who erroneously assumed that Africa was their open territory or open sesame. In this sense, we argue that the core offence of colonialists was not rigidification of African identities - rather the key charge is that colonialists nomadically invaded and looted from Africans. Because of some rigidities of the homeland plan, as already drafted for such territorial authorities in the northern Transvaal, there was exclusion of authority for Tsonga communities. The Tsonga speaking communities were considered a minority, and further, they occupied areas ruled by chiefs of either Venda or Pedi speaking communities. Wherever they had settled homogenously, their numbers could not allow for the formation of a territorial authority (Harries, 1989; Rikhotso, 1984).

This meant that Tsonga communities from various regions were to be assimilated into major cultural groups in their various regions, to form such authorities. For example, the Tsonga of Baloyi who occupied the region near the Balobedu were to be merged with the Pedi of the Balobedu region to form a single authority. The same can be said for the Tsonga of the Malamulele region who were meant to be assimilated into the territory meant largely to be under the control of the Venda cultural group. This further meant that the Tsonga were to be absorbed into those territories as they were then considered a minority group scattered throughout the northern Transvaal. The plan also meant that the minority Shangana groups from the Bushbuckridge Area were to be grouped with and be controlled by the majority Sotho Group of the Mapulaneng Region in Bushbuckridge (Rikhotso, 1984).

The idea did not settle well with the Tsonga/Shangana representatives, Chief Adolph Sundhuza Mhinga, and Regent Chief Isaac Khetho Nxumalo. They both disliked the idea of the Tsonga and Shangana groups being divided and assimilated into majority groups. They then decided to mobilise Tsonga and Shangana chiefs from the various northern Transvaal into forming an alliance and protest against the plan.

On the 23rd July of 1961, 15 chiefs and many headmen and councillors from all over the areas occupied by Tsonga and Shangaan people, as far as Bushbuckridge held a meeting at Chief Mamitwa's village to discuss their predicament. Amongst other things discussed, it was agreed at that meeting that they should, from there onwards, call themselves Shangaan people and refrain from the use of the term 'Tsonga'. This was after a complaint by Chief Nxumalo that the use of the term Tsonga, which was a missionary label, was segregatory of the people from Bushbuckridge (File NTS 321 Ref 23/55). The chiefs from the Bushbuckridge and Malamulele, Giyani and Letaba regions bought into the idea of sending delegates to Pretoria to ask for a Tsonga and Shangana Territorial Authority so that the Tsonga and Shangana could group themselves together and become a single territory.

Chief A. S. Mhinga, together with four other local chiefs, had earlier written a letter, in 1960, to the then Minister of Bantu Administration and Development. The contents of the letter outlined their grievances with respect to Tsonga people and their headmen being placed under Venda Chiefs. The main complaint was that the Venda Chiefs were not treating the Tsonga people under them with fairness and that there should therefore be separation (File NTS 9103 Ref 423/362).

Two years later, a number of chiefs lobbied the then Bantu Native Commissioner J. H. Alberts on the 13th February of 1962 (File: NTS 9103 Ref: 423/362) for their own territory. The lobby included the discussion about the terms of boundaries between themselves and the VhaVenda.

Archival documents, notably File NTS 423 Ref 423/362 discuss the circumstances surrounding the quest by Tsonga speakers for a separate territorial authority. The documents formed the basis for the granting of the Tsonga speakers an own territorial authority. File NTS 321 Ref 23/55 includes a letter signed by Chief A. S. Mhinga, written by ten chiefs to the Bantu Affairs Commissioner on the 18th August 1962. The letter outlines the terms of the boundary between the Tsonga and the Venda south of the Levubu River, and stresses that no Venda chief is to rule over any Tsonga Headman.

In 1962 after a few meetings, the then government of South Africa announced that the Tsonga/Shangana would have their own territorial authority. Their territory came to be known as the Matshangana Territorial Authority (hereafter, MTA). This was declared at Berlin near Tzaneen, on the 19th December 1962 where

Chief A. S. Mhinga was elected by way of ballot to be the chairperson of the MTA. The territorial authority had five districts, namely, Malamulele, Louis Trichardt, Mokoena-Tshangana Nhlanganu (in the Bushbuckridge area), Ndlopfu (in the region adjacent to the Balobedu), and Bankuna in the Letaba/Tzaneen Region.

Fig 1: The Prime Minister of South Africa, Mr B. J. Vorster addressing the first Legislative Assembly of the Matschangana, Tsonga at Giyani. On the right is Mr Mtsetweni, chairman of the Legislative Assembly. (SAB 18361; 1971)

Berlin, the place where the declaration of the MTA was announced, was initially suggested as the capital of the MTA, but because there were more chiefs in the north, that idea was abandoned as it would have proved to be logistically challenging for those chiefs. An area close to Bend Store, apparently where the delegates were briefed, was selected as the capital of the MTA. That area was built up and later called Giyani (Rikhotso, 1984).

Fig 2: *Members of the Matschangana Executive Committee with the then Prime Minister of South Africa, Mr. B. J. Vorster in discussion of constitutional matters in Cape Town. In front left to right: Mr M Mtsetweni (chairperson), Prof H. W. E. Ntsan'wisi (head council member), Mr B. J. Vorster, Head Chief A. S. Mhinga and council member IK Nxumalo. (SAB 16446; 1971)*

The name Giyani was decided upon at a special meeting of the General Assembly of the MTA held at the Nkowankowa Presbyterian Church Hall on the 13th February of 1968. It was chosen ahead of such names as "Fumani, Phaphama, Vuxaka, Kaya, Ganyani, Tsakani" and several others submitted by the general public.

The names were however, deliberated at length until Professor H. W. E. Ntsan'wisi supported "Giyani" which means "to dance in celebration" as the people were dancing in pleasure. The name was supported by Chief R. Mamitwa because for him it was similar to when a person had succeeded in crossing a flooded river and then danced with joy (File: RSA 1976 MTA).

The MTA functioned until 1971. With the deepening of apartheid in 1973, it became the self-governing homeland of Gazankulu (Harries, 1989). The name Gazankulu was derived from the Gaza Empire of the 1800s that initially belonged to Manukosi or

Soshangana, a Zulu warrior who had broken away from the Zulu Kingdom and established an empire to the north, present-day Mozambique (Rikhotso, 1984). The warriors fought and defeated Tsonga "clans" whom they came across and later moved to various other places. Their followers were later called Matshangana after the chief warrior's name, Soshangana.

The Tsonga, Kingship and the Post-Apartheid Nhlapo Commission of Inquiry

The dawn of political independence in South Africa saw the dissolution of homelands, including the Gazankulu Homeland. The dissolution of the homeland also meant the dissolution of the union between Tsonga and Shangaan, which basically formed Gazankulu. Traditional African leaderships that had been trampled upon by the apartheid system were revived. A few of them were contested in courts, and some Kingships were contested on the basis of historical backgrounds, including the Tsonga Kingship. According to the Nhlapo Commission of Inquiry, Chief Eric Mpisane Nxumalo of the Ndwandwe "clan" contested that he was King of all Tsonga speaking groups in South Africa, based on his historical background as a descendent of nineteenth-century Nguni Monarch, Nghunghunyani. His intention was to revive the Gaza Kingdom of his ancestors.

The Kingship claim was rejected by Tsonga Chiefs and even the Nhlapo Commission did not rule in the favour of the Kingship in its findings in 2011. The rejection of the Kingship was reported in the media. Amongst others, an article that appeared in *City Press* (8th January 2006), titled "Nxumalo's claim to the Tsonga Kingship disputed", discussed several related issues including that the Tsonga territories in South Africa should be recognised separately rather than under a single monarchy. Another article that discussed the rejection appeared in *Sowetan* (1st October 2012) titled "Court Case over Kingship" highlighted that the Tsonga speaking community is the only one without a King. Several newspaper articles were written about why the Ndwandwe should not assume the Kingship, including the one that was featured in the *Capricorn Voice* of 15 October 2013 titled: "Nghunghunyani was never a Tsonga King".

Internet Blogs and the Tsonga/Shangaan Dichotomy

There are several post-apartheid internet blogs that have been used in an attempt to address post-apartheid clarity of the dichotomy and possibly the confusion that exists between Tsonga and Shangaan. Some of them discuss issues around the Kingship debate, while others take it a step further to clarify the dichotomy of Tsonga-Shangaan thereby explaining why Chief Eric Mpisane Nxumalo should or should not be King of the people. The titles are striking, inviting, and moreover, self-explanatory. Amongst them are the following:

- The blog "The Tsonga History Discourse" available on the link http://tsonga-history.blogspot.co.za/ (accessed on 14 October 2015) was started in 2007 as a response to the Tsonga-Shangaan Kingship debate, as well as means of clarifying the histories of Tsonga speaking groups in Southern Africa.

- "All Shangaans are Tsonga, but not all Tsongas are Shangaan" available on the link http://gazankulurepublic.blogspot.co.za/2014/09/all-shangaans-are-tsonga-but-not-all.html created on 14 September 2014 (accessed 14 October 2015) is another blog that painstakingly attempts to explain and clarify Tsonga-Shangaan identity.

- "Battle over kingship" with the subtitle "Tsonga speaking people want to have a king as well" available on http://nkhenci.blogspot.co.za/2012/10/battle-over-kingship.html (accessed on 14 October 2015) posted on the 1st October 2012 by Nkhensani Makhuyane, is a blog that discusses amongst other things, the fact that even though the Nhlapo Commission did not rule in Chief Nxumalo's favour, hundreds of people gathered in Giyani in 2012 to celebrate Nghunghunyani Day. For the author, that is a strong indication that Tsonga speaking people do wish to have their own monarchy.

- Fana the Purp's blog "Fana The Purp Version: "Are we Tsonga or Shangaan or VaTsonga-Machangani?" available on the link http://fanathepurp.co.za/fana-the-purp-version-are-we-tsonga-or-shangaan-or-vatsonga-machangani/ (accessed on 14 October 2015) is in many ways similar to the Tsonga-Shangaan history discourse as well as the Gazankulu BlogSpot in that it is about the clarification of the identity and the dichotomy that is Tsonga-Shangaan.

Tsonga Consciousness and Boundaries

When the Tsonga speaking people arrived in South Africa, they were known as "Magwamba" by their neighbours (Harries in Vail, 1989). In the absence of obvious differences, they were all grouped together as Shangaan, people from Soshangana. It was only later with the arrival of the Swiss Missionaries that they came to be known as Tsonga, after Junod (in Harries, 1981). Tsonga consciousness was instilled and heightened at the Lemana Training Institute (Halala, 2012; Harries, 1989). This consciousness turned into 'ethnicity' during the formation of territorial authorities. Tsonga speaking communities who were mainly in multi-ethnic regions were supposed to be incorporated into Sotho and Venda territorial authorities.

It is interesting to note that even though Tsonga speaking communities came from different backgrounds and had migrated into South Africa at different times they were beginning to see one another as allies. They started to draw up boundaries of acceptance of one another and boundaries of exclusion of Sotho and Venda speaking people. The drawing up of boundaries by these groups was based on the sharing of a common language, which is part of their heritage. According to Ross (2001), the heritage is jealously guarded and then used as a gauge as to who belongs to a group and who does not.

It is not surprising that Tsonga speaking communities or groups started to assert boundaries for their hosts. This is quite normal according to Ericksen (1991; 1993) who defines 'ethnicity' as a process by which groups communicate material, political, economic, moral and cultural differences to one another. In a way, a territorial authority meant some political independence but with vassalage to the apartheid government of the time.

At about the same time that Tsonga speaking people were drawing boundaries, other groups were relaxing their own boundaries for the possible formation of a territorial authority.

Amongst the Tsonga speaking groups, there is a common language, and a common history as they were once faced with the common predicament-the Gaza-Nguni. In addition, it should be pointed out that the descendants of the Gaza-Nguni who are based in the Bushbuckridge Area were part of the newly formed alliance, and that further signified that these groups had to stick to the uniting factors for security and survival.

The idea of the formation of the homeland of Gazankulu, formerly Matshangana Territorial Authority saw the relaxation of boundaries for inclusion of disparate groups for the formation of a seemingly united group. That is why in the MTA meeting of 23rd July 1961, one of the issues discussed at length was the name of the group, since they came from different backgrounds. All agreed that they should call themselves 'Shangaans' and refrain from the use of the name 'Tsonga', after a complaint by Chief Nxumalo that the use of the term Tsonga segregated the people from Bushbuckridge (File NTS 321 Ref 23/55), who are descendants of Soshangana, and as such, they are Shangaan. The Tsonga-Shangaan group had to show a united front for the purpose of being granted a homeland, which at the time meant independence from possible rule by others of Sotho and Venda origin.

Conclusion

This chapter has shown that African insecurity does not necessarily arise from rigidities of boundaries or borders, in fact African insecurities have historically arisen from the popularly assumed openness of borders and boundaries. The insecurities arose from colonial settlers who robbed and looted African resources on the erroneous assumption that Africa was so open that there were no distinctions between insiders and outsiders, indigenous owners and foreign looters. In this sense, it is argued that African security will not come from assumptions of fluid/flexible/nomadic identities and subjectivities. Openness – whether assumed or actual - poses vulnerability to (re-)colonisation in a world characterised by the contemporary new scramble for Africa. In this regard, it is argued that the contemporary scholarly and civil society organisations preoccupation with demonisation of African borders and boundaries is strategically meant to facilitate the (re-)opening up of the continent to ease the ongoing new scramble for African resources. It is contended in this chapter that 'ethnic' and 'tribal' conflicts on the African continent are not simplistically a result of rigid boundaries and borders or cultural intolerance – they are, *a fortiori,* a result of (neo-)colonially induced resource competition and scarcity coupled with historical experiences of resource lootings and colonial incitements of hatred of one Africa group by the others. What is needed to stem African conflicts is not simplistically the opening up of boundaries or borders or the assumption of nomadic/fluid identities. Rather what is needed is to ensure restitution of African resources and human essence which was stolen away by the colonists. To restore African human essence requires setting clear parameters of what constitutes the African human and the nonhuman. Contrary to some contemporary arguments, what is needed in Africa is not mindless fluidity/flexibility/nomadology that effaces the distinctions or identities or subjectivities of African humans and nonhuman things. In fact African colonial insecurities originated from the colonisers' consideration and treatment of African human beings as indistinct from animals.

References

Barth, F. (1969) Ethnic Groups and Boundaries, in Hutchinson, J. & Smith, A. D. (eds). Ethnicity. Oxford University Press. United Kingdom.

Blair, T. (2010) *Tony Blair: A Journey.* Arrow Books. London.

Braidotti, R. (2006) The Ethics of Becoming Imperceptible, in Boundas, (ed). *Deleuze and Philosophy.* Edinburgh. Edinburgh University Press.

Braidotti, R. (2012) *Nomadic Theory: The Portable. Rosi Braidotti.* Columbia UP.

Branchesi, L. (2007) *Heritage Education for Europe: Outcome and Perspectives.* Armando Editore.

Cherubini, L. (2008) Aboriginal Identity, Misrepresentation and Dependence: A Survey of the Literature. *The Canadian Journal of Native Studies*. Xxv 111 (2): 221-239.

Clarke, M. *et al.* (2010) *Lozikeyi Dlodlo: Queen of the Ndebele: 'A very Dangerous and Intriguing Woman'*. African Books Collectives.

Cleveland, D A. *et al*, (1997) The Worlds Crop Genetic Resources and the Rights of Indigenous Farmers, in *Current Anthropology* vol. 38(4):477-516.

Conzen, K. N. *et al*, (1992) The Invention of Ethnicity: A Perspective from the U.S.A. *Journal of American Ethnic History*. Vol. 12(1): 4-41.

De Oliveira, E Q. (2012) Protection of Genetic Heritage in the Era of Cloning, in Rev Bras Hermatol Hemoter 334(6) 452-458.

Deng, F M. (2008) Human Rights in the African Context. in Wiredu K. *A Companion to African Philosophy*. John Wiley& Sons.

Engebrigtsen, A. I. (2017) Key Figure of Mobility: The Nomad, *in Social Anthropology*. Vol. 25 (1): 42-54.

Ericksen, T.H. (1991) The Cultural Contexts of Ethnic Differences. *Man, New Series*. Vol. 26, No. 1, pp. 127-144.

Ericksen, T.H. (1993) *Ethnicity and Nationalism: Anthropological Perspectives*. Pluto Press. London.

Ericksen, T.H. (2010) *Ethnicity and Nationalism: Anthropological Perspectives*. Pluto Press.

Fay, D. *et al* (2008) *The Rights and Wrongs of Land Restitution: Restoring What Was Ours*. Routledge.

Fay, D. *et al.* (2008) *The Anthropology of Land Restitution: An Introduction*. Routledge.

Fenton, S. (1988) *Ethnicity: Racism, Class and Culture*. Macmillan Press Ltd. London.

Fenton, S. (2010) *Ethnicity* (2nd Edition). Polity Press. Cambridge.

Galgenbeld, N. (2016) 'We`re Only Particles of Change': Ethnicity, Identity and Authenticity in Continuous Variation, MA Thesis Radboud University Nijmegen.

Geertz, C. (1963) Old Societies and New States, in Yinger, J. Milton. 1985. Ethnicity. *Annual Review of Sociology*, Vol. 11, pp. 151-180. Annual Reviews.

Gqola, P. D. (2016) *Rape: A South African Nightmare*. Jacana Media.

Halala, P. (2012) A Critical Historical Study of the Form and Content of the Response of the Vatsonga to Swiss Christian Missionary Activities: The Case of Valdezia, Elim, Kurhulen and the Surrounding Areas, 1873-1994. Unpublished PhD. Thesis. University of Limpopo. Polokwane.

Hallwood, P. (2006) *Out of this World: Delueze and the Philosophy of Creation.* Verso.

Harmsworth, G. R. *et al,* (2013) Indigenous Maori Knowledge and Perspectives of Ecosystems, in Dymond J. R. (ed). *Ecosystem Serves in New Zealand- Conditions and Trends.* Manaaki Whenna Press, Lincoln New Zealand.

Harries, P. (1981) The Anthropologists as Historian and Liberal: H-A. Junod and the Thonga. *Journal of Southern African Studies.* Vol. 8, No. 1, Special Issue on Anthropology and History, pp 37-50.

Harries, P. (1989) Exclusion, Classification and Internal Colonialism: The Emergence of Ethnicity among Tsonga-Speakers of South Africa. In Vail, L. (ed) *The Creation of Tribalism in Southern Africa.* David Phillip. Cape Town.

Henning, E., Van Rensburg, W. & Smit, B. (2004) *Finding Your Way in Qualitative Research.* Van Schaik. Pretoria.

Hesser-Biber, S. N. & Leavy, P. (2006) *The Practice of Qualitative Research.* Thousand Oaks: Sage. USA.

Hodgkin, K, & Radstone, S. (eds). (2003) *Contested Pasts: The Politics of Memory.* Routledge. London & New York.

Horowitz, D.J. (1977) Cultural Movements and Ethnic Change. *Annals of the American Academy of Political and Social Science*, Vol. 433, pp 6-18.

Hutchinson, J. & Smith, A. D. (eds) (1996) *Ethnicity.* Oxford University Press.

Jaques. A.A. (1984) *Swivongo swa Machangana.* Morija Printing Works. Morija, Lesotho.

Jenkins, R. (1997) *Rethinking Ethnicity.* Sage Publications Ltd. London.

Jok, J M. (2012) Insecurity and Ethnic Violence in South Sudan: Existential Threats to the State? The Sudd Institute: Research for a Peaceful, Just and Prosperous South Sudan Issues Paper.

Jorgensen, C. M. (2016) A Case Study Analysis of Dehumanization in Rwanda. PhD Thesis Nova Southeastern University.

Leedy, P. & Ormrod, J. E. (2010) *Practical Research: Planning and Design.* Pearson Education Inc. New Jersey.

Lentz, C. (1995) Tribalism and Ethnicity in Africa: A Review of Four Decades of Anglophone Research. *Cah.sci.hum* 31 (2):303-328.

MacGonagle, E. (2008) Living with a Tyrant: Ndau Memories and Identities in the Shadow of Ngungunyana. *The International Journal of African Historical Studies.* Vol. 41, No. 1, pp. 29-53.

Malins, P. (2011) An Ethico-Aesthetics of Heroin Chic: Art, Cliche` and Capitalism, in Guillaume, L. *et al* (eds). *Delueze and the Body.* Edinburgh University Press.

Maree, K. (ed) (2010) *First Steps in Research.* Van Schaik Publishers. Pretoria.

Merriam, Sharan B. (2009) *Qualitative Research: A Guide to Design and Implementation.* Jossey-Bass. San Francisco.

Morris, M. J. (2015) Material Entanglements with the Non-human World: Theorising Ecosexualities in Performance. PhD Thesis. The Ohio State University https://etd.ohiouk.edu/etd.send.file?accessing-su1435325456&disposition=online.

Mouton, J. (1998) Using Documents in Qualitative Research, in Ferreira, M., Mouton, J., Puth, G., Schurink, E. & Schurink, W. (eds). Introduction to Social Research. Module 3. Human Science Research Council. Pretoria.

Nagel, J. (1994) Constructing Ethnicity: Creating and Recreating Ethnic Identity and Culture. *Social Problems*, Vol. 41, No. 1, pp. 152-176.

Nash, C. (2017) Genealogical Relatedness: Geographies of Shared Descent and Difference, in *Genealogy* 1(7):1-9. www.mdpi.com/journal/genealogy.

Nash, M. (1989) The Cauldron of Ethnicity in the Modern World, in Hutchinson, J. & Smith, A. D. (eds) Ethnicity. Oxford University Press. United Kingdom.

Niewenhuis, J. (2010) Introducing Qualitative Research, In Maree, K. (ed) *First Steps in Research.* Van Schaik Publishers. Pretoria.

Pashnova, A. (2017) A Nomad from Within? Resilient Identities in an Interconnected World: Russian- speaking Immigrant Woman in Italy- Re-constructing the Self. MA Thesis, University of Jyvaskyla.

Pebley, A. R., Goldman, N. & Robles, A. (2005) Isolation, Integration, and Ethnic Boundaries in Rural Guatemala. *The Sociological Quarterly*. Vol. 46, No. 2, pp. 213-236.

Podrouzkova, J. (2015) Personal Identity in Enchantment in Ostium roc 11c3.

Posselt, F. W. T. (1935) *Fact and Fiction: A Short Account of the Natives of Southern Rhodesia*. Government of Southern Rhodesia.

Ranger, T. (1993) *The Invention of Tradition Revisited: The Case of Colonial Africa*. Harare UZ Press.

Rikhotso, F. (1984) *Matimu ya mfumo wa Gazankulu* (History of the Gazankulu Government). Emmanuel Press.

Ross, M. H. (2001) Psychological Interpretation and Dramas: Identity Dynamics in Ethnic Conflict. *Political Psychology*. Vol. 22, No. 1, pp 157- 178.

Schermerhorn, R. (1970) Comparative Ethnic Relations. Random House. New York, in Hutchinson, J. & Smith, A. D. (eds) Ethnicity. Oxford University Press.

Setumo, T. (2005) *Hosi Ngungunhane of the Tsonga*. J.P Publishers. Polokwane.

Singleton, R., Straits, B. C. & Straits, M. M. (2003) *Approaches to Social Research*. Oxford University Press. New York.

The New Times, (13 March 2014) Dehumanisation: How Tutsis were Reduced to Cockroaches, Snakes to be Killed http://www.newtimes.co.rw/section/read/73836.

Vail, L. (ed) (1989) *The Creation of Tribalism in Southern Africa*. David Phillip. Cape Town.

Van Warmelo, N. J. (1935) A Preliminary Survey of the Bantu Clans of South Africa. Ethnological Publications, Vol. V. The Government Printers. Pretoria.

When, F. (2004) *How Mumbo-Jumbo Conquered the World. A Short-History of Modern Delusions*, Harper Perennial.

Yinger, J. Milton. (1985) Ethnicity. *Annual Review of Sociology*, Vol. 11, pp. 151-180.

Archival Documents
Giyani Archives
NTS 9103 Ref: 423/362.
NTS 321 Ref: 23/55.

Chapter 3

Disabilities and Human Insecurities: Women and Oculocutaneous Albinism in Post-Colonial Zimbabwe

Fidelis Peter Thomas Duri & Alice Makama

Introduction

Insecurity is a concept that encompasses a broad range of vulnerabilities emanating from violent conflict, violation of human rights, bad governance, lack of access to educational and health care, denial of opportunities that inhibits individuals and societies from fulfilling their potential, and inequitable distribution of resources, among other things (Annan, 2000). Insecurity is also characterised by the state of fear or anxiety within individuals, sections of the population or even a whole society that emanates from a real or imagined lack of protection (Beland, 2007). Vulnerability is a central feature of human insecurity (Suhrke, 1999). Vulnerable sections of the population are usually those that experience physical threats to life and denied access to resources that enable them to lead decent lives (Ibid). In April 2001, the United Nations noted the exposure of individuals and societies to various socio-economic vulnerabilities and violence as the major sources of insecurity in the contemporary world (United Nations, 22 April 2001). Accessibility of basic material needs, the absence of threats to one's survival (freedom from want), and a dignified and violence-free existence (freedom from fear) are critical elements of human security (Thomas and Wilkin, 1999; United Nations Development Programme, 1994). This chapter identifies Zimbabwean women living with albinism as one of the most vulnerable sections of the population. It explores their insecurities in various spheres of life and some of the mitigatory strategies they employ.

The term albinism is derived from *albus*, a Latin word which means white (Phatoli *et al*, 2015). It is believed that the word 'albino' was first used in Africa by early Portuguese travellers to refer to 'white' people they came across whom they believed to have partial or complete albinism (Machipisa, 25 November 2002). Some scholars contend that the use of the term 'albino' is demeaning while 'person with albinism' is appropriate since it places a human being before the condition (Baker, 2011; Machoko, 2013). Despite this valuable observation, 'albino' is used in this chapter, without any derogatory connotations, interchangeably with 'person with albinism.'

Albinism is an inherited condition which affects all races. It is brought about by a mutation of several genes which results in a deficit in the production of melanin, the pigment that is responsible for determining the colour of the skin, hair and eyes (Baker, *et al*, 2010; Moyo, 16 July 2015; Mutingwende, 15 June 2016). The condition manifests itself in different forms, the commonest of which are oculocutaneous and ocular albinism (Kagore and Lund, 2005; Lund, 1996). Oculocutaneous albinism is a result of little or no pigmentation in the eyes, hair and skin. In its most severe form, it is characterised by the complete whiteness of the hair and skin throughout life while in its less severe form, the white hair and skin become slightly darker with age (Baker, 2013; Lund, 2001; Machoko, 2013). People with oculocutaneous albinism experience abnormal flickering eye movements (nystagmus) and are very sensitive to bright light. They also experience other eye problems such as poor sight and crossed or squinting eyes (strabismus) (Lund, 2001; Mutingwende, 15 June 2016). Ocular albinism only affects the eyes, which lack colour, but their skin and hair are normal (Mutingwende, 15 June 2016).

Given these critical health-related ailments, constraints and vulnerabilities associated with albinism, the United Nations officially declared albinos as people with disabilities in 2008 (Dawes, 17 May 2012; Mawere, October 2014). In 2013, the United Nations (UN) Human Rights Council passed a resolution calling for the prevention of attacks and discrimination against albinos (Moyo, 16 July 2015). On 18 December 2014, the UN General Assembly passed a resolution proclaiming the 13th of June of every year as the International Albinism Awareness Day. The resolution was effected from the year 2015 (Moyo, 16 July 2015). On 17 June 2016, the UN convened and sponsored Africa's first ever forum to raise awareness on people living with albinism. The event, which was held in Tanzania, was attended by activists and government officials from the continent (Mhofu, 16 June 2016). The Zimbabwe Constitution (Amendment Number 20 of 2013) also recognises albinos as persons with disability and states that "the State and all institutions and agencies of government at every level must recognise the rights of persons with physical or mental disabilities, in particular the right to be treated with respect and dignity."

In 1996, two in every 10 000 people in Zimbabwe's total population of approximately 11.5 million were albinos (Zinhumwe, 25 November 1996). Statistics from the 2002 population census indicated that Zimbabwe had an estimated albino population of 15 000 (Machipisa, 25 November 2002; Ufumeli, 14 April 2015). In 2015, one in every 14 000 Zimbabweans was reportedly living with albinism as compared to one in every 17 000 people in the whole world (Moyo, 16 July 2015). In June 2016, Zimbabwe had about 39 000 people with albinism out of a total population of 13 million (Mhofu, 16 June 2016).

Persons living with oculocutaneous albinism are often ostracised in Africa largely because they are especially conspicuous by their pale skin among dominantly dark-complexioned populations (Baker *et al*, 2010; Lund, 1996; Mawere, October 2014). Since pre-colonial times, the physical appearance of albinos often generated in some African societies, superstitious beliefs and myths which resulted in their stigmatisation, marginalisation and social exclusion (Moyo, 16 July 2015). These age-old negative myths, together with others crafted during the post-colonial period, have largely been responsible for the ostracisation of albinos from the mainstream society worldwide in general and in Zimbabwe in particular. While many of the age-old myths became embodied in the socio-cultural beliefs of some societies, others crafted during contemporary times are not indigenous to Africa, but are largely misrepresentations and misconceptions emanating from lack of scientific knowledge about the condition of albinism. Many people living with albinism are therefore subjected to various insecurities which make their lives very miserable.

While this chapter is primarily concerned with the manner in which myths largely contribute in causing various insecurities on women living with albinism and those who give birth to children with the condition, it is fully cognisant of the fact that 'modern' science has its own tragedies on human life (Nandy, 1988). These include military technological advancements and their consequent losses in human life (Alvares, 1988), the environmental catastrophe caused by industrialisation and 'modern' mining operations (Nandy, 1988), and the negative health implications of Western medicine and genetically-modified foods (Kothari and Mehta, 1988; Shiva, 1988). The findings from 'modern' scientific research that albinism is an inherited condition also aggravates the plight of the generality of the albino population since many people are hesitant to associate with, or marry, them (Baker, *et al*, 2010; Moyo, 16 July 2015; Mutingwende, 15 June 2016). Some medical doctors are known to have caused alarm and despondency by recommending abortions to pregnant mothers carrying babies with oculocutaneous albinism on grounds that the children would not lead healthy and productive lives, and that their life expectancy would be very short (Selepe, 2007).

It is also prudent to note from the onset that superstition is not peculiar to Africa alone. In fact, it is not the intention of this chapter to conflate everything African with myths. Even in several parts of the world such as Europe since historical times, racial myths were, and are still, articulated under the guise of race science discourses. Western anthropological criminology, for example, was based on perceived links between the nature of a crime and the physical/racial appearance, particularly anomalies, of an accused person (Edwin Mellen Press, 2004). Cesare Lombroso, the Italian criminologist and physician who lived from the mid-18th century to the first decade of the 19th century, for instance, held the myth that people with sloping foreheads and receding ears were criminals (Ibid). Another example can be drawn from colonial Rwanda where German and Belgian colonial administrators propagated the Hamitic myth that sought to create racial distinctions among indigenous African people. According to this myth, the Tutsi descended from the Hamites, the light-skinned Black Caucasians from Europe who were believed to be the offspring of the Biblical Noah's son, Ham. The myth credited the Hamites for bringing 'civilisation' to the dominantly 'negroid' populations of sub-Saharan Africa. In line with this myth, the German and Belgian colonisers regarded the Tutsi as being more intelligent than other indigenous African people in Rwanda such as the Hutu and the Twa (des Forges, 1995; Pruner, 2010). Similarly, in Nazi Germany during the 1930s and 1940s, Hitler indoctrinated the youths to regard Aryan Germans as a superior race than the Jews and the Romans (Koch, 2000; Lauridsen, 2004). It should therefore be emphasised that since historical times, many societies and institutions, both in Africa and beyond, have always had myths, some of which, as will be illustrated in this chapter, bring about various insecurities on some sections of the population. In addition, some of the myths are contemporary fabrications which are neither linked to modern science nor traceable to indigenous socio-religious traditions, but are manifestations of ignorance and criminality on the part of the perpetrators.

The condition of albinism in Zimbabwe has attracted the interest of scholars from various disciplines such as Biomolecular Science (Lund, 1996), Anthropology (Baker *et al*, 2010), Psychology (Mutasa, 2013), Sociology (Kagore and Lund, 2005; Lund, 2001; Machoko, 2013), Linguistics (Kadenge *et al*, 2014) and Literature (Baker, 2011; Chinyowa and Chivandikwa, 2017). Many academic works have been devoted to the socio-economic vulnerabilities experienced by people living with albinism in post-colonial Zimbabwe. Baker *et al* (2010), for example, examined the myths surrounding the ostracisation of albino people. Kadenge *et al* (2014) looked at how Shona nomenclature perpetuates the discrimination of people living with albinism in Zimbabwe. Machoko (2013) dwelt on the socio-economic insecurities of albino communities in Zimbabwe with particular focus on their marginalisation in various aspects of life.

It is quite apparent that much of this academic literature views the albino population as a homogenous entity as far as its contemporary insecurities are concerned. Lund (2001) and Kagore and Lund (2005), however, sought to address this weakness in the scholarly literature by focusing on albino children and their challenges in the fields of health and education. This chapter makes a significant contribution to the academic discourse by focusing on the gender dynamics of albinism in post-colonial Zimbabwe. It examines women, both albino and non-albino, in terms of their experiences with albinism paying attention to their victimisation and agency. The chapter contends that while the condition of albinism subjects the generality of the albino population to various insecurities in many aspects of life, women living with the condition and those who give birth to albino children, are the worst affected. Among other things, women with albinism are often seduced, abandoned and raped by unscrupulous men, and shunned by their in-laws, while others are usually blamed for birthing albino children. These challenges largely emanate from age-old superstitions and contemporary myths relating to sexual encounters with albino women. Despite being victimised, harassed and abused in various ways, some women seek to extricate themselves from patriarchal encapsulation. Among other initiatives, some women living with albinism and those who birth children with the condition part ways with abusive husbands and in-laws while others form associations to look into their security in terms of welfare and rights.

Insecurities experienced by the generality of people living with oculocutaneous albinism

In order to fully appreciate the peculiar insecurities of albino women, it is cogent to firstly outline the problems faced by the generality of people living with albinism. This section examines the challenges faced by people with oculocutaneous albinism in Africa in general and Zimbabwe in particular. The insecurities have a lot to do with their health, stigmatisation and marginalisation.

People living with oculocutaneous albinism are vulnerable to a plethora of health ailments and related insecurities. In addition to poor eyesight, their skin is delicate and can easily be damaged under conditions of direct sunlight. As a result, they are always in need of umbrellas, hats, long-sleeved clothing and sunscreen creams (Moyo, 16 July 2015). They are also very vulnerable to skin cancer when exposed to ultraviolet rays (Chinyowa and Chivandikwa, 2017; Machipisa, 14 January 2003; Mawere, October 2014). In February 2013, Richard Nyathi, the Deputy Chairperson of the Zimbabwe

Albino Association (ZIMAS), lamented that the organisation was losing two of its leaders every year due to skin cancer. He added that most people living with albinism in Zimbabwe and the Southern African region did not live beyond 30 years as a result of skin cancer (Nyathi, 13 February 2013). During the period 2004-2014, ZIMAS lost an average of 15 known people living with albinism every year due to skin cancer (Mawere, October 2014). From January to April 2017, 17 ZIMAS members died from skin cancer (Mananavire, 27 April 2017). As a result of these health ailments, people with albinism are often discriminated against in various public arenas and have problems as far as job security is concerned (Lund, 2001). As Adesuyi (20 September 2013: 1) noted:

> Albinos in Zimbabwe are treated as outcasts… Many people also believe that albinism is contagious and avoid contact with albinos. Many albinos have reported disheartening stories of superstition-fuelled discrimination, such as people being afraid to touch them, people denying them services, and people choosing seating far away from them in public places.

The physical appearance of people living with oculocutaneous albinism, particularly the pale colour of their skin, hair and eyes, has resulted in them being ostracised like lepers by the dominantly dark-skinned sections of the African population (Baker *et al*, 2010; Lund, 1996; Mawere, October 2014). This ostracisation is quite evident in some African languages through the use of nomenclature embedded with derogatory connotations on their condition of disability. Among the Shona people of Zimbabwe, as Mashiri *et al* (2002) noted, naming is a communicative tool used to express the culture, belief and values of the society. In Zimbabwe, a person living with albinism is widely known as *musope* (white mysterious figure) and *inkawu* (white monkey) by the Ndebele and the Shona people respectively (Cohen, 1 September 2015). Some Shona people also use the offensive terms *jechwe* (supernatural being) and *murungudunhu* (fake/quasi white person or white person from the village) to refer to albinos (Chinyowa and Chivandikwa, 2017; Kadenge *et al*, 2014; Mutasa, 2013; Mwale, 28 July 2015). Similarly, among the Zulu in South

Africa, they are commonly referred to as *isishawa* (a person who is cursed) and *inkawu* (white baboon) (Phatoli *et al*, 2015). Among the Swahili of East Africa, they are known as *zeru* which denotes a ghost-like creature (Chinyowa and Chivandikwa, 2017).

In many African societies since the pre-colonial period, the insecurity of people living with oculocutaneous albinism has been aggravated by superstitious beliefs that have been generated to explain their light complexion. Baker *et al* (2010: 170) aptly captured the function of myths in many communities since the pre-colonial period:

Throughout the world, myths function to account for phenomena which are out of the ordinary or which cannot be explained in other terms, fulfilling a fundamental human need to make sense of the world. The beliefs surrounding albinism in Southern Africa are often found to compensate for such a lack of knowledge.

In many pre-colonial African societies, the birth of an albino child was often regarded as a mystery. In some cases, the 'mysterious' event was attributed to the machinations of witchcraft and evil spirits (Machoko, 2013). As Bourdillon (1998: 149) noted among the Shona people of present-day Zimbabwe:

Shona (people) often explain disease and misfortune in terms of witchcraft- this belief in witchcraft does not necessarily contradict a belief in natural causes. Natural causes can answer the question of why; why in this particular person and why at the time and place? Europeans are more likely to speak of chance or perhaps divine providence, but the Shona find a more ready answer in terms of witchcraft.

Bourdillon's observation, however, is not entirely accurate as he reduces Shona explanations of events to the machinations of witchcraft. It was common for some Shona people to attribute the birth of an albino child to chance as evidenced by expressions of distress from concerned parents such as *zvangoitikawo* (It has happened against our wish) (Muredzi *et al*, Group Interview, 19 November 2017). Others explained such an occurrence as an aspect of nature or genetics/heritage by saying *ndezvekuberekwa nazvo* (There is nothing we could do since it is part of nature or genetics) or *inotambika* (the contemporary Shona slang for 'it happens') (Ibid).

It should be added that since pre-colonial times, the Shona also attributed some occurrences such as the birth of an albino child to divine providence and not just to witchcraft. Indeed, albinos were often regarded as a curse from God and also a punishment from the ancestral spirits (Adesuyi, 20 September 2013; *Associated Press*, 18 June 2016; Chinyowa and Chivandikwa, 2017; Moyo, 16 July 2015; Waugh, 2005).

Despite these varying explanations, many indigenous African communities regarded the birth of an albino child as an unfortunate event. In particular, the myths advanced to explain such occurrences made it very difficult for albinos to be accommodated in the mainstream society on equal terms. As a result, people living with albinism were regarded as second-class citizens in many communities. Thus, in 2016, during an interview with the *Associated Press* (18 June 2016: 1), Gwen Marange, a Zimbabwean woman living with albinism, stated that "many of us die a little inside each time we step into the public" because many dark-skinned people booed and verbally abused them.

In some pre-colonial African societies, newly-born albino children were killed. Early Portuguese settlers, for example, reported the killing of newly-born albino children in pre-colonial Zimbabwe during the 1580s (Beach, 1999). Ruth Chitara, a 93-year-old woman who witnessed the discrimination of albinism in her childhood, told Ufumeli (14 April 2015: 1), a *Newsday* journalist: "The child would be killed because it was felt that it would bring a bad omen upon the family. The practice was bad because you were made to use your own hands to kill your child. We thank European missionaries for bringing Christianity because it brought an end to this practice." Similarly, in the Zulu Kingdom in South Africa during the 19th century, albino children were "gotten rid of at birth" on grounds that they were "an omen of misfortune" that would "pollute the population" (Dube, 19 November 2015: 1). While some societies killed newly-born albino children on superstitious grounds that they were a bad omen, it is also plausible to argue that they were executed because their skin colour was deemed to resemble that of Europeans who were colonising Africans. Despite these possible explanations, the major point being advanced here is that since the pre-colonial period, the lives of many people born with the condition of albinism were characterised by several vulnerabilities since the pre-colonial period.

It should be noted that the above-mentioned myths, socio-religious beliefs and other explanations of albinism were quite retrogressive because they denied some disadvantaged sections of the population their right to life. As Adesuyi (20 September 2013: 1) argued:

There is no doubt that culture is one of the building blocks of a person's character and moral upbringing. However, when culture dilutes the mind of an individual and devalues the life of a human being because of a physical difference, should this belief be followed? Zimbabwean beliefs of albinos are discriminatory, and this aspect of the culture should be altered. There should be a limit to which culture plays a prevalent role in the overall lives of individuals, especially when it is discriminatory. The discrimination against albinos in Zimbabwe is destroying a group at the expense of cultural beliefs and it is unjust.

Some pre-colonial African superstitious beliefs were, however, ambivalent and self-contradictory in nature. Their lack of uniformity and consistency is illustrated by the fact that while some myths viewed newly-born albinos as a curse that should be killed instantly, others regarded them as supernatural beings whose lives could be sacrificed for ritual purposes to benefit the living. Consequently, an estimated 75 people with albinism were killed in Tanzania during the period 2000-2015 (Moyo, 16 July 2015). In 2015 alone, more than 89 albinos were killed in Tanzania (Ndlovu, 16 June 2016). In Malawi, 18 albinos were killed during the period spanning from early 2014 to mid-2016 (*Associated Press*, 18 June 2016). In many parts of Africa during the 21st century, many albinos were killed for their body parts such as arms, legs, ears and genitals which were believed to transmit magical powers and bring good luck (Ufumeli, 14 April 2015). There is no doubt that the lives of people living with albinism, especially in many parts of Africa, are characterised by fear and insecurity.

As in many other parts of Africa, some contemporary Zimbabweans also believe that body parts from albinos can be used for ritual purposes to bring good luck, among other things. On 23 September 2015, for example, Joyce Katiyo, a pregnant woman, went to give birth at the Domboramwari Maternity Clinic, situated in the south-eastern part of Harare (Machakaire, 15 November 2015). After delivering an albino boy, a midwife immediately instructed her to remain lying down while she took the baby to the next room purportedly to 'examine' his body. After the baby gave out a loud cry, Joyce peeped into the next room, only to find the midwife cutting off one of the baby's testicles. The baby was later referred for treatment at the Chitungwiza General Hospital where doctors confirmed that his testicles had been severed deliberately. It was suspected that the midwife mutilated the testicles of the baby with the intention of using them for ritual purposes (Ibid).

This section has examined some challenges which the generality of people living with albinism in Africa in general and Zimbabwe in particular have been facing since the pre-colonial period. The history of people with albinism was, and is still, largely characterised by a broad range of insecurities. It has been noted that health ailments feature prominently in their experiences as they are vulnerable to skin cancer and other challenges such as impaired vision. It is in view of these health challenges that people living with albinism continue to be discriminated against in various public arenas. In addition, their pale features subject them to further marginalisation. This section has illuminated how myths, socio-cultural discourses and other explanations were crafted to explain their light-skinned complexion. Most of the explanations demonised albinos as mysterious beings, cursed people and an expression of anger by God and the ancestral spirits. Consequently, newly-born albino babies were instantly killed in some pre-colonial African societies. The stigmatisation and ostracisation of albinos, both males and females, has persisted into the present day. The section also noted some superstitious beliefs that regard albinos as supernatural beings whose body parts can be used for ritual purposes resulting in many people living with the condition being mutilated or killed even during the 21st century. On the whole, this section has illustrated the insecurities experienced by people living with albinism since the pre-colonial period which include their victimisation, ostracisation, marginalisation and demonisation. The next section shows that women living with albinism in post-colonial Zimbabwe are worse off as compared to their male counterparts.

Age-old myths and patriarchal chauvinism as sources of insecurity for women living with albinism in Zimbabwe

Many age-old superstitious explanations of albinism have persisted in the post-colonial era resulting in the untold suffering of women living with the condition in independent Zimbabwe. The myths that have been particularly pervasive pertain to albinos being a curse from God, a punishment and angry expression from the spiritual world, and an outcome of witchcraft. As a result, many indigenous communities are reluctant to have albino women married into their families. In addition, their pale skin colour and vulnerability to health ailments, particularly skin cancer, often result in them being regarded as liabilities rather than assets by the relatives of their prospective husbands, both of who also dread that the condition can spread into their present and future generations. In June 2016, for example, some Zimbabwean women living with albinism described their lives as "hell on earth" because of their husbands' "deeply-rooted myths and prejudices" (*Associated Press*, 18 June 2016: 1).

A survey conducted by ZIMAS in April 1997 revealed that very few albinos got married, and that less female than male albinos were likely to engage in any marriage at all (Musiwa, August 1998). The study also found out that it was easier for an albino man to marry a 'black' woman than for an albino woman to marry a 'black' man. To make matters worse, it was very rare for albinos to marry each other for fear of spreading the gene that causes albinism (Ibid). In an effort to find spouses, the survey noted, "albino women think that if they get skin-care lotions to make their skin smooth and beautiful, they will be able to attract men who could marry them" (Ibid, p.1).

In January 2003, Felicity Mwamuka, the then Welfare Officer of ZIMAS, stated that most men were reluctant to marry albino women and girls (Machipisa, 14 January 2003). She added: "Many albino men marry easily than their female counterparts because the society believes that an albino girl will bring albino children. It takes time for albino women, most of whom are single parents, to marry" (Machipisa, 25 November 2002: 1). Consequently, "many albino women are single mothers," she lamented (Machipisa, 14 January 2003: 1). In December 2016, for example, an estimated 69% of Zimbabwean women living with albinism were single mothers (George, 2 December 2016). During the same month, Mercy Maunganidze, an albino woman, explained some insecurities and uncertainties experienced by single mothers living with albinism: "It is tough being a single mother with albinism as you are viewed with fear, superstition and prejudices; it is demoralising" (George, 2 December 2016: 1).

In many cases, family members and relatives discourage men from marrying women living with albinism. In November 2014, for example, Chipo Kumire, a 50-year-old widow from Chirimamhunga Village in the Seke Communal Lands, stated that she was always subjected to harassment by her in-laws who never accepted her condition of albinism even before the death of her husband in 2004 (Chinowaita, 24 November 2014). As Tapiwa Gwen Marange, an albino woman, stated in November 2015:

> We, people with albinism, are stigmatised. We are seen as outcasts; our families are ashamed of us and society does not embrace us. In some cases pregnant women spit in their clothes when they come across a person with albinism as a way of asking their gods not to give them a child with albinism (Marange, 15 November 2015: 1).

This quotation aptly captures the tribulations of women living with albinism. It illustrates their pleas for recognition within their families and communities. It demonstrates that many women dread giving birth to albino children to the extent of asking God and the ancestors (mistakenly expressed collectively as 'their gods') that this does not happen to them.

In a revealing incident that took place in April 2017 in the Mberengwa District, there was pandemonium in the family of Adonia Macheza, a 26-year-old visually-impaired man, who had decided to marry a woman living with albinism. Narrating the incident, the *Zimbabwe Broadcasting Corporation News* (24 April 2017: 1) reported:

> His family and relatives disowned him as they could not come to terms with his choice of marrying a woman living with albinism. Enraged by his nephew's decision to marry a woman living with albinism, Macheza's uncle destroyed the homestead and vandalised property leaving the couple homeless.

The family quarrel forced the newly-married couple to relocate to Shumbashave Village within the same district (*Zimbabwe Broadcasting Corporation News*, 24 April 2017). This incident illustrates the deep-rootedness of some age-old myths and their negative impact on the wellbeing of people living with albinism in contemporary times.

This section has noted how some age-old myths, largely rooted in patriarchal chauvinism, which persist in the post-colonial period make life unbearably insecure for women living with albinism. Among other challenges, many albino women find it very difficult to get married. Those who are fortunate to get married are often ill-treated by their husbands and in-laws. As the next section shows, the vulnerability of women living with albinism in various spheres of life is exacerbated by the formulation of some contemporary myths relating to their condition which further subjects them to a broad range of heinous abuses.

Contemporary myths and the vulnerability of women living with albinism

This section dwells on two contemporary myths that exacerbate the predicament of women living with albinism in independent Zimbabwe. These myths are neither embodied in African indigenous cultural beliefs and practices nor informed by biomedical science, but are largely the machinations of patriarchal chauvinism and veritable manifestations of ignorance, bordering on criminality, about the condition of albinism on the part of some unscrupulous men. One popular myth pertains to the sexual prowess of albino women. The other notoriously superstitious belief is that an HIV-positive man can be cured by having sexual intercourse with a woman living with albinism. These myths result in many women living with albinism being raped and relegated to sex slaves, which also places them at risk of contracting HIV/AIDS and Sexually Transmitted Infections (STIs). These abuses also explain why a considerable number of albino women are single mothers, many of them having been raped, seduced and deserted by predatory men.

There is a widespread myth among some men concerning the sexual prowess of albino women. In addition, numerous cases abound of unscrupulous men who sexually abuse girls with albinism "for experimental purposes, just to compare the difference with black-skinned girls and albinos. They eventually dump them after having fallen pregnant" (Ufumeli, 14 April 2015: 1). Ezeilo (1981), in his study of the Igbo in Nigeria, also noted that some men only become intimate with albino women out of curiosity rather than affection. In addition, as Tapiwa Gwen Marange, a 34-year-old Zimbabwean woman living with albinism, stated in June 2016, "They (traditional healers)…say women with albinism give more sexual pleasure than women who do not have albinism, which is a lie" (Mhofu, 16 June 2016: 1).

Lamentably, this myth demeans albino women and relegates them to sex objects. This partly explains why a considerable number of women living with albinism are either single mothers or choose never to get married. A survey conducted by ZIMAS in April 1997 noted that approximately 20% of the total population of women living with albinism in Zimbabwe were single mothers who had been abused by men who took advantage of their vulnerability and denied responsibility (Musiwa, August 1998). From a sample of 30 women living with albinism in the City of Mutare, Mutasa (2013) discovered that 13 (43%) were single mothers, five (17%) never married, six (20%) had been abandoned by their spouses while five (17%) were married. In late 2016, ZIMAS estimated that 69% of Zimbabwean women living with albinism were single mothers and 59% of them were so frustrated that they would never marry. ZIMAS also stated that about 29% of the single mothers living with albinism in the country were divorcees (Simukai Initiative, 2017). In addition, most of the albino single mothers were in the age group ranging between 25 years and 49 years (Ibid). As ZIMAS noted, most of the single mothers living with albinism lead miserably insecure lives and "suffer psychological, physical, social and economic challenges" (Ibid, p.1).

The experiences of Alice Makama, an albino woman and one of the authors of this chapter, are quite illuminating on how some unscrupulous men abuse women living with albinism. Alice was born in 1991 and was the only albino child out of four children in their family. In 2012, at the age of 20 years, she fell in love with a non-albino man who was a few years older than her. Alice felt privileged to fall in love considering that her skin condition had made it difficult for her "to find someone who loved me because a lot of guys would feel ashamed to be known that they have asked out a person living with albinism, let alone being in a relationship" (Makama, Interview: 2017).

During their relationship, she noted that her partner was not comfortable to be with her in public. As a result, they spent much time at his place. Indeed, her partner often told her "how his friends would laugh at him saying that he was in love with a *musope* (a person living with albinism)…but he always told me that he loved me and he did not care what people said about us and I believed him" (Makama, Interview: 2017).

After dating for three months, Alice formally introduced her partner to her aunt. The man assured her aunt that he wanted to marry Alice. The aunt advised him to approach his relatives and introduce Alice before they proceeded with marriage plans. According to Alice, this marked a turning point in their affair because "months passed by but he never took me to any of his relatives. Each time I asked him when we would meet his relatives, he would just change the topic" (Makama, Interview: 2017). To make matters worse, Alice fell pregnant 10 months into their relationship. When she informed him about the pregnancy, he began to shift goal posts, stating that he was not prepared for marriage but would accept responsibility for the child (Ibid).

When Alice's aunt confronted him, he did not deny responsibility for the pregnancy but insisted that he was not ready to marry. In addition, he also informed Alice's aunt that his parents were not prepared to have an albino daughter-in-law. The aunt then accompanied Alice to his boyfriend's house and left her there (Ibid). As Alice narrated, life at the boyfriend's place was unbearable:

> Life began to change and got tougher each and every day. Kuda had changed. He started behaving awkwardly. He started treating me like a stranger. He would shout at me every day telling me he never loved me and he had a 'normal' girl he wanted to marry. I would cry each and every day regretting falling in love with him. I even started questioning God why l was born with albinism. We stayed together for two months and there was no change. Instead, he would telephone his girlfriends in my presence and I felt like it was the end of the world. I would tell my aunt about what was going on but she would comfort me that things would get better, but things were getting worse each and every day (Makama, Interview: 2017).

After three months, the boyfriend's mother visited them and told her to go back home on grounds that her son was no longer interested and that their family was not prepared to have a daughter-in-law living with albinism. In addition, his boyfriend's mother stated that an albino daughter-in-law was a liability rather than an asset because "l could not help her in the fields since l could not stay in the sun for a long period of time" (Makama, Interview: 2017). Alice felt hurt but there was nothing she could do since she was now six months pregnant (Ibid).

Things got from bad to worse a week after the boyfriend's mother had left. A relative who stayed in the City of Chitungwiza invited Alice and her 'husband' for a birthday party. The boyfriend said that he was wanted at his place of employment but told Alice to go to the party and he promised to follow later during the day. He did not come for the party (Ibid). Alice described the shock of her life after returning home from the party:

He was not there and the house was empty. He had taken all his belongings. There was only a letter he wrote apologising that he had to leave because he was under pressure from his relatives. I was so hurt that l cried. I even thought of killing myself. I felt it was the end of the world but the only thing that gave me hope was my unborn child. I then went back home to my parents who accepted me back and comforted me, giving me counselling. After three months, I was blessed with a 'black' baby girl and l named her Tariro, meaning hope. After two years, I was sent back to school by my parents and right now (2017), I am studying for a Bachelor of Arts Honours Degree in History at Great Zimbabwe University (Makama, Interview: 2017).

Alice Makama's experiences are quite illustrative of the various insecurities faced by women living with albinism. As evidenced by her testimony, the lives of many albino women are characterised by anxiety over whether they would find genuine marriage partners in future. Many are also vulnerable to being seduced and abused by unscrupulous men who become intimate with them solely for experimental purposes. Many of those who get married are not guaranteed of security in marriage as a result of age-old and contemporary myths about people living with albinism.

In contemporary Zimbabwe, there is another pervasive myth that having sex with an albino woman eradicates HIV and other health ailments such as cancer, diabetes and high blood pressure (Machoko, 2013). This has resulted in the rape of many women by men with HIV/AIDS (Moyo, 16 July 2015; UNICEF, April 2010). From 2002, there were widespread reports in Zimbabwe that albino women were increasingly becoming the victims of rape, "a practice fuelled by myths that if an HIV-infected man sleeps with an albino woman, he will be cured" (Machipisa, 14 January 2003: 1). In November 2002, Felicity Mwamuka of ZIMAS expressed concern at the upsurge in such rape cases. She moaned: "With the HIV/AIDS pandemic, most albino ladies are being taken advantage of because of their skin colour. There is this traditional belief that if you sleep with an albino woman, you get cured" (Machipisa, 25 November 2002: 1). This was a disturbing development in a country with a population of 13 million and a high prevalence rate of one HIV-positive person for every four sexually active people (Ibid).

In 2009, a Zimbabwean man living with albinism, quoted by Baker *et al* (2010: 176) acknowledged the vulnerability of his female counterparts to being raped by HIV-positive men:

To be an albino is a terrible thing, but to be a girl albino is the worst of all. You know that the AIDS pandemic, they say the cure is to sleep with a virgin, but if you sleep with a virgin who is albino, then even better. There are many rapes. Because they are so hidden already they do not come forward. And now because of this, we are also dying of AIDS. This rape: it is a terrible thing.

In September 2014, ZIMAS expressed similar sentiments and estimated that 70% of the albino women who were raped succumbed to HIV before reaching the age of 60 years and, out of the fear of being stigmatised, many victims disclosed the rape cases when their health had deteriorated (Huni, 28 September 2014).

Gwenlisa Mushonga, a 33-year-old albino woman and Director of Alive Albinism Initiative, a local non-governmental organisation devoted to improving the lives of albinos, also confirmed the upsurge in such cases of rape in June 2015: "We receive numerous reports of albino girls who are raped because men believe sleeping with a woman with albinism cures HIV and cancer. Sometimes men come for you as if they are in love. They want to exercise their rituals on you, sleep with you and go" Cassim, 24 June 2015: 1). In June 2016, Tapiwa Gwen Marange, 34-year-old Zimbabwean woman living with albinism, stated that this myth was very pervasive in Zimbabwe. She said, "In Zimbabwe, traditional healers lie to HIV-positive men, that if they sleep with a woman with albinism, HIV/AIDS is cured" (Mhofu, 16 June 2016: 1).

An example can be drawn from Melissa Ndongwe (not her real name), a woman living with albinism in the Zimbabwean City of Masvingo and a friend of Alice Makama, the co-author of this chapter (Ndongwe, Interview: 2015). Melissa was married to a 'black' husband for three years from 2012 to 2015 and they stayed together in Masvingo. Melissa recalled that during their three-year marriage, she would see her husband taking tablets every evening. When she asked what the tablets were for, the husband said that they were a remedy for high blood pressure. Sometime in 2015, Melissa took a sample of the tablets and inquired from a nurse what health ailments they cured, only to be told that they were taken by people who were HIV-positive in order to boost their immune systems. Melissa was so frustrated that she abandoned her husband in 2015 to live her own life (Ibid). This case demonstrates that the husband was dishonest to his albino wife for three years and most probably sought to cohabit with her in line with the superstitious belief that his HIV condition could be healed by having sexual intercourse with a woman living with albinism. In addition, considerable numbers of albino women who are abused in this way are at risk of contracting HIV/AIDS.

This section has discussed some of the insecurities experienced by women living with albinism in Zimbabwe that emanate from baseless contemporary myths that they are sexually more satisfying in addition to being a remedy for HIV/AIDS and other health ailments. This conviction results in many albino women being raped, seduced and abused by unscrupulous men, condemning them to lives of perpetual regret and untold misery. In addition to the health challenges consistent with their condition of albinism, such abusive practices worsen their dilemma by exposing them to the risk of contracting STIs and HIV/AIDS.

Victimisation of non-albino women for giving birth to children with albinism

In independent Zimbabwe, longstanding and contemporary myths are often articulated, mostly by husbands and in-laws, to victimise non-albino women who birth children with albinism. In most cases, the women and families from which they came from are scapegoated by being accused of witchcraft, which becomes the explanation for the birth of an albino child. As Lund (2001) observed, whenever a child living with albinism asks the father about the cause of his condition, the blame is often apportioned on his wife's family members. In addition, some women are accused of prostitution and being intimate with white men. As a result, some women are abandoned by their husbands after giving birth to albino children while others endure various forms of harassment at the hands of their in-laws.

There are numerous cases of husbands who blame their wives for giving birth to albino children. As McNeil (9 February 1997: 1) noted: "Many men accuse their wives of infidelity when albinos are born.

Some even accuse them of having had sex with a *tokolosh* (troublesome spirit), a devil's imp who is said to be produced by witchcraft from a tree root and to live under beds." In addition, some mothers who give birth to albinos are often accused of eating or drinking an unorthodox medicine during pregnancy (Kadenge *et al*, 2014). Others are accused of having been intimate with white men (*Zimbabwe Situation*, 5 December 2009). Despite the availability of scientific evidence that both parents can be carriers of the gene that causes albinism (Mashongwa, 13 September 2014), women are often victimised by their husbands and in-laws after giving birth to albino children (Kadenge *et al*, 2014). As Tapiwa Gwen Marange, a Zimbabwean woman living with albinism, explained in November 2015: "In Africa, giving birth to a white child causes confusion, mistrust and in the search of an explanation, superstitions abound" (Marange, 15 November 2015: 1).

Consequently, some women are divorced by their husbands after birthing children with albinism (Kadenge *et al*, 2014). In December 2009, for example, about 90% of albino children in the East African region were being raised by single mothers because their fathers believed that their wives were having affairs with white men (*Zimbabwe Situation*, 5 December 2009). This scapegoating by husbands partly explains why, in June 2016, most albino children in Zimbabwe had single parents, usually mothers (*Herald*, 14 June 2016). A few examples from Zimbabwe will help to illustrate these myths and how they make many albino women to lead miserably insecure lives.

In November 1996, Letwin Karombo, an albino woman, recalled her childhood experiences during which her mother was often blamed for giving birth to two children with albinism. Her mother was often accused of committing adultery with white people. She said: "My uncles and my late father believed that I and my brother were children of sin, born out of extra-marital affairs" (Zinhumwe, 25 November 1996: 1).

Another example pertains to Loveness Mainato, a non-albino woman from the Zimbabwean City of Chitungwiza, who was admitted into a hospital with severe stress after giving birth to a second child with albinism (*Associated Press*, 18 June 2016; Mhofu, 16

June 2016). Her husband was furious at having a second albino child which he blamed on Loveness. In 2007, he married their maid and deserted her (Ibid). Narrating her ordeal, Mainato said, "My husband deserted me just because his family members influenced him that something has to be done, urging us to consult traditional healers. Having experienced such trauma, I suffered heavily from depression, got hospitalised. It greatly affected me, giving me discomfort and embarrassment in the society" (Ufumeli, 14 April 2015: 1). She added:

> My husband's relatives told him that it would be a shame for the family if he continued living with me and that he made the biggest mistake of marrying from St. Mary's (Suburb in Chitungwiza) where I come from because women from that area aborted babies to the extent that the womb would lose pigmentation and babies are born albino. He left me in 2007 and never returned to date. He even refused to name the children. I would also be told by my in-laws that I practised witchcraft and that eating human flesh resulted in albino offspring (Machakaire, 15 November 2015: 1).

In 2010, Richard Nyathi, an albino and member of the Zimbabwe Albino Association, explained how his mother, who did not have albinism, was blamed by her husband's family members and relatives for his condition. His mother was accused of infidelity and subjected to abuse throughout her entire married life (Baker *et al*, 2010).

In November 2015, Trisheiglah Mudume, a Bulawayo mother, who together with her husband were not albinos, stated that she was often harassed by her in-laws for giving birth to two children with albinism. The in-laws argued that the two albino children were a result of her infidelity and a punishment for he 'sins.' She explained:

> It was really difficult for my in-laws to understand that albinism was a medical condition. I just could not fight anymore as I felt dejected. Until now, I hardly talk to my in-laws because they failed to accept my children and believed that I cheated on my husband. What pained me is that they regarded my children as a punishment for 'cheating' on my husband (Dube, 9 November 2015: 1).

This section has noted the misery of non-albino women who are blamed by their husbands and in-laws for giving birth to children with albinism. Thus, as Uzande (10 August 2016: 1) noted, "Mothers of albino children often find it difficult to be fully integrated into their communities because of the negative myths and superstitions which surrounded albinos." It is partly as a result of this victimisation that many mothers allegedly dump their albino babies soon after giving birth. In mid-2016, for example, the dumping of newly-born babies with albinism was reportedly on the increase in Zimbabwe (Ufumeli, 14 April 2015).

The pursuit of security by albino women in post-colonial Zimbabwe

The discussion in the last three sections focused on the victimisation, marginalisation and abuse of albino women and those who give birth to children with albinism. Despite these insecurities, it should be noted, however, that many women are not passive victims who sit idly moaning their predicament. This section examines the individual and collective initiatives which some of the affected women improvise to overcome various insecurities in a superstitious dispensation heavily influenced by patriarchal chauvinism.

At the household level, some albino women who are perpetually abused by their husbands demonstrate agency by liberating themselves through divorce. In 2016, during an interview with the *Associated Press* (18 June 2016), Tapiwa Gwen Marange stated that she had to divorce her husband because he always mocked her about her condition of albinism.

Some women living with albinism seek to dispel myths that demean and demonise albinos by enhancing their status through educational pursuits which they used as a platform to raise public awareness on the rights of their counterparts. In 2008, Bonnie Dudzai Mureyi, a 21-year-old Zimbabwean woman living with albinism, for example, was the country's representative in the Imagine Africa Contest, a campaign that sought to raise youth awareness about HIV and AIDS (Machirori, 20 April 2012). She became the first albino in Zimbabwe to graduate as a pharmacist since the School of Pharmacy was established at the University of Zimbabwe in 1974 (Ibid). At the age of 24 years in 2012, she was a practising pharmacist in Harare. She also devoted much of her time to sensitising the public about the needs and rights of people living with albinism (Machirori, 20 April 2012; Moremi Initiative, 7 July 2016).

From the early days of albino activism in Zimbabwe during the mid-1990s, some women living with albinism became members of associations that championed their cause. On 3 November 1996, for example, Professor John Makumbe, an albino, founded the Albino Trust of Zimbabwe (ATZ) with the initial aim of raising funds to buy sunscreen lotion and spectacles for albinos who could not afford them (Machipisa, 14 January 2003; McNeil, 9 February 1997; Moyo, 16 July 2015). It was soon replaced by ZIMAS, a full-fledged organisation that sought to protect the rights of people living with albinism (Musiwa, August 1998). The membership of ZIMAS was drawn from both men and women living with albinism. In April 2017, ZIMAS had about 13 000 registered members out of an estimated 70 000 people living with albinism in Zimbabwe (Mananavire, 27 April 2017). Its executive committee included women such as Felicity Mwamuka who was the Welfare Officer from 2002 (Machipisa, 14 January 2003). Mercy Maunganidze, another woman living with albinism, served as a counsellor at ZIMAS for 15 years before rising to the position of Director in 2013 after the death of John Makumbe (Mananavire, 27 April 2017; Simuka Initiative, 2016). Soon after its formation, ZIMAS immediately embarked on a campaign, using the then Zimbabwe Broadcasting Corporation's (ZBC) Radio Four Educational Channel, to sensitise people on the rights of people living with albinism (Zinhumwe, 25 November 1996).

In 2016, Mercy Maunganidze spearheaded the formation of Simuka (Arise), a wing of ZIMAS that specifically sought to look into the security of single mothers living with albinism in various spheres of life (Simuka, 2016). Simuka's primary objective is "to assist single mothers with albinism to realise their potential, help them to build their self-confidence and participate fully in economic, social and political issues in their communities without any discrimination" (Ibid, p.1). Mercy Maunganidze (2016: 1) elaborated on how Simuka set out to overcome various insecurities that confronted albino women in Zimbabwe:

> My organisation, Simuka, intends to help single mothers with albinism in Zimbabwe. We want to build their self-confidence and train them in entrepreneurship skills such as business management, marketing strategies etc. In doing this, it will enable these women to participate fully in their communities and earn a living for their families without any discrimination. Additionally, I want to reduce the current percentage of single mothers in my country. This could be achieved by intense campaign awareness programmes to demystify the myths that mainly cause these women to become single mothers.

Some women who are victimised for giving birth to children with albinism also form associations to represent the interests of people living with the condition. A case in point is Loveness Mainato, a former teacher at St. Mary's Primary School in the Zimbabwean City of Chitungwiza, who formed the Albino Charity Organisation of Zimbabwe (ALCOZ) in 2009. She was not an albino but had given birth to two children with albinism which resulted in her husband deserting her and marrying another woman (*Associated Press,* 18 June 2016; Ufumeli, 14 April 2015). The organisation is based in Chitungwiza and aims at looking into the welfare and security of people born with albinism. It is largely funded by private companies and some pharmacists from the city who often pay tuition fees for schoolchildren living with albinism (Ufumeli, 14 April 2015). In November 2014, ALCOZ had a total membership of 887 of which 582 were from Harare and Chitungwiza while 305 were from the surrounding rural areas (Chinowaita, 24 November 2014). In April 2016, 60% of the organisation's members were drawn from Harare and Chitungwiza (Ufumeli, 14 April 2015).

ALCOZ has particular interest in the educational pursuits and rights of children living with albinism. This thrust was articulated by Loveness Mainato while addressing attendants in Harare at an event organised by the United Nations on 15 June 2016 to mark the International Albinism Awareness Day:

> People with albinism are discriminated in many forms of life. Such discrimination and segregation is rampant in the education system especially at primary level where they are teased and laughed at. When these children give excuses that they cannot see properly and request to sit in the front row because of their poor sight, they are not given full attention. In some cases, fellow students shun sitting next to them. There are also many extra curriculum activities where they are discriminated because of their skin. These include athletics and other events and school choir (Ufumeli, 14 April 2015: 1).

She also bemoaned the victimisation of mothers who gave birth to children with albinism: "It is not just in schools where discrimination takes place because there is a myriad of forms of discrimination. The harsh reality is the fact that giving birth to a child with albinism brings all sorts of misery to parents, mostly mothers" (Ufumeli, 14 April 2015: 1).

In addition, ALCOZ also teaches mothers to love and care for their children born with albinism (Ufumeli, 14 April 2015). As Loveness Mainato explained in June 2016: "I am now giving counselling to others, and courage to love their children and to accept their condition as they are. It is not a misfortune. It is not a result of prostitution, neither is it a result of witchcraft" (Mhofu, 16 June 2016: 1).

Loveness Mainato also played a leading role in safeguarding the rights and security of albinos in general. In June 2016, for example, she urged the Zimbabwean government to guarantee the safety of its citizens living with albinism following the recent escalation in cases where people with the condition were killed in Malawi and Tanzania (Ndlovu, 16 June 2016). Addressing a meeting organised by the UN in Harare on 15 June 2016, she said, "The authorities should intervene at a regional level to ensure the safety of people living with albinism. Most albinos are afraid of travelling into the neighbouring countries because of the prevalence of ritual killings" (Ibid, p.1).

Following Loveness Manaito's example, Tapiwa Gwenlisa Marange, Gamuchirai Uzande, two albino women, and Brian Sithole, their male counterpart, formed the Alive Albinism Initiative (AAI) in 2014 (Marange, 15 November 2015; Uzande, 10 August 2016). The organisation seeks to raise the awareness of the public about albinism by dispelling myths and prejudices about the condition. It also aims to economically empower people living with albinism through income-generating projects. Since its formation, the organisation has been actively involved in organising social events for people living with albinism such as Fun Days for children and the UN International Albinism Awareness Day (Ibid).

There are other Zimbabwean women living with albinism who also formed localised organisations in various parts of the country to look into the welfare of albinos. In 2014, for instance, Pastor Rachel Mushonga founded the Wailing Women Trust to help and empower women living with albinism in the Kuwadzana Extension Suburb in Harare (Mashongwa, 13 September 2014).

Indeed, as the UN declared in 2008, albinism is a disability but, as this section has illuminated, disability does not translate to despondency and inability. This section has demonstrated that despite being stigmatised, subordinated, demonised, ostracised and abused by largely male-dominated societies, some women manage to salvage some space to dispel myths associated with albinism. Their agency is manifested by individual pursuits and collective endeavours, both of which seek to bring about a just society in which the security of people living with albinism in various spheres of life is guaranteed.

Conclusion

This chapter has articulated how people's physical features and appearance, particularly skin colour, shape human attitudes and interactions, socio-cultural discourses and the course of history. People living with oculocutaneous albinism are most visible or conspicuous in Africa where the population is dominantly dark-skinned. Since the pre-colonial period, the pale complexion of people living with albinism subjects them to various insecurities in addition to the health ailments that are associated with their condition.

The chapter has examined the insecurities faced by the generality of people living with albinism in Africa in general and Zimbabwe in particular since the pre-colonial era. Both male and female albinos, it has been noted, are vulnerable to similar challenges such as poor vision, sunburns and skin cancer. Their pale skin colour and related health ailments resulted in the formulation of beliefs, attitudes and convictions that are used to discriminate against them in virtually all aspects of life since pre-colonial times.

While the socio-economic challenges encountered by the general albino population in Zimbabwe are adequately captured by a number of scholars (Baker, 2010; Kagore and Lund, 2005; Lund, 2001; Machoko, 2013), this chapter makes a significant contribution to the academic discourse by highlighting the importance of gender as a tool of analysis in studying the insecurities of people living with albinism. The chapter has demonstrated that women living with oculocutaneous albinism endure a host of hardships in addition to the socio-economic challenges they share with their male counterparts.

As noted in this chapter, the additional challenges of albino women are largely rooted in age-old and contemporary superstitious beliefs heavily influenced by patriarchal chauvinism. Most of the longstanding myths stigmatise, demean and demonise people with albinism making it very difficult for women living with the condition to be guaranteed of secure marriages. Those who are lucky to get married are not readily accepted by their in-laws and are often subjected to various forms of harassment. In addition, abusive husbands and in-laws also formulate myths to victimise women who give birth to albino children.

Contemporary superstitious narratives related to sexual encounters with albino women aggravate the situation. Unsubstantiated claims that sexual intercourse with albino women is more satisfying and can also cure HIV/AIDS results in many of them being raped. A considerable number of men, therefore, become intimate with albino women for experimental purposes rather than affection. It becomes very difficult for albino women to identify genuine spouses. Consequently, many albino women are single mothers, having been raped, abused and abandoned by unscrupulous men.

The various forms of victimisation, demonisation and abuse, largely informed by myths crafted by patriarchal societies, often generate agency on the part of women affected, directly or indirectly, by the challenges of living with albinism. As the chapter has shown, some women engage in individual and collective pursuits in an effort to surmount these hardships. Among other initiatives, the divorcing of abusive husbands and the formation of associations to lobby for the security and dignity of people living with albinism by women attest to this.

References

Adesuyi, I. (20 September 2013) 'Albinism in Zimbabwe,' Available at: http://www.emoryglobe.com, Accessed 25 May 2017.

Alvares, C. (1988) 'Science, colonialism and violence: A luddite view,' in: A. Nandy (ed.) *Science, hegemony and violence: A requiem for modernity*, Delhi: United Nations University, pp.68-112.

Annan, K. (2000) 'Secretary-General salutes International Workshop on Human Security in Mongolia,' Available at: www.un.org/News/Press, Accessed 20 October 2017.

Associated Press (18 June 2016) 'Zimbabwe: Ostracised albinos describe life as hell on earth,' Available at: http://www.dailymail.co.uk/wires/ap/article, Accessed 23 May 2017.

Baker, C. (2011) *Enduring negativity: Representations of albinism in the novels of Didier Destremau, Patrick Grainville and Williams Sassine*, Oxford: Peter Lang.

Baker, C. Lund, P. Nyathi, R. and Taylor, J. (2010) 'The myths surrounding people with albinism in South Africa and Zimbabwe,' in: *Journal of African Cultural Studies*, Volume 22, Number 2, pp.169-181.

Beach, D.N. (1999) 'Zimbabwe: Pre-colonial history, demographic disaster and the university,' in: *Zambezia*, Volume XXVI, Number 1, pp.5-33.

Beland, D. (2007) 'Insecurity and politics: A framework,' in: *Canadian Journal of Sociology*, Volume 32, Number 3, pp.317-340.

Bourdillon, M.F.C. (1998) *The Shona peoples: An ethnography of the contemporary Shona, with special reference to their religion*, Gweru: Mambo Press.

Cassim, J. (24 June 2015) 'Zimbabwe's albinos suffer from discrimination, superstition,' Available at: http://news.videonews.us/zimbabwes, Accessed 25 May 2017.

Chinowaita, M. (24 November 2014) 'Women with albinism suffering in silence,' in: *The Daily News*, Harare: Zimbabwe.

Chinyowa, K.C. and Chivandikwa, N. (2017) 'Subverting ableist discourses as an exercise in precarity: A Zimbabwean case study,' in: *Research in Drama: The Journal of Applied Theatre and Performance*, Volume 22, Issue 1, Available at: http://www.tandfonline.com/doi/full, Accessed 23 May 2017.

Cohen, N. (1 September 2015) 'Africa: We need new names,' Available at: http://www.afronline.org/?p=40089, Accessed 23 May 2017.

Dawes, N. (17 May 2012) 'Albinos' lonely call for recognition,' in: *The Mail and Guardian*, Available at: http://mg.co.za/article, Accessed 16 May 2017.

Des Forges, A. (1995) 'The ideology of genocide,' in: *Journal of Opinion*, Volume 23, Number 2, pp.44-47.

Dube, Y. (9 November 2015) 'Albinos in social wars with delusional society,' in: *The Chronicle*, Bulawayo: Zimbabwe, Available at: www.chronicle.co.zw, Accessed 27 May 2017.

Edwin Mellen Press (2004) *Criminal anthropological writings of Cesare Lombroso*, New York: Edwin Mellen Press.

Ezeilo, B. N. (1989) 'Psychological aspects of albinism: An exploratory study with Nigerian (Igbo) albino subjects,' in: *Social Science Medical Journal*, Volume 29, Number 9, pp.1129-1131.

George, L. (2 December 2016) 'The change agents,' Available at: www.thehindu.com, Accessed 26 May 2017.

Herald (14 June 2016) 'International Albinism Day commemorated,' in: *The Herald*, Harare: Zimbabwe.

Huni, S. (28 September 2014) 'HIV positive men rape women with albinism in cure belief,' in: *The Sunday News*, Available at: http://www.sundaynews.co.zw, Accessed 25 May 2017.

Kadenge, M. Mabugu, P. R. Chivero, E. and Chiwara, R. (2014) 'Anthroponyms of albinos among the Shona people of Zimbabwe,' in: *Mediterranean Journal of Social Sciences*, Volume 5, Number 27, pp.1230-1239.

Kagore, F. and Lund, P. M. (2005) 'Oculocutaneous albinism among school children in Harare, Zimbabwe,' in: *Journal of Medical Genetics*, Volume 32, Number11, pp.859-861.

Koch, H. W. (2000) *The Hitler Youth: Origins and development, 1922-1945*, New York: Cooper Square Press.

Kothari, M. L. and Mehta, L. M. (1988) 'Violence in modern medicine,' in: A. Nandy (ed.) *Science, hegemony and violence: A requiem for modernity*, Delhi: United Nations University, pp.167-210.

Lauridsen, J. T. (2004) 'Hitler Youth,' In: P.S. Fass (ed.) *Encyclopedia of Children and Childhood in History and Society, Volume 2: World History in Context*, pp.430-431, Available at:
www.ic.galegroup.com, Accessed 10 November 2016.

Lund, P. M. (1996) 'Distribution of oculocutaneous albinism in Zimbabwe,' in: *The Journal of Medical Genetics*, Volume 33, pp.641-644.

Lund, P. M. (2001) 'Health and education of children with albinism in Zimbabwe,' in: *Health Education Research: Theory and Practice*, Volume 16, Number 1, pp.1-7.

Machakaire, T. (15 November 2015) 'Child living with albinism mutilated in bizarre ritual,' in: *The Weekend Post*, Available at: www.weekendpost.co.zw/articles, Accessed 24 May 2017.

Machipisa, L. (25 November 2002) 'Zimbabwe: The last minority group to find a voice,' Available at: http://www.ipsnews.net, Accessed 25 May 2017.

Machipisa, L. (14 January 2003) 'Albinos hit by Zimbabwe's race divide,' Available at: http://www.africaw.com, Accessed 23 May 2017.

Machirori, F. (20 April 2012) 'My albinism does not define me,' Available at: http://herzimbabwe.co.zw, Accessed 21 May 2017.

Machoko, C. G. (2013) 'Albinism: A life of ambiguity- A Zimbabwean experience,' in: *African Identities*, Volume 11, Number 3, pp.318-333. Available at:
http://www.tandfonline.com, Accessed 23 May 2017.

Makama, A. (31 May 2017) Interview at Great Zimbabwe University, Mashava Campus: Zimbabwe.

Mananavire, B. (27 April 2017) 'Albino cancer deaths rise,' in: *The Daily News*, Harare: Zimbabwe.

Marange, T. G. (15 November 2015) 'Zimbabwe: Albinism - Breaking the myth,' Available at: http://allafrica.com/stories/201511230337.html, Accessed 26 May 2017.

Mashangwa, V. (13 September 2014) 'Albinism: A genetically-inherited condition not a curse,' in: *The Chronicle*, Bulawayo: Zimbabwe.

Mashiri, P. Mawome, K. and Tom, P. (2002) Naming the pandemic: Semantic and ethical foundations of HIV/AIDS Shona vocabulary, *Zambezia*, 29 (2):.221-233.

Maunganidze, M. (2016) 'Book my show,' Available at: www.bookmyshow.com/person, Accessed 29 May 2017.

Mawere, R. (October 2014) 'Fighting albinism's stereotypes,' Available at: http://www.africafiles.org/article.asp?id=27426, Accessed 23 May 2017.

McNeil, D.G. (9 February 1997) 'Black, yet white: A hated colour in Zimbabwe,' in: *The New York Times*, Available at: http://www.nytimes.com, Accessed 22 May 2017.

Mhofu, S. (16 June 2016) 'Activists look to dispel myths driving albino discrimination in Zimbabwe,' Available at: http://www.voanews.com, Accessed 23 May 2017.

Moremi Initiative (7 July 2016) 'Meet Dudzai Mureyi: Outstanding emerged African woman leader,' Available at: https://moremiinitiative.org/wp, Accessed 26 May 2017.

Moyo, L. (16 July 2015) 'Are Zimbabweans' attitudes towards albinism changing?' Available at: http://www.voazimbabwe.com, Accessed 23 May 2017.

Muredzi, D. Nendoro, S. Nyariya, L. and Nyirenje, W. (19 November 2017) Group Interview, Sherukuru Business Centre, Mutasa District, Zimbabwe.

Musiwa, S. (August 1998) 'Zimbabwe: Albinos: Black yet white,' in: *African News*, Available at: http://web.peacelink.it/afrinews/29_issue/p5.html, Accessed 25 May 2017.

Mutasa, F.L. (2013) 'An investigation into the psychosocial implications of oculocutaneous albinism: A case study of the Manicaland Albino Association,' Master of Social Work Dissertation, Harare: University of Zimbabwe.

Mutingwende, B. (15 June 2016) 'Albinism continues to be treated with stigma and discrimination,' Available at: http://spiked.co.zw/?p=1510, Accessed 22 May 2017.

Mwale, T. (28 July 2015) 'United Nations Information Centre-Harare commemorates the first-ever day for albinism awareness,' Available at: http://harare.sites.unicnetwork.org, Accessed 24 May 2017.

Nandy, A. (1988) 'Introduction: Science as a reason of state,' in: A. Nandy (ed.) *Science, hegemony and violence: A requiem for modernity*, Delhi: United Nations University, pp.1-23.

Ndlovu, M. (16 June 2016) 'Zimbabwean albinos concerned about Malawi killings,' Available at: http://thesoutherndaily.co.zw, Accessed 23 May 2017.

Ndongwe, M. (22 May 2017) Interview at the Civic Centre, Masvingo: Zimbabwe.

Nyathi, R. (13 February 2013) 'Battling skin cancer, stigma,' in: *The Zimbabwean*, Available at: www.thezimbabwean.co, Accessed 29 May 2017.

Phatoli, R. Bila, N. and Ross, E. (2015) 'Being black in a white skin: Beliefs and stereotypes around albinism at a South African university,' in: *African Journal of Disability*, Volume 4, Number 1, Available at: http://dx.doi.org/10.4102/ajod.v4i1.106, Accessed 23 May 2017.

Pruner, G. (2010) *The Rwanda crisis: History of a genocide*, London: Hurst and Company.

Selepe, D.M. (2007) 'Teenagers of oculocutaneous albinism in Polokwane: Their self-esteem and perceptions of societal attitudes,' Unpublished Master of Arts Dissertation, University of Limpopo, Republic of South Africa.

Shiva, V. (1988) 'Reductionist science as epistemological violence,' in: A. Nandy (ed.) *Science, hegemony and violence: A requiem for modernity*, Delhi: United Nations University, pp.232-256.

Simukai Initiative (2017) 'About us,' Available at: www.simukai.org, Accessed 29 May 2017.

Suhrke, A. (1999) 'Human security and interest and security of states,' in: *Security Dialogue*, Volume 30, Number 3, pp.265-276.

Thomas, C. and Wilkin, P. (1999) *Globalisation, human security and the African experience*, London: Lynne Rienner Publishers.

Ufumeli, A. (14 April 2015) 'People with albinism face various discrimination,' in: *The Newsday*, Harare: Zimbabwe, Available at: www.newsday.co.zw, Accessed 25 May 2017.

United Nations (22 April 2001) 'UN Secretary-General Millennium Report, Chapter 2,' Available at:
www.un.org.millennium/sg/report, Accessed 20 October 2017.

United Nations Development Programme (1994) *Human development report: New dimensions of human security*, New York: Oxford University Press.

UNICEF (April 2010) *Children accused of witchcraft: An anthropological study of contemporary practices in Africa*, Dakar: UNICEF.

Uzande, G. (10 August 2016) 'Albinism is beautiful,' Available at: http://www.hararenews.co.zw, Accessed 28 May 2017.

Waugh, J. (2005) 'Social and emotional aspects of albinism,' Available at: http://www.tsbvi.ed/outreach, Accessed 1 June 2017.

Zimbabwe Government (2013) *The Zimbabwe Constitution Amendment (Number 20) Act of 2013*, Harare: Government Printer.

Zimbabwe Broadcasting Corporation News (24 April 2017) 'Mberengwa man disowned by relatives after marrying wife living with albinism,' Available at: http://iharare.com, Accessed 24 May 2017.

Zimbabwe Situation (5 December 2009) 'The voice of the oppressed,' Available at: www.zimbabwesituation.com/old, Accessed 26 May 2017.

Zinhumwe, T. (25 November 1996) 'Zimbabwe- Human rights: Not black enough,' Available at: http://www.ipsnews.net, Accessed 23 May 2017.

Chapter 4

A Religious Survey of Technological Oddity: Humanoid as a Case Study

Raymond Ogunade & Gbenga Zaccheaus

Introduction

There is a profound anxiety about the fate of the world, taking cognizance of the fleeting inventions of life with regard to the continuous engagements between religion and technology. Ostensibly, technology is a basic aspect of humanity, but its functionality is expected to be within a framework of moral values and religious factors of the people it serves. It therefore becomes problematic when technological breakthroughs pose underlying threats to moral sensibilities and the religious order, of which humanoid robots with Artificial Intelligence (AI) is a focal paradigm of this discourse. Employing the multiple approaches of socio-cultural, anthropological, and analytical methods, this chapter provides a survey of humanoid robots, exploring the spirituality of the same in Yoruba Religion and Christianity respectively portraying these religions as monitors towards technological oddities in our society. This chapter reveals that the moral implications of unmonitored technologies especially the humanoids have greater defects than the benefits they are intended to offer.

Technology is not value free; it is developed through scientific choices which imply value judgments. It reflects the values of its society and in turn technology shapes and reshapes the society and vice versa. Religion, being the bedrock of morality has a profound responsibility towards technological oddities, saddled with the role of a 'watchdog' to enhance values which would encourage the development of responsible technologies in relation to both humanity and God's creations as a practical outworking of religious principles.

It is axiomatic that religion, high or low, sophisticated or primal should have a role in any society it is practiced… Finally, the spiritual heritage of humanity is a potential resource for a more humane feature of humankind. Science and Technology may give human beings advanced means of living, but human beings still require an attendant spiritual voyage as exhibited in the living religions of mankind (Dopamu 2006:16).

It is painstaking that technologists (with their apophatic and cataphatic knowledge) are on a limitless quest of explaining life mysteries and breaking natural laws, if possible. This is evident in their inventions and intensification of Artificial Intelligence (AI) domain and humanoids, i.e. (technologies created like human physicality). In view of morality, there is an urgent point of concern because recent humanoids are so developed that some are being garnered to replace humans in the nearest future, given human-like pulses, intelligence and sensuality. As a matter of fact, individuals may now decide to own or marry these unconscious humanoids as domestic partners, sex dolls, crime agents, private spies and so forth. The most recent example of *Jia Jia* humanoid of China readily comes to mind. This premise of comparing religion and technological advancement can be called "religio-techno" intricacies. By religio-techno intricacies, one refers to the innovations that give vent to religious oddities, religious and moral questionings. It is in view of this understanding that Ogunade avers: "…the enmity between science and religion has been so volatile, the past fourteen years has witnessed a gradual romance of these two aspects of human existence (Ogunade 2010: 43). There is no doubt that science and technology have made life easy but the excesses of scientists appear equivocal with morality in view. These selected developments might contribute to natural degradation and abruption of normalcy in human society. Science connotes profound knowledge but technologists have the prerogative of galvanizing that knowledge to functionality, which makes them answerable to humanity about their technical decisions. Little wonder, Alamu describes scientists as "high priests of a new technological culture (Alamu 2010: 1), they might be unconsciously perpetrating a culture of competing with the supreme attributes of God as the omniscient, omnipotent and omnipresent Being. Many a technologist is at the verge of creating the formula of life and to conquer the mystery of mortality. All these are exemplified in their bewildering inventions which we are witnessing today. Therefore, it is not erroneous when Tim Lahaye and Jenkins stipulate that this 21st century seems to be the most exciting days to be alive, because it has witnessed breathtaking advances in technology (Lahaye and Jenkins 1999: 9), this includes humanoids.

It is perturbing that when technological trials get to its apex and having conquered the universe, making everything accessible and attainable to humans at the snap of our fingers, then the docile populace may no longer see the necessity of religion or need to approach God as subservient beings. Be that as it may, the moment humans become extremely comfortable with technology; God might be given an indefinite leave from human minds. All these necessitate religion and morality in this subject matter, to serve as a monitor to technological advancements in our society before it becomes too late'

Meaning of Humanoids

A humanoid, from the English words "human" and "oid" resembling is something that has an appearance resembling a human being (Wikipedia 2017). The earliest recorded use of the term, in 1870, referred to indigenous peoples in areas colonized by Europeans. By the 20th century, the term came to describe fossils which were morphologically similar, but not identical, to those of the human skeleton. Although this usage was common in the sciences for much of the 20th century, it is now considered rare. More generally, the term can refer to anything with uniquely human characteristics and/or adaptations, such as possessing opposable anterior forelimb-appendages (thumbs), visible spectrum-binocular vision (having two eyes), or biomechanical digitigrade- bipedalism (the ability to walk on heels in an upright position).

A humanoid robot is a robot that is based on the general structure of a human, such as a robot that walks on two legs and has an upper torso, or a robot that has two arms, two legs and a head. A humanoid robot does not necessarily look convincingly like a real person, for example the ASIMO humanoid robot has a helmet instead of a face.

An android (male) or gynoid (female) is a humanoid robot designed to look as much like a real person as possible, although these words are frequently perceived to be synonymous with humanoid (Wikipedia 2017). While there are many humanoid robots in fictional stories, some real humanoid robots have been developed since the 1990s, and some real human-looking android robots have been developed since 2002. Similarly to robots, virtual avatars may also be called humanoid when resembling humans.

In African worldview, deities are often imagined in human shape (also known as "anthropotheism"), sometimes as hybrids (especially the gods of Ancient Egyptian religion). A fragment by the Greek poet, Xenophanes, describes this tendency that Men make gods in their own image; those of the Ethiopians are black and narrow-nosed, those of the Thracians have blue eyes and red hair (Wikipedia 2017). In animism in general, the spirits innate in certain objects (like the Greek nymphs) are typically depicted in human shape, for example, spirits of trees (Dryads), of the woodlands (the hybrid fauns), of wells or waterways (Nereids, Necks), and so on. With regard to extraterrestrials in fiction, the term humanoid is most commonly used to refer to alien beings with a body plan that is generally like that of a human, including upright stance and bipedalism. Many aliens in television and science fiction films are presented as humanoid. This is usually attributed to budget constraints, as human actors can more easily portray human-like aliens. According to Isaac Asimov, the popular three laws of Robotics are:

i.   A robot may not injure a human being nor allow a human to come to harm through inaction.

ii.   A robot must obey orders given by humans when they do not contradict rule one.

iii.   A robot must protect its own existence, so long as such protection does not conflict with rules one and two (Asimov 1950: 40).

These three laws of robotics appear very credible and have since occupied a place of pride since time immemorial.

Historical Antecedent of Humanoid Robots

Since time immemorial, humans have shown a perennial desire to emulate God, to create in our own image. Creating images of the human body in paintings, clay, metal and stone; images of human activities were described in literature and the arts. Humans created machines that mirror human activities through their own actions. While aware that these images were both partial and superficial, they still have exerted a tremendous influence on how we view ourselves and our place in the world. In 1495, famed inventor, Leonardo Da Vinci, designed a suit of armour that moved as if there was a real person inside. It was operated by a series of pulleys and cables, and could stand, sit, move its arms, and even raise its visor to reveal nothing inside (Freedberg 1989: 18). The goal was merely to amuse Milanese royalty, but modern recreations of the device have shown that it was fully functional. In 1774, Swiss watchmaker, Pierre Jacquet-Droz, his son Henri-Louis, and Jean-Frédéric Leschot built a trio of automata that are still in use today. The first is "the musician," a female robot that plays a custom-built organ by pressing the keys with her fingers. The second is "the draughtsman," a young child robot that can draw four different images and the third is "the writer," another child robot capable of writing any custom text up to 40 characters long using a quill on paper. All three are startlingly lifelike. Their eyes follow their actions, and the musician even breathes while playing.

The first digitally controlled anthropomorphic robot was built in 1970 at Waseda University in Tokyo (Wikipedia 2017). It had a limb-control system with tactile sensors for walking and gripping, a vision system that could measure distances, and a conversation system that could communicate in Japanese. The researchers estimated that it had the mental faculties of a child aged about one and a half. In 2000, one of the world's most famous robots was first assembled. Honda designed and developed Asimo as a multi-functional mobile assistant that could help people with poor mobility. It could recognize objects, gestures, sounds, and faces, allowing it to interact with humans, and was capable of fully autonomous navigation with a top speed of 1.8 m.p.h. Later upgrades bumped that to 3.7m.p.h. and added the ability to climb stairs—something it spectacularly failed to do in its first demonstration in December 2006 but successfully completed a month later. Today, development of humanoid robots continues apace and the latest and most sophisticated robot is known as Jia Jia in China (Wikipedia 2017).

Fig. 1:   *JiaJia* Source: Google

Effects of Humanoids on the society

It is important to pay attention to the underlying effects of humanoids technology in the society. Following Bill Joy's warning that:

> Advances in robotics and in humanoids could result, as soon as 2030, in a technology that may replace the human species, Hans Moravec, of the artificial intelligence (AI) lab at Carnegie Mellon, pushes the time back to 2040 but agrees, by performing better and cheaper, the robots will displace humans from essential roles. Rather quickly, they could displace us from existence (Moravec 1998: 56).

This is to say that the development of humanoids has enormous effects on society. It is therefore important to pay a rapt attention to this phenomenon. Just late last year it was posited that the humanoid robot was poised to take a leap from a mere facsimile of human behaviour, to one that futurists suggest, will walk like a human and possess self-awareness as well as a full range of high-tech computational spectrum analysis and capabilities and emotions. Some are predicting that robots of all types could fully replace humans by 2045 (Herzfeld 2002: 61). Artificial intelligence is now advancing to a point where a new type of brain can be offered to complement the relatively menial tasks of modern-day robotics, hinting at the next stage of machine evolution.

One worry that people are having about humanoid robots is that they will replace jobs. Although this could be potentially beneficial to certain companies, it would hurt those who have jobs in certain fields, such as nurses, pharmacists, secretaries, etc. Japan is known to be the leading nation in humanoid robot development, coming up with new robots rapidly to work in offices. Middle class people should be concerned that humanoid robots will one day replace their jobs. It is estimated in about 75 years that humanoid robots will take over nearly all traditional labour roles in society such as manufacturing, agriculture, construction, firefighting, food service and even community policing. If humanoid robots take over middle class citizens' jobs, the economy will be negatively affected.

Another effect of humanoid robots could be the material cost, depending on how advanced the robot is. As humanoid robots start becoming more and more available to society it will be mostly the wealthy who will be able to afford them. For example, Kumotek VisiON 4G is a humanoid robot costing roughly USD44, 000 but able to complete a variety of tasks, many more tasks than a humanoid robot that costs USD1, 500. For middle class and low income families, this is an expense not many people would be able to afford. The price tags of humanoid robots are high enough that not everyone except the elite would be able to own one.

Furthermore, if these robots do these everyday jobs, humans will become too dependent on robots. People are going to become lazy, and dependent if we have such robots doing our chores for us.

117

Immorally, some individuals utilize humanoids as sexual dolls to satisfy their sexual desires. Humanoids built with functional genitals have been created for 'shy' men who cannot woe the female folks and for some others who are willing to buy, own and marry a robot for sexual explorations. This connotes a sense of moral decadence confronting the society as a result of human abuse of humanoids and this negates God's command about sexual obligations and reproduction. It is worrisome when Levy, author of *Love and Sex with Robots* said:

> I have no doubt some will find it creepy, but the arrival of sexually responsive robots will have enormous consequences. We have already seen rapid changes in human relationships thanks to the internet, mobile devices and social media. The next major advance will enable us to use our technology to have intimate encounters with the technology itself- to fall in love with the technology, to have sex with robots and to marry (Levy 2017: 1).

As many people will supposedly benefit from the emerging humanoid robot, there will also be those who are greatly suffering. As noted earlier, one group of those that will be negatively affected by the humanoid robot is the people whose jobs will be replaced. Middle class and low income families will also be negatively affected by the robots economically. Also, perverts will be encouraged and there will be a high chance of marital disruption when people become comfortable to marry robots than the female folks.

Factors promoting Humanoids in the society

Research Tools
Humanoid robots are used as research tools in several scientific areas. Researchers need to understand the human body structure and behaviour (biomechanics) to build and study humanoid robots. On the other side, the attempt to the simulation of the human body leads to a better understanding of it. Human cognition is a field of study which is focused on how humans learn from sensory information in order to acquire perceptual and motor skills. This knowledge is used

to develop computational models of human behaviour and it has been improving over time.

Performance of Tasks

Humanoid robots are being developed to perform human tasks like personal assistance, where they should be able to assist the sick and elderly, and dirty or dangerous jobs. Regular jobs like being a receptionist or a worker of an automotive manufacturing line are also suitable for humanoids. In essence, since they can use tools and operate equipment and vehicles designed for the human form, humanoids could theoretically perform any task a human being can, so long as they have the proper software. However, the complexity of doing so is deceptively great.

Entertainment

They are becoming increasingly popular for providing entertainment too. For example, Ursula, a female robot, sings, play music, dances, and speaks to her audiences at Universal Studios. Several Disney attractions employ the use of animatrons, robots that look, move, and speak much like human beings, in some of their theme park shows. These animatrons look so realistic that it can be hard to decipher from a distance whether or not they are actually human. Although they have a realistic look, they have no cognition or physical autonomy. Various humanoid robots and their possible applications in daily life are featured in an independent documentary film called *Plug and Pray*, which was released in 2010 (YouTube 2017).

Special Missions

Humanoid robots, especially with artificial intelligence algorithms, could be useful for future dangerous and/or distant space exploration missions, without having the need to turn back around again and return to Earth once the mission is completed.

Companionship

Humanoid robots are seen as domestic companions to some. They aid with errands and petty house chores.

Implications of Humanoids on the Society

Virus Invasion

It is apparent that humanoids stand a great risk of virus invasion. Artificial intelligence (AI) has struggled with this great challenge of virus vulnerability for a long time. A humanoid infected with virus will effortlessly perform unscrupulous acts and misconducts that could be harmful or disastrous to the people around.

Crime Agents

Similarly to the above, humanoid robots can be programmed as crime agents to terrorize the people. This have been suggested and demonstrated in some science fictions like Terminator, Robocop etc. that we have seen.

Sexual Discrepancy

Sex robots with fully functioning genitals have hit the market costing €12,000 (Levy 2017: 1). They have built-in heaters which so they have genuine body warmth and sensors that can react to touch. RealDoll is made by Abyss Creations, a company based in California. They claimed "We want to have people actually develop an emotional attachment to not only the robot but the actual character behind it- to develop some kind of love for this being".

Unexpected Malfunction

Humanoids are prone to malfunctions based on its technical vulnerability which can lead to electrocution and sudden death, as in the case of sex robots. There is no perfection in human products compared with God's product.

The Religious Implications of Humanoids

Humanoids hold religious implications for both our self-understanding and our Godly co-existence with our own creation. It is germane to examine the following points of consideration:

i. God's Commandment

According to the book of Genesis 1:28, God commanded Adam and Eve to multiply and fill the earth. This great reproduction commandment explains the sexual proclivity of humans to give birth to young ones who take much resemblance of their parent. God in His infinite wisdom understood the importance of procreation and continuity through biological process which necessitated that commandment (Oral interview, Odofin: 25/01/2017). Considering the creation of humanoids, one might be tempted to argue that this technological leap negates to some extent the ideology of God's reproductive plans. God could have commanded that humans should create humanoids and fill the earth if He deemed it fit, but His sense of continuity is found in natural reproduction process and not creation of humanoids and the likes. Also in the Decalogue, God negates the moulding of graven images as symbols of worship.

ii. Divine Conscience

The argument on humanoids' consciousness remains highly interesting. It is worthy of note that conscience constitutes a divine attribution of an innate sense of judgment in human beings. The advent of humanoid is apparently eroded of the attribution of divine conscience to this creation (Ogunade 2017: 39). This is to say that humanoids have no conscience and cannot be held responsible for atrocities or wrong deeds. Humanoids are not given a sense of judgment like that of humans; they only operate on programs installed in them. As a result, their functionality is based on the wishes of the inventor not that of God. In other words, humanoids can be programmed to commit crimes and cannot be judged or queried for obeying without human feeling or conscience. This is an abuse of human freewill (Herfeld 2002: 69) as a robot cannot be held morally, religiously or rationally responsible for its actions but its creator.

iii. God's Mystery of Life and Death

Life and death remains a mystery and can only be unravelled by the Supreme Being. Cybernetics stand a great chance of immortality as the case is today (Herzfeld 2002: 70). For example, humanoids are not birthed and cannot die like humans do. They can only be destroyed or terminated. This idea poses a great threat to the code of the mystery of life and death which God has put in place right from time. Also, the intensification of humanoids today is in a sense an attempt to beat the mystery of life and death. However, this remains an everlasting task for technologists as far as religion is concerned.

iv. Afterlife Judgment

Religion is conversant with after-life judgment where every soul will be judged according to their deeds. It is expedient to note that this is not related to humanoids because no matter how human-like they may be; they do not possess a soul that will be held accountable on the judgment day. Hence, humanoids are earthly and ephemeral machines that cannot be likened to humans.

v. Worship and Liturgical Responsibilities

Humans have a sheer belief that we are created to worship God and perform certain socio-religious obligations, like liturgical practices and so on. Humanoids are not embedded with this mindset of recognizing the God factor. Even if they do, their inventor instils himself as the creator. *Jia jia,* for instance, refers to her inventor as "my lord," (Wikipedia 2017: 1) which in religious circles is considered blasphemous.

Christian Theological Evaluation of Humanoids

The theological evaluation of humanoid takes as a starting point, scriptural references to the creation of human beings in the 'image of God'. Given the important role the concept of our creation in the image of God has played in Christian doctrine, it is therefore pertinent to ask varying questions about humanoid as a form of recreation in humans' image. The fact that human beings are created in the image or likeness of God is stated explicitly in only three passages in the Old Testament, all of which occurred in portions of Genesis attributed to the Priestly writer (P): Gen. 1:26-28, 5:3, and 9:6. Gen. 1:26-28 is the text from which the others are derived and has, historically, been the most oft-cited reference to the *imago Dei*. Then God said, let us make mankind in our image, according our liken; and let them have dominion over the fish of the sea and over bird of the air, and over the cattle and over all the wild animals of the earth, and over every creeping things that creeps upon the earth. So God created humankind in His image, in the image of God He created them male and female. God blessed them, and God said to them: "Be fruitful and multiply, fill the earth and subdue it; and have dominion over the fish of the sea and over the bird of the earth and over every living thing that move upon the earth".

As we human beings attempt to create in our own image through artificial intelligence, the *imago Dei* becomes an even more important symbol. As a litmus test of humanity, the image of God not only contributes to defining what it is to be human but also to determining our relationship to the non-human. This image serves to distinguish humans from the rest of creation, conferring upon humans a special dignity and value. The bone of contention remains that invention of humanoids is an attempt by humans to copy and play God. Since it has become pleasurable for technologists to create in humans' images also i.e. image creating image. Hence, the yardstick of measuring the image of God in humanoids is apparently lost in oblivion (Herzfeld 2002: 30). The big question is: "Are we not playing God?"

Theologically, it is imperative to give recourse to the great commandment in the Decalogue which negates creation of graven image of worship. Hence, the possibility of humanoids to be worshipped or not is only a matter of time, given the fact that they are vulnerable to be worshipped and venerated. The stance of *Shigidi* in Yoruba Religion (Yorel) (Ogunade 2017: 98) and Science readily comes to mind because they are sometimes described as idols by Western religions, even though Yorelians (adherents of Yoruba Religion) only see them as emblems of worship (Ogunade 2017: 98). It is critique able to witness the vast spread of Sexual humanoids in the society. This is against every religious tenet because God created females for males and do not expect males to marry or co-habit with lifeless humanoids. Therefore, caution should be exercised in order to check this unruly invention before it is too late.

Humanoids in Yoruba Religion (Yorel)

In the true sense of the meaning of the word humanoid, agreeably, it has been in existence in Yorel since time immemorial. Taking a quite different mechanical dimension, humanoids can be interpreted as the spiritual effigies of Yoruba Religion. Yorelians view effigies with so much sacredness and religious values, which cannot be overemphasized as far as African Traditional Religion is concerned. Taking cognizance of the structure of Yorel, the belief in God, Divinities, Spirits, Ancestors, Magic and Medicine are all embedded in the reality and spirituality of humanoids in Yorel. Yorelians especially, demonstrate profound belief in the efficacy of humanoid to bring about spiritual manifestations.

The sacredness of these humanoids, attain their spiritual prowess from the Divinities that constitute their efficacy. In other words, humanoids which are mostly carved wooden images or emblems in human shapes are given spiritual powers by devotees of Divinities, who consecrate those humanoids with Spiritual powers, drawn from their Divinities. Certain spirits inhabit the images and they lend credence to spiritual manifestations (Oral interview, Fagbemi 13/02/2017). Taking the exemplary ebb of Yoruba Religion, humanoids range in sizes and human shapes, in accordance with their designated spiritual mission or function. They are known as *Shigidi, Omolangidi* and *Osanyin* (effigies). They are found in various localities carved as males, females, children, couples, pregnant woman, twins and so on.

Spirituality of Humanoids in Yoruba Religion

Yorelians, regularly utilise these small carved and moulded three dimensional human figures in their medicines. These figures are used by individuals in purposeful acts of magical mimesis to manipulate the social world. These humanoids act as surrogates, messengers and they are used to activate forces affecting individual lives (Oral interview, Fagbemi 13/02/2017). The Yoruba carve and mould human images as parts of their technology of indigenous medicine in a system in which both natural and supernatural causation are recognized. These humanoids in the shape of the human body are one type of the many essential ingredients, natural and artificial, used by Yoruba medical practitioners to diagnose, cure, protect from, and, in some cases, cause illness and misfortune. Among the many ingredients utilized in the preparation of medicines in a specialist's repertoire are human images moulded and carved from natural materials and used as conduits to channel the powers of nature toward goals in acts of "magical mimesis" which involves both copy and substantial connection, both visual replication and material transfer (Oral interview, Fadipe 30/03/2017).

Shigidi, An example of Humanoid in Yoruba Religion

Fig. 2 *Shigidi* Source: Google

Shigidi is a spiritual humanoid in Yoruba Religion. The name literarily means something "short and bulky". This humanoid is represented as an image with short stature and short head, made of clay, or, more commonly, by a thick blunted cone of clay or wood, which is ornamented with cowries or red/black piece of cloth and is no doubt emblematic of the head (Oral interview, Elebuibon 16/02/2017). The Yoruba often describe *shigidi* with the pity saying that: *ti Shigidi ba fe te, a ni ki won gbe ohun lowe lodo* (When *shigidi* is ready to be disgraced, it will be taken to the river for a bathe). This implies that *shigidi* can easily get displaced if thrown in the river, considering its component and small stature.

Shigidi is often associated with evil telepathy, when someone wishes to hurt another, s/he offers sacrifice to *shigidi* who then proceeds at night to the house of the person indicated and kills him. According to this research, its mode of procedure is to squat upon the chest of its victim and "press out its breathe", but it often happens that the tutelary deity of the victim, comes to the rescue and wakes him, upon which leaps off, falls upon the earthen, and disappears, for it only has power over man during sleep. The person, who employs *shigidi* and sent it out to kill, must remain awake till the humanoid returns. For if he was to fall asleep, *shigidi* will at the moment turn back and the mission will fail. *Shigidi* either travels on the wind or raises a wind to waft him along; the first of being attacked by *shigidi* is a feeling of heat or oppression at the pit of the stomach. If a man experiences this when asleep, it behoves him to get up at ones and seek the protection of God (gods) he usually serve (Oral interview, Oloya 25/02/2017).

Houses and enclosed yards can be placed under the guardianship of *shigidi*. In order to do this, a hole is dug in the earth and a fowl, sheep or in ancient times, in exceptional cases, a human victim was slaughtered so that the blood drains into the hole and is then buried. A short conical mound of red earth is next built over the spot and an earthen saucer is placed on the summit to receive occasional sacrifices. When a site has been placed under the protection of *shigidi*, it kills in its typical manner, those who injure the building or who trespass there with bad intentions (Oral interview, Fagbemi 13/02/2017).

Religious monitory roles towards technological advancements

Through Cultic functionaries: The cultic functionaries are custodians of religious values and traditions. They are the *dramatis*

126

personae of various religions in the world today. Therefore, they are saddled with the responsibility of guidance. Cultic functionaries are expected to scrutinize the usage of technologies that lack guidance values in order to checkmate their functionality and to guide their followers on their usage. By doing this, they implore their religious outplays towards monitoring technological advancements in the society.

Through Sacred Texts: The sacred texts of various religions are compendiums of moral injunctions that guide against oddities of life. The sacred texts of religions usually set precedents for proper behaviour in common situations. It does not matter whether the sacred stories or myths of a religion actually occurred in every detail but they are still illustrative of correct thought and behaviour. It is therefore a profound necessity to galvanize scriptural injunctions towards monitoring technological advancements.

Through Rites and Rituals: Rites and rituals are basic features of every religion. They are exhibitions of the belief system of various religious adherents. Consequently, upon this, rites and rituals should reflect our technological beliefs and practices in the society.

The Relationship of Isaac Asimov's laws of Robotics with *Shigidi* in Yorel

According to Isaac Asimov, the popular three laws of Robotics are:

i.   A robot may not injure a human being nor allow a human to come to harm through inaction.

ii.   A robot must obey orders given by humans when they do not contradict rule one.

iii.   A robot must protect its own existence, so long as such protection does not conflict with rules one and two (Asimov 1950: 40).

This chapter advances that these laws of humanoid robotics can be interpreted in relation to the spiritual robots '*Shigidi*' in Yoruba Religion in the following order:

i.   A *Shigidi* may not injure a human being nor allow a human to come to harm through inaction.

ii. A *Shigidi* must obey orders given by spiritualists through telepathy when they do not contradict rule one.

iii. A *Shigidi* must protect its own existence, so long as such protection does not conflict with rules one and two.

Contributions to Knowledge

i. Religious Implication is a pivotal consideration for Technological Inventions

There is no doubt that technological inventions in our society are inevitable, as a matter of fact they contribute to the rapid development of the universe. Nevertheless, it is pivotal that technologists should take cognizance of the religious implications of these technologies before their invention. This chapter posits that technologies like humanoids are quite delicate as far as morality and religion are concerned. For the sake of posterity, religious clarifications should be made available for every technological invention and their functionality. Be that as it may, any technology that fails the test of religious and moral sensibility should be prohibited because it will cause more harm than the intended good. Guidance values should therefore be put in place to control the production and use of humanoids.

ii. Guidance Values on Humanoids:

Whether we like it or not humanoid technologies have been saturated in our society especially in western hemisphere. It is imperative and obliging for their inventors to provide their guidance values. Humanoids without guidance values can be catastrophic and disastrous for humanity. We have seen examples of such calamities in fictional movies like Terminator, Star Wars, etc. To avoid a realistic outplay of these movies humanoids should be provided with guidance values and ethical codes for the society.

iii. Caution to technological quests of breaking Natural mystery:

Science is known for discoveries and bewilderments, exemplified in the various inventions that we are witnessing in this generation.

Scientists often go out of their way just to break natural laws and mysteries. As laudable as this is, it is important for scientists to exercise caution with regards to their endless quests. This is so because natural mysteries are part of life and are put in place by God Who owns the sole attribute of Omniscient, Omnipotent and Omnipresent Being. Thus, God is God because only He can decode life mysteries and this shows His supremacy overall and sundry.

iv. Academic engagement between Religion and Technology is a necessity:

Hitherto, religion has been all encompassing and pervading, this is because religion cuts across every other discipline including science and technology. In this chapter, religion is shown to have a great interplay or connection with technology because they represent a shaping force of our society. The romance between these two entities deserves a continuous academic enjoyment. Suffice it to say that religion and technology's engagement is a necessity that cannot be over emphasized.

v. 'Host and Virus' Illustration

Taking a swipe at the monitory role religion is to play herein, the "host and the virus" monitory theory, will serve as an attempt to connote that the host (which is the universe) is "infected" and "inflicted" with the viruses of obnoxious human inventions and technological oddities like humanoids in this instance. This infected cosmos was initially certified perfect after creation by a good God (Cosmodicy) however due to the concept of freewill, human beings; especially scientists decided to explore and tamper with the universe (Anthropodicy). This monitory theory therefore explains that the universe can only get rid of the virus if God, who is the owner of the universe takes an action in His infinite wisdom to check the technological oddities (to think of the case of the Tower of Babel) and bring about a manifestation of the various religious eschatological prophecies. Otherwise, one could guess that if scientists and technologists get the formula of life and the clue to immortality, then "the virus" has conquered "the host". What this means in essence is that the hidden divine power of God and the mystery of life and death is what made God to be qualified as "God". This can be illustrated diagrammatically as below:

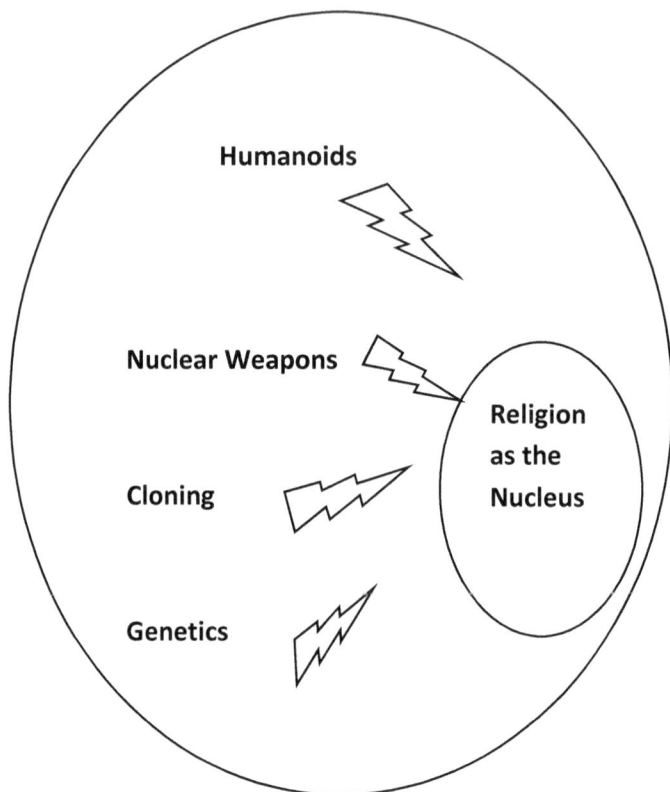

Fig.3 Host and Virus Illustration diagram (Source: Original)

The figure above shows the universe in its spherical shape as the host, engulfed with examples of technological oddities which are likened to threatening viruses in the universe. Here, religion is shown as the nucleus of the universe because religion is all encompassing, pervading all human affairs; also serving as the keynote of life. The cracks suggest the striking forces of the technological oddities in the universe which calls for close religious monitoring.

Conclusion

The cut and thrust of this chapter has been an illumination of the interdisciplinary domain of religion and technology. It has been garnered that religion and technology occupy a place of pride as far as humanity is concerned. As humans, we have shown a perennial desire to create humanoids the way God created us. This task is in itself understandable but if without a moral and religious framework, it becomes a threatening cankerworm and so must be monitored duly. This work has attempted to present religion as the monitor saddled with the responsibility of checking technological oddities.

Having considered the true sense of the word, humanoid has been shown to also exist in Yorel, using *shigidi* as a typical example. *Shigidi* suggests an idea of a spiritual robot that also requires monitoring to avoid malevolent usage. This research has attempted to explore the two sides of the coin i.e. the benefits *vis-à-vis* the defects of humanoids, making this a situation of more harm than good. A functional view of humanity raise interesting questions like, will the future be one of happy religious co-existence with humanoids or will it be one in which humans are threatened? What would be human responsibilities towards humanoids, how should technology, intelligent or not, be integrated into our human society? If humanoids reach a point at which they function better than humans, on what grounds could human beings retain dominion over the earth? Hence, religion bridges the gap here as a monitor to check the technological oddities of humanoids. Should we fail how to learn how to live in authentic relationship with our God, with each other and with the natural world, religion will take the blame.

References

Alamu, A. G. (2010) 'On Dopamu's God Loves Variety and Hates Monotony,' In: Adam K. Arap, *et al* (eds.) *Human Views on God: Variety not Monotony (Essays in Honor of Ade P. Dopamu)* Kenya: Moi University Press.

Asimo - Available at https://wtvox.com/robotics/top-10-humanoid-robots/ Accessed on 19th March, 2017.

Asimov, I. (1950) *Robot,* New York: Double day Publication.

Dopamu, A. (2006) 'African Religion (AFREL) and the Humanist Perspective in the Global Age', Olu Obafemi *et al*, (eds) *Science and Humanities* Vol. 1 No. University of Ilorin: Unilorin Press.

Freedberg, D. (1989) *The Power of Images: Studies in the History and Theory of Response* Chicago: University of Chicago Press.

Herzfeld, N. (2002) *In Our Image: Artificial Intelligence and Human Spirit*, Minneapolis: Fortress Press.

'History of humanoids', Available at https://howwegettonext.com/watch-a-history-of humanoids 9708a4a0d42#.1wmrxou5mAccessed on 12th March, 2017 by 1:21pm. http://jpang8.blogspot.co.ke/?m=1Accessed on 9th November, 2016 by 05:10am.

http://jpang8.blogspot.co.ke/?m=1Accessed on 2nd December, 2017 by 8:20am.

http://www.naijaloaded.com.ng/others/see-sx-robots-with-functionalvagina-made-for shy-men-photo Accessed on 5th January 5:05pm, 2017 by 11:20am.

https://melissaoberferst.wordpress.com/3-disadvantages/Accessed on 7th November, 2017 by 4:20 pm.

http://www.naijasinglegirl.com/meet-harmony/ , Also available at

http://www.lailasblog.com/2017/05/photos-meet-harmony-realisticerotic.html?m=1#.WRn549ZJWNg.facebookAccessed on 4th April, 2017.

http://m.economictimes.com/slideshows/tech-life/meet-jia-jia-she-can talk-express but-she-is-not-real/most-realistichumanoid/slideshow/56498684.cms Accessed on 1st May, 2017.

'Humanoid Robots' available at https://en.m.wikipedia.org/wiki/Humanoid Accessed on 25th February, 2017.

Jia-Jia- Available at https://www.engadget.com/2016/04/17/jia-jia-robot/Accessed on 3rd January, 2017.

Lahaye and Jenkins, J. (1999) *Are We Living in the End Times?* Illinois: Tyndale House Publishers.

Moravec, H. (1998) *Robot: Machine to Transcendent Mind* Oxford: Oxford University Press.

Ogunade, R. (2010) 'The Scientific Universe in Yoruba Religion' In: Adam K. Arap, et al (eds) *Human Views on God: Variety not Monotony (Essays in Honor of Ade P. Dopamu)* Kenya: Moi University Press.

Ogunade, R. (2017) *Ori: Yoruba Personality Guide* San Francisco: Pacific Phoenix Press.

Ogunade, R. (2017) "The Resilience and Challenges of Yoruba Religious Worship in Modern Context" in Munyaradzi Mawere, *et al* (eds.) *The African Conundrum: Rethinking the Trajectories of Historical, Cultural, Philosophical and Developmental Experiences of Africa* Cameroon: Langaa RPCIG.

Oral Interview, Baba Ifadipe Ola, 72 years, Odo Egbe, 30th March 2017.

Oral Interview, Chief Fagbemi Yusuf Alabi, The Oleye logun (*abun omo aje niko*) of Offa, 67 years, Ile Awudere compound, Offa, Kwara, 13th February 2017.

Oral Interview, Henry Odofin, 45 years, 3, Taiwo Street Tinubu, Lagos, 25th January 2017.

Oral Interview, High Priest Chief Ifayemi Elebuibon, the *Araba* of *Osogbo,* informant on African Religion, 13 *Elebuibon* Street, Osogbo, Osun State, 70 years,16th February 2017.

Oral Interview, Iya Oloya, 85 years, Oke Egbe Sango Shrine, 25th February, 2017.

Plug and Pray Movie - https://m.youtube.com. Accessed on 6th February, 2017.

Chapter 5

The Vacuity of the Responsibility to Protect in Africa? Insecurities and Social Protection in Zimbabwe

Clement Chipenda & Tom Tom

Introduction

Social policy in the developed countries, including late industrialisers in Northern Europe and Eastern Asia, has for the past two centuries been concerned with multiple and complimentary functions to bring about development. These multiple functions have included production, reproduction, protection, redistribution, social cohesion and social protection. According to Mkandawire (2011), UNRISD (2006), Adesina (2014) and Yi and Kim (2015), social policy based on these multiple functions is concerned with enhancing the productive capacities of citizens (their economic potential and labour market participation), protecting citizens from the vagaries of the market, reconciling the burden of reproduction with that of other social tasks (for example, facilitating the participation of women in the economy) and redistributing from the economy (for example, vertical and horizontal redistribution of resources). In order for social policies, for countries in the global south, to have as much impact as they have had in the developed countries and in the late industrialisers, it is imperative that social and economic policies be interconnected and symbiotic. They should be defined by shared normative commitments with vertical and lateral norms of social solidarity and equality. Social policies in these countries need to play a productivity role rather than the reductionist and residual role which characterises social policies in the global south.

It is against this brief background of social policy that will be explored in greater detail in subsequent sections of this chapter exploring social policy in sub-Saharan Africa with specific focus on Zimbabwe. With social policy in the global north being framed in the approach to social policy highlighted above which is anchored in the relationship between social and economic policies and the multiple functions of social policy, in this chapter we argue that this cannot be said for the social policy regime that is preponderant in most countries in the global south. In this chapter, we explore the social policy architecture that has been dominant in countries in sub-Saharan Africa with special reference to Zimbabwe which has shown social policies that have been heavily influenced by the legacy of post-settler colonialism and a neo-liberal dispensation which has influenced the direction and context of social policy. Overall, in Zimbabwe and other parts of Africa, the acceptance and implementation of the social policies exhibit vacuity and non-recognition of the states' responsibility to protect their citizens. Focusing on social protection which is one of the multiple functions of social policy in the Zimbabwean context, this chapter looks at how it has been largely market-based, individualised, fragmented and it has dealt with vulnerability *ex-post*. Unlike in countries like Germany, Finland, Malaysia, South Korea, Taiwan, Japan and Singapore; social policy, with its multiple functions has not been used as a vehicle for development. The social protection paradigm has tended to be dominated by multilateral agencies like the Bretton Woods Institutions (the World Bank and International Monetary Fund) as well as United Nations Agencies, international non-governmental organisations (INGO's), non-governmental organisations (NGO's) and a multiplicity of actors who are usually funded by bilateral agencies. These players have played prominent roles in advocating and pushing for national policies and social policy reforms which have shaped the social policy architecture in developing countries. Internationally, in the past two decades we have seen countries adopting, through the United Nations, the concept of the responsibility to protect. Consequently, countries in the global south find themselves having social policies which focus on vulnerability, precarity and extreme poverty which do not in any way stimulate development.

Due to the undue preponderance of the Bretton Woods institutions, as well as European countries and the United States of America, countries in sub-Saharan Africa have a history in social policies which is heavily influenced by these countries. This influence has impacted them to date. This chapter explores the extent to which this undue influence resulted in countries adopting the largely neo-liberal economic structural adjustment programmes (SAP's) in the 1980's and 1990's which saw the adoption of provisioning based on the concept of 'social safety nets'. This saw the creation and adoption of responses framed as the social costs of adjustments which attempted to alleviate the suffering of the vulnerable and poorest who bore the brunt of economic structural adjustment (ESAP). The second intervention on social policy which has gained prominence in sub-Saharan Africa in contemporary times, which is also heavily influenced by the countries and the institutions mentioned above, has been the use of the targeted cash transfer system. This system has been used as an instrument to respond to vulnerability with the rolling back of the state in welfare provisioning based on a neo-liberal ideology.

These issues are addressed in this chapter. This chapter shows that over the past decades, there has been a gradual move by dominant global agencies like the Bretton Woods institutions and developed countries to dictate social policies in countries in the global south. Social policy instead of being a conduit for development has actually contributed to insecurity and available mechanisms of social protection have contributed to what Titmus (1974) refers to as 'diswelfares'. Social policy has been vacuous; and has not been prophylactic and has failed to enhance the productive capacities of citizens. Thus, the demographic dividend and human capacity available in the global south which could have gone a long way in advancing African countries socially and economically has not been used to its fullest potential and in some instances, it has benefitted countries in the global north for example through unprecedented migration of both skilled and unskilled labour from Africa to western Europe in the past decade. Natural resources are still open to exploitation by the global north as the political leaders in the global south have tended in most instances to export them in their unprocessed form to the global north at very low prices in a historical exploitative relationship. This historical process was highlighted by Immanuel Wallerstein in his World Systems Theory which appeared in his works *The Rise and Future Demise of the World Capitalist System: Concepts for Comparative Analysis* (1974) and The *Modern World System: Capitalist Agriculture and the Origins of the European World-Economy in the Sixteenth Century* which appeared in three volumes (1974, 1980 and 1989).

Due to this and other reasons, Africa has been constrained in fully utilising its resources to benefit its citizens. This contrasts with the late industrialiser in Northern Europe, East Asia and the Nordic Countries who are on record for using their social policies to enhance the productive capacities of their citizens and to exploit their natural resources for national development (Adesina 2007, UNRISD 2006, Yi and Kim 2015). All these issues are explored in detail in this chapter which argues that the current social policy regime is favourable for the continued strangulation of Africa's development, and the status quo is favourable for the continued entrenchment of Euro-American hegemony. Spaces for interference and control in national public policy exist in the face of threats and sanctioning and a consequence of this has been the dictating of the social policy architecture which has had impact on development. It is these issues, which are numerous and cross cutting that we explore in this chapter. Important to understand in this introduction is that the resultant social policies were vacuous and lacked practice of the responsibility to protect.

Responsibility to Protect (R2P) Concept

The Responsibility to Protect, also presented as the R2P has assumed increasing importance in governance and development. Several scholars, notably Powers (2015), Borgia (2015) and Deutscher (2005) focused on the emergence and application of the responsibility to protect principle. The Responsibility to Protect, first coined by the International Commission on Intervention and State Sovereignty in 2001, is intended as a political and policy tool to halt mass atrocities. However, prior to 2001, the need for citizens' protection became alive with the end of the Cold War when the international community was faced with humanitarian tragedies and loss of civilian life in Kosovo, Bosnia, Rwanda, Somalia and so forth.

The deplorable level of failure to safeguard human security led these countries to fall in the failed states category. Generally, during this phase, the responses by the international community to mass atrocities have been inadequate, inconsistent, controversial and completely lacking. This lacuna had to be addressed.

An obligation to respond to mass atrocity crimes developed from the concepts of 'sovereignty as responsibility', the 'right to intervene' and 'two sovereignties' (a sovereignty of the people and sovereignty of states) due to the failures of the state to provide human security in countries such as Rwanda and Srebrenica. Powers (2015: 1258) argues that this obligation shifted the conception of sovereignty from an absolute and sacrosanct right of states to acknowledge that with sovereignty comes responsibility to the people of a state.

The R2P has three pillars. Firstly, each state has the primary responsibility to prevent or halt atrocities. Secondly, other states and the international community have a duty to assist in this effort. Thirdly, should the state fail to prevent or halt mass atrocities, the international community has a responsibility to act collectively, including with force if necessary. Based on these three pillars, Deutscher (2005) argues that the state has a right and responsibility to its people. The primary responsibility to protect citizens rests with the state but if the state is unable or unwilling to protect its citizens, or the state is itself the perpetrator, the international community has the responsibility to temporarily step in, even forcefully depending on the situation.

The ascendency of the Responsibility to Protect in terms of importance and acceptance can be noted in its inclusion in the UN Secretary General's 2004 Report *(A More Secure World, Our Shared Responsibility)*. The report was unanimously adopted by the UN Security Council (UNSC) in Resolution 1674 in 2006. In addition, the UNSC Resolution 1973 (2011) used the responsibility to protect to justify the coercive use of military force in Libya for the protection of civilians from imminent atrocities. Accordingly, the Responsibility to Protect has become a norm in global governance. There is wider consensus for peace and security, and the implementation of this responsibility for the wellbeing of the civilians (Deutscher 2005).

The responsibility to protect is conceptually sound. However, when analysed in relation to the global political order and governance practice, a lot of issues arise. For example: What is the scope of mass atrocities and the responsibility to protect? Given the deep-seated global inequalities, are states equal in defining mass atrocities? Why are some states not punished for gross infringement on the rights of civilians? Overall, the responsibility is shrouded with inconsistencies, controversy, laxity of some states, hegemony by some global economic powers, national and global capitalist interests, socio-political and economic crises.

In this chapter, we extend the responsibility to protect from warfare and military intervention to all the social policy obligations of the state to its citizens. Our central argument is that viewing the responsibility to protect narrowly in terms of mass atrocities that are perpetrated by the state through its repressive state apparatus (RSAs) is too narrow and unacceptable. Accordingly, protection of citizens also incorporates initiating and sustaining wellbeing through social policies. Enhancing wellbeing is a major obligation of the state therefore if a state falls short of meeting this obligation, it has failed to meet its responsibility to protect. Such failure could emanate from internal or external factors.

The Social Policy Concept

Social policy is a widely used concept in the academic and policy world. Just like most academic concepts there is no commonly accepted definition. Yi and Kim (2015) see it as a philosophical principle, as a product of collective action, as a framework for action as well as a process of action. Mkandawire (2001) has defined social policy as collective actions directly affecting transformation in social welfare, social institutions and social relations. For most scholars, social policy is seen as working in tandem with economic policy. They see it as also being embedded in economic policy and it works towards the pursuit of national social and economic goals. Social policy contributes to the welfare of the society as a whole and it does not merely deal with vulnerabilities and casualties that arise due to social change and processes. Through direct government interventions there is the provision of welfare through education, health, pensions, social security, progressive taxation, land reform as well as other redistributive policies. Thus, social policy plays a role in the transformation of economic relationships and improving people's lives. In addition to these functions, social policy is also a vehicle through which gender, racial and other social relations are transformed. This is usually through for example anti-discrimination legislation, marriage laws, laws on families and affirmative action (Adesina 2011, 2014; UNRISD 2006).

Central to the social policy concept is the issue of citizenship. Marshal (1950) cited in Titmus (1974) has argued that citizenship is essential in ensuring that members of society are treated fully and equally. This equality is achieved by increasing the number of social rights that are available to a citizen. For Marshal (ibid) citizenship is divided into civil, political and social rights. If citizens are granted these rights, they have access to public education, unemployment insurance, healthcare and old age pensions. This is seen as being achieved through social policies which are crafted to meet the needs of citizens (Kmylicka and Norman 1994). With citizenship being central, scholars of social policy view its purposes and objectives differently. Some like Titmus (1968) and Townsend (1969) see social policy as being concerned with social conditions and having wider objectives. For them, it covers more than social services and it is concerned with social conditions, equality, justice, wealth redistribution and wealth adjustment. For others like Rein (1970), social policy results in redistribution with the equitable distribution of social benefits and social services being central. In this context, it impacts on agriculture, social welfare policies, the economy and physical development. Yi and Kim (2015) further argue that if social policy is only centred around the provision of services and income such as social insurance, public assistance, health services, welfare services and housing it has limited impact.

Approaches to Social Protection

Social protection is one of the multiple functions of social policy and it is our major concern in this chapter. Just like other concepts in academia, the social protection paradigm is a subject of much contention and debate. When we look at the debate in development, the social protection paradigm is seen as having emerged as a critical response to the social safety nets approach which was dominant in the 1980's and the 1990's. Social safety nets dominated the social protection landscape of countries in the global south and were part and parcel of ESAP. Countries that were considered as being too poor or which had administrative weaknesses and could not put in place comprehensive social welfare architecture were considered as ideal candidates for these SAP policies. While the intention behind having safety nets in place was noble, it did have its challenges. When we look at these safety nets, we can see that they were temporary, short term, discretionary and residual policy instruments. They are contrasted to social protection measures used in contemporary times which are seen by their proponents as being long term, guaranteed and entitlement based.

Another interesting dimension of the social protection paradigm which feeds into the debate in academia is the extent to which social protection and the welfare state have an impact on a country's economy. Social protection for some is seen as costly. This is in a context where it is viewed in the context of short term financial sustainability and spending. The other dimension of this is that from an economics point of view, social protection if properly designed is considered to be an economic investment which can be an instrument to stimulate economic growth. There is a gradual shift in viewing social protection as having a scope that is limited to protecting citizens from shocks and the vagaries of the market. Emphasis is now being placed on how social protection can enhance the capabilities and productive capacities of citizens, playing a promotive and transformative role. Social protection is seen as having a role and employing strategies which strengthen vulnerable groups while addressing structural inequalities. In addition, social protection is considered as a stabilizing instrument in times of crisis, as positively impacting on production and as having short term investments through social spending which is seen leading to long-term investments in human capital. It is due to these perceived positive aspects of social protection, with poverty reduction and economic growth being central, that it is considered as a policy of choice for developing countries hence the push for its adoption by international institutions and dominant countries in the global north. They can be seen pouring billions of dollars in this initiative.

The social protection paradigm is quite dominant especially in literature which has been produced by Organisation for Economic Development (OECD) scholars. This literature advocates for programmes like cash transfers which are seen as reducing poverty and this is achieved through sustained income which promotes social mobility and provides opportunities for citizens to escape poverty. Mkandawire (2005) and Adesina (2011) have argued that this literature has an OECD bias. Social protection is seen as having a neo-liberal influence in which it is reduced to social assistance and social safety nets. Social policy in this context is seen as being reduced to mono-tasking with emphasis being placed on *ex-post* interventions rather than *ex-ante* interventions. The other challenge is that when it comes to social protection, global actors fund some of these initiatives as well as economic support to developing countries. They use this as a basis in which they demand accountability and take a position of moral high ground. Through it, they demand the observance of human rights, the rule of law and democratic processes and respect of democratic institutions. This usually results in the interference in the domestic affairs of countries and if one looks at the history of developing countries over the past three decades, this has been a contentious issue for a long time. Social protection can be best understood using two approaches – the social risk management framework and the transformative social protection framework which we will now briefly look at.

The Social Risk Management Framework (SRM)

This is the approach that has dominated the social protection discourse in the global south over the past decades. It is important to note that social protection in Zimbabwe as shall be shown in subsequent sections has largely been informed by this framework and it is important to bear this in mind as we discuss this framework. The SRM framework is a World Bank inspired framework which is primarily used by the Bank in its programmes and policy recommendations. According to Holzman and Kozel (2007), SRM is a framework that is used to reduce vulnerability and poverty. It targets countries that are considered as not having the instruments and space to manage risks. Holzman *et al* (2000) elaborate on these risks and contend that the basic thrust of the SRM framework is based on two assessments. Firstly, they see the poor as being more typically exposed to diverse risks which range from the natural disasters like flooding and earthquakes and man-made risks such as war and inflation. Secondly, they see the poor as having the fewest instruments at their disposal to deal with these risks. These instruments are seen as ranging from access to government provided income and market based instruments which can be in the form of insurance. In such a scenario, the risks can impact on individuals, communities and regions in an unpredictable and unavoidable way leading to an increase in poverty.

This approach is seen as having weaknesses and these weaknesses have given rise to the development of an alternative approach to dealing with social protection which is known as the transformative social protection framework. Moser (1998) and Mkandawire (2005) have argued that the SRM fails to deal with the root causes of poverty. It views the poor as a static group in society and it categorises them into the ultra, the deserving and the undeserving poor. Emphasis is placed on means testing which Johannsen (2006), Van Oorschot (2002) and Mkandawire (2005) have written on highlighting its weakness as well as its strengths. Wilensky and Lebeaux (1958) have criticised means testing and they have argued that it is aimed at ensuring that applicants or the deserving poor do not get more help than they should. Moser (1998) further argues that the other challenge with SRM which cannot be ignored is that it does not build on strategies that strengthen people's own initiative solutions to their vulnerabilities. Building on the weaknesses of the SRM approach Moser (ibid) developed what she terms the 'asset vulnerability framework'. This framework demonstrates that even the poorest of all people cannot be classified as being helpless victims. Rather, they have resources which they can use to build resilience against vulnerability.

The Transformative Social Protection Framework

The framework was developed by Devereux and Sabates-Wheeler (2004) and it rose due to dissatisfaction with the SRM framework. Sabates-Wheeler and Devereux (2004) have defined the transformative social protection as initiatives that are in place to transfer income and assets to the poor. Through this transfer, the poor are protected against livelihood risks, their social status is enhanced, the rights of the marginalised are realised as well as an extension of the overall benefits of economic growth to the economically or socially vulnerable poor (both individuals and groups). According to Devereux (2004, 2009), this approach is aimed at addressing power imbalances which create and sustain economic inequality and social exclusion. These transformative interventions also include legal and judicial reforms, legislative reforms and adherence to legislative processes, policy review and monitoring, social, behavioural as well as attitudinal change.

It is from this understanding of the basic tenets of the transformative social protection framework that we see it as being geared towards providing *ex-ante* social protection. Unlike the SRM framework which provides social protection *ex-post*, the transformative social protection framework can be seen as addressing power imbalances as well as social and economic exclusion and marginalization providing social protection *ex-ante*. It is from this framework that we see initiatives being put in place by the governments of developing countries to have social protection mechanisms which are not only welfare based but which are transformative and developmental. We will touch on this when we look at options for social protection in contemporary Zimbabwe.

Social Protection in Zimbabwe

Zimbabwe provides us with an excellent example of the neo-liberal dispensation in social protection which has dominated the social protection paradigm in the global south. In this chapter, we argue that this social protection paradigm has failed to improve people's lives or bring about any meaningful development. It has in fact entrenched poverty and failed to address inequalities and insecurity affecting the vulnerable. The interventions that have been in place over the past half a century have addressed vulnerability *ex-post* and not addressed the root causes of vulnerability. The welfare system despite piecemeal reforms has continued to be residual and it has failed to be prophylactic which Alva and Gunner Myrdal posit should be the objective of any welfare intervention. We will begin by giving a brief historical background of the social welfare system in Zimbabwe followed by a brief synopsis of contemporary interventions aimed at protecting the vulnerable.

The Pre-and Post-Colonial Social Protection System

Zimbabwe has always had some form of social protection or social security system historically. For example, pre-colonial Zimbabwe had a social protection system based on the traditional system (Chikova 2013, Kaseke 1988). Kaseke (ibid) argues that the social security and social protection system found in Zimbabwe was time tested. It ensured that an individual's social, emotional and economic needs were met within the family setup. Chikova (ibid) adds that traditional societies in Zimbabwe were characterised by formal and informal social protection that was located within the family and its extended relationships. Through this system the orphaned, the aged, the sick, the destitute and vulnerable were provided with care and support. The nature and extent to which social protection was provided was reliant on the strength of relations among kinsmen. Membership to the family was an important criterion for assistance, creating a sense of togetherness and solidarity among people who shared a common kinship base. The society as well as the traditional authority also had a role in the provision of social protection to those in need. Social cohesion was the underlying theme that ensured that the system remained intact. Social cohesion was found in families and in communities and it was from this that families and societies galvanised support for those in need. This resonates well with the observation made by Mafeje (2003) in sub-Saharan Africa that the clan, the lineage and the household have always acted as units of production, reproduction and as a means of controlling and accessing resources. In addition, the unit was important in providing a welfare system, for family members, which was unfortunately disrupted with colonialism and the introduction of the money economy.

Colonialism brought with it urbanization, industrialisation and the introduction of the money economy which impacted on the traditional system (Kaseke 1988). Amin (1972) and Arrighi (1973) point out that colonisation saw Zimbabwe being turned into a labour reserve economy for the minority white capitalists. Due to the demand for taxes and the monetisation of the economy, the indigenous Africans were compelled to work on farms and mines. The working conditions were poor and they received meagre wages but they were forced to work and participate in the economy, contributing their labour in order to meet the demands of the colonial capitalist economy. According to Kaseke (1998), the introduction of the capitalist economy in Zimbabwe meant that the indigenous Africans became exposed to risks which are associated with the cash economy and these included unemployment and workplace injuries. These realities introduced a shift in the nature of social protection in the country given the rise of a large working class.

The development of social policies in Zimbabwe and the provision of social services to the vulnerable was closely tied to the country's colonial history (Kaseke 1991 and Mhiribidi 2010). In its orientation, it reflected a wholesale transfer of the British system. As Zimbabwe was a British colony its social policy architecture during the colonial and even post-colonial period was deeply steeped in the British Poor Laws as well as the Beveridge Social Insurance System. The system was slightly different in respect of the fact that in a context of racial segregation it was aimed at balancing the needs of the settler minority and the indigenous African majority. For Kaseke (2011), the social welfare system was developed as a response to social ills. These included crime, destitution as well as prostitution. From the colonial governments' perspective, if such ills were left unattended, they were seen as having the potential to create instability and to undermine order. In this context, social work was used as an instrument of control. It did not address the underlying causes of the social ills. Religious and voluntary organisations were the first to provide social relief to societal members. Recipients of social relief were considered to be objects of pity and Kaseke (2011) notes that charitable acts were not celebrated as they were seen to encourage the development and reinforcement of a hand-out mentality. Recipients of social relief were seen as having chosen a life of poverty and social relief was considered to be a privilege extended to the poor and over the years this characterisation has continued and persisted. It is important to note that the influence of the colonial power in shaping social policies was not peculiar to Zimbabwe but it was a common feature in colonised countries. Asamoah (1995) notes that the basic institutions of the colonisers which included the political, social, legal, educational and economic influenced institutions in the colonies. The approaches adopted in the colonies were not compatible with local cultures and traditions and this made them discordant with local contexts. Great Britain for example according to Asamoah (ibid) influenced its colonies to adopt a remedial model in its focus on the challenges faced by vulnerable. Rehabilitation for example was the main focus in the attention which was given to the vulnerable. In contrast, social policies in the former French colonies and territories can be seen to be more reflective of the comprehensive approach which was embodied in the French Overseas Labour Code (Asamoah, ibid).

In colonial Zimbabwe, some of the notable legal enactments that provided for the protection needs for the indigenous Africans included the Native Labourer's Compensation Ordinance No:15 and Workmen's Compensation Ordinance No: 22 of 1922. These provided for the payment of labourers who had suffered injury or death as they performed their duties (Clarke, 1977). Subsequent amendments made it to cover more workers. There the emergence of self-organised mutual aid associations as the colonial period was characterised by rural to urban migration and migrants could no longer rely on traditional support systems in urban areas. During the colonial era, there was no formal social security for the indigenous Africans. This was in a context where many had been pushed to the unproductive communal areas which had a high population density. The Old Age Pensions Act introduced in 1936 provided old age pensions but only for non-Africans aged over 60 years who had resided in the country for more than 15 years. According to Kaseke (2011, 2013) and Clarke (1977), the motivation behind providing social assistance was to attract and retain the European settlers. The provision of pensions to the settlers was meant to alleviate poverty among the older settlers excluding the indigenous Africans. The Rhodesian National Farmers Union introduced a pension scheme for agricultural workers but it has limited coverage as only beneficiaries over 60 were eligible at a time when life expectancy was at 50. In Rhodesia, social distress for Africans was catered for by the Department of Native Affairs until it was transferred to the Department of Social Welfare in 1965. The Department granted assistance to the aged, the blind and the sick. This was on condition that they had severed relations with their relatives in the rural areas. If it was seen that they still had links with relatives, they were repatriated immediately to their rural areas.

Post-Independence Social Protection in Zimbabwe

The new Zimbabwean government in 1980 inherited a country that had some socio-economic challenges. The economy was racially biased and the new government had to deal with the thorny issue of the philosophy of white supremacy which was cross cutting across the social and economic landscape (Chitambura 2010; Chitambara 2012). In the early years just after independence, the government followed policies which were meant to promote equity and socio-economic development. These included the Growth with Equity Policy (1981), the Zimbabwe Transitional and National Development Plan and the First Five Year National Development Plan (1986-1990). The Department of Social Welfare provided social assistance to the destitute or those deemed to be in need of care from the 1980's. In Zimbabwe, social assistance then and now is means tested and based on the residual concept of social welfare. According to Patel (2005), such a concept suggests that the state can only provide assistance to individuals if it established that they are unemployed and unable to receive support from their families. It rests on an assumption that individuals are responsible for their welfare and their needs should be met through the family and the market.

In Zimbabwe in the 1990s, the social sector was quite active. The World Bank driven ESAP saw the reduction of government spending on the social sectors. It resulted in the government introducing the Social Dimension of Adjustment whose main programme was the Social Development Fund (Chitambara 2012). This programme was aimed at cushioning the vulnerable from the negative impacts of economic adjustment but it failed to achieve its objectives as there was an increase in poverty. It was succeeded by the Poverty Alleviation Action Programme (PAAP) in 1994 which had a range of social protection measures which included institutional development of targeted social programmes, informal sector development and enhancement of social policy development and monitoring (Chinake 1995). The government then launched the Enhanced Social Protection Project (ESPP) in 2000 which has had a lasting legacy on social protection in Zimbabwe. The ESPP was a social protection strategy that had components which included the Public Works Component, Children in Especially Difficult Circumstances Module as well as Essential Drugs and Medical Supplies Component. They were aimed at protecting communities by providing social safety nets and alleviating the losses which had been experienced in human capital in the areas of health, education and food security (Government of Zimbabwe 2003 cited by Maushe 2014). The most important legacy of the ESPP was that it resulted in the creation of the Basic Education Assistance Module (BEAM) which still exists in Zimbabwe today and it provides educational assistance to vulnerable children.

When it comes to actual services which are provided to the people, since the 1980's Zimbabwe has provided Public Assistance (PA). PA has been used to target sections of the community that are deemed to be vulnerable and in need of state support. Using the Social Welfare Assistance Act, Chapter 17:06 of 1988 (amended in 2001), the government of Zimbabwe has provided public assistance to those over the age of 60 years, the chronically ill, persons with disabilities and indigent persons. It also supports children and supports those in need including children of the beneficiary, a step or legally adopted child and orphans (Chinyoka 2017; Munro 2001). Other forms of assistance which the government has provided have included assistance to destitute households, children in difficult circumstances (largely orphans), support to persons with disabilities, support to the elderly, Assisted Medical Treatment Orders (AMTO) and the Basic Education Assistance Module (commonly referred to as BEAM). Assistance to destitute families, children in difficult circumstances and the elderly is in the form of cash transfers whilst support to persons with disabilities is in the form of cash transfers, assistive devices and project loans (Kaseke 2013: 1; Kanyenze *et al*, 2011). AMTO allows for the poor to receive free medical treatment at public clinics and hospitals. BEAM is used to provide educational assistance to children who cannot afford and it is the largest social protection intervention by the Department of Social Services. In addition to these mainstream social assistance programmes, the government through the Department of Social Services has distributed food aid mainly to rural households facing food deficits and this usually occurs in times of drought (Department of Social Services 2010). Social assistance which is provided in Zimbabwe is means tested and is provided to those in need who meet the qualifying criteria.

Contemporary Social Protection in Zimbabwe

The social protection regime in Zimbabwe can be roughly divided into three phases with the first phase occurring between 1980 and 1990s, the second phase between 2000 and 2008 and the third phase from 2009 to date. The first phase was from 1980 to the late 1990's, the ruling ZANU (PF) was politically secure and it did not face any strong opposition politically. This had an impact on its policy in government. The state could be seen providing assistance to the indigent on the basis of poor laws at the time with public assistance as the main vehicle used. It was during this period that there was economic restructuring and there were numerous initiatives which were put in place to protect the vulnerable citizens which we have discussed in sections above. The government also provided food aid and there was a land redistribution programme which although it had

151

limited success was aimed at providing for the poor. The second period was between the year 2000 and 2008. During this period ZANU (PF) dominance was severely threatened by the opposition Movement for Democratic Change (MDC) which was formed in 1999. ZANU (PF) sought to consolidate its waning political fortunes and a warning sign of this came through an ominous defeat on a new constitution in 2000. Faced with this setback, it sought to consolidate its power and support base. Through a radical and unprecedented land reform programme, ZANU (PF) managed to consolidate its political power but this coincided with a deepening economic crisis which is attributed to different causes. During this period on the social protection front, the government introduced BEAM which targeted orphans and other vulnerable children in 2001. In response to recurrent droughts, the government partnered with the United Nations (the World Food Programme) as well as other NGOs to roll out an expansive food aid programme (Munemo 2009; Munro 2003). As part of its targeting of communities ravaged by droughts, the government introduced a public works programme which was temporary in which communities undertook different projects (like infrastructural rehabilitation) in return for food. As the economic situation in the country worsened, there was an increase in initiatives to try and make poor communal farmers to be self-reliant and to increase their productive capacities. This period marked a slight change in focus with emphasis being placed on input transfers for communal area dwellers and the newly resettled farmers. There was the introduction of the Presidential Input Scheme as well as a number of initiatives to boost agricultural productivity through the Reserve Bank of Zimbabwe. The overall objective was to enhance the productive capacities of the poor and not to make them overly reliant on public assistance at a time when there was high inflation with the country's currency losing value.

From 2009 to 2013, Zimbabwe had a Government of National Unity (GNU) between ZANU (PF) and the two MDC formations (this had split from the original united MDC). A major highlight of this period was the introduction of the poverty targeted cash transfer programme, the Harmonized Social Cash Transfer programme (HSCT). The target for the HSCT has been indigent households. It provides support to vulnerable groups who include the elderly, child headed households, the disabled and the orphans. The programme was an initiative under the National Action Plan for Orphans and Vulnerable Children (NAP for OVC) 2011-2015 as well as the broader programming under the Department of Social Services. The HSCT is means tested and it targets food poor and labour constrained households (Mtetwa and Muchacha 2013). It has continued to date and it marked a period in which the government reverted towards cash transfers as the GNU brought some relative economic stability. It needs to be understood that the HSCT was adopted at the instigation of donors. The socio-economic situation was conducive for the programme and the dynamics in the GNU in which the MDC had control of the social welfare ministry resulted in its adoption. The HSCT programme came about in 2009 in the face of lack of funding on other long-standing government assistance programmes like food for work, assisted medical treatment and public assistance. The first cash transfer pilot project was implemented from December 2009 to February 2012 under the Programme of Support (PoS) financing mechanism. The HSCT programme can be seen using what Cornia and Steward (1995) and Thomas (1993) call a traditional micro-economic model of households which consist of individuals who are utility maximizing. Using this utility model, even if cash is disbursed to a household without any specific targeting, every member of the household is assured of a share. This however rarely happens in reality as different household members have different preferences and priorities. In Zimbabwe, the HSCT programme uses food-poor and labour constrained households as its targeting criteria and households receive anything between US$10-US$25 a month depending on level of need established during means testing. This kind of social protection programme is not unique to Zimbabwe but it can also be found in other countries which include Nicaragua, Zambia, Malawi, Ghana and Kenya among others.

In addition to social assistance as one of the pillars of social security in Zimbabwe it is important to take note that social insurance also makes up one of the pillars of social security. It includes a social insurance schemes administered by the National Social Security

Association (NSSA). NSSA is a semi-public organisation which administers the National Pensions Scheme (NPS) and the Workers Compensation Insurance Scheme (WCIS). Under the NPS anyone in Zimbabwe who is employed and above 16 and is below the age of 65 is compelled to join and contribute to the pension scheme. They benefit from it upon retirement. On the other hand, under the WCIS, the families of workers are provided with financial relief in instances where an employee who is covered under the scheme is killed while at work or suffers an accident. The scheme also pays for rehabilitation services in cases of injury at work (Chitambara 2010; Kaseke 2013). The last pillar of social security in Zimbabwe according to Kaseke (2013) includes voluntary arrangements which comprise of private insurance and occupational pension schemes. Just like social insurance, this pillar of social security in Zimbabwe is funded by people in formal employment through worker contributions. As a result of high unemployment in the country, a lot of people are not able to participate in social insurance. Those in need are dependent on social assistance but unfortunately only a few can benefit.

Challenges with Social Protection in Zimbabwe

While Zimbabwe has had social policies aimed at cushioning the vulnerable a lot of challenges remain which have contributed to the vacuity in social protection and, instead of contributing to security, they have actually caused insecurities. Chitambara (2010: 9) notes that '…social protection interventions have remained largely inadequate and exclusionary.' Mtetwa and Muchacha (2013) argue that there is lack of predictability, consistency, transparency and sustainability in most of the schemes. Kaseke (2011, 2013) argues that when it comes to social security, there is limited coverage and in most instances, there is no social insurance to speak of. While social assistance provides the basic protection for the population, it is not adequate to cover for all those who need it. The use of the term 'social welfare' by government officials and the public in reference to social assistance has had negative connotations making it to be viewed negatively. In the 1990s Munro (2003) noted that public assistance

154

faced challenges due to its low coverage, poor funding and its irregular and unpredictable payments. The decline in the number of beneficiaries from 69 308 in 1994 to 20 562 in 1998 confirms this observation. Kaseke (2013) notes that there are problems arising from the legal framework guiding the provision of social assistance in Zimbabwe. He notes that the legislation is silent on the right to access social assistance and this inadvertently conveys the notion that access to social assistance is a privilege. Secondly, he argues that the language which is used is not in tune with the discourse on human rights. This is exemplified by the Act referring to those wishing to claim social assistance as applicants and not claimants. The use of the term claimant is seen suggesting that citizens can claim their right to access social assistance if their circumstances so demand it. The use of the term is also not seen as conveying a sense of entitlement.

The other challenge which Kaseke (2013) notes is that officials who administer social assistance have a lot of discretional powers and they decide who benefits and who does not. A challenge with the social assistance system in Zimbabwe was noted by Kaseke (2003) in which social assistance only became active if the intended beneficiaries visit the offices of the department to lodge their applications. This has been restrictive as it assumes that intended beneficiaries must know about the programme. Secondly there are restrictions as beneficiaries have challenges travelling to offices. While there has been decentralisation of offices, travelling remains a barrier and long distances are restrictive to receiving benefits. Lastly a lot of exclusion occurs due to the categorisation of vulnerable people who benefit. While the act has provisions for extended assistance to persons in need of assistance the categorisation of people into the elderly persons with disabilities, the chronically ill children in difficult circumstances and children of indigent persons limits access to social assistance. In addition to these challenges, Chinyoka (2017) has noted that under the constitution of Zimbabwe, social protection is a vague right and it is not enshrined in legislation. Article 30 of the Constitution provides for social welfare and it requires the state to provide social security and care to those in need. In this context, the right to social assistance in Zimbabwe is seen remaining hollow and elusive (Kaseke 2013).

Insights on Social Protection and the Emergence of Social Insecurity in Zimbabwe

The discussion above has briefly touched on the social policy architecture in Zimbabwe from the pre-colonial, colonial and post-colonial periods. The importance of this narrative was to provide a background on the progression which was made over the years in developing contemporary social policy interventions in present day Zimbabwe. It is our contention that social policies which have been found in the country have never been locally developed or 'home grown' except during the pre-colonial phase. During the colonial phase, we have shown that the social welfare system was to a large extent shaped by the British Poor Laws as well as the Beveredgian system of social insurance. As Zimbabwe, then called Rhodesia was a British colony it followed that its social policy architecture borrowed heavily from the British system. With the coming of independence, the social welfare system changed slightly as Zimbabwe pursued a socialist ideology. Emphasis however was still placed on providing welfare to the destitute who included the sick, the aged, the disabled and the unemployed. Racial segregation was removed and the assistance was non-contributory and financed from taxation. It was also means tested and given as a last resort if it was noted that the family was unable to provide support to the vulnerable.

The early 1990s mark a period which is of concern to this chapter which shows how the influence of external actors and disastrous policy prescripts have resulted in a vacuity in social protection and caused social insecurity in Zimbabwe. At the heart of the social protection paradigm in post-independent Zimbabwe has been the concept of means testing which has transcended all interventions on social protection in the country and which we argue is an 'alien' concept that has inadvertently caused gaps in social protection and insecurities. Patel (2005) argues that means testing can be understood as coming up due to the adoption of a residual approach to social welfare. The concept suggests that the state can only provide assistance to individuals if it is proved beyond any reasonable doubt that they are destitute and the family cannot support them. Due to

156

the rigorous nature of means testing it is considered as one of the most humiliating processes that one can go through and in some developed countries those in need may even opt not to seek assistance due to the embarrassments caused by means testing. ESAP which Zimbabwe undertook in 1991 not because of an economic crisis but as a loan (totalling US$484 million) to energize the country's rapid economic growth marks an important turning point in the country's social policy trajectory. Structural adjustment was undertaken not only in Zimbabwe but in other African countries like Cote d'Ivoire, Uganda and Senegal. These programmes were imposed by the IMF and the World Bank as a precondition for financial support. The loans were given to enable the developing countries to be able to repay their foreign debts and this was at a time when their global market share was falling and they had reduced imports and more imports. They entailed the rolling back of the state and promotion of the private sector in what has been termed 'neo-liberalism' or 'free market fundamentals. The objective was to improve the living standards of the people. The fact that this programme was driven by the IMF and the World Bank for us is problematic. This is because when we look at the history of these two institutions, they have since their formation been dominant in global trade as well as finance. Western countries especially the United States and Western Europe have dominated these institutions in terms of voting and policy direction. As pre-conditions for loans or financial support as exemplified by the SAP programmes we can see that the institutions have been used to recommend policy prescripts which have been used to entrench economic domination by developed countries over developing countries. The policies under the guise of the neo-liberal dispensation have opened up the economies of developing countries to the developed countries. Markets have been penetrated and local industries have failed to compete. There has been the flooding of imported goods on local markets and an increase in the export of primary resources to the developed countries at very cheap and uncompetitive prices. Case studies in different countries like Zimbabwe, Ghana and Cote d'Ivoire bear witness to these trends which arguably have led to the economic subjugation of the developing countries (Ismi 2004).

Critics of these policies have argued that the policies contributed to an increased debt burden, unemployment, poverty and economic polarisation which all impeded sustainable development. This is in a context where it is opined that Africa's endemic poverty and pervasive underdevelopment is a consequence of decades of development policy experiments with the vagaries of the external environment especially policies of developing countries playing a role to undermine development (see Kingston *et al*, 2011).

The impact which the SAP's had on social services and the economy in Zimbabwe is well documented and we would argue that it sowed the seeds of underdevelopment and insecurity in social protection. The country was left vulnerable to economic exploitation through adoption of policies based on the neo-liberal ideology. There was the establishment of user fees for health care services which led to a dramatic increase in health costs for patients. This has continued to date and in some instances, it has led to small margin of the population managing to access comprehensive medical services with many people not having medical insurance and having to use out of pocket payments in order to access health services. The same also occurred in the educational sector where there was a reduction in subsidies which made education more expensive and out of reach for some sections of the population. In Zimbabwe, just like in Kenya the push by the SAP's for there to be privatisation of some sectors of the economy for example in the education sector meant that there was less access to education by the poor as education became a commodity on the market subject to the forces of supply and demand. It was only after seeing the limitations of this approach after the SAPs that the Kenyan government reintroduced free education, and ironically it was supported by the same donors which had advocated for the SAPs (Mwenzwa and Maweru 2016).

In Zimbabwe emphasis on leaving public services in the hands of the forces of market and demand occurred in a context were there was progressive falling of the GDP and Zimbabwe's productive capacity was destroyed resulting in massive unemployment and poverty. Furthermore, reforms which cut on social service spending further impoverished Zimbabweans. When it came to agriculture which was the major economic mainstay for the country, the removal of subsidies on agricultural inputs, reduction in government spending on roads and infrastructure as well as high interest rates meant that agricultural performance declined. A consequence of this was high food prices, lay-offs for some in the food sector and related industries and increased impoverishment. Whilst SAPs are no longer there, they have had a lasting impact on the social policy architecture in the country. Priority is still being given to productive sectors, by the government at the expense of the social services sector. This is because the social services sector is seen as wasteful and unproductive. While the programmes are no longer in place, it can be noted that the government has continued cutting on public spending especially on medical care and education. There has been the gradual downscaling and removal of food subsidies and this has in turn worsened poverty. State owned enterprises which played a role in providing affordable goods and services to citizens have either been privatised or are in the process of being privatised. Efforts can be seen in attempts to reduce barriers to trade and foreign investments and to generate export-led growth which is seen as being a catalyst to attract foreign direct investments which can be used to reduce poverty and debt. These strategies have been shrouded in a neo-liberal dispensation which unfortunately has negatively impacted on the poor.

While the neo-liberal trajectory in Zimbabwe's social policy has contributed to the shortcomings of social protection, other factors have also contributed. Of interest is the influence which countries and institutions in the global north have played in undermining the national economy and negatively impacting on public spending on the social sector. In order to contextualise this we need to understand that since 1980, Zimbabwe was confronted by a racially skewed land tenure system with there being seen to be an urgent need for land reform. This land reform was considered as essential in order to alter the racially biased land tenure system, which the country inherited, that favoured the minority of foreign descent at the expense of the majority indigenous Zimbabweans. Failure of the post-independence land reform programmes of the 1980's and mid 1990's as partly blamed on the non-delivery of the free market based economic model which the country adopted under ESAP. Due to these failures of the land reform programme and increasing impatience, there were farm occupations from 1998. These culminated in the highly contested and controversial fast track land reform programme which the government launched in 2000. The objective of the programme was equitable land redistribution in order to avail the means of production to the majority, reverse a racially skewed agrarian structure and to stimulate agricultural production and industrialisation by the indigenous Zimbabweans.

This policy trajectory which Zimbabwe took had its consequences. Unilateral economic sanctions by the United States of America and some European countries at the behest of the United Kingdom and general bilateral donor disengagement was witnessed. This severely crippled the economy of Zimbabwe especially during the period 2000-2008. The United States of America was in the forefront of imposing the sanctions with the enactment of the Zimbabwe Democracy and Economic Recovery Act (ZDERA) in 2001. The European Union, Canada and Australia also imposed sanctions. For the social sectors, the impact was catastrophic given the economic meltdown and unprecedented hyper-inflation which was experienced in the country. Due to these sanctions as well as some internal factors like poor governance, the education, water and sanitation as well as health sectors faced near collapse. These sectors lost most of their financial support and this made it challenging for them to deliver on their mandate. The social infrastructure was there but it found itself being overburdened and it was only through resilience and innovative livelihoods by the population that the system did not collapse and began to recover after 2009. This was due partly to the adoption of a multiple currency system as well as the GNU.

Due to these factors and the impact of the actions of the international community in Zimbabwe, poverty deepened and increased. The different and innovative social policies implemented by the Zimbabwe government were not as effective as they should have been due to socio-economic constraints. This is shown by the fact that despite social protection interventions, Zimbabwe internationally has scored very low in the human development category. According to the GoZ and UNDP (2016), and Zimstat

(2001 and 2013), between 1980 and 2014, Zimbabwe's Human Development Index (HDI) increased slightly in value from 0.437 in 1980 to 0.509 in 2014, with an HDI of 155 in 2014 out of 188 countries globally. This was in the backdrop where from 1980-1985 it had risen but had declined between 1991 and 1999 mainly due to the economic reforms. It had reached its lowest point during the recession period from 2000 to 2008 and has slightly recovered between 2009 and 2014. Another sign of the challenges faced by the Zimbabwean population and the shortcomings of the social protection initiatives can be seen in the trends in national poverty witnessed in the country over the past three decades. A report on progress made on attainment of the millennium development goals by Zimbabwe (GoZ and UNDP 2016), showed that while some achievements had been recorded, income poverty still remains high. The population below the food poverty line which had been decreasing has in the past few years increased. The food severity index, although it has decreased is still very high especially in the rural areas which continue registering high levels of poverty. The statistics are as follows:

- Rural areas continue registering high levels of income poverty. In 2001, it was 82.4% and 84.3% in 2011/12. In contrast in the urban areas it was 42.3% and 46.5% during the same period.
- The population below the food poverty line declined from 41.5% in 2001 to 22.5%. Those who could not meet non-food expenditure increased from 29.4% to nearly 50% in 2011/12.
- Nationally, the servicing of poverty was seen as having remained relatively high although the poverty gap index (PGI) had declined from 38.3% in 1995 to 35.4% in 2001 and 34.1% in 2011/12. The rural population was seen as having a PGI of 47.1% in 1995 which had fallen to 42.8% by 2011/12. For the urban population, the PGI's were at 20.2% in 1995 and had fallen to 15.5% in 2011/12.
- At a national level, the poverty severity index (PSI) had also remained relatively high at 23.2% in 1995 to 21.4% in 2001 and 19.6% in 2011/2012.

Statistics in the health sector are also reflective of the challenges which the country has been facing. It also shows some of the shortcomings in its social policy architecture. The genesis of these challenges can be traced to cuts in public spending and socio-economic constraints. When it comes to health financing, the government of Zimbabwe through taxation is the major financier of public health. The health budget in the country fluctuated between 7 and 9.8% between 2009-2014 which was low compared to the 15% target set by the Abuja target on health financing. Since 2009, the health budget has fluctuated. In 2009 it was 8.7%, 7% in 2010, 9.3% in 2011, 8.2% in 2012, 9.8% in 2013 and 8.2% in 2014.

Alternative Approaches to Social Protection: The Way Forward

In the discussion above, we have painstakingly traced the historical development of social protection in Zimbabwe and we have highlighted some of the challenges with the social protection paradigm. These have been shown as stemming from historical processes as well as the influence of the neo-liberal ideology in social policy. A consequence of this has been that the social policy framework has failed to address vulnerability and has in fact caused insecurities. Social protection interventions have to a large extent been palliative, residual, remedial and reductionist and they have failed to address the challenges of social inequality, poverty and under development. This situation is not unique to Zimbabwe but it can be found in other countries in the global south. An exploitative system can be seen existing which is supported and sustained by a network of international and local NGO's and countries in the global north which control official development assistance and the global monetary authorities. This system has effectively controlled and directed the social policy architecture that now exists in some countries in the global south. Of interest is that the very same countries and institutions that pushed for the adoption of neo-liberal economic structural adjustment projects that worsened vulnerability and arguably saw increased dependency by the countries on the global south on the countries in the global north are now championing new social protection initiatives. In this context, the concept of the responsibility to protect which views the state and the international community as custodians of the rights of citizens has been shown as being flouted as the very same custodians have acted in ways that have skewed the social policy architecture of countries in the global south thus perpetuating inequality and vulnerability. For Zimbabwe, the historical trajectory in social protection discussed in this chapter has shown that over the years in terms of social policy, Zimbabwe has become what Gough (2014) calls an 'insecurity state' in which the state can be seen to have (in some instances) taking decisions and policy trajectories which have seen it undermining the welfare of its people. This has been influenced by the preponderance of foreign donors who now provide the bulk of funding for social protection programmes and hence have leverage in dictating the direction of social policies.

Over the years in Zimbabwe, there has been witnessed a steady decline in the capacity of the state to provide welfare. Efforts to revamp state welfare capacity for example though the HSCT scheme has met with limited success. The push for the adoption of the HSCT scheme has further entrenched the position of external agencies in their participation in social policy provision in some countries in the global south. We would argue that this has contributed to some extent to the erosion of the principle of the responsibility to protect by states which they have partly surrendered to international humanitarian organisations. This is exemplified by Zimbabwe in 2016 were it was noted that in the context of economic challenges facing the country over the years the state has been severely constrained in its support for social protection initiatives. The situation has worsened over the years such that in the 2016 national budget the Ministry of Public Service, Labour and Social Welfare was allocated US$174.24 million with social welfare programmes being allocated US$4.74 million. This was seen as being insufficient with the bulk of the budget going to wage related costs and administration (UNICEF 2016, Ministry of Finance and Economic Development 2016). As a consequence of this the HSCT scheme which was confronted with 504 000 extremely poor households needing assistance was insufficient. This scenario has seen the burden of social protection in the face of state failure being shouldered by development partners, families and extended families. UNICEF for example in 2015 provided US$9.9 million which benefitted 53 509 households which was almost a five-fold increase compared to the US$2 million provided by the government of Zimbabwe (UNICEF 2016).

With these challenges in social protection questions now arise on what should be done to ensure that the social protection framework in Zimbabwe is not only prophylactic but it is also an instrument that can enhance the productive capacities of the beneficiaries. This ensures that citizens are not insecure, overly dependent on charity and are not vulnerable with the state assuming its responsibility to protect and filling up the vacuity in social protection which have been witnessed over the past few years. Several initiatives can be put in place to enhance social protection in Zimbabwe and we will briefly highlight these. In order for the state to reclaim its position as being in the forefront of providing support to the vulnerable proportion of the population it is essential that the economy recovers and the link or interface between social and economic policy which Gumede (2016) has argued as being essential being restored. Gumede (ibid) has argued that for there to be inclusive development, it is essential that there be a link between social and economic policies with social policy having intrinsic (normative) and instrumental functions. These functions are built on the bedrock of the nation building agenda and thus the social and economic policies interface to bring about inclusive development. For countries in the global south, strategies need to be formulated on how investments can be made from funds which are kept for social protection purposes like social insurance and pensions unlike the situation that currently prevails in which these funds are at times not invested or if they are the types of investments which are made (for example on shopping malls) serve no significant production and developmental purposes. Lessons can be learnt from the late industrialisers in the Nordic countries and Eastern Asia were such funds were used to build infrastructure, industries and electricity generation plants. They thus acted as a stimulant for industrialization.

Zimbabwe needs to relook at its social policy architecture with a view of weaning itself away from extensive reliance on donor support for its welfare system. As long as it is dependent on this support, it will always find itself having its social policy direction dictated on by the main funders. The international community will always try to influence the social policy direction of the country as there are vested interests in that area. But this can be avoided as long as the country has a principled stance on its policies and the direction which they expect them to take as well as being the principal actors with the responsibility to protect. The country also needs to move away from the historically defined social policy architecture which has its roots in the colonial dispensation in which it was heavily inspired by racism and the Beveridge model of social policy and the Poor Laws. The social policy architecture needs to be redefined and to borrow from some positive aspects from the Nordic and East Asian models which have positively uplifted the life of citizens on one hand while being a stimulant for economic development.

While it is noble to support the vulnerable and those unable to care for themselves, the approach that is used has had its weaknesses which we will not explore in detail save to say that they have failed to improve the lives of those who benefit, they are wholly inadequate and have actually trapped them in a cycle of dependency. Households have remained poor and insecure (as support can be withdrawn at any time) and it has been erratic and unreliable and this has been in a context of severe economic challenges. Alternatives to supporting poor households for example through land and agrarian reform (by providing land as a resource to poor households) as well as agricultural input transfers instead of cash transfers need to be looked at with models being developed to ensure their sustainability. Such an approach can be beneficial as it will enhance the productive capacities of poor households (in the communal, old resettlement, new farming as well as urban areas). These social transfers (in this context, agrarian transfers) are important as Yi (2013) has argued that social transfers strengthen individual and social resilience as well as capabilities. They also empower the weak and the vulnerable and are the basis for equitable, democratic and sustainable economic growth. It is our contention that the issues highlighted above are a few of the many initiatives that can be done to ensure social protection in Zimbabwe that is inclusive and ensures the state regains its position as the principal welfare provider. It is only this way that the state will assume its position and 'responsibility to protect'. Social policy in this context will not only serve a social protection function but it will also be an instrument for inclusive development.

Conclusion

This chapter has been exhaustive in highlighting some of the important historical milestones in the development of social protection in Zimbabwe with reference to other countries in the global south. We have shown that the social policy architecture in the country has progressed from the pre-colonial to the colonial and post-colonial period in which despite different positions, social policy in Zimbabwe has not been prophylactic and it has failed to enhance the productive capacities of citizens. By all fair assessments foreign-induced social policy in Zimbabwe has been vacuous and detrimental to the wellbeing of the majority of the citizens. Accordingly, Zimbabwe has failed to uphold the responsibility to protect. Countries and powerful institutions and agencies in the global north have been shown as playing an important role in shaping the social policy architecture in the global south which in most instances has tended to perpetuate a long standing historical relationship of exploitation and dependency. If caution is not taken, this exploitative relationship will continue in the foreseeable future. An immediate consequence of this has been that social policies in some countries in the global south have failed to live up to their fullest potential of stimulating socio-economic development. Despite these challenges we have indicated that there are alternative trajectories in social policy which countries can pursue. These are centred on revising the deeply entrenched historical social policy practices which we find in contemporary initiatives. There are a lot of lessons and insights which countries can learn from the traditional systems of social protection which were based on the family, the clan, the lineage and kinship ties. This system was quite effective and a lot of lessons can be drawn from it. In the same vein, countries like Zimbabwe (in the long term when there is economic stability) there are important lessons which can be learnt from the Nordic and East Asian countries which have impressive records on how social policy in tandem with economic policy can be a conduit for inclusive economic development.

References

Adesina, J. O. (2011) 'Beyond the social protection paradigm: social policy in Africa's development', *Canadian Journal of Development Studies,* Vol. 32, No. 4, 454-470.

Adesina, J. O. (2014) 'Accounting for social policy: Reflections on recent developments in Sub-Saharan Africa', *Paper prepared for the UNRISD Conference on New Directions in Social Policy: Alternatives from and for the Global South,* 7-8 April, 2014, Geneva: UNRISD.

Amin, S. (1972) *Neocolonialism in West Africa,* Harmondsworth: Penguin.

Arrighi, G. (1973) 'The political economy of Rhodesia'. In G. Arrighi and J.S. Saul (eds), *Essays in the Political Economy of Africa,* New York: Monthly Review Press, 336-77.

Asamoah, Y. W. (1995) Africa. In: T. D. Watts, D. Elliot and N. S. Mayadas. (eds) *International Handbook on Social Work Education,* Westport CT: Greenwood Press, 223-239.

Borgia, F. (2015) The responsibility to protect doctrine: between criticism and inconsistencies, *Journal on the Use of Force and International Law,* Vol. 2, No. 2, 223-237.

Chikova, H. (2013) 'Social protection in Zimbabwe', *Paper presented at SASPEN-FES International Conference on 'Social Protection for Those Working Informally. Social & Income (In)Security in the Informal Economy',* 16-17 September. Johannesburg, SASPEN-FES.

Chitambara, P. (2012) 'Social protection in Zimbabwe'. In: R. Kalusopa, R. Dicks & C. Osei-Boateng. (eds). *Social Protection Schemes in Africa,* Windhoek: African Labour Research Network.

Chitambara, P. (2010) *Social protection in Zimbabwe,* Harare: Labour and Economic Development Research Institute of Zimbabwe.

Chinyoka, I. (2017) *Poverty, changing political regimes, and social cash transfers in Zimbabwe 1980–2016,* UNU-WIDER Project, WIDER Working Paper 2017/88, Helsinki: UNU-WIDER.

Clarke, D. G. (1977) *The economics of african old age subsistence in Rhodesia,* Gweru: Mambo Press.

Deutscher, M. (2005) 'The responsibility to protect Medicine', *Conflict and Survival,* Vol. 21, No. 1, 28-34.

Ismi, A. (2004) *Impoverishing a continent: The World Bank and the IMF in Africa,* Canadian Centre for Policy Alternatives and Halifax Initiative Coalition. Available at www.asadismi.ws, Accessed 23/12/2017.

Johannsen, J. (2006) 'Operational poverty targeting in Peru? Proxy means testing with non-income indicators', *International Poverty Centre and UNDP Working Paper No. 30,* October 2006.

Kanyenze, G., Kondo, T., Chitambara, P. and Martens, J. (2011) *Beyond the enclave: Towards a pro-poor and inclusive development strategy for Zimbabwe,* Harare: Weaver Press.

Kingston, C., Irikana, S., Dienye, G., Kingston V. and Kingston, G. G. (2011) 'The impacts of the World Bank and IMF Structural Adjustment Programmes on Africa: The case study of Cote D'Ivoire, Senegal, Uganda and Zimbabwe', *Sacha Journal of Policy and Strategic Studies,* Vol. 1, No. 2, 110-130.

Kymlicka, W. and Norman, W. (1994) Return of the citizen: A survey of recent work on citizenship, *Theory in ethics,* Vol. 104, Iss. 2, 352-381.

Mkandawire, T. (2001) 'Social policy in a development context', *Social Policy and Development Paper No. 7,* Geneva: UNRISD.

Mkandawire, T. (2011) Welfare regime and economic development: Bridging the conceptual gap. In: V. Fitzegerald, J. Heyer & R. Thorp (eds). *Overcoming the persistence of poverty and inequality,* Bangistoke: Palgrave MacMillan.

Devereux, S. and Sabates-Wheeler, R. (2004) 'Transformative social protection', *IDS Working Paper 232,* Brighton: IDS.

Devereux, S. (2009) 'Seasonality and social protection in Africa', *FAC Working Paper 11,* Brighton: University of Sussex.

GoZ and UNDP (2016) *Zimbabwe Millennium Development Goals 2000-2015 Final Progress Report,* Harare: UNDP.

Gumede, V. (2016) *Vusi Gumede Academy Professional Network.* [Online] Available at:

http://www.vusigumede.com/content/2016/JUN%202016/La test%20Academic%20Paper.pdf

Holzman, R. and Kozel, V. (2007) The role of social risk management in development: A World Bank View, *IDS Bulletin*, Vol. 38, No. 2, 8-13.

Kanyenze, G. (2011) *Beyond the enclave: Towards a pro-poor and inclusive development strategy for Zimbabwe*, Harare: Weaver Press.

Kaseke, E. (1988) 'Social security in Zimbabwe', *Journal of Social Development in Africa*, Vol. 3, No. 1, 5-9.

Kaseke, E (1991) 'Social work practice in Zimbabwe', *Journal of Social Development in Africa, Vol.* 6, No. 1, 33-45.

Kaseke, E. (2011) ' The poor laws, colonialism and social welfare: Social assistance in Zimbabwe. In: J. Midgely & D. Piachaud, (eds). *Colonialism and Welfare: Social Policy and the British Imperial Legacy* (pp. 119-130). Cheltenham: Edward Elgar.

Mafeje, A. (2003) 'The agrarian question, access to land and peasant responses in Sub-Saharan Africa', *UNRISD Civil Society and Social Movements Programme Paper Number*, 6 May 2003. Geneva, UNRISD.

Maushe, F. (2014) 'In search for the right to education: The role of the Basic Education Assistance Module (BEAM) in promoting access to education in Zimbabwe', *Journal of Development Administration* 1 (1): 1-20.

Mhiribidi, S. T. (2010) 'Promoting the developmental social welfare approach in Zimbabwe: challenges and prospects', *Journal of Sustainable Development in Africa*, Vol. 25, No. 2.

Mkandawire, T. (2005) 'Maladjusted African economies and globalisation, *Africa Development*, 30(1): 1-33.

Munemo, N. (2009) 'Social protection in post-crisis Zimbabwe'. In Chimhowu, A. (ed.), *Moving forward in Zimbabwe: Reducing poverty and promoting growth*: *95-102*. Manchester: Brooks World Poverty Institute, University of Manchester.

Powers, M. (2015) 'Responsibility to protect: Dead, dying or thriving? *The International Journal of Human Rights* 19 (8): 1257-1278.

Titmus, R. (1974) *What is social policy?* London: Allen and Unwin.

Titmus, R. (1968) *Commitment to welfare*, London: Allen & Unwin.

Townsend, P (2004) From universalism to safety nets: The rise and fall of Keynesian influence on social development. In: T. Mkandawire (ed). *Social policy in a development context* (pp. 37-62), New York: Palgrave MacMillan.

UNICEF (2016) *Zimbabwe 2016 Social Protection Budget Brief*, Harare: UNICEF.

UNRISD (2006) *Transformative social policy: Lessons from UNRISD research*, Geneva: UNRISD.

Wilensky, H. L. and Lebeaux, C. N. (1958) *Industrial society and social welfare*, New York: Sage Publishers.

Yi, I. and Kim, T. (2015) 'Post 2015 Sustainable Development Goals (SDGs) and Transformative Social Policy (TSP)', *OUGHTOPIA: The Journal of Social Paradigm Studies*, Vol. 30, No. 1, 307-335.

Zimbabwe National Statistics Agency (2001) *Income Consumption and Expenditure Survey (ICES)*, Harare: ZIMSTAT.

Zimbabwe National Statistics Agency (2013) *Poverty, Income, Consumption and Expenditure Survey 2011/12 (PICES) Report*, Harare: ZIMSTAT.

Zimbabwe National Statistics Agency (2013) 'Poverty and poverty datum line analysis in Zimbabwe 2011/12', In *Poverty Income and Expenditure Survey (PICES) 2011/12*, Harare: ZIMSTAT.

Chapter 6

Entangled in the "New World Order": Africa's (In-) Security Quandaries and Prospects

Aluko Opeyemi Idowu

Introduction

The world is in a power matrix where some countries especially from the Global North engage themselves to harness benefits, including core national interest achievements and personal egocentric motives. These domineering roles are championed by a single country (United State of America). Its global role is trimming and tilting the world to a One World Government regime. It is important to note that the global political and economy order during the cold war era (1988-1990) was the bipolar world order where the now defunct Soviet Union led by Russia was in dual control with the United States of America. In the late nineteenth century up to now (1999 to 2017) the 'new world order' gradually becomes structured to a more powerful Unipolar world order where a single country that is the United States of America champions the control of the politics and economy of the world in terms of economic diplomacy, military threat capability, political international relations, technology developments and social negotiations.

Other countries of the world including African States are caught in the unipolar world order wind of change negatively because of the plethora of problems the continent had been entangled with which has overwhelmed it. These problems are post-colonial spill over and neo-colonial entanglements are the causes of insecurity of the continent in the 'new world order'. This chapter utilises the game theory to explain how most African countries had been down played in the global politics and as well clarifies the sequential and simultaneous games in the international relations. The methodology utilises World Bank data on African countries' entanglements into debt crises due to the status of their political-economy owing to neo-colonialism and existing colonial structures. Also, Africa Development Bank data on Africa's development are considered. Six African states (Botswana, Ghana, Côte d'Ivoire, Kenya, Nigeria and Zimbabwe) are randomly selected across the continent to analyse some of the most important problems Africa has entangled with in the 'new world order'. Therefore, what is the extent of development and policy focus do Africa countries need attain in order to break-off from the global politics entanglements and become a power broker in the current world politics? This chapter argues that a sustainable development intervention is needed to be able to effectively disentangle the continent from an insecure mode in the world politics instead of political propaganda.

The world is in a power matrix where various countries are entangled and mangled. The core national values and interests are the focal points in all kinds of relationships among the nations of the world. Each nation seeks to derive the maximum achievements or utmost satisfaction from all bargains so as to induce its desired growth and development. Seldom in such relationships among nations, the personal egocentric motives of each country come to the fore as countries try to out-play one another. The self-interested representatives of the countries may also want to derive some personal aggrandisement from the negotiation (Cox, 2016; Sunkel and Inotai, 2016; Nelson-Pallmeyer, 2017). Therefore in whatsoever international relations, there is an element of power interplay be it soft power or hard power interplay.

Prior to the outbreak of the World War One (WW1) in (1914-1918), African continent had been scrambled and partitioned upon by the European therefore rendering the continent unsafe, unsecure, economically miserable, politically unviable, socially devastated and grossly unfit to compete effectively and efficiently in the global politics. After the outbreak of the World War One (WW1) in (1914-1918), there emerged the unipolar world order system where most of the countries were controlled and pay allegiance to a single country (United State of America). The United States had both the hard power and the soft power to push, pull and compel any country in the world to bid its instructions. Any country that fails to comply is treated as a pariah nation among the comity of states. However, each country was slowly but gradual learning diplomacy, allies' tactics, developing their technologies (Fukuyama, 2017; McFate, 2017). This internally slow but sustainable growth, developments and socio-political and economic readjustments gradually made some countries of the world to attain soft power and hard power technologies They acquired power over who/what?.

Therefore, the world order changed to the bipolar world order in the cold war era (1945 to mid-1970's) where the now defunct Soviet Union led by Russia was in dual control of what with the United State. The now defunct Soviet Union which was a combination of states in the Eastern Europe became the power contender with the United States of America. Both states arrogated power over the other states of the world to the extent that both literally divided the world into two big halves and a little fraction (Chafer and Jenkins, 2016). The other fraction is the group of non-aligned countries. The non-aligned countries sought to exercise their sovereignty without becoming satellites of the two big powers.

In the late nineteen century to date, the new world order changed to a more solidified unipolar world order where all other countries are solely under the prejudice of the United State of America. This is grossly evident in terms of economic diplomacy, military threat capability, political international relations, technology developments and social negotiations which had the United States far ahead of all other states in the world. America have a large influence as the major or sole power bloc on other nations whereby it bully other states, dictate the sizes of militaries for other states, preventing other states from developing competing nuclear weapons, imposing sanctions on other states, determines which action is terrorism or genocide, determines which regime will be pull down and which one will be enthrone around the world, unilaterally and illegally imposing sanctions as well as declaring wars on other sovereign countries. (Bourantonis and Wiener, 2016; Greenblatt, 2017). Thus, the new world order is made up of the United State of America as the major powerful nation, in terms of the economical capability, socially stability, political sovereignty and military capability. This fitness was achieved through intense and consistent technological development with a realistic political economy policy plan. A few other countries are emerging across Europe, Asia, and Africa but are all under the firm grip and subversions of the United State of America's One World Government agenda.

Africa on the other hand is cut in this wind of change negatively because of the plethora of problems the continent had been entangled with which has seriously overwhelmed it due to the Euro-America trounced African sovereignty, is holding Africa in check preventing it to rise. When other countries are enhancing their development sustainably, Africa is battling with series of problems which prevents it from competing favourably with other countries. These problems are the Euro-American deliberate policies induced to weaken Africa, it include political instability, long military rule, weak or unrealistic policies, poor policy implementation, weak or selfish leadership, poor economy management, high rate of unemployment, ethno-religious crises among others. These problems are foundational causes of the insecurity in Africa continent in the new world order. Many countries in Africa are at the mercy of power interplay of the other powerful countries across continents. Therefore, in political economic negotiation, many African countries are marginalised using 'might is right', sequential games or simultaneous games principles in the game theory.

This chapter utilises the game theory to justify the sequential games or simultaneous games principles in the international relations. The methodology utilises World Bank data on Africa countries entanglements into debt crises due to the status of their political-economy owing to neo-colonialism and existing colonial structures. Also, Africa Development Bank data on Africa's development from six African states (Botswana, Ghana, Côte d'Ivoire, Kenya, Nigeria and Zimbabwe) are randomly selected across the continent to analyse some of the most important problems Africa has entangled with in the 'new world order'. Therefore, what extents of accelerated development do African countries need to break-off from the insecure global entanglements? This chapter opined that a sustainable development measure is needed to be able to effectively disentangle the continent from an insecure world politics.

Conceptualising new world order

The New World Order (NWO) is a notoriously vague conspiracy theory which claims that some powerful groups are either secretly running the world, or on the verge of gaining such control. A 'New World Order' is that of a secretive power elite with a globalist agenda conspiring to eventually rule the world through an authoritarian world government—which will replace sovereign nation-states—and an all-encompassing propaganda whose ideology hails the establishment of the New World Order as the culmination of history's progress (Gurudas, 1996). The term "new world order" has also been used to refer to any new period of history evidencing a dramatic change in world political thought and the balance of power. Before the early 1990s, 'New World Order' 'conspiracism' was limited to two American countercultures, primarily the militantly anti-government right and secondarily the fundamentalist Christianity concerned with the end-time emergence of the Antichrist (Rivera 2003).

The earliest standalone uses of the phrase 'New World Order' was by Frederick C. Hicks. The phrase had previously been used by N.M. Butler in his 1917 book *A World in Ferment*. To Hicks and Bailey, the term meant a benevolent social democracy that would soon emerge, whilst Butler used the term to describe the First World War as it was being waged. Ewoh, (1997) opined that the 'new world order' is both a political and economic configuration. Politically it is the death of the bipolar world that existed during the cold war and World War between the Eastern bloc and Western bloc to give rise to a unipolar world order guided by the United State of America. Economically, it connotes the emergence of trade blocs and institutions regulating them which monitors the world trade under the watch of the United State of America.

Different groups have opined that the term 'new world order' have different connotations. The conspiracy theorists opined that the 'new world order' conspiracy centres on the role of the United Nations. This theory claimed that the United Nations was merely a tool of the Communists, and that the end goal was the complete subjugation of the United States to the United Nations. This would then set up a world government in which all of the freedoms that Americans hold dear would be abolished. However, in the most recent times, more liberal versions of the 'new world order' opined that instead of the United Nation taking sovereignty away from the United States, the United States of America through the platform of the United Nation plans to conquer the entire world.

It is difficult for anyone to determine which organization, institution and individual are parts of the 'new world order'. However, International organizations such as the World Bank, IMF, European Union, the United Nations, and North Atlantic Trade Organization are often listed as core 'new world order' organizations. Presidents and prime ministers of nations are routinely included in the conspiracy. It is important to note that 'new world order' conspiracy theories opined that the Bible as well has prophesied about it. This comes from pages in the Books of Ezekiel, Daniel and Revelation, stating a New World Order will occur for seven years, and then Jesus will returns and defeats the Antichrist. As well the Latin phrase "*novus ordo seclorum*" appearing on the reverse side of the Great Seal since 1782 and on the back of the U.S. one-dollar bill since 1935, translates to "New Order of the Ages". This alludes to the beginning of an era where the United States of America is an independent nation-state and the "New World Order".

Africa in the dynamic world order

Development in human society has many sides. At the level of the individual, it implies increased skill and capacity, greater freedom, creativity, self-discipline, responsibility and material well-being. At the level of the state, it implies political, economic and social growth. Africa over the years has made substantial efforts to grow in this dynamic world. First, the continent has the general combined body of states (the Africa Union) that makes general policy for the growth and development in the continent. Second, the continent has various regional bodies that cater for the specific needs of each region such as the Economic Community of West African States (ECOWAS), the Southern African Development Community (SADC) among others (Hettne, 2016). Third, each country has governments that take up the various developmental policies from the various organizations they belong so as to integrate and domesticate them. Lastly each country in Africa belong to the world political-economic and cultural organization (the United Nations) and other various socio-political and economic organization such as the Organization of Petroleum Exporting Countries, World Bank, International Monetary Fund, International Court of Justice among other international institutions (Breslin and Hook, 2016).

All of these efforts are to ensure that the African continent break even among the comity of nations. However, it is conspicuous that there are large development[and attendant looting] gaps between the Global North and the Global South. The Global North countries are the highly "industrialised" nations in Europe, America and part of Asia [that take unlimited liberty to plunder Africa] while the Global South countries include Africa, part of Asia, the Middle and Far East Asia countries among others. These development [and plunder] gaps are obvious in terms of economic and fiscal growth, military capabilities, high political influence, good health policy, general infrastructure development, high technological development and enhanced human and social capital development. Rodney (1973) noted that a society develops economically when its members increase jointly their capacity for dealing with the environment. This is dependent on the extent to which they understand the laws of nature (science), the extent to which they put that understanding into practice by devising tools (technology), and on the manner in which their work and society is organised. In the true sense of natural development, Euro-American states never have such clean basis of development because they plundered Africa, enslaved Africans, looted African resources and other forms of exploitations. They did not purely develop simply as a result of 'understanding the laws of nature' but by subverting the laws of God, good neighbouring and nature (Mawere and Nhemachena, 2017).

Some of these lacunae that cause entanglement to Africa in the global politics include the colonial exploitation. Colonial Africa fell within that part of the international capitalist economy from which plundering, looting and exploited Africans lost their livestock, land, minerals and human resources to feed the metropolitan sectors in

Europe. Proceeds of colonial plundering were repatriated to the so-called 'mother country'. There were expatriations of plundering, looting, human resources and exploited Africans lost their livestock, land, minerals produced by African labourers or slaves out of African resources. It meant the development of Europe is a part of the same dialectical process in which Africa was looted and plundered. The "development" of the capitalist economic world has involved the creation of the "modern" world economy institutions (Aluko, 2015). The Euro-American institutions invariably reshape Africa's economy by imposing a number of conditionality before they could give "loan" to most African states. These include; currency devaluation, privatization and commercialization of public owned establishments among others (Aluko, 2017). These structural adjustment programs make the receiving nations to be at the mercy of the "donor" nations.

Aluko (2017) as well noted that the African economy was essentially a socialist system whereby public welfare is the order of the day and mutual development of individuals was of the utmost priority. However at the onset of capitalist structure as far back as the colonialism era, exploitation of the work force by owners of the means of production became prominent. The "rich" [plunderers] are getting "richer" while the "poor" [plundered] are getting "poorer". The ownership by plunderers replaced ownership by the African original owners. The economy of mutual growth and development changed to plunderous personal aggrandisements and egocentric motives. After independence, Africa states produced new manifestations of capitalists who eventually sustained the colonial legacy of domination, subjugation..

Entanglements with premeditated problems created by Europeans colonial creations become more prominent when many African countries gain puppet independence and yet depend heavily on just one or two raw materials for export and economy survival. The exportation of such agricultural and mineral resources to Europe, Asia or America is as well dependent on the importers' conditionality. Africa remains at the mercy of the importing nations that in many cases determine what quantity they want and the price they can afford. If African states reject the conditionalities, the economy may run into recession (Nhemachena, 2016). Therefore,

African valuable raw materials are exported to other continents and the same materials are transformed into finished goods which are later exported back to Africa. At this point, the finished goods are very important to the survival of the African economy for food sufficiency. Sadly, the by-products of Africans raw materials which are harmful and injurious to both humans and the environment are repackaged and exported back to Africa in the form of e-waste, substandard electronics, dump ground for old model cars, substandard drugs among others. This 'tie down syndrome' makes many Africa states to be dependent on the plunderous "developed" states of the world and yet unable to favourably compete with them in terms of technology strength, trade prowess, military capability, human capacity development, political negotiation power and infrastructural developments.

This in turn led many of African states into a heavy dependency on foreign aid, foreign direct investments and economic bailouts. The timeless sovereignty of the African states is under threat as the "donor" groups will have a say on what to use the money for, how to spend it, where and when to spend it, as well as who should spend the money and the expected outcome of the fund. The governments of the receiving countries will therefore be much more careful not to offend the "donors" but to align with them in almost all policies and dance to their prejudice so as to be able to get more of such funds (Lindberg and Sverrisson, 2016). Therefore, some African political leaders becomes puppet leaders and 'yes sayers' in the international politics coupled with their unpatriotic and low political will to grow their home economy, stop corruption and embezzlement of public funds.

Due to unsustainability and instability of Africa's financial status, many countries become unprecedentedly externally "and human resources indebted". The services of the "debts" as well sap off huge financial resources which could have contributed to Africa's domestic growth and development. The World Bank and the International Monetary Fund (IMF) defined total external "debt" as "debt" owed to non-residents. Total external "debt" is the sum of public, publicly guaranteed and private non-guaranteed long-term "debt", short-term "debt" and the use of IMF "credit". Short-term "debt" includes all "debt" with an original maturity of one year or less and interest in arrears on long-term "debt" (World Bank, 2015). Although UNCTAD (2015) notes, the distinction between domestic and external "debt" is becoming blurred as there has been a shift in "debt" instruments since the early1990s away from loans in foreign currency held by non-residents towards bonds that may be denominated in a foreign currency but held by residents. African is entangled in these "debt crises".

In 2011–2013, the annual average external "debt" stock of Africa amounted to $443 billion (22.0 per cent of GNI) compared with $303 billion (24.2 per cent of GNI) in 2006–2009 (UNCTAD 2016). On average, Africa's external "debt" stock grew rapidly, by 10.2 per cent per year in 2011–2013, compared with 7.8 per cent per year in 2006–2009. The annual average growth rate of Africa's external "debt" stock exceeded 10 per cent in eight heavily "indebted" poor countries and 13 non-heavily "indebted" poor countries. Due to the trend of push and pull factors, such as the recent sharp decline in commodity prices and resulting lower revenues (pull), and the global financial crisis, the external "debt" stock grew most rapidly in Mozambique (by, on average, 30 per cent per year), Cameroon (26 per cent per year) and Gabon, Nigeria, Rwanda and Seychelles (24 per cent per year each) (World Bank 2015; UNCTAD 2016).

Definitely, these entanglements in the plunderous global political economy will never make Africa or other continents such as Asia to be able to grow out of the woods and effectively compete. Africa's scorecards and jokers in the game of international politics are usually pre-empted by the other plunderous players in Europe, America, and Asia that squeeze the continent.

Theoretical framework

Game Theory
Game theory is the branch of decision theory concerned with interdependent decisions. The problems of interest involve multiple participants, each of whom has individual objectives related to a common system or shared resources. Because game theory arose from the analysis of competitive scenarios, the problems are called

games and the participants are called players. But these techniques apply to more than just sport, and are not even limited to competitive situations (Manshaei, Zhu, Alpcan, Bacşar and Hubaux, 2013). In short, game theory deals with any problem in which each player's strategy depends on what the other players do. Situations involving interdependent decisions arise frequently, in all walks of life. A few examples in which game theory could come in handy include: Friends choosing where to go and have dinner, parents trying to get children to behave, commuters deciding how to go to work, businesses competing in a market and diplomats negotiating a treaty among others. All of these situations call for strategic thinking and making use of available information to devise the best plan to achieve one's objectives.

Moreover, all players are .intelligent in the sense that they understand the structure of the economy. A game is as well referred to any social situation that involves two or more participants (Colman, 2013). Specifically a game always has three components; first, when specifying a game we need to be explicit about who the participants are. These are called players. Depending on the application, a player may be a seller in a market, a consumer, a general at war, or even diplomat representing a country at the United Nations General Assembly. Second, we also need to be explicit about what every player can conceivably do. Myerson (2013) and Ichiishi (2014) opined that their capability and extent of threat they can foment against other players. The third component in a game is the payoff function for each agent that specifies how each player evaluates every strategy profile. The tradeoffs or payoff includes what an actor losses to gain another thing. That is to figure out what each agent wants to do and what they should expect others to do. At this stage each players or actors need to know the utility for every choice of the agent as well as every choice of everyone else. However the actors that are dependent on the other or that had been made to be dependent due to uneven playing ground is entangled.

In world politics of all eras, be it the unipolar, bipolar or the current 'new world order', game theory operates as either sequential games or simultaneous games. In a sequential game, actors react based on the information they have at hand over the other party in question. In this case, mapping out of all the possibilities is done by looking ahead to the very last decision, and assume that if it comes to that point, the deciding player will choose his/her optimal outcome. Actors at this point usually back up to the second-to-last decision, and assume the next player would choose his/her best outcome, treating the following decision as fixed and as well continue to reasoning back in this way until all decisions have been fixed. Stronger nations in most cases would have predetermined what gift will be used to entice or entrap the weaker nations so as to derive a maximum benediction from such relationship. This is a typical case in Africa whereby stronger nations outplay the continent's bargaining and profiteering deals thereby generating political, economic, cultural and epistemic unevenness.

The simultaneous game on the other hand involves the quick decision making because there is not necessarily any last move. Actors cannot look ahead and reason back, since neither decision is made first (Myerson, 2013; Dresher, Shapley and Tucker, 2016; Cornelissen, Cheru and Shaw, 2016). They just have to consider all possible combinations. This is most easily represented with a 'table game' listing the players' possible moves and outcomes. In the new world order, both sequential games and simultaneous games strategies are employed. Stronger countries use sequential games model to relate with the less powerful states (Africa and other developing nations). They pre-empt their last outcome and present their joker to win the best of the negotiations. However, relationships that connect strong states utilize the simultaneous games which put each actor in dilemma of what the other might do if a certain decision is taken. This is because the last joker of the first actor is equal or almost equal to the others on the negotiation table. Therefore there is no last move but consequential simultaneous actions.

Methodology, data presentation and discussion of findings

The methodology utilises World Bank data on Africa "debt" crises and Africa Development Bank data on Africa's development. Six African states (Botswana, Ghana, Côte d'Ivoire, Kenya, Nigeria and Zimbabwe) are randomly selected across the continent to analyse some of the most important problems Africa has entangled with in the 'new world order'. Six African states (Botswana, Ghana, Côte d'Ivoire, Kenya, Nigeria and Zimbabwe) are randomly selected across the continent to find out why the continent is entangled in the global wave of change, growth and development otherwise known as the 'new world order'. Descriptive statistics is used in the analysis and interpretation of the data and subsequently the findings.

World Bank Data on Africa Development and Debt Rates

Selected African Countries	% of Total External Short Term Debt		% of Total External Long Term Debt	
	2006-2009	2011-2013	2006-2009	2011-2013
Botswana	8.7	17.0	88.8	77.2
Ghana	24.8	22.7	68.1	68.1
Côte d'Ivoire	7.2	2.8	83.9	66.5
Kenya	11.4	15.0	88.3	74.3
Nigeria	0.0	0.0	30.7	35.8
Zimbabwe	29.8	29.8	64.9	48.4

Table I

Source: World Bank 2016

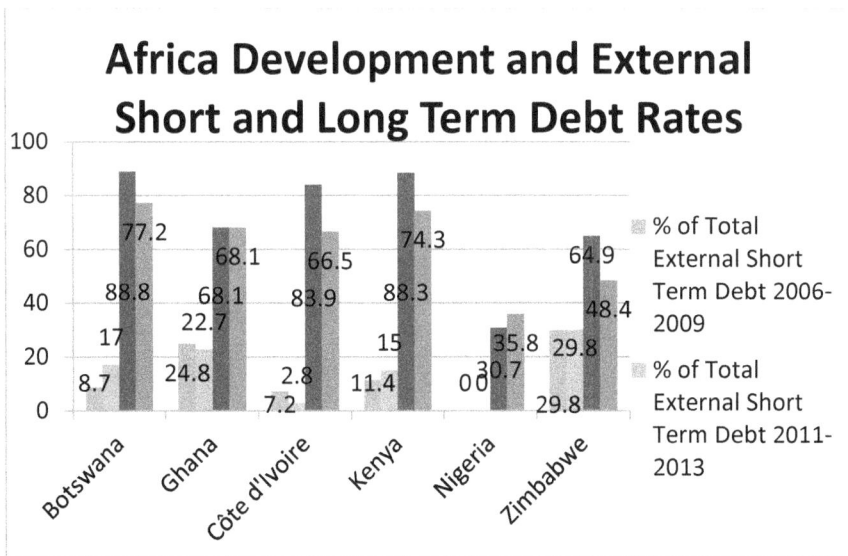

Figure I

Source: World Bank 2016

183

The table I and figure I above show the World Bank data on Africa development in terms of credit worthiness or "debt" rates. The total percentages of external short term "debt" from 2006 to 2013 are provided. This revealed that between 2006 and 2013, Botswana's total external short term "debt" increased by 8.3% that is, from 8.7% to 17% while the percentage of the total external long term "debt" decreased by 11.6%. This implies that the country access to international credit facilities is reduced. The credit worthiness status has reduced and the required huge amount of money for the political economy development which usually comes from long term loans has reduced. This will further lead to slower economy growth in which the country will not be able to compete effectively in the 'new world order'. This slow economic growth is also corroborated by the Africa Development Bank 2016 data in table II and figure II below that the country percentage of real Gross Domestic Product is below five percent (2.9%) while the inflation rate is above five percent (6.3%).

The "debt" profile from World Bank data on Ghana -another African country indicates that the total external short term "debt" decreased by 2.1% that is, from 24.8% to 22.7% while the percentage of the total external long term "debt" remains constant at a high level of 68.1%. This implies that the country is "indebted" to international credit facilities providers. The amount of money for the political economy development which usually comes from long term loans is constant. This will lead to a steady or gradual economy growth in which the country will not be able to effectively compete and remove the country from the developmental "debt" required to cope with the 'new world order'. This slow economic growth is also corroborated by the Africa Development Bank 2016 data in table II and figure II below that the country percentage of real Gross Domestic Product is below five percent (3.2%) while the inflation rate is far above five percent (18.1%).

The "debt" profile from World Bank data on Côte d'Ivoire-another African country indicates that the total external short term "debt" decreased by 4.4% that is, from 7.2% to 2.8% while the percentage of the total external long term "debt"alsodecreasedfrom83.9% to 66.5%. This implies that the country is still greatly "indebted" to international credit facilities providers. The amount of money for the political economy development which usually comes from long term loans is decreasing. This will lead to a slow but gradual economic growth in which it is not sufficient to instantaneously remove the country from the developmental debts and entanglements of 'new world order'. This slow economic growth is also corroborated by the Africa Development Bank 2016 data in table II and figure II below, the country percentage of real Gross Domestic Product is below ten percent (7.5%) while the inflation rate is just below five percent (2.8%).

Africa Development Bank Data on Africa's Development 2016

Country	Real GDP %	Inflation %
Botswana	2.9	6.3
Ghana	3.2	18.1
Côte d'Ivoire	7.5	2.8
Kenya	6.0	6.3
Nigeria	-1.5	16.1
Zambia	0.5	20.7

Table II

Source: World Bank 2016

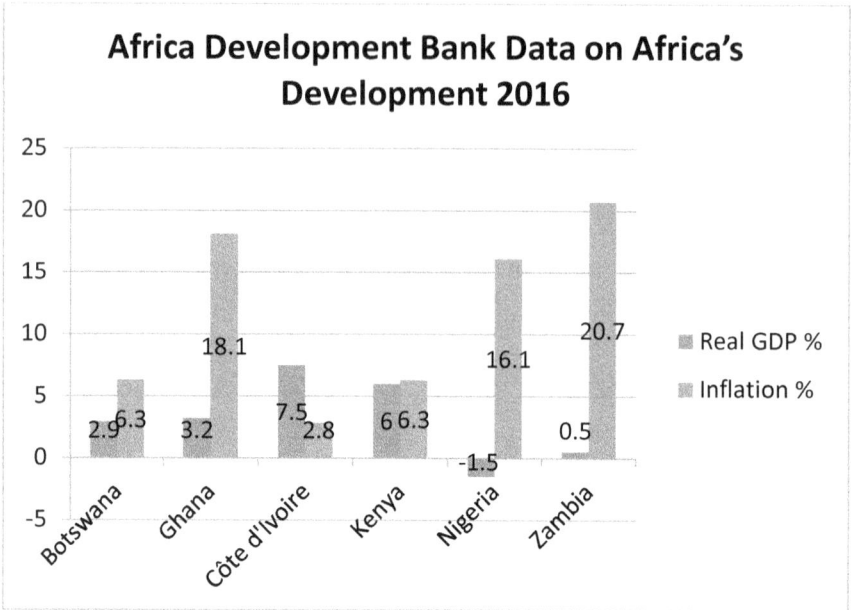

Figure II
Source: World Bank 2016

The "debt" profile from World Bank data on Kenya - another African country from the table I and figure I above indicates that the total external short term "debt" increased by 3.6% that is, from 11.4% to 15.0% while the percentage of the total external long term "debt" also decreased from 88.3% to 74.3%. This implies that the country is still greatly "indebted" to international credit facilities providers and its concern about long term development plan financing is reducing. The amount of money for the political economy development which usually comes from long term loans is decreasing. This will lead to a slow or gradual economic growth in which it is not sufficient to instantaneously remove the country from the developmental "debts" and entanglements of 'new world order'. This slow economic growth is also pointed out by the Africa Development Bank 2016 data in table II and figure II above. The country percentage of real Gross Domestic Product is above five percent (6.0%) while the inflation rate is as well above five percent (6.3%).

The "debt" profile from World Bank data on Nigeria - a country in African from the table I, figure I above indicates that the total

186

external short term "debt" has no value or not indebted while the percentage of the total external long term "debt" also increased from 30.7% to 35.8%. This implies that the country is still slightly "indebted" to international credit facilities providers or the country's credit worthiness has reduced along sides with its concern for financing long term development plan. The amount of money for the political economic development which usually comes from long term loans is slightly increased. This will lead to a slow or gradual economic growth in which it is not sufficient to sustainably remove the country from the developmental "debts" and entanglements of 'new world order'. This slow economic growth is also pointed out by the African Development Bank 2016 data in table II and figure II above. The country's percentage of real Gross Domestic Product is below one percent (-1.5%) which shows an economy in distress or recession. The inflation rate is as well is far above ten percent (16.1%).

The "debt" profile from World Bank data on Zimbabwe - an African country from the table I, figure I above indicates that the total external short term "debt" has remained constant at 29.8% while the percentage of the total external long term "debt" also decreased from 64.9% to 48.4%. This implies that the country is still slightly "indebted" to international credit facilities providers or the country's credit worthiness has reduced so also its desire for financing long term development plan. The amount of money for the political economy development which usually comes from long term loans is drastically decreased. This will lead to a slow or gradual economic growth which is not probably insufficient to sustainably remove the country from the developmental "debts" and entanglements of 'new world order'. This slow economic growth is also corroborated by the Africa Development Bank 2016 data in table II and figure II above. The country's percentage of real Gross Domestic Product is below one percent (0.5%) which shows an economy in distress or recession. The inflation rate is as well is far above fifteen percent (20.7%).

Conclusion

There is a plethora of problems facing Africa's development in the 'new world order'. One can even ask whether Africa can ever be able to come out of these [sham] global developmental entanglements. Africa needs a sustainable and accelerated development so as to break-off from the global political entanglements and become a power broker in the world. A sustainable development measure is needed to be able to effectively disentangle the continent from an insecure mode in the world politics. African leaders have a lot of political propagandas which are not backed up with practical actions. A lot of money and human resources has been allocated to enhance infrastructural development but the presence of weak leadership, coupled with weak institution and corrupt personnel had render African countries handicap of growth and development.

The United Nations (UNCTAD) 2014 Report revealed that Africa requires estimated financing investments of between $600 billion and $1.2 trillion per year. This huge amount of money might be needed continuously for about twenty to thirty years so as to be disentangled from global developmental debts. Infrastructure alone would cost $93 billion so as to be able to achieve the desirable Sustainable Development Goals. Therefore for Africa to successfully achieve this major development finance needs a thorough public budgetary resources is required. Every yearly fiscal budget must be incremental and must address specific developmental infrastructure projects. The budget so drafted must be realistic and the rate of its accomplishment must be above ninety five percent (95%).Therefore any Africa country that wants to escape the developmental entanglement of the 'new world order' must have an incremental budget which provides good infrastructural and technological priority.

African countries must make collaborative efforts to reduce Africa's external "debt". The current African "debt" record is on the rise and is mainly related to reduce export revenues, a widening current account deficit and slower economic growth. The main drivers of this "debt" accumulation are associated with a growing current account deficit and slower economic growth. This situation got worse due to heavy reliance on export of raw materials instead of finished goods which will provide a chine of employment for the teeming population and drive the country to a sustainable development. This scenario can be reduced if sustained investments are made on technology and industrialization. Sustainable efforts must be made on transforming raw materials into finished goods for export purposes instead of exporting raw materials.

There must be robust control of illicit financial outflows from Africa. If this is curtailed, it could become a source of development finance, as long as efforts to tackle them at the national and international levels are sustained. This implies that other countries of the world should prosecute individuals or leaders that illicitly repatriate money away from their homeland to the foreign land. This is crucial, as World Bank and the African Union records revealed that Africa lost about $854 billion in such outflows from 1970 to 2008.Over that period, about USD217.7 billion is estimated to have been illegally transferred out of Nigeria, USD105.2 billion from Egypt, more than USD81.8 billion from South Africa, while Kenya is reported to have lost about $1.51 billion between 2002 and 2011 (AU/EAC 2015).

This sum is nearly equivalent to all official development assistance received during that period. Yet the figures double every decade. Forum on Transparency and Exchange of Information for Tax Purposes and the Stolen Asset Recovery Initiative should be fully brought on board to avoid duplication of expenses while utilising their experiences and best practices. Lastly, the vital role of anti neo-imperialist minded civil society in monitoring transparency should be recognized, reinvigorated and used it to provide additional societal vigilance. All of these action plans and policy oriented pragmatic steps are fundamental to the growth of the African continent out of the 'new world order' entanglements.

References

Aluko, O. I. (2017) Political Economy of Crony Inequality among Nations: A Study on Capitalism and Socialism *Journal of Community Development Research (Humanities and Social Sciences) Naresuan University*, Volume 10, No. 2.

Aluko, O. I. (2015) Political Economy of Crony Capitalism: The Prospect and the Bane *Journal of Economics Library* Volume 2 Issue 3

AU/ECA (2015) Track it! Stop it! Get it! Illicit Financial Flows, Report of the High Level Panel on Illicit Financial Flows from Africa, *Conference of Ministers of Finance, Planning and Economic Development.*

Bourantonis, D., & Wiener, J. (Eds.). (2016) *The United Nations in the new world order: the world organization at fifty.* Springer.

Breslin, S. & Hook, G. (Eds.). (2016) *Microregionalism and world order.* Springer.

Butler, N. M. (1917) New World Order*: A World in Ferment* http://archive.org/stream/aworldinferment00butlgoog#page/n120/mode/2up/search/world+order

Chafer, T., & Jenkins, B. (Eds.). (2016) *France: from the Cold War to the new world order.* Springer.

Colman, A. M. (2013) *Game theory and its applications: In the social and biological sciences.* Psychology Press.

Cornelissen, S., Cheru, F., & Shaw, T. (Eds.). (2016) *Africa and international relations in the 21st century.* Springer.

Cox, R. W. (Ed.). (2016). *the new realism: Perspectives on multilateralism and world order.* Springer.

Dresher, M., Shapley, L. S., & Tucker, A. W. (Eds.). (2016) *Advances in Game Theory. (AM-52)* (Vol. 52). Princeton University Press.

Ewoh, A. I. (1997) Africa and the New World Order *East Africa Geographical Review* Vol 19 No1.

Frederick C. Hicks (1920) *The New World Order* http://archive.org/details/newworldorderin00hickgoog.

Fukuyama, F. (2017) *State building: Governance and world order in the 21st century.* Profile Books.

Greenblatt, S. (2017) *Marvelous possessions: The wonder of the New World.* University of Chicago Press.

Gurudas O. (1996) *Treason the New World Order* Cassandra Press San Rafael, California.

Hettne, B. (Ed.). (2016) *The new regionalism and the future of security and development* (Vol. 4). Springer.

Ichiishi, T. (2014) *Game theory for economic analysis.* Elsevier.

Lindberg, S., & Sverrisson, Á. (Eds.). (2016) *Social movements in development: The challenge of globalization and democratization.* Springer.

Manshaei, M. H., Zhu, Q., Alpcan, T., Bacşar, T., & Hubaux, J. P. (2013). Game theory meets network security and privacy. *ACM Computing Surveys (CSUR), 45*(3): 25-32.

Mawere, M. and Nhemachena, A. (2017) "Humanitarian" Fundamentalism: Interrogating "Global" Processes of Fishing in African Troubled Waters, in Nhemachena, A. and Mawere, M. (eds), *Africa at the Crossroads: Theorising Fundamentalisms in the 21st Century.* Bamenda: Langaa RPCIG.

McFate, S. (2017). *The modern mercenary: Private armies and what they mean for world order.* Oxford University Press.

Myerson, R. B. (2013). *Game Theory.* Harvard university press.

Nelson-Pallmeyer, J. (2017). *Brave new world order: must we pledge allegiance?.* Wipf and Stock Publishers.

Nhemachena, A. (2016) (Post-)development and the Social Production of Ignorance: Farming Ignorance in 21st Century Africa, In: Mawere, M. (ed), *Development Perspectives from the South: Troubling the Metrics of [Under]development in Africa.* Langaa RPCIG: Bamenda p 77-118.

Rivera D.A. (2003) *Final Warning: A History of The New World Order* Conspiracy Books An Imprint of Inteli Books Oakland: California

Rodney W. (1973) *How Europe Underdeveloped Africa.* Bogle-L'Ouverture Publications, London and Tanzanian Publishing House, Dar-Es-Salaam
http://www.marxists.org/subject/africa/rodney-walter/how-europe/index.htm.

Sunkel, O., & Inotai, A. (2016) *Globalism and the new regionalism* (Vol. 1). Springer.

UNCTAD (2015) *Trade and Development Report, 2015: Making the International Financial Architecture Work for Development.* United Nations publication. Sales No.E.15.II.D.4 New York and Geneva.

UNCTAD (2016) The *Economic Development in Africa Report 2016: Debt Dynamics and Development Finance in Africa*,
UNCTAD/ALDC/AFRICA/2016.

United Nations, www.unctad.org/Africa/series.

World Bank (2015) *International Debt Statistics 2015* Washington, D.C.

Chapter 7

Rethinking Security and Global Politics:
The Tethering of Africa in an Era of Globalisation

Munyaradzi Mawere & Costain Tandi

Introduction

The notion of human security has vigorously influenced the academic and political debate on contemporary global studies. The view that Africa has suffered greater economic, political, environmental and technological insecurity in the hands of the Global North than any other region of the world cannot be dismissed by a wave of a hand. The continent has, over the years, been prone to political abuse, deepening poverty, food and nutritional insufficiency, health and educational crises, bad governance, violent and intractable conflicts, rising number of refugees and internally displaced persons, and environmental bankruptcy, among other calamities, mainly as a result of the influence of external 'forces'. Owing to this obtaining reality, human insecurity in Africa as elsewhere in the Global South has heightened at a sporadic pace. Globalisation along with other external forces such as modernisation and westernisation continue to exert unimaginable pressure on Africa that attenuate the continent's capacity to alleviate human insecurity. As a result, insecurity remains a continental problem as it is also a global problem.

This chapter explores the causes of human insecurity in Africa. It argues that pressures unleashed by global forces in the form of liberalisation, privatisation, debt and globalisation, among many others, undermine Africa's development in general and human security in particular. In advancing this argument, the chapter interrogates conventional assumptions on human security and surmises that in a heavily dependent region like Africa, fortunes are intricately tied to development in the wider global economy. As such, human insecurity in Africa cannot be realistically divorced from development in the international system. In problematising human security, the chapter examines external factors in the aggravation of Africa's human security crisis.

While part of the causes of human insecurity in Africa is arguably internal deriving from among other factors such as conflicts, corruption, inauspicious public policies, mismanagement and sometimes environmental factors such as famine, deforestation, desertification and many others, this chapter submits that global politics play a seemingly inconspicuous role in aggravating these factors.

Conceptualising human insecurity in the Global South

The causes of human insecurity in Africa can be categorised as either international or local. Internationalised causes are those causes emanating from the Global North inspired state system and values including the globalisation of Western democracy. On the other hand, the localised causes are those specific to local situations such as terrorism, inequalities, inauspicious state policies as well as conflicts (Akokpari 2007). We should underline here that most of the causes of insecurity in Africa are externally inspired. We expand this argument in the section below where we discuss the uncertainties and insecurities imposed on Africa as a result of globalisation.

Globalisation and its uncertainties: Paradigms in African Security

Globalisation remains highly contested, devoid of an intellectual consensus on its definition, conceptualisation and interpretation. Scholars are not sure as to when the period of globalisation commenced, and whether it has ended or it still continues. For instance, according to Hirst and Thompson (1996), there is no one accepted model of the globalised economy and how it differs from the past. This resonates with Bairoch and Kozul-Wright (1996) who opine that, most contemporary observers have differed in their description of the globalisation process, and have failed to construct a consistent theoretical explanation of what is driving it and where it might be going.

However, the period we focus on here relates to when many of the writings on the subject of globalisation emerged, and the period generally discussed or referenced in these writings. As a starting point to explaining the phenomena of globalisation, most definitions make reference to openness, integration or flows. Openness relates to individual countries participating in, or being willing to participate in and integrate in international economic activity. Integration refers to combining or amalgamating elements across countries, which predominantly occurs through cross-border activity and international division of production (Gundlach & Nunnenkamp 1994). Flows as they pertain to globalisation encapsulates the movement of goods and services through trade, financial transaction through investment and foreign exchange markets and the sharing of ideas, intellectual property as well as technology.

In relation to what has been observed within the more recent period of international economic activity, Hay and Marsh (2000) assert that there has been a gradual evolution toward globalisation rather than a quantum leap at any particular point in time, while Hirst and Thompson (1996) note that what has emerged is not a genuinely global economy, but rather a high level of interaction between individual players within the international economy. The economic components of globalisation pertain to production, trade, investment, finance, competition and demand. All of these factors have exhibited increased international integration over the past two decades.

We note that many scholars who have discussed globalised seem to have narrowed it economic interaction neglecting other forms of interaction such as cultural, political, religious and educational. In this chapter, we focus on globalisation mainly as it pertains to issues of security in developing countries. The exploration of the subject of security is prompted by the fact that much of the globalisation literature makes reference to the processes of globalisation as an uneven and unequal phenomenon (see for example, Baker, Epstein & Pollin 1998; Kiely 1998; Morris, 1996; Mawere, 2013; 2016; 2017). Due to varying effects of globalisation on different spheres of life in

Africa, Mawere (2016: 1-2) for instance, has described globalisation as "a bitter pill that one takes with a crinkle face". His argument is that globalisation as a process has a double effect – what he calls "the paradox of globalisation" (Mawere 2017: 92): it should be treated with care as it has the potential to yield both positives and negatives. Others describe globalisation as "the latest stage of imperialism" (Bello 2003; see also L5L 2003). More others conceive it as "Euro-American imperialism" (Aborishade 2002) that results in either "cultural atrophy" (Ekwuru 1999) or "cultural crisis" (Akindele 2002). Indeed, the globalisation experience has differed between developing and developed countries, and among developing countries. Furthermore, the experience has varied within individual countries (CEPAL 2002). There have been regional differences with respect to developing countries during the most recent period of globalisation.

Over the past two decades, Africa has consistently portrayed the image of a continent in distress, taunted as deeply troubled and on the road to self-destruction (Gberie, 2005; Bischoff 2005), but mainly as a result of globalisation which seems to disadvantage other countries of the world. It is piteous to note that, at a time other continents are counting their achievements, Africa is counting more losses; backsliding steadily in virtually all human development indicators. It is assumed that its peoples are poorer now than in 1960; most of them living on income level below one dollar per day (Didia 2015). At the same time, the continent's share of global trade is just around 2%, contributing even less (about 1%) to total global economic output (Bracking 2003). We cannot refrain from asking questions: why is Africa so poor? What is preventing the continent from growing and developing? In addition to that, what is hindering the progress of democracy in African societies? Was globalisation introduced to help the so-called developing countries or to subjugate them? Many theories might explain why Africa has been the poorest continent despite its many valuable resources, vast tracts of land, and the finest talent in the world. There is currently much optimism about economic development in Africa, and the ability of globalisation and western policies to promote growth on the continent. This optimism is however misplaced as it is self-serving of G8 and other donor interests; it also goes to the heart of how 'the West' views 'Africa', and does little more than promoting a patronising view of Africa (and Africans), while promoting a subordinating practice of development (Federici 2004). In fact, what others view as optimism for Africa, we view it as the widening gap of Africa's insecurity.

Globalisation and the international economic order have systematically generated human insecurity throughout the world over the years especially in Africa as well as other regions of the advanced industrial countries in the Global North. Most pertinently, globalisation and the international economic order have undermined economic-human security –that is economic, food, political, cultural and health security– which in turn has contributed to the generation of personal, community and political insecurity. This general deterioration of human security throughout much of the Global South lays the causal groundwork for widespread societal unrest; the undermining of state power and legitimacy; the emergence of parallel criminal economies managed by rival warlords; the mutual corruption and militarisation of the state and society; and ultimately the eruption of violent conflict fuelled by war economies. In this way, globalisation and the international economic order, generating economic-national insecurity, fundamentally destabilise the national security of countries in the Global South. This systematic undermining of security across national boundaries amounts to a veritable globalisation of insecurity at human and national levels. The sheer, relentless scale of this process demonstrates that the international economic order and the neoliberal paradigm on which it is based must be fundamentally transformed if this process is to be reversed in the interests of the security of the majority of the world's population.

The various facets and impacts of globalisation on Africa cannot be contemplated in this short chapter: it requires a book dedicated solely to it. Globalisation as is known today did not cause Africa's contemporary predicaments; even though it, in numerous ways, exacerbated them. The logic driving Africa's developmental challenges could be traced to a variety of external and internal factors, mostly relating to the manner and processes through which the continent of Africa was, in the guise of globalisation, engulfed (or captured) forcefully into the global capitalist order around the mid-1500. How this long colonial adventure continues to implicate Africa's current development has fascinated African scholarship and worrying Africanists and moralists alike. Ihonybere (2000: 3-4) summarised Africa's experiences during that historical moment as:

> the experience of slavery; the termination of endogenously driven patterns of state and class formation; the imposition of colonial rule; the balkanisation of the continent and imposition of alien values, tastes, and institutions; the creation of a repressive corrupt, unproductive, unstable, and illegitimate state; the creation of a highly fractionalised, factionalised, dependent, corrupt, and weak elite; the domination of the African economy by profit-and-hegemony-seeking transnational corporations dedicated to making profit at all cost; the total denigration of local cultures, values, and institutions, and the introduction and promotion of primordial differences and suspicions; and finally, the structured incorporation of the African economy into the periphery of the global division of labour and power as vulnerable, dependent, underdeveloped, weak, and largely raw material-producing region, to mention a few.

With this in mind, it is quite veritable to make a standing observation that the manner in which globalisation is affecting the Global South in general and Africa in particular is not only painful for Africanists but worrying security-wise (Nnoli 2003; Juhasz, 2002; Meagher, 2003; Morton, 2004; Swyngedouw, 2004; Mawere 2017). Nevertheless, only the extent to which globalisation is complicating Africa's security problems will be of interest in this chapter. As a matter of fact, it is possible to discern that different historical epochs have laid their own different and unique 'globalisation'. Nevertheless, what may be different about the current era can be explained in terms of its scope (global spread), intrusivity (the degree of penetration) and intensiveness (the resultant changing effects). For Africa, globalisation may have been delivered in different forms but the effects were essentially the same. As colonialism, globalisation represented (and continue to represent) political and administrative domination mainly to facilitate extraction and accumulation. After independence in many countries of the South, globalisation manifested itself as imperialism by helping to deepen accumulation even further, allowing the persistence of human indenture, magnifying the inequality of capitalist expansion, increasing human insecurity, and generally provoking violent disorders (Bracking2003; Field 2004). During the 1980s, globalisation was represented by the activities of the Breton Woods institutions and international donors under the IMF/World Bank structural adjustment program (SAP). Presently, it is vividly shown by the contraction in time and space, the ease of capital mobility and the radical transformations in the organisation of human affairs and social life (Bischoff, 2005; State 2003). For most weak and developing countries, each of these phases of globalisation simply reinforced the other thereby accelerating the decline or collapse of welfare and security safe nets.

Those who celebrate globalisation point to the phenomenal increase in the movement of peoples, coupled with unprecedented flows of goods, services and capital around the world (Olukoshi 2003; Richard 200). Those critical of globalisation insist that the agency of the process of globalisation has become too destructive and consuming as it widens social disconnections, social dislocations and violent conflicts at every point and space that it strives to negotiate a presence (Nnoli 2003). For countries in the Global South, then, globalisation provokes a return to familiar conditions of subordination – much like those which marked the insertion of the continent into the global capitalist system fully around 19[th]century by European colonialism (Richard 2000). The Ugandan political analyst, Catherine Odora Hoppers described the current phase of globalisation and the neo-liberal ideology driving it as simply a continuation of the war that began with colonialism and never ended (Gberie, 2005).

Scholars such as Field (2004) challenge the pro-globalisation thesis relating to the question of space and territoriality. His main point is that while it may be genuine that the physicality of space no longer hinders interactions and movement of factors of production, globalisation has turned out to be another euphemism for westernisation in direct opposition to multiculturalism presented as the discourse of differences and diversity. What globalisation seem to be doing to developing economies such as those of Africa, then is intensifying age-old group antagonisms: sublime racial politics, regional economic disparities, and worsening global poverty. It disguises the true nature of the North-South divide and generates the illusion that to transcend differences is to overcome it. According to Field (2004), globalisation does not and cannot foster equity owing to the fact that its technology is driven by the same exploitative trade regimes which it supposedly called out of order (Field, 2004).

Interestingly, scholars such as Olukoshi (2003) observe that globalisation is celebrated even when it is uncertain whether the global uniformity that is projected is desirable, beneficial or even possible in the final analysis. The outlines of globalisation, according to him, is revealing that some regions of the world have been associated with the collapse of the middle class, side by side with the collapse of the middle ground in the national and regional politics, the widening of the social gulf between the rich, whose numbers are radically thinned out, and the poor whose numbers are swelling by the day, as well as sharp increases in armies of unemployed people, mostly young school leavers. Olukoshi (Ibid) acknowledges the legitimate worry arising from globalisation as the world continues witnessing the worst and most extensive process of social exclusion ever known, occurring side-by-side with the single-minded, ideologically-motivated retrenchment [and de-energising] of the state and the erosion of its capacity. The provocative reality about globalisation therefore is that at the same time that developed countries are claiming to be putting in place robust policies to cushion the side-effects and threats from globalisation, they are dissuading, even coercing, their weaker counterparts in the South from pursuing their own independent interests on the pretext that the State must roll back its presence and allow the market to mobilise and allocate social capital. Since decay seems to outweigh renewal therefore, Olukoshi (2003), warns us that the biggest challenge facing Africa consists of renewing and retooling the State in order to enable it resume a meaningful role in the developmental process. This is where the irony about globalisation and African security problematic most reveals itself: at the same time that globalisation is undermining the capacity of the State and the State itself is reeking under the weight of its own internal contradictions: it is still expected to be the major force for stability and security in contemporary Africa.

Globalisation by-passing the Global South

A number of scholars have also argued that globalisation has largely by-passed countries in the Global South. Dollar and Kraay (2001) for instance, opine that developing countries which have not participated in globalisation suffered significant slowdown in their economic growth. This resonates with Lindert and Williamson (2001) who suggest that globalisation has been a largely positive experience for many countries. Nevertheless, the countries which have become worse-off are those that have not participated. Additionally, the inequality previously noted has been proposed to occur because globalisation has not spread far enough (Johnson 2002). This shows that inequality and non-participation are inextricably linked.

Interestingly, countries in the Global South do not participate by choice, but owing to occurrences within the international economy, for instance, the low demand for the exports of developing countries, which makes it virtually impossible for such countries to participate in international economic activity. Other areas where countries in the Global South largely do not have a choice pertains to where there are standards or requirements for certain goods or services which these countries are not able to meet, in attracting foreign direct investments (FDI) and in the establishment of production facilities by multinational enterprises (MNEs). Notably, there are domestic elements that make Third World countries less able to participate in global trends, for instance, economic stability and the quality of infrastructure available to support industry and production.

Hoogvelt (1997) adopts the dependency theorist terminology of core and periphery to describe the pattern of separation and exclusion that has emerged within the most recent period of globalisation, where core pertains to the Global North and periphery to the Global South. Specifically, a small number of relatively advanced developing countries have been able to move from the periphery to the core, such as Taiwan, Singapore and South Korea. Nevertheless a significant number of countries in the Global South have remained in the periphery, especially those located in the African continent. Therefore, trading patterns within the international economy have remained largely unchanged from the period prior to globalisation. Furthermore, trading patterns are largely similar to what they were at the beginning of the Twentieth Century (Bhaduri 1998), for those countries that have remained in the periphery. Hoogvelt (Ibid) makes reference to there actually being less interaction between the core and periphery than in the past. For the developing countries that have moved into the core, improvements in income and growth have been observed (Hirst & Thompson 1996), however, for developing countries that have not moved into the core, their relative position within the international economy has deteriorated as a consequence of the growth of other countries. Notably, the countries that have moved into the core represent a small proportion of the overall population of the so called Third World countries. A number of trends have contributed to the Third World countries being unable to participate in the process of globalisation, and the perpetuation and strengthening of the core and periphery structure within the international economy. Relevant trends include the growth of MNEs, the increase in protectionism by developing countries, and the emerging production trends. Oman (1994) argues that because of the trends associated with globalisation, the division between developed and developing countries has been more prevalent than in other periods in economic history.

Why globalisation worries countries in the Global South?

A second school of thought has advanced that countries in the Global South have not been by-passed by the most recent period of globalisation. Participation in international economic activity has largely disadvantaged developing countries, putting them in a worse position than would otherwise have been the case. The problems faced by developing countries participating in the international economy are due to the high level of concentration brought about through specialisation, and to the unattractiveness of the industries being specialised in, for instance, agricultural commodities and simple manufacturing.

Globalisation has brought about Third World countries participating in international economic activity according to comparative advantage. The so-called poorest countries in the developing world tend to export a narrow range of low value-add products, typically dominated by one or two key exports which exhibit relatively low growth rates within global export markets. Such countries therefore lack export diversification. This has its own associated challenges owing to the fact that it creates vulnerability and instability in revenue, arising from any external shocks. Any number of events could put an export at risk, with severe implications for export earnings. For instance, the introduction of a less expensive substitute could diminish export earnings considerably. Rifkin (1996) argues that genetic engineering could also pose a threat to a narrow export structure. Where there is concentration in agriculture, a crop failure or natural disaster could adversely impact on export earnings for a given time period.

Much of the criticism pertaining to developing countries and globalisation relates to the industries that Third World countries have a comparative advantage in, and therefore the goods that are exported by these countries when participating in international economic activity. Global South countries are largely stuck in unattractive industries with low scope for growth (Porter 1990; Didia 2015). The industries that countries in the Global South predominantly specialise in are primary commodities, and simple manufacturing, often processing these primary products.

The main problems inherent with industry and exports dominated by primary commodities did not emerge during the most recent period of globalisation, with economists such as Prebisch (1950) and Singer (1950) warning against such a structure several decades earlier. Nevertheless, the problems highlighted by these economists have continued to exist, and have potentially even increased in relevance in recent years, with increasing evidence to support the initial theories proposed. Over the last forty years, there has been evidence of the sustained decline in terms of trade for commodities, which Prebisch and Singer predicted. Most importantly, commodities have largely exhibited instability and short-term price fluctuations (UNCTAD 2001).

In recent periods, including the globalisation period, agriculture has exhibited low, and for some products, negative growth rates (UNCTAD 2002). There are a number of factors that have contributed to the observed trends including population growth rates, income elasticity of demand for agricultural goods, and the emergence of substitute products (Maizels 2003). Owing to low population growth rates in developed countries, the export market size for agriculture is declining. Agricultural commodities exhibit low income elasticities of demand relative to manufactured goods, and therefore, as incomes rise in developed countries there is not a proportionate increase in demand for agricultural commodities. Agriculture also exhibits low price elasticity of demand, so that movements in price do not have significant impact on demand. At the same time, agriculture exhibits high price elasticity of supply, so that when multiple countries export the same commodity, prices fall. In recent times, a growing number of substitutes for certain agricultural commodities have been introduced, which has increased the vulnerability of producers of these commodities. Trends of increased protectionism toward agriculture and other commodities and the emergence of product differentiation for agricultural commodities, previously discussed, add to the issues that make specialising in agriculture problematic for developing countries.

In terms of manufacturing, the trend of breakdown of value chains has provided opportunities for developing countries to participate in manufacturing, albeit at the lower end of the value chain where a smaller amount of value is typically added relative to the total value of the good or service being produced (Krugman 1995). The problems associated with this kind of participation is that developing countries are not developing the skills necessary for advancement and export income is minimal, reflective of the relative value the output of developing countries brings to the overall production process.

The growth of FDI and global expansion of MNE activity have been referenced as some of the key aspects of globalisation. FDI and MNE activity in developing countries is suggested to disadvantage developing countries in a number of ways. Because MNE activity is driven by profit motivations of shareholders, their presence in developing countries potentially leads to surplus extraction with limited benefit to the developing countries (Chang 1998). As developing countries compete to attract FDI, a so-called race to the bottom can emerge, as a consequence of developing countries lowering and compromising standards to attract FDI (Obstfeld 1998).

Standards that have the potential to be eroded include labour, health and environmental standards (Crotty, Epstein & Kelly 1998). Another problem associated with FDI and MNE activity is that governments either provide concessions, thereby reducing income, or spend to meet the infrastructure requests of MNEs, diverting spending away from development areas such as health and education. Technologies introduced by MNEs have displaced local technologies, and the technologies introduced are potentially less aligned with the resources and skills that exist within developing countries. Finally, the FDI that is directed toward developing countries may not go toward sectors that are conducive to economic development, for example, investment may be made in agriculture and mining (Baker, Epstein & Pollin 1998).

A number of environmental issues have been associated with globalisation and activity within developing countries. Specialisation has caused excessive use of non-renewable resources (Goldsmith, 1996). Ecological problems highlighted throughout the literature include soil erosion and land degradation due to over-farming, and destruction of marine life due to over-fishing of rivers and oceans (Cole 2000). Pollution has been caused by emergence of industry, and inadequate sanitation to cope with rural-urban migration. Health problems have also increased as a consequence of rural-urban migration. There have also been adverse social and cultural impacts of developing countries participating in globalisation, such as loss of natural cultures and the introduction of alternative values such as materialism (Scholte 1996).

Theorising the nexus between globalisation and security

Generally speaking, the concept of security has been articulated in neo-realist terms, where the primary unit of analysis is the

205

sovereign state whose territorial integrity and internal cohesion must be protected. A rather different –though not wholly unrelated– conceptualisation of security that is centred primarily on the individual or community can be understood as human security. It is worth mentioning that the concept of human security is centred more directly on the protection of people, the scope of their freedom within communities, their access to market and social opportunities, and whether their society is in a state of peace or conflict. Although economic security is, therefore, a particularly vital component of human security, the latter encompasses many other aspects of human existence. In 1994, the United Nations Development Programme (UNDP) argued that:

Human security can be said to have two main aspects. It means, first, safety from such chronic threats as hunger, disease and repression. And second, it means protection from sudden and hurtful disruptions in the patterns of daily life -whether in homes, in jobs or in communities (p. 3).

The UNDP (2004) identified seven key components of human security. These include:

- Economic security (e.g., assurance of a basic income).
- Food security (e.g., access to food).
- Health security (e.g., access to health care and protection from diseases).
- Environmental security (e.g., protection from harmful effects of environmental degradation)
- Personal security (e.g., freedom from threats by the state, groups, or individuals).
- Community security (e.g., freedom from harmful community practices).
- Political security (e.g., enjoyment of human rights, and freedom from political oppression).

Interestingly, these areas of concern illustrate that globalisation is intimately connected to the concept of human security, since they are affected by a wide variety of global processes, including for example: the depletion of non-renewable resources; drug trafficking; human trafficking; the rapid spread of communications technology; the growth of unsanctioned capitalist markets; poverty and inequality; and the HIV/AIDS pandemic.

The concept of human security attempts to provide an overarching framework by which to understand the fundamentally interconnected and cumulative nature of these global processes and their detrimental impact on people's security on a world scale. While globalisation has on the one hand created new opportunities, it has also generated political and economic instabilities and conflicts within states. Whereas over 800,000 people a year lose their lives to violence, about 2.8 billion suffer from poverty, ill health, illiteracy and other maladies (Ahmed 2004). Human security recognises the linkage between conflict and deprivation –the latter provides a causal context to many conflicts. Conversely, conflict increases poverty and crime, and devastates economies. A broad all-encompassing and integrated approach is therefore required to account for these complex interconnections.

As Ahmed (Ibid) notes, the concept of human security is perhaps too broad. Its all-inclusive nature means that it serves as an unwieldy instrument for policy makers due to positing such a diverse variety of threats and sometimes incompatible solutions to them. This also lends the concept a definitional elasticity that potentially hampers its application as a concrete analytical tool. Nevertheless, despite these flaws, human security provides the beginnings of a theoretical framework for primarily analysing non-military threats to the safety of societies, groups, and individuals. Rather than focusing on military threats to the state, human security emphasizes the need to examine military and especially non-military threats to individuals. Arguably, the broad complexity of the concept is actually intrinsic to the wide variety of factors affecting the security of the object of reference – individuals– rather than indicative of a failure of the concept itself. Therefore, because one of our primary concerns here is to understand the economic impact of globalisation on individuals and communities across national boundaries, as opposed to the state alone, human security provides a useful conceptual launching point for this chapter.

From a human security perspective, there are two fundamental forms of violence. These include the direct violence which relates to killing swiftly through war and indirect violence which means killing slowly and invisibly through poverty, hunger, disease, repression and ecocide. Both forms of violence cannot be seen merely as the outcome of isolated, random and discrete process. Rather, they constitute a function of interlocking dominant processes and structures at both intra-national and international levels.

Here, we are primarily concerned with the three economic components of human security (economic-human security). Using the UNDP criteria established in 1994, it is clear that the first three components –economic security, food security and health security– are all directly interconnected. Both food security and health security can be directly undermined by the generation of economic insecurity. These three areas of ultimately economic concern are, thus, forms of indirect or structural violence. Trickner (1987) argues that, the indirect violence done to individuals when unjust economic and political structures reduce their life expectancy through lack of access to basic material needs. Lack of income (economic insecurity) equals lack of purchasing power necessary to obtain sufficient food (food insecurity), clean water and healthcare (health insecurity), all of which constitutes structural violence, the violence of starvation and malnutrition [which] accounts annually for the death of upwards of 18 million people and primarily affects individuals based in the Global South.

As Rodgers (1992) argues, this is a consequence of the hierarchical structure of the international system of states operating in the framework of a global capitalist economy, whereby economic security for the transnational poor is increasingly undermined by economic security for transnational capital. Structural constraints on the attainment of economic security for individuals based in the poorest states are established by uneven development within the global capitalist economy. This is because a state's position in the international division of labour determines its ability to respond to global market forces. Gilpin (1992), states –such as those largely based in the Global North– are impervious to the potential negative impact of external market forces, and instead are able to channel these forces to the advantage of their own economies. On the contrary, soft states are unable to manage their economies effectively and are subject to the dictates of external market forces. While economic globalisation has resulted in only limited benefits to the majority of individuals and groups in soft less developed countries, it has simultaneously exacerbated deeply-rooted structural problems. This has led to slow or negative growth rates, extreme inequalities in the distribution of income, drastic falls in standards of living, and increasing poverty. We can therefore argue that globalisation and the international economic order undermine economic-human security in less developed countries.

Conflicts, poverty and insecurity in Africa

There is absolutely no doubt that conflicts and poverty present one of the most daunting threats to human security in Africa. Africa's conflicts are however unique in the sense that they have become much frequent and intense. For instance, a considerable proportion of the 80 conflicts recorded in sub-Saharan Africa between 1960 and the 1990s occurred in the post-cold war era (Adedeji 1999). Most importantly, the majority of the conflicts are intra-state. Of the 16 wars that occurred on the continent between the years 1990 to1997, only two- the Chadian/Libyan and Rwandan/Ugandan conflict were interstate. So far, quite a few countries in sub-Saharan Africa have been spared of war. Adejumobi (2001) opines that in 1994, no fewer than 12 of the 48 countries in sub-Saharan Africa were at war, two countries were at the post-war phase while 14 had a previous or current experience with political violence. To confirm its prominence as a theatre of conflicts, Africa had the largest peacekeeping contingent – 17000 strong in the DRC- by the close of 2006, while there are calls for additional peace keepers in Darfur and Somalia where conflicts have been raging unabated for the past 5 and 16 years respectively. Zimbabwe which was until 1990 full of promise for political stability is now teetering dangerously on the brink of violent inter-party conflict.

Generally, these conflicts have devastating impact on human security. Quite a number of conflicts for instance in Uganda and Sierra Leone have drafted children as combatants. Besides, they have generated refugees and internally displaced persons. The UNDP noted that by 1992, conflicts in various African countries had spawned large numbers of refugees including 870000 in Somalia, 850000 in Ethiopia, 67000 in Liberia, 40000 in Angola and 274000 in Sudan (UNDP 1994:32). Akokpari (2007), states that the correlation between poverty and general economic despondency on the one hand was most poignantly stated by Therese Paquet Sevigny (1990), the former UN General Secretary for public information:

> Deepening poverty is already leading to instability. The widespread unrest, turmoil and violence which is now afflicting an unprecedented number of countries is linked to one common thread of growing economic malaise, regardless of the ethnic and political guises it adopts. In Liberia, Rwanda and the horn of Africa, poverty is the tinder which ignites the resentments and fears that all people and communities harbour (p.27).

The inescapable reality is that conflicts linked to distribution of resources are often exacerbated by economic crises typified by unemployment, inflation and prolonged periods of recession. The preponderance of poverty in Africa is beyond question. Over 40% of the 800 million people especially in sub-Saharan live below the poverty line-earning less than US2 dollars a day (UNDP 1999). Africa is the only region in which absolute poverty is expected to increase over the current level (UNDP 2000). The gravity of poverty is exemplified in nearly all the indicators of human development. For instance, as of 2002 the percentage of sub-Saharan Africans with access to improved sanitation, water sources and literate were 36%, 58% and 61. 3% respectively (Akokpari 2007). Most importantly poverty limits access to health and nutrition where these are available and thus increase the susceptibility of people to diseases. The adverse implications of poverty for human security however transcend the vulnerability of people. Political corruption and abuse of human rights by governments are high under conditions of poverty as people become more pre-occupied with basic survival. The ignorance of the poor is often exploited by the predatory state which misinforms them and compounds their vulnerability to insecurity.

Environmental insecurity

There is little doubt about the escalation of environmental degradation in Africa. The threat to human security posed by this phenomenon is dire as over 70% of sub-Saharan Africans depend on the forest for livelihood. The extent of environmental decay in the region is too familiar to be recounted here. Nevertheless, suffice is to mention that the region's ecology has been plagued by rapid deforestation, desertification, soil erosion, pollution, drought and famines. Besides, sub-Saharan Africa is faced with an intractable population growth rate of about 3.1%, the highest in the world despite the prevalence of the HIV/AIDS pandemic. The pollution of land and rivers by multinational companies is on the increase while drought and famine have repeatedly hit sub-Saharan in the last four decades. The environment in sub-Saharan Africa is unsuitable, imparting severe threats not only to the present but also to the future generation. The pressure to liberalise national economies and create space for MNCs in response to the dictates of globalisation along with enhanced powers of capital to tame the state has forced the latter to relax or even waive environmental laws. In the following environmentally bankrupt policies, African states seem to be obvious to the intricate connection between environmental protection, sustainable development and human security. Thus although unobtrusive external factors play a role in the escalation of environmental insecurity in Africa.

Terrorism and insecurity

Terrorism is a source of human insecurity for the simple fact that it breads fear, uncertainty, destruction as well as death. Quite a number of countries in the Global South especially those of Africa have been victims of terror. Countries with radical Islamists such as Algeria, Egypt and Morocco have had to deal with terrorist acts perpetuated by groups opposed to the state or its policies on a regular basis. Although such violent acts are common and indeed frequent in North Africa, they are by no means confined exclusively to that part of Africa. Some countries south of the Sahara including Somalia,

Ethiopia and Nigeria have in recent decades witnessed various forms of terrorist acts. The most publicised terrorist acts in Africa were the near simultaneous attacks on the US embassies in Nairobi-Kenya and Dar es Salaam – Tanzania on 7 August 1998 that claimed 213 and 10 lives respectively. The causalities in the Nairobi attack were predominantly Kenyans including 34 who were employed by the embassy and 167 who were either passing or working near the embassy at the time of the blast (Akokpari 1997). As well another 5000 people received medical treatment while extensive damage to buildings and other infrastructure were recorded. Similarly, in Dar es Salaam attack, 70 additional people were injured. Against this background, anti-terror legislations have been passed in most African countries. Nevertheless, this development has endangered critical implications for human rights in particular and human security in general in the Global South. While the passing of anti-terror legislation was hailed in some countries, as an assurance of the state's commitment to secure the personal security of people, there are concerns on the other hand about the sweeping powers being assumed by the state under those legislations. Such powers make it easier for governments to manipulate the rule of law to crush and annihilate opposition or people agitating for democratic reforms. In Akokpari's (1997) view, Uganda's anti-terror laws have enabled the state to arrest and detain Dr Kizza Besinge who poses the strongest challenge to the presidency of Yuweri Museveni. In general, it is getting increasingly clear that the mechanisms used to prosecute the war on terror in Africa are threatening human security perhaps more seriously than terrorism itself.

Mitigating human insecurity in sub-Saharan Africa

Clearly the human security challenges facing the Global South are enormous, ranging from conflicts, poverty, bad governance, refugeeism to environmental degradation. The enormity of human security challenges requires the collective efforts of Africa, MNCs, NGOs, Africa's credit community and the international community at large if they are to be effectively addressed. The popular aphorism of African solution to African problems which came to vogue at the beginning of the century has limited relevance in the context of human insecurity. The axiom was evoked in the context of conflicts on the continent and was made to galvanise African states to assume responsibility for preventing, containing and managing conflicts on the continent. Given the sheer magnitude of the human security crisis, the international community has to be part of the solution.

Conclusion

Africa's insecurity is enormous and visible. Its poverty levels are high and set to increase. Poverty feeds into HIV/AIDS pandemic which is rocking the region. Furthermore, intra-state conflicts have become frequent and protracted while environmental degradation, religious and cultural conflicts have become more pronounced. These have both heightened human insecurity and stymied efforts at reversing these undesirable conditions. While welcoming the contribution of the international community to alleviate human insecurity, we have argued in this chapter that Africa should consider itself an integral part of the solution. To this end, it should reverse policies that tend to create conditions for conflict such as bad governance and marginalisation of its people in various sectors and communities.

References

Adjeji, A. (1999) "Comprehending Africa's conflict" in Adebayo Adeji (ed), *Comprehending and Mastering Africa's conflicts: the search for sustainable peace and global governance*, London, Zed books (p3-21).

Adejumobi, S. (2001) Citizenship, Rights and the problem of conflicts and civil wars in Africa, *Human Rights Quarterly* 23 (1): 148-170.

Ahmed, M. N. (2004) *The globalisation of insecurity: How the international economic order undermines human and national security on a world scale*, United Kingdom, Institute for Policy Research and development.

Akindele, W. (2002) 'Drawback of cultural globalisation,' Available at: www.org/globalisation.com.

Akokpari, J. (2007) *The political economy of human insecurity in sub-Saharan Africa*, Japan, Institute of Development Economics.

Aborishade, F. (2002) Effects of globalisation on social and labour practices in privatised enterprises in Nigeria, *A Research Report Submitted to the Centre for Advanced Social Sciences*, Port Harcourt: Nigeria.

Bello, W. (2003) 'Globalisation: The latest phase of imperialism,' Speech Presented to the One World on 10/07/2003, The Global South: India.

Bischoff, P. H. (2005) A Reflection on Peace Agreements in Africa, *Conflict Trends*, Vol 1 (2) p 7-11.

Baker, D., Epstein, G. & Pollin, R. (1998) "Introduction", in D. Baker, G. Epstein & R. Pollin (eds), *Globalisation and Progressive Economic Policy*, Cambridge University Press, Cambridge.

Bhaduri, A. (1998) "Implications of Globalisation for Macroeconomic Theory and Policy in Developing Economies", In: D. Baker, G. Epstein & R. Pollen (eds), *Globalization and Progressive Economic Policy*, Cambridge University Press, Cambridge.

Bracking, S. (2003) *Africa, Imperialism and New Forms of Accumulation*, *ROAPE*, Issue No 95 p 5-10.

CEPAL. (2002) Globalisation and Development, *Paper presented to ECLAC*, Brazil.

Chang, H. J. (1998) "Globalisation, Transnational Corporations, and Economic Development: Can the developing economies pursue strategic industrial policy in a globalised world economy?" in D. Baker, G. Epstein & R. Pollen (eds), *Globalisation and Progressive Economic Policy*, Cambridge University Press, Cambridge.

Crotty, J., Epstein, G. & Kelly, P. (1998) "Multinational Corporations and the Neo-liberal Regime", In: D. Baker, G. Epstein & R. Pollen (eds), *Globalisation and Progressive Economic Policy*, Cambridge University Press, Cambridge.

Didia, D. O. (2015) *Ten reasons why sub-Saharan Africa has failed to develop economically: Can Africans succeed by themselves*, The Edwin Mellwn Press, USA.

Dollar, D. & Kraay, A. (2001) Trade, Growth and Poverty, *Development Research Group*, Washington, The World Bank.

Ekwuru, G. (1999) *The pangs of an African culture in travail*, Totan Publishers Limited: Owerri.

Federici, S. (2004) Globalisation and Professionalisation in Africa, *Social Text* 79, 22 (2) p 81-100.

Field, S. (2004) "Introduction" in Field, S, *Peace in Africa: Towards A Collaborative Security Regime*. Johannesburg, South Africa: Institute for Global Dialogue, p19-26.

Gberie, L. (2005) Africa: The Troubled Continent, *African Affairs*, Issue No (10) 5 p 337-342.

Gilpin, R. (1987) *The Political Economy of International Relations*. New Jersey, Princeton, Princeton University Press.

Goldsmith, E. (1996) "Global Trade and the Environment", In: J. Mander & E. Goldsmith (eds), *The Case against the Global Economy*, Sierra Club Books, San Francisco.

Hirst, P.Q. & Thompson, G. (1996) *Globalisation in Question*, Polity, Cambridge.

Hoogvelt, A. (1997) *Globalisation and the Postcolonial World*, Macmillan Press Ltd, London.

Ihonvbere, J. O. (2000) *Africa and the New World Order*. New York: Peter Lang.

Kiely, R. (1998) "Introduction: Globalisation, (Post-) Modernity and the Third World", in R. Kiely & P. Marfleet (eds), *Globalisation and the Third World*, Routledge, London.

Krugman, P. (1995) Growing World Trade: Causes and Consequences, *Brookings Papers on Economic Activity*, Vol. 1995, no. 1, pp. 327-77.

Johnson, D. G. (2002) Globalization: What it is and who benefits, *Journal of Asian Economics*, vol. 13, pp. 427-39.

Juhasz, A. (2002) The Failure of Globalisation, *Cambridge Review of International Affairs*, 15, (3) p88-91.

Lindert, P. H. & Williamson, J. G. (2001) Does Globalisation Make the World More Unequal?, *Working Paper No. 8228*, National Bureau of Economic Research.

Maizels, A. (2003) "The Role of the Commodity Sector", In: J. Toye (Ed.), *Trade and Development Directions for the 21st Century*, Cheltenham, UK.

Mawere, M. (2013) *Lyrics of reason and experience*, Langaa RPCIG Publishers: Bamenda.

Mawere, M. (2016) 'Colonial heritage, memory, and sustainability in dialogue: An introduction,' In: Mawere, M. & Mubaya, R. T. (Eds). *Colonial heritage, memory and sustainability in Africa: Challenges, opportunities and prospect*, Langaa RPCIG Publishers: Bamenda.

Mawere, M. (2017) *Theorising Development in Africa: Towards Building an African Framework of Development*, (2017). Langaa Publishers: Bamenda.

Meagher, K. (2003) A Backdoor to Globalisation? Structural Adjustment, Globalisation and Transborder Trade in West Africa, *ROAPE*, 95, p57-75.

Morris, D. (1996) "Free Trade: The Great Destroyer", in J. Mander & E. Goldsmith (eds), *The Case Against the Global Economy*, Sierra Club Books, San Francisco.

Morton, A. (2004) New Follies on the State of Globalisation Debate?, *Review of International Studies*, 30 (5) p133-147.

Nnoli, O. (2003) Globalisation and African Political Science, *African Journal of Political Science*, (8) 2 p11-32.

Obstfeld, M. (1998) The Global Capital Market: Benefactor or Menace? *The Journal of Economic Perspectives*, 12 (4): 9-30.

Olukoshi, A. (2003) *Governing the African Development Process: The Challenge of the New Partnership for Africa's Development*, Holger Brent Hansen and Maj-Britt Johannsen eds., The Challenge of the New Partnership for Africa's Development. Copenhagen: University of Copenhagen North/South Priority Research Area, p11-44.

Oman, C. (1994) *Globalisation and Regionalisation: The Challenge for Developing Countries*, Development Centre of the Organisation for Economic Co-operation and Development, Paris.

Porter, M. (1990) *The Competitive Advantage of Nations*, The Free Press, New York.

Prebisch, R. (1950) *The Economic Development of Latin America and its Principle Problems*, The free press, New York.

Richard, J. (2000) Managing Africa's violent conflicts, *Peace and Change*, Vol 25 (2) p208-224.

Rifkin, J. (1996) "New Technology and the End of Jobs", in J. Mander & E. Goldsmith (eds), *The Case Against the Global Economy*, Sierra Club Books, San Francisco.

Rogers, P. (1992) *A Violent Peace: Global Security After the Cold War.* London, Brassey.

Scholte, J. A. (1996) "Beyond the Buzzword: Toward a critical theory of globalisation", in E. Kofman & G. Youngs (eds), *Globalisation Theory and Practice*, Pinter, London.

Singer, H. (1950) U. S. Foreign Investment in Underdeveloped Areas: The distribution of gains between investing and borrowing countries, *American Economic Review*, Vol. 40, no. 2, pp.473-485.

State, R. J. (2003) Governance and Insecurity in Africa: Democracy and Development, *Journal of West African Affairs*, 3 (2) p7-16.

Swyngedouw, E. (2004) Globalisation or 'Glocalisation'? Networks, Territories and Rescaling, *Cambridge Review of International Affairs*, 17 (1) p45-52.

Tickner, J. A. (1987) Re-visioning Security, in Booth, Ken; Smith, Steve (eds.), *International Relations Theory Today.* Oxford, Polity Press p18.

UNICTAD. (2001) Economic Development in Africa: Performance, *Prospects and Policy Issues*, New York.

UNICTAD. (2002) *Trade and Development Report 2002*, UNCTAD/TDR/(2002), United Nations.

United Nations Development Programme. (1992) *Human Development Report.* New York, Oxford University Press.

United Nations Development Programme. (1994) *Human Development Report.* New York, Oxford University Press.

United Nations Development Programme. (1999) *Human Development Report.* New York, Oxford University Press.

United Nations Development Programme. (2000) *Human Development Report.* New York, Oxford University Press.

Chapter 8

United Nations Agencies and Management of Humanitarian Crisis of Internally Displaced Persons (IDPs) in Nigeria's Abuja Camps: Reflections on the Security of Igbo Migrants in the North (2010-2016)

Orji Boniface Ifeanyi

Introduction

The plight of internally displaced persons (IDPs) has over the years become a formidable problem of global significance and implications (Oduwole and Fadeyi, 2013). Around the world, as at the end of 2013, about 33.3 million people were said to be internally displaced as a result of conflicts and generalized violence sub-Saharan Africa, however, recorded the highest number of IDPs with about 12.5 million persons (RRID, 2015). Nigeria has been grappling with the issue of insecurity and insurgency in the northern part of the country, orchestrated mostly by ethno-religious conflicts and terrorist attacks. The situation in the Northeast geo-political zone, where the emergence of Boko Haram insurgent emanates, has led to wanton destruction of properties, loss of lives, displacement of people from their place of origin, and acute segregation of community and ethnic polarization of once generally mixed population.

Following the dispersal of the inhabitants especially Igbo migrants in the North as a result of the emergence of Boko Haram since 2011, a lot of Igbo found refuge at various locations and camps in Abuja, Nigeria Capital City where access to adequate food, shelter and safe drinking water is increasingly difficult for the majority of the dispersed population. As at February 2014, it was reported that Nigeria recorded about 3.3 million people who were displaced internally (Premium Times, 2015). The ever-increasing number of IDPs including the Igbo creates enormous challenges to both the international community and the Nigeria government. This is

219

because, basic requirements such as food, shelter, medical care and hygiene create huge logistical problems in terms of procurement, adequate and equal distribution of these basic needs (RRID, 2015).

The United Nations General Assembly in 1998 adopted a set of guiding principles as a tool for the prevention and management of internal displacement:

i. These Guiding Principles address the specific needs of internally displaced persons worldwide. They identify rights and guarantees relevant to the protection of persons from forced displacement and to their protection and assistance during displacement as well as during return or resettlement and reintegration.

ii. For the purposes of these Principles, internally displaced persons are persons or groups of persons who have been forced or obliged to flee or to leave their homes or places of habitual residence, in particular as a result of or in order to avoid the effects of armed conflict, situations of generalized violence, violations of human rights or natural or human-made disasters, and who have not crossed an internationally recognized State border.

iii. These Principles reflect and are consistent with international human rights law and international humanitarian law. (UNOCHA: 2003)

Nations all over the world use these principles as a guide to all governmental and non-governmental humanitarian actors working with internally displaced persons (National IDP Policy, 2010). In October 2009, the African Union in its convention for the assistance and protection of internally displaced persons in Kampala, Uganda adopted the UN guiding principles on displacement *(Ibid)*. The adoption of the Kampala Convention (the African Union Convention for the Protection and Assistance of Internally Displaced Persons in Africa) by the African Union was in line with the realization of the gravity of tension IDPs pose to the continued security of African states (RRID, 2015).

Although millions of persons' all over the world are currently internally displaced as a result of the rise of violent conflicts across the globe, the preponderant number is in Africa (start-network, 2015). In Nigeria for instance, the increase in the activities of the Boko Haram group in the Northeastern part of the country forced some of the IDPs to move into the Federal Capital Territory (Ibid).

Going by the United Nations' Guiding Principles of Internally Displaced Persons (IDPs) of 1998, this chapter interrogates the role played by international agencies in alleviating the plights of IDPs in some selected camps of the Federal Capital Territory. The chapter examines the security of the Igbo migrants (who controls a good number of investments in the North, but are always the target of attacks in the northern parts of Nigeria) and contemporary discourse on the plight of the Igbo who are among the internally displaced persons (IDPs) in Abuja. It reveals that although some of the UN humanitarian agencies are making efforts to ameliorate the plight of the IDPs, the Nigerian officials are sabotaging the efforts by diverting and selling relief materials provided by the agencies for the IDPs. This threatens the social security of the migrants as well as their economic livelihoods. The chapter adopts both oral and secondary sources to argue that there is considerable neglect of IDPs by the Nigerian government and her agencies, highlighting the security implications of such on the city of Abuja.

Despite some of the efforts made by the International Communities to alleviate the sufferings of the IDPs, so far, the efforts have been jeopardized by Nigerian officials who divert the relief materials for their personal aggrandizements (Hassan, 2016). Using some selected camps in the FCT, this chapter explores how the agencies of the United Nations have failed in addressing the plights of Internally Displaced Persons' (IDPs). These camps include, Durumi Area One Camp, New Kuchnigoro, Waru, Wassu, Nyanya/Karu/Orozo/Marraba Axis, Kuje and Gwagwalada/Kwali Axis Camp located at Dobi.

Background to Displacement in Nigeria under the forth Republic

Internal displacement has become an issue of serious concern to many scholars because of the human tragedy and insecurity associated with it. Besides, conflicts induced displacement which is mainly caused by ethno-religious, inter-ethnic, political and intra and inter-communal conflicts mostly dominate discussion on issues of internal displacement at the global, continental and national levels (Adesote and Peters, 2015). Conflicts among Nigeria's ethnic groups have been part of its history ranging from the Kano Riot of 1956, Nigerian Civil war (1967-1970), Sharia crisis of the 2000s and of lately Boko Haram crisis. The systematic and overlapping patterns of inequality in the country have been described as "breeding grounds" for conflict (Okpeh, 2008; CRISE, 2007). As a result, the country is faced with the ongoing challenge of responding to fluctuating but always sizeable internally displaced population. Nigeria is made up of a web of ethnic, linguistics and religious, social groupings.

Conflicts have been triggered by disputes over access to land, kingship, cultural, residual citizenship and broader questions of identity. Identities have been particularly important in the shaping of both the political and social arena in Nigeria both during colonial and post-colonial times. Under British colonial rule, religious, ethnic and regional differences were given prominence, which eventually exacerbated divisions between Muslims and Christians, Northerners and Southerners, and Hausa-Fulani, Yoruba and Igbo groups (Okpanchi, 2010). Such differences, particularly between people considered indigenous to an area and those regarded as settlers, became instrumental after independence in the manipulation of identities for political ends (Jega, 2000). During the Biafra War of 1967-1970, in which the old eastern region attempted to secede from Nigeria, over one million Nigerians, mostly Igbo, were internally displaced.

Successive military governments of General Babangida (1985-1993) and Abacha (1995-1998), often using brutal tactics, generally kept ethnic rivalries in check. However, since the election of a democratic government in 1999, ethnic conflicts have surged in both number and intensity, leading to sizeable numbers of internally displaced people (IDPs).

Table 1: Population caseload of IDPs in Adamawa Yobe and Borno.

ADAMAWA				YOBE				BORNO			
LGA	LGA BASE	IDP Caseload	%	LGA	LGA BASE	IDP CASELOAD	%	LGA	LGA BASE	IDP CASELOAD	%
Madagali	1,3514,2	31316		Damaturu	16281	16281		Gwoza	288446	16117	
Michika	1,552,38	5772		Postisum	11988	11988		Bama	278353	13484	
Mubi North	1,515,15	2152		Fune	4042	4042		Mobbar	116631	2350	
Mubi South	129,956	3586		Fika	3659	3659		Damboa	249298	20540	
Gombi	114,761	9389		Gujiba	15226	15226		Konduga	190951	35810	
Yola North	196,197	5460		Tarmuwa	3540	3540		Kaga	3496	2086	
Yola South	199,675	5346		Gashua	10172	10172		Mafa	3496	3496	
Fufore	363	363		Geidam	11446	11446		Biu	7040	7040	
Lamurde	2339	2330						Jere	51,720	1864	
Total	1,085,186	66,826	6%	Total	771368	76,354	9%	Total	1,199,222	106,098	11%

Source; NEMA 2014

A critical analysis of displacement in Nigeria reveals that internal population displacement is caused by various categories of violence ranging from inter-ethnic, ethno-religious, communal and political links. Nigeria has a rapidly growing population of about 160 million with over 400 ethnic groups (IDMC, 2014). With its composition, it is made up of an extremely complex web of ethnic, linguistic and religious groups (IDMC, 2015). Even though the full scope of displacement in Nigeria is unknown *(Ibid:10)*, the cause of IDPs can be traced to many events and factors. While some of these displacements are said to be caused by religious or ethnic differences which is often time triggered by the increasing level of poverty, hunger, ignorance and arbitrary powers among others (Ibeanu, 2015), others are said to be triggered by disputes over access to land, citizenship and the broader question of identity (IDMC, 2015).

The return to civilian rule in 1999 opened up new opportunities for people to express their grievances that were brutally suppressed by military regimes. New areas of conflicts were created in the freedom of speech and expression which democratic rule provides (IDP Project, 2005). The effect of this is the recurrent internal conflicts and generalized violence which have resulted in the displacement of many across the six geo-political zones (North-East, North-Central, North-West, South-East, South-South and South-West) of the country (Adesote and Peter, 2015).

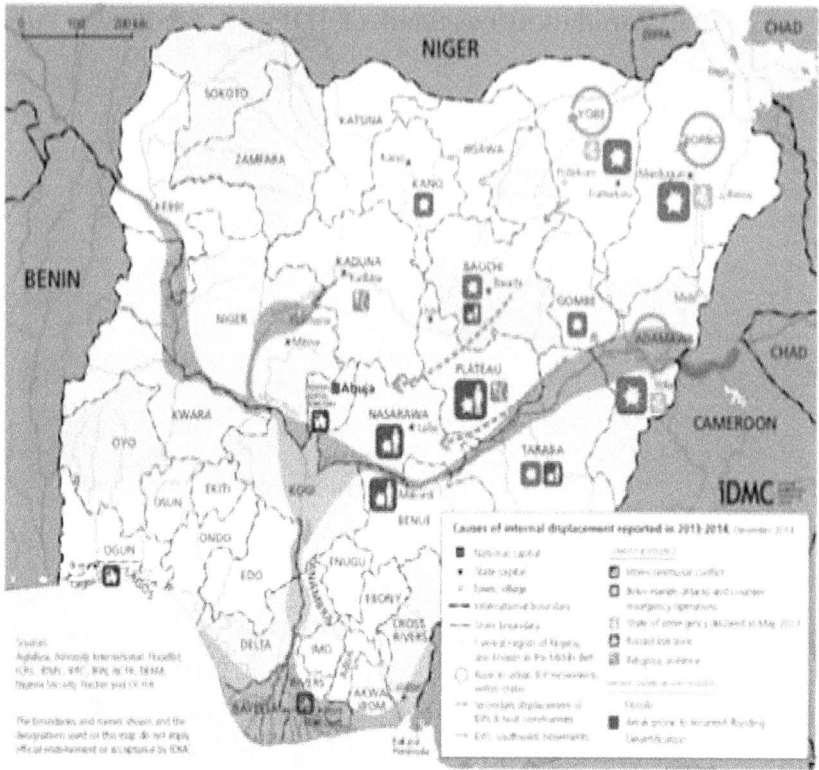

Figure 1: Map of Nigeria showing crisis areas

The Northern region as well as the north central equally witnessed series of inter-ethnic violence in Taraba, Plateau, Nasarawa and Benue states and ethno-religious violence in Kaduna, Zamfara, Kano, and Bauchi, just to mention but a few. These facets of violence led to the displacement of thousands of persons across the country and even beyond. In fact it has been argued that from 1999 - 2005, about half a million people were displaced (Ibid). Similarly between 2003 to 2007 inter-ethnic, ethno-religious, political and a number of violence which could be communal featured across the country. For instance, clashes over farmland in Adamawa and Gombe states produced over 30,000 displaced persons (Ibid).

Displacement Matrix in the North East Geo Political Zone

Current Location	IDP Individuals	IDP Households	Average HHs size
Adamawa	220,159	25,807	8.5
Bauchi	60,555	9,881	6.1
Borno	672,714	76,842	8.8
Gombe	24,655	3,335	7.4
Taraba	74,125	11,599	6.4
Yobe	135,810	21,893	6.2
Grand Total	**1,188,018**	**149,357**	**8.0**

Source: UNHR 2015

The impact of these conflict induced violence (Ethno-Religious) to the development of any nation cannot be overemphasized. In the words of the then president Olusegun Obasanjo "violence has reached unprecedented levels and hundreds have been killed with much more wounded or displaced from their homes on account of their ethnic or religious identification. Schooling for children has been disrupted and interrupted; businesses have lost billions of Naira and property worth much more destroyed" (This Day 2011). By 2005, statistics of the Global IDP Project showed that the number of IDPs in Nigeria range between 200,000 and 800,000. In February 2009, a dispute between two different religious communities in Bauchi state led to the displacement of about 5,000 persons (Ibid). The lists of cases of internal population displacement in the Nigeria context are endless.

The Role of International Organizations in addressing the plight of Internally Displaced Persons (IDPs) in some selected camps in the Federal Capital Territory

Internal population displacement has become one of the human tragedies confronting Nigeria. The conflict induced displacement which could either be, ethno-religious, inter-ethnic; intra and inter-communal or politically motivated in nature appears to the major cause of IDP in the country (Adesote and Peter, 2015). Since

225

Nigeria's return to democratic rule, successive governments of Obasanjo, Ya'Aradua, Jonathan and Buharia have failed to adequately address the growing insecurity challenges that confront the country. In order to address this challenge, ethnic militias, separatist groups and faith-based movement have mobilized to defend their communities and to conduct violent campaigns to assert their cultural, religious or ethnic dominance and control resources in the vacuum left by authorities weakening presence (IDMC, 2015). To buttress this, Ayodele argue that different reasons and circumstances which are the weak character of the Nigeria state and the inability of its equally weak institutions to engender order and security are responsible for these conflicts and violence in the country.

Prior to the Declaration of the United Nations Guiding Principle on internally displaced persons in 1998, the principal responsibility of providing for the well- being and security of IDPs rested with the government of the countries involved. However, the governments were most times unable or unwilling to assume this obligation, and the international organizations didn't have clear rules of engagement with the rapidly growing numbers of IDPs in need of assistance. Thus, the need for an international document that would address these challenges becomes necessary; hence, the United Nations guiding principles of IDPs (Couldry and Herson, 2008). To further reaffirm this, Principle 5 of the guiding principle states that "all authorities and international actors shall respect and ensure respect for the protection of IDPs under international law, including human rights and humanitarian law" (UNOCHA, 2003).

Under this section, internally displaced persons are recognized as part of the civilian populations of any country and must therefore, be protected by the respective authorities. This is because due to circumstances, the IDPs are often vulnerable as they lose their properties and means of livelihood, experience family separations, lack of identity, and access to basic services, discrimination in some cases, loss of their political rights, and high level of sexual abuses, among others.

Though the Responsibility to Protect (R2P) mechanism asserts that sovereign states have the responsibility to protect their populations, but when they are unable or unwilling to do so, a responsibility of the broader community of states comes to play (Ibid). Furthermore, the Nigeria government's adoption of the United Nations Guiding Principles equally reaffirms the role of international organizations in adhering to the minimum standard in providing protection and assistance to IDPs in areas of water, sanitation, hygiene, food security, shelters, health services which is entrenched in its national policy on internally displaced persons (NPIDP, 2013).

Furthermore, the specific role of international organizations and agencies within the framework of the United Nations is the continual protection and assistance of IDPs (AUCPAIDP, 2008). Similarly, protecting IDPs is the responsibility not only of authorities in victims' country but also of the international community. However in addressing the plight of IDPs, the focus of the international community has been unsuitable (Couldry and Herson, 2008). Even though it is been argue that the international community is better organized to provide basic needs of the IDPs in the form of shelter, access to health care facilities, and water, among other needs. With regards to the IDPs camps in the Federal Capital Territory, the presence of any agencies of the United Nations in the form of support and assistance has not been adequately felt. The tales and confessions of the IDPs in these camps shows neglect by government, and sabotage of UN/other international agencies efforts in addressing the plights of the IDPs.

According to the National Emergency Management Agency (NEMA) as at February 2014, around 3.3 million people have been displaced by conflict and violence since 2010. As a result, nearly 10,000 Igbo were forced to flee violence within the Northeastern states of Borno, Yobe and Adamawa states on one hand (NEMA, 2015). Inter communal violence, on the other hand, has also continued to cause displacement in northern areas and the middle belt region. Cattle rustling raids and clashes between herders and farmers over land have equally caused deaths and the destruction of property and crops and leading to the displacement of thousands of people in Zamfara, Benue, Taraba, Plateau states, just to mention but a few. The impact of these displacements is the massive wave of migration from these areas into the Federal Capital Territory, resulting into the setting up of some camps for the IDPs.

New Kuchingoro Camp: This is a new temporary camp set up to address the continue influx of IDPs from the North, which comprised of temporary, scrapped shelters which house about 1,006 IDPs comprising Igbo from the north-east as well as the north-central. The composition of these IDPs based on their states of origin, gave rise to the existence of strong state lines which creates a very tense atmosphere amongst the IDPs in the camp. The distribution of donations from UN donor agencies to the IDPs, usually create much animosity among the rest of the IDPs populations (Protection Monitoring, 2016).

With regards to the vulnerabilities of IDPs, the UN agencies usually sends funds and relief materials to address the needs of existing good number of unaccompanied and separated children, persons with special needs like the elderly, pregnant mothers, lactating as well as teenage mothers. Other challenges the IDPs are faced with which the UN agencies tries to tackle includes the violation of the IDPs right to good and quality education; as children were seen having lessons under an open area (Ibid). Furthermore, the availability of portable water is to say the least not available as IDPs were seen fetching water from a nearby stagnant stream. Similarly, the lack to quality health care facilities is equally a major challenge to IDPs in the camp.

Figure 1: IDPs Struggling for Food

Source: Field Observation 2016

228

Figure 2: IDPs Scampering for Water

Source: Field Observation 2016

Durumi Area One (1) Camp: It is located at Agwan Dagwa Site after the Dunamis Church. The camp boosts of Igbo IDPs from Borno with about 1,582 persons, Yobe 532 persons and Adamawa with about 234 persons (Yusuf, 2016) living in poor shelters that depict the sphere standard. Just like the Kuchigoro IDPs Camp, the plight and challenges of IDPs at the Durumi Camp is equally the same. With regards to the distribution of relief assistance from UN agencies and other donors, the coordination of these materials is not carried out by any proper structure. Therefore, unscrupulous individuals exploit this gap to divert relief materials. Also it is been argued that security operatives had arrested and detained some of those involved in the act, but nothing has since been heard from them (Protection Monitoring, 2016).

Wassa Camp: is located in a village which is about 20 kilometres away from Apo Mechanic Spare Parts Market. A total of 4, 602 IDPs from Plateau, Nassarawa and those from the north east takes refuge in abandoned low cost housing units. Just like the New Kuchingoro and Durumi camps, the tales of Igbo IDPs in Wassa Camp is not different. Taking abode in abandoned and uncompleted buildings, IDPs had to use sacks and clothes to cover the doors and windows; with the presence of overcrowded shelters as an average of eight IDPs live in one room.

Figure 3: IDPs Temporary shelter

Source: Field Observation 2016

Figure 4: IDPs Relief Materials

Source: Field Observation 2016

To further compound their plight, IDPs pay annual rent ranging from 25,000 to 40,000 Naira to the local Wassa resident as failure to do so mean eviction (Ogbonna, 2016). In addition, access to quality health care, better sanitary facilities as well as access to clean drinking water for the IDPs is considered a mirage. Consequently, IDPs drink water from the local stream, which is also used for cooking, bathing as well as washing.

Sabotaging the Humanitarian Efforts of UN Agencies in FCT IDP Camps

Over the years, progress has been made in raising funds and relief items for persons who have been displaced from their ancestral homes by insecurity caused by the Boko Haram insurgency and other forms of insecurity in the country. But the federal government has not done much to ensure that the donated resources get to their intended beneficiaries. The Victims Support Fund, which was launched on July 31, 2014 by former President Goodluck Jonathan, is a veritable means of ensuring accountability in the collection and distribution of money and aid for the IDPs. The federal government tried to summon the needed political, social, and legal support for the victims' fund. The former government authorized the incorporation of the fund into a trust fund to, among other things, "insulate it from political interference."

A lot of goodwill was achieved within and outside Nigeria including UN donor agencies in terms of response to appeals for relief resources for the victims of insecurity. There are individuals and government officials involved in the wicked act of diverting IDPs' relief materials. There were reports about some officials of the National Emergency Management Agency caught changing the bags in which rice procured by government, benevolent Nigerians, and foreign donors for the IDPs were sold, on purpose to resell them (Obia, 2016).

The Nigerian Security and Civil Defence Corps (NSCDC) in Borno state arrested some men alleged to have duped IDPs in the state into buying fake forms for relief materials to the tune of about N27 million (Vanguard, 2012). The suspects were said to have sold 9,000 forms at N300 each to IDPs in some camps in Maiduguri with the promise of providing them special relief materials from the federal government. It is disturbing to note that while the funds and items meant to bring some succour to the IDPs are being siphoned, conditions in the camps are worsening every day.

NSCDC report showed what it called a shocking incidence of prostitution in IDPs camps in a desperate survival bid by the people (The punch, 2011). The IDPs were being lured into the act because of the situation they found themselves. That prompted the House of Representatives to resolve to investigate allegations that donor funds and materials meant for the displaced persons were being diverted. In a similar vein of annoyance at the exploitation of IDPs, Economic and Financial Crimes Commission (EFCC) expressed worry over complaints of corruption in the IDPs camps which came from international humanitarian organizations and other civil society organizations that were donating relief materials to victims of the Boko Haram insurgency in the North-east, camped in different camps in the country.

Conclusion

Internal population displacement is one formidable challenge confronting Nigeria. Even though Nigeria has experienced this challenge in the past, the magnitude with which conflicts induced displacement especially since her return to democracy is alarming. Nigeria who became a signatory and domesticated the United Nations Guiding Principles on internally displaced persons as well as the Kampala Convention, is yet to find a lasting solution to the challenges posed by internal displacement.

The research for this chapter found out that despite the efforts of the UN donor and other international organizations to ameliorate the plight of the IDPs in Nigeria, with reference to FCT camps, agencies, some individuals ranging from government officials down to NGOs representatives are making life difficult for the IDPs that they are supposed to cater for. The chapter therefore, posits that the authorities must rise to the occasion, and proactively move to save the IDPs from those who are out to profiteer from their situation. Government must demonstrate that they are committed and able to protect the IDPs from persons who have sold their souls to the devil.

The federal government needs to harness the domestic and foreign goodwill to make a difference in the lives of the IDPs. This it can do by streamlining the process of relief management through the Victims Support Fund, which is manned by a group of prominent and dependable Nigerians. Empowering the Victims Support Fund to manage the issue of relief for the IDPs donated by the UN/international organizations donors would be an excellent way to eliminate the disheartening and shameful reports of corruption in the IDPs aid system.

References

Adesote S. A. and Peters A. O. (2015) A Historical Analysis of Violence and Internal Population Displacement in Nigeria's Fourth Republic, 1999-2011', *International Journal of Peace and Conflict Studies*, 2(3): 13-21.

Centre for Research on Inequality, Human Security and Ethnicity (CRISE), (2007) University of Oxford, Institutionalizing Ethnic Representation: How effective is the Federal Character Commission in Nigeria Retrieved from: Internet: http://www.crise.ox.ac.uk/pubs/working paper 43. pdf.

Couldrey M. and Herson M. (2008) Ten Years of the Guiding Principles on Internal Displacement, December, p. 4-12.

Hassan A., 40 years, Civil Servant, interviewed at Abuja, on February 1, 2016.

IDMC. (2013) "Nigeria: Increasing violence continues to cause internal displacement A profile of the internal displacement situation". Internal Displacement Monitoring Centre, Norwegian Refugee Council.

Internal Displacement Monitoring Centre (2014) 'Multiple Displacement Crises Overshadowed by Boko-Haram', Nigeria: 9th September www.internaldisplacement.orgpdf.

Internal Displacement Monitoring Centre IDMC (2015) Nigeria Simmering Tensions Cause new Displacement in the "Middle Belt": A Profile of the Internal Displacement Situation, www.internal-displacement.org/assets/publications/2015/09-corp-IDMC-annual-report-en.pdf.

Ibeanu O. (2015) "Between Refugee and Rights: Internally Displaced Persons and Inclusive Electoral Process in Nigeria" (paper presented at the Electoral Institute, Independent National Electoral Commission, Abuja, Nigeria, 15th December), p.18

Internal Displacement in Nigeria: A Hidden Crisis, February 1st 2005 in www.idpproject.org p.8

Jega, A. (2000) The State and Identity Transformation under structural Adjustment in Nigeria in "Identity transformation and identity politics under structural adjustment in Nigeria" Kampala Convention (2008). 'African Union Convention for the Protection and Assistance of Internally Displaced Persons' in Africa,' Kampala.

National Policy (2010) On Internally Displaced Persons' (IDPs) in Nigeria in www. Infopointmigration.org.ng/wp-content/uploads/NATIONAL-IDP-POLICY.pdf.

Nigeria: Displacement; Need for International Assistance in www.start-network.org/wpcontent/uploads/2015/04/150408-ACAPS-START-Nigeria-Displacement.pdf.

Obia V. (2016) 'The Disturbing Reports about Diversion of IDPs Funds and Materials'. https://www.thisdaylive.com › Politics. July 24.

Oduwole T., and Fadeyi, O. (2013) 'Issues of Refugees and Displaced Persons in Nigeria', *Journal of Sociological Research*, 4 (1): 1-14.

Olagunju, O. (2006) 'Management of Internally Displaced Persons in Nigeria'. Working paper #35. *Legal Anthropology*, Brandeis University.

Okpanachi, E. (2010) "Ethno-Religious Identity and Conflict in Nigeria: Understanding the Dynamics of Sharia in Kaduna and Kebbi States". Retrieved from: Internet: http://www.ifra-nigeria.org/spip.phpanticls/107.

Okpeh, O.O. (2008) Inter-group Migrations, Conflicts and Displacement in central Nigeria (in Population Movements, Conflicts, and Displacement in Nigeria, (ed.) T. Falola and O. Ochayi Okpeh, Jr).

234

Premium Times (2015) "Nigeria sets new record; now has Africa's highest number of displaced persons." Accessed from Http:/www.premiumtimesng.com/nows accessed on 8/4/2015.

Premium Time (2015) 'In the Community Court of Justice of Economic Community of West African States (ECOWAS) Holding at Abuja'. Nigeria:
www.media.premiumtimesng.com/wp-content/files/2015/05/SERAP-VS-FG-Internally-Displaced-Persons-Case-Before-The-Ecowas-Court.pdf.

Protection Monitoring Report (2015) on IDP sites in the Federal Capital Territory, July 15th-16th in
www.reliefweb.int/sites/reliefweb.int/files/resoures/protection monitoringReportonIDP-sites in FCT.PDF p.5.

Responsibility to Respond (2015) 'Internal Displacement in the ECOWAS Region: Case Studies of Cote D'Ivoire, Liberia and Nigeria'. *The Ministry for Foreign Affairs of Finland Publication*, March, p.1-8.

The punch, (2011) "18 killed in Abuja UN Bombing" The Nigerian Tabloid, vol. 7086, pg. 2.

This Day Newspaper (2015) "With Insurgency and Communal Clashes, Nigeria sees more Internally Displaced Persons in 2014." http//www.thisdaylive. com/article.

United Nations Human Rights (1995). UN, New York, USA.

UNOCHA (2014) "The Monthly Humanitarian Bulletin." July, 2015.

United Nations Office for the Coordination of Humanitarian Affairs, OCHA (1998) Guiding Principles on Internal Displacement, E/CN.4/1998/53/Add. 1, February 11, New York: United Nations.

United Nations Office for the Coordination of Humanitarian Affairs, OCHA (2003) Guiding   Principles on Internal Displacement, 2nd ed., UN, New York, USA.

UNHCR, (2007) *Internally Displaced Persons: Questions and Answers.* UNHCR: Geneva, p. 4.

Vanguard Newspaper. (2012) "Boko Haram in the North." July14, 2012.

www.world/ii.org/int/Journals/ISILYBIHRL/2001/10-rtf.

Yusuf B. (2016) Camp Secretary, 35 years, interviewed at Durumi Abuja, on February 1.

Chapter 9

Religions and Insecurities:
Heritage Contestations and Religious Praxis in
Mberengwa and Masvingo, Zimbawe

Edmore Dube

Introduction

Heritage contestation among Jews and Arab Muslims, offspring of Abraham through Sarah and Hagar respectively, has caused sustained insecurity in Israel. After the destruction of the replacement of the Temple of Solomon, during the Jewish-Roman war of 66-70 CE, the Arabs eventually built The Dome of the Rock on the same spot in the seventh century so that the land consecrated to God through Abraham and Solomon might be put to good use. Now the Jews want the temple land back resulting in serious security concerns currently dominating the 'Middle East crises'. Of particular concern to the current research is the fact that Jews and Muslims have had serious disagreements or rather conflicts in Masvingo Province and Mberengwa area in particular, each side claiming Remba praxis as its own heritage, resulting in serious identity and insecurity crises. This has been accompanied by a new evangelistic zeal only paralleled by the ante-colonial Christian missionary fervour which was eventually diagnosed as a precursor to colonialism. In light of this historical precedent regarding missionary activities in Zimbabwe, the chapter warns that this could as well be the genesis of a new religious imperialism. The chapter particularly refers to the possible manipulation of the constitution with regards freedom of worship, which some Remba believe could be a source 'religious re-colonisation.'

Jews and Muslims have built up synagogues and mosques in Mapakomhere in Masvingo District, Chinyika in Gutu and Mposi in Mberengwa. In this regard the researcher has been motivated by fear of the repeat of the Jerusalem crisis caused by heritage dispute, which

237

the ordinary Remba citizens have openly expressed. It is within the ambit of this research to evaluate the theories that validate the Jewish-Arab truth claims that put the lives of believers in danger, through possible violent defence of contentious heritage.

Jewish sympathizers have deployed science and technology to strengthen Jewish claims over Remba praxis. This has been done through genetic research, which has resulted in claims of foreign Remba paternity. Foreign paternity is a dangerous claim because it questions Remba citizenship in a country Muzondinya (2007: 331) describes as displaying negative attitudes towards aliens.

Fears of insecurity are further exacerbated by Zionist Israel's deployment of missiles, missile defence systems and satellites to defend Jewish religious positions against those of their Arab cousins in Israel. In this case science and politics have become servants of religion. The Remba who are against both Jewish and Arab genealogies express fear that Jews and Arabs may import such an 'abuse' of science and politics pitying Jewish and Arab minorities in Zimbabwe. Such a scenario revives memories about the nefarious logics of the 'cold war' fought on foreign soil as the United States of America and the Soviet Union tussled for world dominance. Worse still, Jews and Arabs may recruit the Remba for their war at home, which also revives bitter memories about Zimbabweans who perished in the 'Whiteman's two world wars.'

The chapter starts by examining the sources of the Jewish-Arab acrimony from both Biblical and historical narratives. This helps the reader to contextualize the Jewish-Arab conflict and the parameters of Remba security concerns.

Biblical Narrative

First we need to understand the relationship between Jews and Arabs from the Biblical narrative, which is also replicated in the Quran. We need to understand the source of the bitter rivalry between them. We also need to trace the development of the Temple narrative from the Biblical side, as well as from history in order to understand how the Arabs came to dwell on the *Jews'* sacred Temple land. The whole narrative starts with the promises Abraham received from God and the challenges in fulfilling them.

Abraham lived to the age of eighty-five (Genesis 16:15), sharing a childless life with his seventy-five year old wife Sarah despite God's promise that he would be father to a populous nation numbering as much as the 'sand of the sea' or 'the stars of Heaven' (Genesis 15:5). He became desperate, and his wife with him. As was customary, Sarah proposed that he takes Hagar her Egyptian maid to bear children on her behalf (Ramsey 1982; Bishau and Nenge 2010). Abraham agreed and Ishmael was born, to the great relief of this couple (Genesis 16: 4, 15). The relief was short-lived though, as Sarah then conceived and bore Isaac. Sarah became jealousy and influenced Abraham to send off Hagar with her 'thirteenth-year circumcised son,' Ishmael, into the torturous Arabian Desert with no provisions. Deep in the Arabian Desert, Hagar nurtured Ishmael who fathered the Arab nation, the repository of Islam. Meanwhile Isaac, 'the child of the promise' (Genesis 17: 19-21), also grew to become the father of Esau, and Jacob the father of the Jewish nation.

The Jewish nation grew to formidable heights at the hands of King David. David proposed to build a thanksgiving Temple for God. The Ark of the Covenant was to be permanently removed from its traditional tent and be reposited in the proposed elegant Temple, but the prophet Nathan forbade him. God would not allow the king to build him a sacred house because of his bloody hands. Instead his successor Solomon would do it on his behalf when David was deceased (2 Samuel 7: 12-13). That is what exactly happened. But before David died, he made thorough preparations for the building of the Temple he had proposed for the top of Mount Moriah (Zion) (1 Chronicles 22:14; 29:4; 2 Chronicles 3:1). Such preparations included the purchase of Araunah's threshing floor for the Temple site (2 Sam. 24:21ff), as it was believed to be the site of Abraham's pristine sacrifice. The Temple's Holy of Holies was to be built on the spot traditionally believed to be the sanctuary where Abraham intended to sacrifice Isaac (Genesis 22: 9) or Ishmael according to Muslim tradition. This is a major source of the dispute. The shrine being Abraham's makes it heritage for both Jews and Arabs, but whoever was to be sacrificed (Isaac or Ishmael) 'bought' God's favour for his descendants to inherit the shrine. Isaac's descendants got possession of the shrine first.

Consequently, Solomon went on to build the first Temple on Abraham's shrine in the tenth century BCE (I Kings 5). That Temple was destroyed by the Babylonians around 586BCE, creating a traumatic experience among the Jews. That painful experience is today commemorated as a holiday referred to as the fast of Tisha B'Av *(Telushkin, 1991)*. Ezra and Nehemiah witnessed the construction of the second Temple by Zerubbabel on the same Temple mound from 520-515 BCE (Schiffman, 2017). It was built at the decree of the Persian king Cyrus II (Ezra 1:1-4), re-establishing the ancient Israelite worship as specified in their Holy Scriptures. The rebuilding of the Temple was encouraged by prophets Haggai and Zechariah. This was a restoration of the most important Jewish ritual centre whose ecclesiastical purity Ezekiel foretells. This is the Temple we are familiar with in the New Testament, as refurbished by King Herod the Great. Temple sacrifice was seen by most Jews as the most efficacious way of reaching God. During special festivals (Passover, Boots, Pentecost etc.) Jews and proselytes converged at the Temple from all over the Ancient Near East (ANE). Pilgrims were content with the presence of God in the Holy of Holies, as the purity code was closely related to the Temple (Grabbe, 2010: 19-29).

The New Testament portrays an array of Jewish political parties including Pharisees, Sadducees, Herodians, and Zealots who agitated for political independence from the Romans. This nostalgia for Jewish independence epitomised by the Davidic 'Golden Era', eventually led to a protracted Jewish-Roman armed conflict in the seventh decade of the current era (66-70 CE). The result was the utter defeat of the pro-independence Jewish elements at the hands of Emperor Titus, then a Roman general. The termination of Jewish resistance saw the complete destruction of the Second Temple and the dispersion of the Jewish nation into the known world as far as Europe. But the Temple remained treasured in Jewish art and the in hearts of many, who dreamt of the messiah who would one day restore the kingdom of Israel and the glory of Solomon's Temple *(Kershner, 2015)*.

The Historical Narrative

The historical narrative gives us the birth of the name Palestine, an Arab coated name, in place of Judea. It also brings out the birth of the protracted Arab-Israeli conflict which still rages on, sucking in the whole Middle East. At the centre of the conflict is the Temple site and the 'land of the promise' granted by the same God who resided in the Temple Holy of Holies.

When the Romans suppressed the third Israeli revolt in 135CE they lost patience with the Jewish people. They expelled Jews from Jerusalem and its surroundings; selling many of them into slavery (*Arab-Israeli conflict* 2008). The province was then renamed Palestine, which strengthened Arab claims to the land largely evacuated by Jews. The Israelite claim to the land was further complicated by the conquest of Jerusalem by Arabs in the seventh century CE. Many Israeli and Palestinian locals were subsequently assimilated into Islam, though large Christian and Jewish minorities remained especially in the proximity of Jerusalem. Muslims went on to construct The Dome of the Rock, an Arab shrine for Muslim pilgrims on the Temple Mount (688-691 CE). The Dome of the Rock is an octagonal structure which supports a golden dome over a rock, hence its name. It is understood that the Muslim shrine was built directly over the Holy of Holies of both the Temple of Solomon and the Second Temple. This is the presumed place (rock in the dome) where Abraham prepared to sacrifice Ishmael/Isaac and the place from which Muhammad ascended to the seventh heaven (Quran Surah 17: 1). The Dome of the Rock was therefore constructed in a place coveted by both Arabs and Jews, creating another source of bitter heritage dispute (*Islam and Al-Hamad, 2007: 109–128*).

The magnificent Arab shrine, the oldest surviving Muslim monument, can be viewed from any part of Jerusalem, overshadowing all Jewish prayer houses, to the great chagrin of the Jews (*Slavik, 2001: 60*).It is 'Jerusalem's most recognisable landmark', and a UNESCO World Heritage Site (*Goldberg, 2001) lying in the Old City* important to the three Abrahamic religions (Judaism, Christianity and Islam). The area has been the most contested in the entire Holy Land. Muslim tradition has it that the angel shall come to sound the trumpet of judgments from the same rock in the Dome of the Rock (Brockman, 1997: 129).Departing from this tradition, some Muslim scholars, however, teach that Muhammad ascended from the Al-Aqsa Mosque adjacent to The Dome of the Rock, which also lies on the sacred Temple Mount (Yakub of Syria, 2012).

Some scholars, like Murphy-O'Connor (2017: 85-89), claim that Muslims wished to make a bold statement on their architectural abilities to both Jews and Christians, in a space sacred to both Jews and Christians. The Doom of the Rock therefore represented triumphalism, demonstrating that Arabs had conquered Jews, their 'cousins', and taken over the Abrahamic holy place. The place had been desecrated by the triumphalist Romans who had built a Temple to Jupiter Capitolinus in the Holy place, after the Bar Kokhba revolt pacified in 135 CE (Grabbe, 2010: 29).In a similar feat, when the crusaders wrestled the city of Jerusalem from the Muslims in 1099, they turned the Dome of the Rock into a Catholic church. It only reverted to Arab shrine-hood with its re-conquest in 1187. The Israeli triumph in the seven 'days war' of 1967 saw the Israeli flag dangling from the Dome. Orthodox Jews still cannot understand why their government allows the Muslim structure to stand on the Holy of Holies, where ordinary Jews dare not tread.

Roger Cohen (2014) notes that the dispute was worsened by counter claims to the land beyond the Temple. The understanding was that the same God who granted the land was the same God who resided in the Temple. The Temple was actually a thanksgiving offering for the granting of the land. The land claimed by Israel is generally regarded by the Pan-Arab movement as historically belonging to Palestinians (*The National Palestinian Charter – Article 6*).

The nineteenth century saw the rise of Zionism aimed at reclaiming the homeland for the Jews and rebuilding its Holy sanctuary (*Arab-Israeli conflict,* 2008). Restoration of the house of the Lord and national independence were seen as the only viable answers to anti-Semiticism and Jewish persecution in the Diaspora. Jews from all over the world, especially from Eastern Europe and Yemen, started going back to Palestine in large numbers. The first Zionist congress of 1897 had a great nostalgia for rejuvenating the Israeli nation as 'a light unto the nations'. The Jewish Holocaust spurred the need for the restoration of the Jewish nation and the aura around Jerusalem, Mount Zion and the Temple.

When the British annexed Palestine from the Ottoman Empire in 1917, they promised Zionists a homeland, which they eventual found difficult to do. As Nazi power gained momentum in the world, many Israelis were expelled, and the first port of call was always the proposed Jewish homeland. With Palestinian Arab resistance and growing British hesitance, Jews became violent from 1937, hitting both Arab and British targets. Palestinians upped their resistance forcing the British to concede to their demands for halting further Jewish immigration. Now Arab violence was met with counter violence from Jews fighting to gain a foothold in the only remaining 'safe haven' in the world. No other country was prepared to take Jewish refuges with the simmering threats of reprisals from Nazi states.

On 29 November 1947 the United Nations resolved to create two separate states; one for Jews and the other for Palestinians. The UN resolution 181 creating the State of Israel separate from the Palestinian state allocated 55% and 45% of the former Palestine to Jews and Arabs respectively. This subsequently created serious Arab-Israel hostilities following Israel's declaration of statehood the following year (Morris, 2008: 79). Five Arab nations (Lebanon, Syria, Iraq, Egypt and Saudi Arabia) declared war on the nascent Israel nation following its declaration of statehood on 14 May 1948. The Arab League coordinated Arabs who were united by common language and religion (Bell, 2001: 176).

Resolution 181 failed to resolve the status of the Temple Mount and the greater Jerusalem. Israel wanted to make Jerusalem its capital. The Palestinian authority maintained East Jerusalem fell under its jurisdiction and proposed to make it their capital. This was further complicated by another dispute over Bethlehem, the Biblical city of David, who originated the building of the first Jerusalem Temple. The United Nations proposed that both Jerusalem and Bethlehem be internationalised, to neutralise the Jewish-Arab conflict over control of the two cities. Most Israelis remained opposed to a Palestinian state with its capital in East Jerusalem (*Arab-Israeli conflict*, 2008). As a result there continues to be no meaningful progress to the numerous peace efforts by the international community to date (Schulze, 1999: 12). The Remba are therefore wary that this impasse could be transferred to Zimbabwe, through the Jewish-Arab contestation over Remba praxis.

The Deployment of Technology to Bolster Positions

Both Israelis and Palestinians have deployed technology to bolster their positions, with regards to counter claims over the Holy Land and its shrines. The Israelis are believed to possess nuclear weapons as a deterrent to Arab inversion. They have one of the world's most feared security services named Mossad. Together with Russia's KGB and America's CIA, it remains one of the most talked about secret service; very often for the wrong reasons. It is believed to control complex technology which may be used even in the rigging of elections in order to determine favourable outcomes. NIKUV, believed to be a branch of Mossad, was vociferously accused of rigging elections in favour of Zimbabwe African National Union (Patriotic Front) in the 2008 harmonised elections in Zimbabwe. The Remba fear that the infamous secret service may eventually be deployed against those of their kin who have opted for Islam. Such a scenario would inadvertently wreak havoc among those who have shunned both Islam and Judaism, since neutrality is as dangerous as opposition in a war situation. To be non-committal is generally interpreted by McLaughlin (1996:4) to mean supporting one's enemy. It is more worrisome because Mossad shares sensitive materials with the dreaded CIA, in addition to keeping sophisticated surveillance equipment in communities of its opponents (Thomas, 2009: 312, 314). It also works in collusion with intelligences of such powerful nations as France, Britain and Germany, which makes its alliance formidable for a small country like Zimbabwe. Worse still, the Israel Defence Forces "responsible for coordinating all intelligence ... from time to time gives Mossad specific tasks" (Thomas, 2009: 416). Some Remba are therefore critical of the two theories connecting them to Semitic paternity.

Remba Jewish-Arab Paternity Theories

Two schools of thought remain irreconcilable on the Remba paternity. This has been a huge pull factor for both Jews and Arabs to Zimbabwe. Synagogues and mosques have sprouted in Mposi in Mberengwa, and Chinyika and Mapakomhere in Masvingo Province, on the strength of the two paternity theories. The two theories are considered briefly below, starting with the 'fallacious Jewish theory' (Mandivenga, 1986: x) as the thesis and the Arab theory as the antithesis.

Mativha (1992) and Tudor Parfitt (2002) have been the most fervent proponents of the Jewish theory in the recent years. Their heads of argument are as follows. The Remba circumcise their sons, which Parfitt (2002) considers as 'not African at all,' despite a consensus that *lupanda* (Yao circumcision) is indigenous to Malawi and Mozambique (Dube, 1995: 47; Thorold, 1993: 80; Rangerly, 1962: 45-6). This makes the diffusionist theory advanced by the duo problematic. They maintain against the theory of Africa being the cradle of mankind, that the Remba must have copied circumcision from the Jews who were told by God to circumcise all male members of their households including the thirteen year old Ishmael (Genesis 17: 25). This is despite the fact that 'the results of genetic research provide scientific evidence that humans living today share a common origin' (Oberfrank and Falus (2013: 204), with Tanzania and Ethiopia producing the oldest forms of human life. The argument for Jewish paternity is not clear on the Jewish-Remba connection with regards female 'clitorisation' (*komba*) which is done concurrently with male circumcision *(murundu)* every winter. Male circumcision is done in temporary booths in the bush. Although the use of booths in the bush may be an intimation of the pristine world, the Bible neither mentions booths nor attaches circumcision to protracted traditional teaching. Instead the Bible mentions standard circumcision on the eighth day (Genesis 17: 12; Luke 2: 21) as a birth rite.

When circumcision was revealed to Abraham, Ishmael was already thirteen years old. In line with the circumcision of Ishmael in the thirteenth year (Genesis 17: 25), Muslims circumcise their sons between the seventh and the fifteenth year (Dube, 2013: 32). The

Remba likewise circumcise their sons between seven and fifteen years of age. In light of that, while circumcision is a birth rite among the Jews it is a rite of maturation among Muslims and Remba people. In terms of purpose therefore, circumcision among the Remba and Muslims is aimed to achieve the same end.

Mativha (1992) and Parfitt (2002) further assert that endogamy among Remba practitioners was borrowed from the Jews, though it is pertinent to both Jews and Arabs. They put endogamy side by side with food taboos common to Remba, Jews and Muslims. Although they attribute these to Jews, they are not oblivious of their existence among Arabs and the Muslim fraternity. With regards food taboos, the three groups avoid pork, carrion, mice, carnivores and meat animals not slaughtered by internally recognized members among each of the three groups (Dube, 2013: 23). The origin of taboos cannot be resolved as there is no intrinsic aspect swinging it in either Jewish or Muslim favour. All claims of religious utterances during animal slaughter are recent additions caused by either Muslim or Jewish influences (Chiromo, 2013).

The protracted argument has resulted in the deployment of science and technology to authenticate the Jewish theory, which in itself may harbour imperial politics. Tudor Parfitt (2002: 49) discusses the genetic test results on the Remba carried out in Britain in 1999, which show DNA links between the Remba and the people of Hadramaut. Specialists in genetic science maintain that "due to comprehensive, multifaceted, long-term and unforeseen effects, however, in addition to the pragmatic approach, further analysis, social dialogue and consistency are also needed" (Oberfrank and Falus, 2013: 198). This is particularly important where there is a significant private interest in terms of actors, funds and goals, because genomics may be manipulated. There is, therefore, need for more tests to authenticate the results, but until then, it is difficult to set aside the results on the basis of theoretical possibilities. Oberfrank and Falus (2013: 201) maintain that on paternity issues 'the application of gene diagnostics is more accurate and precise'.

Parfitt (2002: 49) argues that a large Jewish minority is historically linked to the city of Sanaw in Hadramaut. This Jewish minority has largely been depleted by wars and emigration since the founding of the Jewish state in 1948. A definitive genetic linkage with these minority Jews has been difficult, owing to the fact that the same genetic configuration is also true for Arab populations both in Hadramaut and the greater Middle Eastern region. The genetic theory has proved that there is only paternal linkage between the Remba and the Abrahamic tribes of Isaac and Ishmael. Beach (1980: 213), Mandivenga (1983: 2) and Mudenge (2011: 363) maintain that the Remba mothers were Shona. Shoko (2012: 99-100) further specifies that their mothers were Karanga, a southern dialect of the Shona people. This specification of Remba maternity leaves the two theories with the latitude to deal with the disputed Remba paternity only (Dube, 2017: 232).

The two schools of thought are faced with the task of unravelling how the genetic configuration common to Jews and Arabs was imported into Africa. Parfitt's (2000) original diffussionist theory negates African origins. His contentious statement therefore maintains that the Remba are Jews who emigrated from Jerusalem to Africa via Hadramaut and Pusela. Since this would have entailed the importation of both male and female genes rejected by the medical tests, he has modified it to a single male Jew who sojourned in East Africa where he sowed the Remba seed. This lone Jew is unknown in history. What is known to history is the presence of Muscat Arab traders from Hadramaut in the vicinity of Great Zimbabwe, an ancient Shona capital city (Beach, 1980: 417; Dube, 2017: 227). These Muscat as well as Swahili Arabs, whose artefacts have been confirmed by archaeologists of Great Zimbabwe, traded for gold with the Shona producers and traders of the central plateau. Asante (2007: 157) notes that 'the gold trade between the Shona and the Swahili drew the attention of the Portuguese in the sixteenth century. Quite kindly, the Portuguese sought to divert the trade from the coastal Swahili to their own trading posts along the Indian Ocean. This brought then into conflict with the Swahili'. Though most of the Shona traders worked autonomously some are known to have served the Arabs as middlemen *(vashambadzi)* (Beach, 1980: 40, 417; Mudenge, 2011: 44). As Arab praxis allowed *mutah* (temporary marriages) at that time, Arab Muslims are known to have sired many children on their trade excursions, resulting in the spread of Islam together with some Arabic (Alpers, 2000: 303).

Concluding Parfitt's (2000: 40-42) original argument on the Remba as immigrants from Jerusalem via Pusela, was the inclusion of the Ngomalungundu, a Remba sacred relic, as the lost 'Ark of the Covenant.' This argument is premised on the diffusionist theory which is problematic. In reality, it runs contrary to the assumption that if God is the source of knowledge as recorded in the Bible, then he could as well vouchsafe the same knowledge directly to the Africans. In that regard the Remba would not rely solely on diffusion knowledge from Semites. Although this has proved to be the weakest part of the argument, it has been maintained. In reality there is no connection between the Ngomalungundu and the Ark of the Covenant apart from the transportation procedure and that they both housed sacred objects of particular peoples. It baffles the mind to say that the Ngomalungundu, 'the drum that thunders,' can be equated to the Ark of the Covenant which had no mechanism for making sound. If we take 'thundering' to mean enormous sound, then the Ngomalungundu made a lot of sound, perhaps equivalent to that made by trumpets in Israel. The linkage has therefore been maintained in order to outpace the Arab theory. The argument is that the Arabs had no object sacred to their God which they carried around as did the Jews and the Remba. The Ngomalungundu is currently reposited in the Harare Museum of Human Sciences as a national heritage.

Considering the Remba nomenclature, scholars find it plausible to associate the Remba with the Arab stint with the local population prior to 1500 (Mandivenga, 1983: 1). The Remba and the Arabs use such commons names as Hamisi, Seremani, Sadiki, Sarifu and Chihora, which can only be a result of some Arab-Shona interaction in pre-colonial Africa (Dube, 2013: 25). This interaction between Muscat Arabs and the local Shona population was terminated by the Portuguese colonists who dominated Mozambique at the close of the sixteenth century. Their presence at the coast prevented Arabs from interacting with the interior Shona groups. The renewed interaction between the Remba and the Muslims only came as an accidental discovery early in the latter half of the twentieth century.

Remba interaction with Muslims and Jews in Zimbabwe

The current Muslim-Remba discourse historically emanates from a mutual discovery of similar Muslim-Remba practices made by a Muslim traveller and a Remba of Maeresa family in Buhera in 1961 (Mandivenga, 1983: 30). Muslims immediately deployed the contentious diffusionist theory discussed above, to conclude that the Remba were 'renegade Muslims' in need of re-Islamisation. From that time on, the Muslims have made efforts to 'reintegrate' them into mainline Islam (Mandivenga, 1989: 99). In the early 1990s Muslims made some influence on Remba circumcision in Mberengwa (Ravengai, 2017: interview). This has since been neutralised. Muslim officials have been barred from officiating during Remba circumcision (Maramwidze, 2016: interview). Muslims have, however, built mosques for the Remba in Buhera, Gutu and Mapakomhere prior to the coming of Jews targeting Remba in these areas. Although some members of these Muslim communities are non-Remba their main target was Remba.

Up to the advent of Parfitt with his genetic tests in 1999, it seemed Remba people would gradually be absorbed into either Islam or Christianity. The situation completely changed with the publication of the Ngomalungundu in Harare in 2010. Tudor Parfitt, Zimbabwe government ministers and Remba leaders graced the occasion; authenticating the Jewish theory as it were. From then on American Jews developed interest in the Remba; running directly into the same field coveted by Muslims, who for years had made groundwork for the 'reconversion' of the Remba (Mandivenga, 1983: 31). Their main focus was Mberengwa the 'spiritual home of all Remba' people (Mativha, 1992: 47) as well as Chinyika in Gutu.

This brought Muslims running into Mberengwa to forestall Jewish advances, resulting in the building of two mosques to match two synagogues. The confused situation in which Muslims sought to set up a mosque for every synagogue, divided the Remba into four distinct groups comprising followers of African indigenous religions, Judaism, Islam and Christianity. For some time it seemed as though Christianity would be the biggest loser. Many former Christians vied for either Islam or Judaism. This resulted in the building of two synagogues North West of Mberengwa and two mosques South West of Mberengwa.

Jewish medical doctors from the United States of America camped at Danga Mposi Clinic, at the heart of Remba land, offering free consultation and medication to bolster Jewish claims to Remba praxis. Multitudes turned up for healing resulting in doctors being overwhelmed. They employed local guides for guiding patients into special queues to see specific doctors on relevant ailments (eye problems, tooth aches, respiratory etc.). Such guides were paid handsomely which sent strong signals to locals, persuading many Remba to associate with Jewish genealogies through Yemenite Jews. This further attracted community members to Judaism in order to be employed as guides. Members of the local synagogue had the first priority. Apart from being employed as guides, synagogue members were also given assistance in cash or kind which improved their lives, raising envy among non-Remba. In the resultant competition for the uptake of Judaism, quite a number of prominent Remba are believed to have lost their lives through mysterious poisoning. Though this was never brought before any competent court for adjudication, it brought a lot of fear to the Mposi community; Remba and non-Remba alike. Though this chapter concentrates on the projected fear of the religious recolonisation and its repercussions, Warikandwa, Nhemachena and Mtapuri (2017: 2-3) already note connections between the resurgence of Greek mythology with the second scramble for African resources in this way:

> 'Thus, recolonizing Africa under the pretext of having been commissioned by the resurgent Greek goddess gaia, the transnational corporations and their foreign governments can be understood as merely repeating history in which colonists colonised Africa under the pretext of their religions; only that this time they are not using God as the pretext but they are using gaia as the figure of a merciless goddess-commissioner of the current violence of re-colonisation'.

Muslims took advantage of the allegations of mysterious poisoning among early Remba converts to Judaism, to wrestle a number of Remba from the Mharepare and Chaza synagogues.

Though Muslim assistance to new members may have been rated less than that of the synagogues, they did attract enough Remba and *senzi* to build two prayer mosques at Masaga and Zebra on the South Western fringes of Mposi. As the situation appeared to be calming down after the great turbulence, Christianity appeared to emerge overall winner. Many former Christians who were shocked by the poisoning allegations chose to return to Christianity than join Islam. This was mainly due to the 'dominant discourse narrative' which tended to favour the Judeo-Christian 'template' against the Muslim discourse (Mazarire, 2013; Dube, 2017: 221). Anything not resonating with Jewish-Christian values was looked down upon, with terrorism used as deterrence against Muslim fellowship.

Through the influence of an erudite Mativha protégé, a synagogue has just been constructed in Mapakomhere, following on the foothills of the Mberengwa synagogues. This synagogue stands in opposition to the Muslim mosque constructed in 1969. Now this competition of non-indigenous religions over the Remba praxis as their heritage has necessitated this research. Of particular importance has been the non-Muslim Remba narrative which is wary of the Middle East crisis. There is no doubt that the current fears have been caused by the negative media portrayal of Islam particularly in relation to Boko Haram, Al Quaeda, and Al Shabab; in addition to the Middle East Crisis. These narratives are often broadcast on television and social media out of context, due to the heavy influence of the Judeo-Christian 'superior discourse', which generally says nothing against Zionism. In this respect media has become a major driver of fear of insecurity, often propagating unfounded theories of violence.

Mashavakure (2017: interview), a Remba elder, noted that the situation has been worsened by Lazarus Dokora, the former Minister of Primary and Secondary Education, who has made Islam compulsory in the new curriculum. Mashavakure (2017: interview) noted that 'Lazarus Dokora has been bought by Jews and Muslims for the provision of recruiting ground for the Middle East conflict.' Rambuwana (2017: interview) added that his father fought in the Second World War when Zimbabwe (then Rhodesia) was made recruiting ground by the British. "At the conclusion of the war against the Germans, my father was honoured with a useless war veteran medal, while whites were rewarded with farms and suburbs including Mt Pleasant in Harare", noted Rambuwana (interview), with a clear nostalgic hatred for the British on his face. He shook his head at the understanding that the Falashas of Ethiopia had already embraced Jewish identity and relocated to Israel. He believed that they would never be treated as equals; rather they would only be used for the benefit of white Jews. He noted that they would be standard bearers for the 'Whiteman's war with Muslims.'

Chitando (2011) agrees that there is evidence of acrimony between white and black Jews on the social level, both in Israel and in Zimbabwe. Ultra-orthodox Jews view the genetic theory with great suspicion, and are not willing to embrace it as a reason for integrating with the Remba, or any other black Jews. This leaves the Remba in a difficult position. The genetic theory has already made them non-indigenous, but their supposed kin and kith do not accept them as equals, and would rather exclude them as 'gentiles.' Kessler (1996) confirms the unease relationship between white Jews and the Falashas who have relocated to Israel.

The genetic theory has been a source of psychological trauma for those Remba who have been excited by it into joining Judaism. The new black synagogue members face 'intra-Judaism segregation', while those that joined Islam find themselves at the mercy of the 'dominant discourse' that indiscriminately labels all Muslims 'potential terrorists' (Salume, 2017: interview). Psychologists have for time immemorial found labeling to breed negative results in the community. The salient counter-accusation among Jews and Muslims as well as the community perceptions are brewing a time bomb which will explode at any time (Gijima, 2017: interview). The greatest fear lies with the future, in the event that both Jews and Muslims have enough numbers to threaten each other. The rest of the population fear fatalities as collateral damage in the event of armed hostilities between the two groups. Gijima (2017: interview) is of the view that hostilities may be triggered by one side recruiting its believers to fight in the Middle East war. The other one would attack Zimbabwe in retaliation. Either the Zimbabwe Defence forces, which are known for heavy handedness in times of crisis, will come heavy on the community as a reprisal for the wrong side, or the two sides will confront each other putting the whole community at risk. Despite this potential risk caused by the head-to-head conversion to Judaism and Islam, the constitution would not allow any forced moratorium on such conversion as preferred by some Remba. The open democracy proposed by the constitution in the areas of faith and belief is seen as a source of insecurity by many Remba in Zimbabwe.

Constitutional Provisions

The Constitution of Zimbabwe Amendment No 20 of 2013, gives right to all citizens to freely choose their faiths and beliefs. It guarantees freedom of association. Citizens are free to retain indigenous African religions or to take up any missionary religion of their choice including Judaism and Islam. The difficulty at the moment lies with declaring conversion to Islam and Judaism *free* on the basis of part time employment and assistance in cash or kind. Muparuri (2017: interview) observes that most of those who have converted have done so 'under duress. Poverty and needfulness have compelled them to convert with their enunciated stomachs, meek faces and humble open hands.' Mparuri is a thriving Remba master farmer, with a strong traditional flair.

Jews have clearly deployed science and technology as evangelistic tools. Medicine has been the major pull factor, even though healing and giving out of spectacles is not segregatory. This deployment of medical science including the genetic tests has divided the communities in Mberengwa, Mapakomhere and all other areas with large Remba minorities, including Chinyika in Gutu district.

Conclusion

Judaism and Islam among the Remba have proved to be sources of conflict exposing believers to serious insecurities caused by *alienism* resulting from foreign paternity claims. Religious beliefs have proved non-negotiable with Jews and Muslims fighting endless wars in the Middle East over Abrahamic and Solomonic heritage. Religion has deployed science and technology to defend its truth claims unadulterated. State authority and politics have become subject to religion, with respect to Jews and Arabs. That scenario has brought fear to Remba communities in Mberengwa and Masvingo Province, where theocratic Jews and Muslims are competing over Remba praxis as their heritage. Those neither in the mosque nor in the synagogue communities need serious assurance that this Arab-Jewish competition will not result in the importation of the Arab-Jewish Middle East crisis intransigent to any form of mediation. Yellow reporting by the media and historical allusions to the Cold War have heightened security concerns among Remba communities. Religious freedom and the new primary and secondary schools curricula have been seen as harbingers of the coming Arab-Jewish crisis in Remba dominated communities currently 'besieged' by Jewish and Muslim evangelists.

References

Alpers, E. A. (2000) 'East Central Africa', in Levitzion, N. and Pouwels, R. L. (eds) *The History of Islam in Africa,* Athens: Ohio University Press.

Arab-Israeli conflict (2008) *http://www.israel-palestina.info/arab-israeli_conflict.html.*

Beach, D. N. (1980) *The Shona and Zimbabwe 900-1850,* Gweru: Mambo Press.

Beach, D. N. (1986) 'NADA and Mafohla: Antiquarianism in Rhodesia and Zimbabwe with Special Reference to the Work of F.W.T. Posselt', *History in Africa,* Vol.13.

Bell, P. M. H. (2001) *The World Since 1945 – An International History,* London: Bloomsbury Publishing Plc.

Bishau, D. and Nenge, R. T. (2010) *Interpreting the Old Testament,* Harare: ZOU.

Brockman, N. (1997) *Encyclopedia of Sacred Places,* Oxford: OUP.

Chitando, E. (2011) 'VaJudha (African Jews) in Harare: Expressing Contested Identities in Tight Spaces', *Journal of African Studies* Vol. 64, No. 2, pp.135-155.

Cohen R. *The New York Times,* 30 January 2014.

Constitution of Zimbabwe Amendment (No 20) Act 2013, Harare: Fidelity Printers and Refiners.

Dube, E. (1995) 'The Impact of Proselytising Religions on Traditional Beliefs and Practices: A Study of the Interaction between Islam and the Chewa and Yao Traditional Religions in the Inter-Lakes Region in Malawi', unpublished MA Dissertation, University of Zimbabwe.

Dube, E. (2013) *A Tradition of Abstinence and Ritual Identity: The Ruling Sadiki Remba of Mposi in Mberengwa,* LAP Lambert Academic Publishing.

Dube, E. (2017) 'The Great Zimbabwe Monuments and Challenges in African Heritage Management', in Green, M. C., Hackett, R. I. J., Hansen, L. and Venter, F. (eds) *Religious Pluralism, Heritage and Social Development in Africa,* Stellenbosch: African Sun Media, pp. 221-237.

Goldberg, J., The New Yorker, 29 January 2001.

Grabbe, L. L. (2010) *An Introduction to Second Temple Judaism: History and Religion of the Jews in the Time of Nehemiah, the Maccabees, Hillel, and Jesus,* New York: A&C Black.

Holy Bible (2008) Revised Standard Version, British and Foreign Bible Society.

Islam, M. A. and Al-Hamad, Z. F. (2007) 'The Dome of the Rock: Origin of its Octagonal Plan', Palestine Exploration Quarterly, Vol. 13, No. 2, pp. 109–128.

Kershner, I. New York Times, 8 December 2015.

Kessler, D. (1996) *The Falashas: A Short History of Ethiopian Jews,* London: Frank Cass.

Mandivenga, E. C. (1983) *Islam in Zimbabwe,* Gweru: Mambo Press.

Mandivenga, E. C. (1986) Islam in Zimbabwe: A study of the Religious Developments from the Sixteenth to the Twentieth Century, PhD Thesis, University of Aberdeen.

Mandivenga, E. C. (1989) 'The History and "Re-conversion" of the Varemba of Zimbabwe', *Journal of Religion in Africa,* Vol.19, No. 2, pp.99-120.

Mativha, M. E. R. (1992) *The Basena, Vamwenye, Balemba,* Johannesburg: Morester Printers.

Mazarire, G. C. (2013) 'Mberengwa, Zimbabwe – Home to the Lemba Tribe: Are they the descendants of Yemenite Jews?' A paper presented at the Historical Dimensions of Development in the Midlands Seminar, Fairmile Hotel, Gweru, 2001.

McLaughlin, J. (1996) *On the Frontline: Catholic Missions in Zimbabwe's Liberation War,* Harare: Baobab Books.

Milton-Edwards, B. and Hinchcliffe, P. (2001) *Conflicts in the Middle-East since 1945*, London: Routledge.

Morris, B. (2008) *A History of the First Arab-Israeli War*, Yale: Yale University Press.

Mudenge, S. I. G. (2011) *A Political History of Munhumutapa c1400-1902,* Harare: Africa.

Murphy-O'Connor, J. (4th ed) (1998) *The Holy Land: An Oxford Archaeological Guide*, Oxford: OUP.

Muzondidya, J. (2007) 'Jambanja: Ideological Ambiguities in the Politics of Land and Resource Ownership in Zimbabwe', *Journal of Southern African Studies*, Vol. 33, No.2, pp.325-341.

Oberfrank, F. and Falus, A. (2013) 'Bioethical and Research Ethical Issues in Genetic Research', in Szalai, C. (ed) Genetics *and Genomics Genetics and Genomics,* Budapest: Typotex Kiadó, pp. 198-206.

Parfitt, T. (2000) *Journey to the Vanished City,* New York: Vintage Random House.

Parfitt, T. (2002) 'The Lemba: An African Judaising Tribe', in Parfitt, T. and Trevisan-Semi, E. (eds) *Judaising Movements: Studies in the Margins of Judaism,* London: Routledge Curzon.

Ramsey, G. W. (1982) *The Quest for the Historical Israel,* London: SCM Press.

Rangerly, W. H. J. (1962) 'The Arabs', *Nyasaland Journal,* Vol. 15, No.2, pp. 11-46.

Schiffman, L. H. (2017) *Building the Second Temple: The Historical Importance and Practical History of Rebuilding Ancient Judaism's Sacred Center,* Kveller: JTA.

Schulze, K. E. (1999) *The Arab-Israeli Conflict,* Harlow: Pearson Education Ltd.

Shoko, T. (2012) 'Karanga Men, Culture, and HIV and AIDS in Zimbabwe', in Chitando, E and Chirongoma, S. (eds) *Redemptive Masculinities: Men, HIV, and Religion,* Geneva: WCC Publications, pp. 91-112.

Slavik, D. (2001) Cities through Time: Daily Life in Ancient and Modern Jerusalem, Geneva: Runestone Press.

Telushkin, J. (1991) Jewish Literacy: The Most Important Things to Know About the Jewish Religion, its People, and its History, New York: William Morrow.

Thorold, A. (1993) 'Metamorphoses of the Yao Muslims', in Brenner, L.(ed) *Muslims Identity and Social Change in Sub-Saharan Africa,* Bloomington: Indiana university Press, pp.79-90.

Warikandwa, T. V., Nhemachena, A. and Mtapuri, O. (2017) 'Transnational Corporations, Land Grabs and the On-going Second Mad Scramble for Africa: An Introduction', in Warikandwa, T. V., Nhemachena, A. and Mtapuri, O. (eds) *Transnational Land Grabs and restitution in an Age of the (De-)Militarised New Scramble for Africa: A Pan African Socio-Legal Perspective,* Bamenda: Langaa.

Yakub of Syria (Ka'b al-Ahbar), (2012) *Last Jewish Attempt at Islamic Leadership Committee for Historical Research in Islam and Judaism,* Accessed 9 November 2017.

Young, J. W. and Kent, J. (ed) (2013) *International relations since 1945,* Oxford: Oxford University Press.

Primary Sources

Gijima Mposi, Chamawanga, 27 December 2017

Maramwidze Tadzoka, Danga Mposi, 22 April 2016.

Mashavakure Bwerinofa, Great Zimbabwe Monuments, 2 December 2017.

Rambuwana Mafirikureva, Mupandawana, 4 December 2017.

Ravengai Tavavona, Masaga, 26 December 2017.

Salume Musa, Mapakomhere, 2 December 2017.

Chapter 10

Electoral Politics and (In-) Securities in Africa: Thinking the past and the present for the future of Africa

Costain Tandi & Munyaradzi Mawere

Introduction

The (re-)introduction of multiparty politics especially in Africa is viewed by many as a positive step towards democratisation on the continent. Elections have been lauded as the pinnacle indicator of state moving towards a more secure democratic future. Electoral competition for state power has become the order of the day and quite a number of countries have held a significant number of elections. The multi-million dollar question is that, while voting has become a regular occurrence in many of these countries, has it been accompanied by an improvement in democratic quality? It is piteous to note that, whereas the frequency of elections barometrically spelled advancements in the quality of democracy, this development has been closely accompanied by another, much more worrying trend of election-related human insecurity. In some African countries, the holding of elections is often not as simple as it may first appear, with many practitioners and academics identifying them as flashpoints for violence and insecurity. The prevalence of such human insecurity reflected a plethora of reasons. These include the intensification of the competition for access to the state, perceived as a channel of accumulation, poor organisation of elections, government interference in the work of election management bodies (EMBs), the insatiable desire of some presidents to seek third terms in contravention of constitutionally mandated two terms, and in some cases because the electoral model excluded loosing parties from parliament. The gist of this chapter is to interrogate the factors that increase human insecurity during elections, consequences of electoral violence as well as ways of combating electoral violence in Africa.

The study will carry out a general survey of the areas in which the causes and enabling conditions of election related human insecurity in African countries can be underpinned. The chapter therefore concludes that elections in Africa, if not well monitored, can be flashpoints and hotspots for violence and human insecurity. This will retard developmental efforts in the continent. Policy recommendations to solve electoral human insecurity take into consideration this analysis.

Conceptualising human insecurity, elections and electoral violence

The concept of human security emerged from the traditional notion of security considered to mean the absence of threats to core values (Wolfers, 1952). This concept was popularised as a result of the efforts of the United Nations in 1994 through its UNDP report. The report tried to broaden the concept of security, which had historically been associated with the state to include people. In this case, threats to the state were largely external in source and military in nature. Baldwin (1997) argues that military responses were resorted to during security threats. According to Henk (2005), the inherent weakness of this notion was the exclusion of people as a referent of security. It was paradoxical that at a time when states were spending colossal sums of money in building military arsenals in response to external threats – both real and imagined – people within the territorial state, who were constant victims of diseases, internal conflicts and human rights abuses among other adversities, were left peripheral to the security discourse (Akokpari 2012). As the UNDP report noted:

The concept of security has so far been interpreted narrowly as a security of territory from external aggression, or as protection of national interest in foreign policy or as global security from the threat of nuclear holocaust. It has been related more to nation states than to people .... Forgotten were the legitimate concerns of ordinary people.... For many of them, security symbolised protection from the threat of disease, hunger, unemployment, crime, social conflict, political repression, and environmental hazards (UNDP 1994: 22).

The United Nations (UN) aimed to change this perception by distinguishing the state from government. We note that state should be understood to include everything within a territory, people included, whereas a government is narrower than the state. Arguably, the notion of human security defines people as targets of security threats. This means that [African] human security suffers as soon as state security vanishes. The UNDP's 1994 report identified a number of possible and visible areas of human security threats. These included economic, food, health, environment, personal, community and political. This range of insecurities was redefined into two main areas, namely freedom from fear and freedom from want. Akokpari (2012) observes that, the former referred to conditions such as conflicts, violence and crime that induced fear and deprived people of the stability in life, while the latter referred to deprivations such as the lack of employment, education, housing, medical care, sanitation, and so on, which undermined dignified life. We add that some of the human security threats that Africa experiences emanate from international institutions such as the Bretton Woods and others that cause "collateral" damage as was in the case in Iraq and Libya.

However, the concept of human security faced a number of criticisms from scholars (Roland Paris, 2001; Pettman, 2005; Henk, 2005; Tomuschat, 2003). These scholars denounced the concept as being too broad and including virtually any kind of unexpected or irregular discomfort. Interestingly, some see the concept as too narrow and focusing too exclusively on humans. This view recommends an expansion in the focus of the concept to cater for traditional ways of living (Pettman, 2005). Henk and Tomuschat (Ibid) question whether human security is ever achievable in a world facing various forms of security threats, while feminists argue that the articulation of the concept has not gone far enough to address the concerns of women. In spite of these criticisms, human security remains a useful concept that has guided policies, especially in Global South. In its 64th General Assembly Plenary session, the UN noted that human security was intimately linked to the achievement of the Millennium Development Goals (MDGs) and other human development goals (UN, 2010). The adoption of the MDG initiative in 2000 was thus part of the broader efforts to alleviate human insecurity.

In the current discussion on electoral politics and insecurity in Africa, the focus is on the freedom from fear and more specifically, on violence, conflicts and personal security. Without doubt, conflicts and violence – some of which are caused by the interference and meddling by external actors including Euro-American states and their institutions – have remained defining features of African politics in recent years. Many of Africa's conflicts are related to the dearth of democracy and good governance – human rights abuses, corruption and the partisan posture of the state in distributing resources among competing constituencies (Adedeji, 1999; Le Billon, 2001; Sawyer, 2004, Akokpari, 1998). The deepening of democratic governance was expected to mitigate the continent's conflicts. However, in much of Africa, electoral politics, which are central to democratic politics, seem to create or exacerbate conditions for conflict, violence and human insecurity.

On the other hand, Gabriel (2016: 2), defines elections as "the symbolic competitive, periodic, inclusive, definitive processes [organised in independent, free, fair and transparent frameworks] in which the chief decision-makers in a government are selected by citizens who enjoy broad freedoms to criticise government, to publish their criticism and to present alternatives." There are three types of elections namely: proportional representation, majority proportional representation, majority system and the mixed electoral system (Gabriel, 2016). However, it is worth mentioning that none appears to be more democratic than the other. The definition of elections given above describes democratic elections, whether in a proportional, majority or mixed system. Undemocratic elections usually lack one or more of the adjectives used to describe elections above. Generally speaking, when people use the term election, they more often mean Democratic Elections.

While elections are clearly a means of choosing representatives, they are not a straightforward means of conflict prevention and/or resolution or simply of conflict management as this is conditioned by their being free, fair, frequent enough and highly transparent and independent. Where these conditions are not met for their proper management/administration, the election itself can lead to violence and human insecurity.

It is worth mentioning that numerous explanations are offered in the available literature to conceptualise electoral violence. Ogundiya and Baba (2007), for instance, opine that electoral violence is used inter-changeably with political violence. Nevertheless, it has been noted by these authors that political violence is much broader than electoral violence which transpires in different kinds of political systems that may not necessarily be democratic. Anifowose (1999) advances that, political violence can be distinguished from electoral violence owing to the fact that political violence is the use of threat or physical act carried out by an individual or individuals within a political system against another individuals or property with the intention to cause injury or death to person and damage or destruction to property whose objectives are to modify the behaviour of others in the existing arrangement of power structure that has some consequences for the political system.

Ogboaja (2007) observes that electoral violence means all forms of organised acts or threats, physical, psychological and structural, aimed at intimidating, harming, black mailing political opponents before, during and after an election, geared towards influencing the electoral process to one's selfish desire. This means an unsystematic or planned action that seeks to control, postpone results, or else sway an electoral procedure by means such as intimidation, coercion, hate language, propaganda, physical attack, damage of belongings, or killings (Fisher, 2002; Albert, 2007). This resonates with UNDP (2009: 4) which defines electoral violence as:

> Acts or threats of coercion, intimidation, or physical harm perpetrated to affect an electoral process or that arise in the context of electoral competition. When perpetrated to affect an electoral process, violence may be employed to influence the process of elections—such as efforts to delay, disrupt, or derail a poll—and to influence the outcomes: the determining of winners in competitive races for political office or to secure approval or disapproval of referendum questions.

Interestingly, election-day violence is the most celebrated and documented electoral violence. At the structural level, election-day violence includes deliberate use of security personnel, political opponents and their supporters. Besides, politicians also use this to destroy electoral materials and prevent voters perceived to be in support of their opponents from voting (Ogboaja, 2007). According to Jegede (2003), there are different manifestations of electoral violence such as murder, arson, adduction, assault, violent seizure and destruction of electoral materials. These acts are committed by individuals and groups with the intention of influencing the outcome of elections or deter elected officials from consolidating their positions after elections.

Electoral violence has features that make it distinct from other sorts of political violence. Firstly, it should be noted that such violence is utilised in order to realise specific political objective that is to affect the various aspects of the electoral process and thus its outcomes. Most importantly, it may occur at all stages of the electoral process. These are the pre-election period, the Election Day and the post-election period (Sisk, 2008). Thirdly, it involves different actors like government forces, that is, the police and military, political parties (leaders, members and sympathisers) and non-state armed groups like militias, rebels and paramilitaries (UNDP, 2009). Fourthly, it includes various activities such as threats, coercion, obstruction, abduction, detention, assault, torture and murder as well as rioting, plundering and destroying properties, distracting campaign activities and materials, disturbing public gathering and educational activities, shutting down offices, establishing 'no-go' areas etc. (UNDP, 2009). Fifthly, it has specific targets. These include electoral partakers such as electorates, candidates, election officers, observers and media groups, electoral materials such as ballot boxes, campaign stuffs, registration data, polling results, electoral facilities such as voting and tallying stations and electoral events such as campaign meetings and demonstrations, journeys to voting stations.

Electoral violence has an effect both on democracy and peacebuilding. From the standpoint of democratic politics, violence and insecurity may influence the result of elections in many ways. Actors may use threats and coercion to prevent electorates from registering to vote and to discourage them from casting votes. Party candidates may abandon the electoral process due to threats and killings during campaigns or may act against measures taken to conduct elections (UNDP, 2009). From conflict management view point, violence may have an adverse effect on the society. It will polarise the voting public along conflict margins and in the worst case could lead to an outbreak of violent conflict. Radical or fanatic groups may also get the opportunity to assume state power through violence (ibid). Studies have shown that electoral violence has increased significantly in Africa in recent years (Hyde & Marinov, 2012). The following factors have been identified:

Stakes

The incumbents in electoral authoritarian regimes usually have strong incentives for staying in power, but due to internal and/or external pressure for democratisation they are forced to expose themselves to the uncertainties of elections. However, long years of autocratic rule may leave behind a legacy of deep-rooted cleavages and tensions within the society that may turn against the incumbents in the face of a regime change should they lose the elections. Losing would not only mean a loss of political power but also a loss of legal impunity as well as the loss of financial/material benefits the incumbency has provided. In Zambia, when Levy Mwanawasa assumed power, his government took a swipe on the crimes committed by his predecessor Mr F Chiluba when he was in office. Sometimes a regime change can even lead to the death of a former autocrat despite any possible concessions he/she has made during his/her final years in power. From the opposition's point of view there is often much more to win than to lose in the elections since losing would most often just mean the continuation of business-as-usual whereas winning would promise tremendous changes and thus opportunities for both the opposition politicians and their constituencies.

Competitiveness

As the opposition strengthens and is allowed to operate more freely, the competition between the incumbents and the opposition is likely to increase. High levels of competition mean that even small shifts in the share of votes can determine who will be the winning party. Thus, the contenders are likely to use any means available to boost their share of votes. When the stakes are high and competition stirs up, it may become increasingly tempting to resort to illicit tactics to win the electoral race. High stakes and competitiveness reinforce the political culture of winner-take-all that is usually associated with plurality/majority electoral systems that operate under the principle of first-past-the post. In Africa some 28 countries use the plurality/majority system in elections whereas proportional representation system is used by 15 countries (Atoubi, 2008).

Besides, electoral violence in Africa is caused by impoverishment. Impoverishment in Africa is very alarming and this gives room for the disinherited and unemployed majority to be manipulated to perpetuate all forms of electoral violence. Impoverishment is the state of been extremely ravaged and disinherited. It is a situation whereby the individual is not possessed of heritages and is thus not able to meet the basic necessity of life. An individual exposed to these hardships is more likely to engage in electoral violence than a rich person in society. When the economic hardship becomes too unbearable, the propensity for violence increases. "Army of unemployed youth" then becomes a tool for electoral violence.

Again, it could be captured across the streets of Africa that electoral violence is being instigated as a result of the culture of impunity. The ineffectiveness and malfunctioning of the security forces also give people the impetus to stage electoral violence. The ineffectiveness especially on the part of the police service is a major factor which encourages electoral violence. Pre-electoral violence is often associated with killings but the police service always fails to get to the root of those killings. This failure seems to be creating a culture of impunity and motivation for recurrence of crimes and violence in our society.

Electoral violence is not being met with strong criminal codes in Africa. Weak penalties or punishment for violators of electoral process also give room for more crimes to be committed. Penalties or punishment are intended to achieve correction, retribution and deterrence. Most countries in Africa lack legislation against perpetrators of certain electoral offences. This renders African elections amenable to all forms of crimes and violence.

Weak governance and corruption can also instigate electoral violence. Corruption can set the stage for structural violence. Weak governance and corruption make people feel desperate enough to seek any means of revenge against political authority including violence. Small arms proliferations in African countries are on the increase. Possession of arms leads to the perpetuation of violent conflicts and the creation of new cycles of violence and crime.

Perpetrators of electoral violence

There are many perpetrators of electoral violence. These include among others the military, the police, private security forces, paramilitary, hired thugs, as well as hard-core supporters of the political parties. Although not exhaustive, this list provides a good starting point for understanding the nature of the people that are involved in electoral violence and their motives. Because electoral violence is by nature politically motivated, the perpetrators are, in most cases, likely to be linked to party politics in one way or another. More often than not, electoral violence is directly orchestrated by one or more of the political parties involved, or it occurs with its/their assent. Thus, political parties, both those in power and those in the opposition, have a pivotal role in the emergence and continued occurrence of electoral violence. However, politicians do not always have full control over the perpetrators of types of? Political violence (listed above), even when they operate under the direct payroll of the politicians. Sometimes things get out of the politicians' hands and escalate. However, the more organised and trained the perpetrators are, the less likely they are to disobey the orders issued by a political authority.

Victims

Victims of electoral violence are usually political rivals and their election campaigners, potential supporters and voters of political rivals and election officials. Political rivals are often the most direct targets of electoral violence during the pre-election phase. After all, one of the most reliable ways to win an election is to knock other contenders out of the race. The incumbents usually tend to focus their intimidation efforts primarily on rival politicians rather than on other potential victim groups, since they often have other means for influencing election officials, and they often do not want to intimidate voters (unless absolutely necessary) in order to make the elections appear more legitimate in the eyes of the general populace. Political rivals do not necessarily have to come from the opposition, but they can also be fellow party members, that is, people within the ruling party. For example in Nigeria, intra-party violence during the primaries of the 2007 gubernatorial, general and presidential elections was particularly fierce, causing several casualties (HRW, 2007a). Intimidating or assaulting political rivals directly may have more straightforward implications than targeting their voters, firstly because it might be difficult to identify these potential voters of the rival candidates, and secondly, because targeting them could result in loss of votes from the swing voters that would otherwise give their vote to the potential offender. On the other hand, intimidating political rivals may cause them to retaliate, thus compromising the offender's own safety. Therefore, voter intimidation tends to be a safer route for devious politicians, and thus they might prefer to utilize electoral violence against voters rather than other politicians. This would mean taking fewer risks in terms of personal safety, although at the same time, political risks (in terms of popular support) might increase.

According to Paul Collier & Pedro C. Vincente (2008), voter intimidation may not be very effective in turning people into voting against their personal preference, mainly due to the fact that the ballot is cast anonymously and in secret, so it may be impossible to know for sure who the intimidated people actually will vote for, and in addition, the intimidated people might also decide not to vote at all. Although in the majority of cases people tend to be fairly confident about the secrecy of the ballot, Afro-barometer results show that in Africa between 2008 and 2009 almost one out of four persons believed that it is somewhat or very likely that those in power could actually find out how they voted.

Yet, as potential swing voters may be difficult to identify, their voting behaviour—in terms of whom they vote for—may likewise be difficult to control. However, if potential supporters of the political rival(s) can be identified, devious politicians and their thugs can relatively easily monitor whether these people vote or not. It may be considerably easier to repel potential opposition/rival voters from the ballot box than to force them to vote against their preferred candidate. However, voter intimidation almost always leads into a decrease in voter turnout which in turn reduces the perceived legitimacy of the election. In authoritarian electoral regimes, the whole point of running elections, from the incumbents' point of view, is to legitimise the prevailing regime, that is, the status quo. The goal is to secure an election victory, and at the same time to make the victory appear as legitimate as possible. Therefore, voter intimidation is more or less incompatible with the aims of the incumbents so long as there are other alternatives available for securing a victory in the elections. For the opposition, who often are the underdogs, undermining the legitimacy of the elections may be a worthwhile strategy, especially if they are likely to lose the elections anyway. So long as the incumbents are also playing unfair, they may even manage to turn the tide in popularity, should the incumbents resort to retaliation through the same violent tactics.

Consequences of failing to combat electoral violence

Electoral violence is associated with a huge cost. A cost which must be paid by member states and Africa as whole. Electoral violence leads to political instability. Electoral violence is both the causative and symptomatic … in Africa. It is the causative factor because it feeds the political crises that manifest regularly. Political violence is a threat to building a strong, efficient and visible democratic Africa. It leads to anti-human acts as basic human rights, issues of gender equality; cultural rights and identities are often either ignored or trampled upon. These adversely affect the human security and social development of Africa.

Electoral violence breeds insecurity as it is often characterised by loss of life and properties. It forms the catalyst for human and property insecurity. Over millions of people are killed; billions of people displaced and properties worth billions have been burnt, looted and destroyed. Where will all these lead us to as a continent? Aside leading to political, social and economic insecurity, there are attendant costs of ensuring security, repairs of damaged infrastructure. These resources could have been put into an alternative use to better human and social development.

It is very pathetic to observe in dismay that development cannot occur in the absence of peace and security due to electoral violence, yet day in and day out, we witness them across the continent. Africa suffers from an atmosphere of insecurity and political instability. Electoral violence drives away prospective foreign "investors" due to the lack of adequate security for their "investments". Private domestic "investors" will also lose confidence in their respective countries and opt for foreign investment.

Electoral violence leaves so many people across the streets of Africa homeless. No place to lay their head and lack of access to food and portable drinking water. Electoral violence renders some Africans orphans; some become physically handicapped; hunger and death are the least. At least, this should not be the portion of the black African. There must surely be a change in the trend of our electoral processes as a continent.

Electoral politics and (in) security in Africa: a general survey

Quite a number of political analysts have raised concern over Africa's capacity and political will to conduct free, fair, and peaceful elections. In some African countries such as Kenya, Nigeria and Zimbabwe, violence and myriad irregularities have persistently marred the process of electing the country's leaders. Political leaders in these countries, having adopted vices such as corruption, violence and vote rigging from their former colonisers and some NGOs operating in their countries (Hancock 1989), have become habituated to fraud, corruption, intimidation, and violence, as if they consider these the necessary weapons of political winners. Sadly, the voters have been denied the chance to count and be counted and, disturbingly, the trend has worsened. Most importantly, the key drivers of election violence remain unaddressed and during the election period, underlying social and economic concerns collide with hopes and fears of change, raising tensions and the likelihood of violent competition. This is particularly true in countries such as Zimbabwe, Kenya and Nigeria where chronic instability, poor governance, communal disputes, gang-related fighting, and violence sponsored by power brokers fosters long-standing grievances.

Kenya has a long history of electoral violence and human insecurity. When it got its independence in 1963, its political system was pluralist, with two dominant parties: the Kenya African National Union (KANU) and the Kenya African Democratic Union (KADU). Although there were incidences of electoral violence during this period as a result of ideological differences, they were minimal. The period 2007-2008 caught the country and the international community by surprise. Over 1,500 fatalities were reported across multiple identity-based clashes that created widespread population displacement, especially in the Rift Valley (Wepundi, 2012). Despite promises from Kenya's leaders to reform, the country's political system remains haunted by human insecurity as a result of electoral violence. This owes to the fact that the rewards of political office, include protection from criminal prosecution, are huge. As such, some candidates in the past have gone to great lengths to achieve power, including unleashing violence on their opponents and their supporters.

From the 1950s, elections in Nigeria approximated a war that is often waged to determine political power. According to Andohema *et al* (2014), all weapons are always available for politicians in Nigeria to use religion, ethnic sentiments, out-right bribery, the power of incumbency, corruption, the abuse of electoral process, etc. to unleash violence and threaten the security of lives and property in the country in such a way that in such election-related crises, it is estimated that over 10,000 Nigerians have lost their lives, hundreds of thousands have been displaced while property worth billions of Naira have been destroyed due to election-related violence in the country. Consequently, the prevailing security challenges in contemporary Nigeria have equally had some link to the hostile political atmosphere in Nigeria created by election-related conflicts.

In Zimbabwe, the existence of electoral violence emanates from the party system structure such that the elections have become a mere concession to pressure to democratise, a gross form of lip-service to democracy characterised by the ZANU-PF regime's use of authoritarian tactics, violence and intimidation to coerce the electorate to support it. During the first independence decade, ZANU PF government was heralding towards the establishment of a de facto one party state (Mandaza and Sachikonye, 1991; Sithole and Makumbe, 1997). Nevertheless, such a one party state desire and establishment was vehemently criticised and crushed by the influential opposition political figures such as Edgar Tekere who led the vibrant Zimbabwe Unity Movement (ZUM). This then meant that the one party state agenda was defeated in the *de jure* sense, but not in the *de facto* sense, as Zimbabwe's political landscape continued to resemble the dominance of a one party state (see Mandaza and Sachikonye, 1991).

Interestingly, the entrance of the MDC in the political scene in 2000 increased the risks of election related human insecurity in Zimbabwe. The ZANU PF election campaigns invoked the selective memory of the liberation struggle. These violent memories and images of a nation that was born out of violence (liberation struggle) is used during election time as an opportune time for voters to defend their country that is always at odds fighting against re-colonisation and the agents of Western imperialism as fronted by the Morgan Tsvangirai led (MDC) party. This has been a strategy that has been used to win the hearts and minds of the electorate. Moyse (2009: 43) succinctly observes that, "ever since the birth of meaningful political opposition to the ruling ZANU (PF) party in Zimbabwe, elections have become a battleground". This clearly explains how electoral contestations remains to be the source of human (in) security in Zimbabwe. What have elections been like during the colonial era?

Violence has become endemic to Zimbabwean politics - to an extent that it has become synonymous with elections in Zimbabwe as noted by Bratton and Masunungure (2008:50) when they argued that: "code-named Operation Mavhotera Papi ("How Did You Vote?") was rolled out during the post March 2008 polls. This operation was aimed at rooting out, victimising and targeting all people suspected of supporting or voting for the opposition MDC in the March 2008 elections (ibid:50). Surprisingly many of the perpetrators of violence were immune from arrest and walk freely in their respective communities till today. You may balance this up with a critique of impunity for colonial era and enslavement era crimes.

Both ZANU PF and MDC have been legitimising political violence through hate speeches, songs and slogans increasing electoral human insecurity. In the year 2000 Morgan Tsvangirai the leader of the opposition party is reportedly to have said: "What we would like to tell Mugabe is please go peacefully. If you don't want to go peacefully, we will remove you violently" (Mwonzora, 2014). Evidently these utterances entice violence and is an anti –thesis to the principles of his party that is the principles of social democratic non-violence and peaceful change. Eight years down the line President Mugabe reportedly echoed the same message that could intimidate the electorate. In 2008 President Mugabe is quoted in one of his campaigning speeches as saying, "We are not going to give up our country for a mere X on a ballot. How can a ballpoint pen fight with a gun?" (Mwonzora, 2014).

Such a statement clearly shows how the political leadership in Zimbabwe has been negating the principles of electoral democracy and the respect of the popular will by calling for violence. Unfortunately, this call to violence has been couched and phrased in nationalistic and liberation war narratives. Former MDC – T Minister of Constitutional Affairs Advocate Eric Matinenga, as Mwonzora (Ibid) postulates, succinctly critiqued the socialisation of hate and violent language through messages and symbols in the MDC especially the sloganeering. Mr Matinenga's message of non-violence was quoted in the Newsday and he is reported to have said: "We say hit someone against the ground. Of what help to us is that slogan?"[…] "We want constructive slogans." Loosely translated into the Shona language the MDC-T slogan read as follows – *'musimudzei mudenga, murowerei pasi bwaa'* (trans: 'Lift him/her up in the air, smash down to the ground'). Such a slogan has been widely used by the MDC at political rallies for denouncing their opponents in campaigning periods.

In the same vein, ZANU PF is to a larger extent guilty of having resorted to hate language and speech both during and out of campaign periods. In its slogans, ZANU PF uses the symbol/image of a clenched fist, which resembles militancy. It also uses slogans such as *'pasi navanopikisa'* (down with the opposition). Further, ZANU PF uses phrases like *'ZANU ndeyeropa'* (meaning the party is associated with blood). The period leading to the June 2008 elections saw the emergence of a new crop of singers who came up with songs and jingles that captivates and were pregnant with revolutionary messages. Such messages largely contributed to human insecurity.

Whilst the March 2008 elections were largely free of violence, the legacy of violence might have been still ingrained in the psyche of the Zimbabwean populace. At least there were no incidences of naked violence as opposed to the 27 June 2008 runoff elections. The March 2008 elections by all standards were viewed by the local observers and regional observers to have passed the legitimacy test of free and fair elections as enshrined by the SADC Principles and Guidelines Governing Democratic Elections (1992) which was adopted in Mauritius in (2004). Generally speaking, all political parties were 'free' to campaign in rural communities although the electoral playing field was still skewed in favour of the incumbent (ruling) ZANU PF. Nonetheless, there was some degree of a façade of 'freeness' especially comparing how the opposition MDC was able to enjoy some airplay on the national television selling its electoral message. However, it should be noted that the electoral playing field has always been uneven and in favour of the incumbents especially in post - conflict elections (Lyons 2002) in most African countries with Zimbabwe being no exception.

Preventing election related human insecurity in Africa

Electoral violence is an ill wind of social phenomenon, which blows no one any good. In its aftermaths both its perpetrators and victims are losers. Also, that violence is not native to man but rather a consequence of his fallen nature, his frequent transgressions against the grains of his nature. Against this background, politicians should conduct their campaign on the basis of issues rather than attack on political opponents or mobilisation of religious, ethnic and regional sentiments. The campaign should focus on the implementation of the critical national economic, political, social cultural, educational and health services. Political parties should evolve as mechanism of democratic governance rather than servicing as an organised criminal enterprise used for seeking, gaining and retaining power in order to rob public treasury. The antidote to electoral violence in any society is justice. African countries should allow justice –both the need to redress colonial era and contemporary injustices – to rule.

The culture of impunity that encourages political violence should be discouraged by scrupulous enforcement of indigenous expression of *Ubuntu/Unhu* which prohibit political violence and illegal arms trade, possession and use. The civil society organisations should intensify their efforts and make all their activities more transparent in the area of civic education so that the citizens can understand the essence of politics, the values of democratic governance and practices, and to eschew ethnic and religious sentiments in political participation. There is need to stop overzealous ambition, lost for power, selfishness, voluptuousness, pride, anger and revenge in African politics. We should learn to have a passion of leadership no matter what will be our political need. Dialogue should be allowed to prevail over the language of violence.

Local and international stakeholders draw on an array of strategies to safeguard the integrity of the electoral process to prevent human insecurity in Africa. Electoral monitoring and observation have become the most frequently employed interventions since the 1990s, playing a prominent role in ensuring accountability and reducing the chances of impunity. They aim to produce assessments concerning the fairness and legitimacy of the polls based on solid documentation. As OSIWA (2012); EISA (2010), observe, these are passive observation activities, with limited or no capacity to promptly react to episodes of violence or other irregularities.

More recently, there has been recognition of the need to supplement electoral monitoring with more proactive conflict prevention strategies (IPI, 2012; OSIWA, 2012). According to UNDP (2009), they can range from electoral mediation and the implementation of rapid response mechanisms, to programs that foster social cohesion in electoral contexts. The UNDP (ibid) notes that, the promotion of social integration is one of the most effective mechanisms to build trust in the electoral process and to curb tensions that can lead to the outbreak of violent episodes leading to human insecurity. Key activities include voter education, peer-to-peer peace advocacy, engagement with the media, creation of structures of dialogue among stakeholders, and direct engagement with vulnerable populations.

Preventive strategies can be more effective if combined with the use of information and communication technologies (ICTs). Civil society initiatives have been particularly creative in making technology a key ally against electoral violence and human insecurity (Bardall, 2013) though the same (technology) has also been abused in many countries to foment violence. For example, they rely on crowdsourcing in election monitoring, increasing citizen participation in election observation. Besides, by sending reports via SMS, social media platforms, or specific websites, ordinary citizens can actively participate and report election-related human insecurity and other bad electoral conduct, such as fraud and vote buying.

Most importantly, mobile technology can facilitate communication between actors and the delivery of real-time reports from the ground. By speeding up the flow of information through SMS messaging or internet-based platforms (email, or social media like Twitter and other websites), ICT help expedite responses to violence or misconduct, thus contributing to a peaceful and fair election process. The particular features of election-related violence thus point to the relevance and potential of initiatives that combine social inclusion, crowdsourced election monitoring, and mobilisation of youth and women.

Way Forward

• There must be tolerance to opposition in African political practices. Political power and positions in African countries should not be seen as open sources to wealth, which often leads to electoral contests as "win-or – die" affairs. Elections should not be "win-or-die" affairs in Africa.

• The imposition of candidates on the electorate during elections should be discouraged. This would allow the citizens to freely choose their representatives during elections without resorting to violence.

• Election riggings, falsification of election results, multiple voting, acts of thuggery and the intimidation of the opposition in the electioneering process should be completely eradicated in African politics. Killing and maiming of political opponents in Africa's electioneering and political process should be discouraged.

• Security measures should be tightened in Africa to checkmate re-occurrence of election-related violence and always curtail the high rate of insecurity of lives and properties that has increasingly become a recurring decimal in Africa's socio-economic, religious and political systems. Perpetrators of election-related violence should be treated and punished according to the existing laws.

• Meanwhile, gainful employment opportunities should be made available to the teeming unemployed youth in Africa to avoid their being idle, which makes them to be easily used to perpetrate violence by desperate politicians in the country before, during or after elections.

• There is need to implement conflict-prevention policies and strategies in advance as opposed to post, ad hoc and reactionary measures.

• Most importantly, African nations should establish systems/institutions to monitor, prevent, mitigate and manage election violence throughout the electoral cycle- pre, during and post-election.

• There is need to conduct a conflict analysis of the local context for a clear understanding of the local dynamics. Electoral violence is not limited to overt and large-scale physical violence, but rather includes other coercive means such as threats of violence, intimidation and harassment. By-elections are particularly vulnerable to violence in countries marked by close political competition.

- Address the underlying structural causes of electoral violence; decentralise the power of the executive office including a separation from the security forces, strengthen the role of parliament and implement broad-based socioeconomic development programmes.
- Establish the electoral systems and administrative units that encourage broad-based and inclusive strategies for mobilising voters.
- Discourage winners-take-all and first-past –the post electoral systems in divided societies.
- Strengthen the governance and independence of electoral institutions-including election commissions to increase their political integrity, transparency and efficacy.
- Then again the security sectors have a major role to play in ensuring law and order in any society. The security sector must be well structured, equipped and motivated enough to play its role in ensuring the consolidation of democracy in Africa.
- There is a need for capacity building for the police force and other security agencies in the areas of small arms proliferation to enable effective performance of their duties.
- There must be some level of co-operation between the police service and the other security agencies. The electoral body which is the electoral commission must be well equipped and resourced with both human and physical capital. Electoral officers must be well trained and motivated. The security sector must educate the public on the consequences of violating the electoral laws.
- Moreover, there must be some level of electoral reforms and good governance. The underlying problem of political instability in our society is the lack of good governance. Hence to resolve political violence, accountability, social justice, transparency, rule of law, gender equality and due process must guide governance and leadership in Africa. Electoral reforms must include other things as mass education. There must be some level of education for the citizenry to know who is a registered and considered as an eligible voter under the laws of the land.

Conclusion

Africa has witnessed significant democratic progress over the past two decades, although there is still great variation between various sub-regions and countries. Conversely, much remains unchanged in regard to the underlying socio-economic structures of society and the nature of politics in many African states. Precisely due to the increasing reliance on elections as a means to distribute and regulate political power in society, the stakes of such elections are often high. The socio-economic realities of losing power in societies where almost all political power and economic resources of the state is lost to neoliberalism such as privatisation of economic resources, coupled with exclusive electoral systems and weak or biased electoral institutions, risk turning elections into a do-or-die affair. This is intensified in societies divided along ethnic and other socio-economic cleavages. Reforms to improve the lives of ordinary citizens and provide alternative socio-economic assurance to those in power are required in order to move beyond simply establishing formal "constitutional" democracy.

References

Adedeji, A. (1999) "Comprehending Africa's Conflicts" in Adebayo Adedeji (ed.) *Comprehending and Mastering African Conflicts: The Search for sustainable peace and good governance* London: Zed Books, p3-21

Afrobarometer. (2012) *Online Data Analysis,* URL: http://www.jdsurvey.net/afro/afrobarometer.jsp (visited on Nov. 7, 2017)

Akokpari, J. (1998) The State, Refugees and Migration in sub-Saharan Africa, *International Migration Review*, 36(2): 211-231.

Akokpari, J. (2012) Is electoral politics a new source of human insecurity in Africa, *Afro-Asian Journal of social sciences,* Vol 3 (3.2) pp2229-5313.

Albert, I. O. (2007) *Reconceptualising electoral violence in Nigeria.* In Albert, I.O., D. Marco & V. Adetula (Eds.). Perspectives on the 2003 elections in Nigeria. IDASA and Sterling-Holding Publishers: Abuja.

Anifowose, A. (1982) *Violence and Political in Nigeria: Yoruba Experience*, London: Nok Publishers.

Aondohema, S.S. *et al. (*2014) Election related violence and security challenges in Nigeria: Lessons from the Aftermaths of the 2011 General election, *IOSR Journal of Humanities and social sciences*, 19 (12): 59-68.

Atoubi, S. M. (2008) Election-Related Violence in Africa. *In Conflict Trends* 2008/1. ACCORD.

Baldwin, D. (1997) The concept of security. *Review of International Studies* 23: 5–26.

Bardall, G. (2013) Gender-specific election violence: the role of information and communication technologies. Stability: *International Journal of Security and Development* 2, (3) p23-39.

Collier, P. & Pedro, C. (2012) Violence, Bribery, and Fraud: The Political Economy of Elections in SubSaharan Africa. *In Public Choice*, Vol. 153, No. 1–2, pp. 117–147. Springer Link.

Electoral Institute of South Africa (EISA). (2010) *When elections become a curse: Redressing electoral violence in Africa.* EISA Policy Brief 1 (2): 91-99.

Fischer, J. (2002) *Electoral Conflict and Violence: A Strategy for Study and Prevention.* IFES White Paper.

Gabriel, N. (2016) *Causes of electoral violence in Africa*, Cameroon, Democracy chronicles.

Hancock, G. (1989) *The lords of poverty: The power, prestige and corruption of the international business*, Atlantic Monthly Press.

Henk, D. (2005) *Human Security Relevance and Implications Parameters*: US Army War College 35(2): 91-106.

Hyde, S. D. & Nikolay, M. (2012) *Which Elections Can Be Lost? In Political Analysis*, Vol. 20, No. 2, pp. 191–210. Oxford University Press.

HRW 2007a. Criminal Politics: Violence, "Godfathers" and Corruption in Nigeria. *Human Rights Watch Report*, Vol. 19, No. 16(A).

International Peace Institute. (2012) Elections and stability in West Africa: the way forward. *IPI Policy Brief.*

http://reliefweb.int/sites/reliefweb.int/files/resources/Full_D ocu_2.pdf

Jegede, S. (2003) "Inter and Intra - Party Conflicts and the Future of Democracy in Nigeria". In Olasupo, B. A. (ed), *Electoral Violence in Nigeria: issues and Perspectives*. Lagos: Fredrick Ebert Stiftung (FES).

Le Billion, P. (2001) The political ecology of war: natural resources and armed conflicts, *Political Geography* 20(5): 561-584.

Lyons, T. (2002) Post-conflict Elections: War Termination, Democratisation, and Demilitarising Politics. *Institute for Conflict Analysis and Resolution*, George Mason University.

Mandaza, I. & Sachikonye, L. M. (1991) *The One-Party State and Democracy: The Zimbabwe Debate*. Sapes Books Harare.

Moyse, A. (2009) The Media Environment Leading Up to Zimbabwe's 2008 Elections, *Defying The Winds of Change* (1) P 43-60.

Mwonzora, K. (2014) *Towards peacebuilding? Mapping efforts of the Government of National Unity to prevent electoral violence in Zimbabwe*, The Hague, Netherlands, SJP.

Ogboaja, C. (2007) Political Violence in Nigeria: *The Ill Wind*, Abuja: Wordsmiths Communications Services

Ogundiya, I. S. & Baba, T. K. (2007) "Electoral Violence and Prospects of Democratic Consolidation in Nigeria", in Jega, A. and Ibeanu, O. (eds), *Election and the Future of Democracy in Nigeria*. Nigeria, Political Science Association.

Open Society Initiative for West Africa (OSIWA). (2012) *Making elections count: a guide to setting up a civil society election situation room*. OSIWA. Available at: http://osiwa.org/IMG/pdf/osiwa-guide situation room bd.pdf

Paris, R. (2001) "Human Security: Paradigm Shift or Hot Air? *International Security* 26(2): 87-102.

Pettman, R. (2005) Human Security as Global Security: Reconceptualising Strategic Studies *Cambridge Review of International Affairs* 18(1): 137-150.

Sawyer, A. (2004) Violent conflicts and governance challenges in West Africa: the case of the Mano River basin area, Journal *of Modern African Studies*, 42(3): 437-463.

Sisk, D. T. (1998) "Elections and Conflict Management in Africa: Conclusions and Recommendations" in Sisk D. T & Reynolds A, *Elections and Conflict Management in Africa.* Washington: United States Institute for Peace.

Sithole, M. and J. Makumbe. (1997) Elections in Zimbabwe: The ZANU (PF) Hegemony and its Incipient Decline, *African Journal of Political Science/Revue Africaine de Science Politique* : 3 (12) 122-139.

Tomuschat, C. (2003) *Between Idealism and Realism: The Collected Courses of the Academy of European Law* 3(1) Oxford: Oxford University Press.

UNDP. (1994) *Human Development Report New York*: Oxford University Press.

UNDP. (2009) *Elections and Conflict Prevention: A Guide to Analysis, Planning and Programming.* New York: UNDP.

Wolfers, A. (1952) National Security as an ambiguous symbol, Political *Science Quarterly* 57(4):481-502.

Chapter 11

Espousing Global "Civilisation" in "Social Networking":
Linguistic Vulnerability and Techno-paranoia among Tshivenda/Xitsonga Speakers in Zimbabwe

Prosper Hellen Tlou & Aleck Mapindani

Introduction

Multilingualism tops as a living reality in most African countries, including Zimbabwe. In multilingual situations, the need for language policies that clearly stipulate the equality, equity and unbiased usage of languages cannot be overstated. This, in a sense, serves to guard against both premeditated and inadvertent formulations of language stratum, domination and loss. Languages do not serve merely in enabling communication, but they also function as conveyers of culture and identity. Traditionally, language loss emerges in multilingual settings in which a language spoken by the majority progressively replaces the range and functions of a language spoken by a smaller group so that, steadily, the speakers of the language spoken by a smaller number of speakers shift to speaking the language of the majority group (Schmidt, 2008). Basing on Sapir-Whorf hypothesis (1929) that language determines thought and culture and that language influences thought and culture, the chapter will deliberate on the impacts caused by the usage of English language as a medium of communication on social media. It problematises the use of English (as embraced in contemporary technological gadgets) by speakers of indigenous languages in informal settings by arguing that its use poses threats and insecurities to indigenous languages and their cultures.

This understanding is triggered by the fact that English is mostly used on social platforms such as Facebook, WhatsApp, twitter, just to name a few – acronyms are formed and shorthand is adopted. It maintains that non-usage of indigenous languages in important domains leads to their underdevelopment, loss of culture and uninformed espousal of foreign cultures that spell loss, including insecurities of African heritages. In this regard, losing one's language and culture entails nefarious global processes of [becoming or] being turned into an animal without linguistic and cultural heritages. Phillipson (1992:47) precisely unravels the predominance that the English language has gained over and above the indigenous peoples and their languages in the ensuing way:

> ...education serves the imperial centre by having three functions: ideological, economic and repressive. The ideological function serves as a channel for transmitting social and cultural values. In this role English is regarded as a 'gateway for better communication, better education and higher standards of living.' The second function – economic – legitimizes English as a means of qualifying people to contribute to their nation and operate technology that the language provides access to. The third function – repression – serves to dominate indigenous languages

The tragic scenario insinuated above provides for the easy and unnoticed domination of speakers of both Tshivenda and Xitsonga languages in Zimbabwe. English comes as an iron hand in a velvet glove – an insidious weapon methodically intended to subdue, multifariously, the virility of the indigenous prowess through the instrument of a language. In such cases, the youths are branded as the misplaced, ruined or pilfered generation for their tendency to eschew all that is from their culture and gleefully attach themselves to alien (neo-)imperial cultures (Trudger, 2000). Such (neo-)imperial cultures have been noted as being led by English although they also encompass the Chinese, Spanish, or French language (Schimdt, 2008). This scenario of linguistic encroachment, as further noted by Schimdt (2008:1), is a notable transnational trend "that has been observed over the past decades as clearly (encroaching) towards smaller languages, particularly minority and indigenous languages (so that they) die out because of the spread of a few world languages" mentioned above.

Worth underscoring also is the effacement of indigenous languages as engineered by a deliberate but covert policy of the New World Order that is aimed at creating a one world government and hence, to efface indigenous sovereignty and the languages. Hinted briefly from Professor Adam Weishaupt in his writing entitled *Proofs of a Conspiracy* (nd), the Illuminati aimed covertly to gradually "…to rule the whole world. To achieve this it was necessary for the Order to destroy all religions, overthrow all governments and abolish private property" (Epperson 2009:66). Having America and Britain as major giants in the exercise, English will then unquestionably have a complete dominion and overwhelm the rest of the world languages. Once they are without indigenous languages they are easier not only to assimilate but to put all the people on the same plane as animals.

Theoretical Framework

The subject of how a dominant language can influence thought and culture of an 'ethnic' group or people who use a particular language cannot objectively be inferred in the absence of a relevant hypothesis or conceptual ideology; hence the application of Sapir-Whorf's theory in enunciating the entrails of this chapter. During the early and mid-20th century, notable linguistic anthropologists Benjamin Whorf and Eric Sapir proposed that language is not merely an interface but also play a formative role in shaping thought itself. Two broad categories entailed in the hypotheses which are the linguistic- relativistic view and the linguistic determinism are to anchor the deliberations of the discussion. According to the hypotheses, the idea that language, to some extent determines the way we think about the world around us is known as linguistic determinism, where "strong determinism" is limited to the ability of a language to determine thought and "weak determinism" being restricted to the implicature that human thoughts are influenced by language (Campbell, 1997). In this light, the theory will enhance the critical scrutiny of the allegation that English as a dominant language imposes new linguistic and cultural practices to indigenous languages and thus, affecting people's perspectives on how they view the world. This has strong links with the view that many African values, morals and virtues have been lost in exchange of Western substitutes, in the name of using the so-called "Queen's language". It is through this overt channel that many Western cultural practices were brought to Africa through language, hence the argument that language influences the linguistic continuum of indigenous African thinking.

Linguistic Stratification: (In)Voluntary Language Choice, Preferences and the Dominancy of English

Society is categorised into classes, where a plethora of instruments are employed to set up the strata. Language being a critical aspect of humanity is held as vital in the classification of individuals and groups through different social platforms. The language one chooses to use suits him or her to a certain social class. Choice of language is also determined by class categories in the society. For Karl Max, social class is determined by the ownership of and non-ownership of the means of production. Those who own the means of production are bourgeoisie and those who work for these bourgeoisies are the proletariat. Everyone wants to be associated with the higher class and thus the use of English for the language is associated with power and money.

Language loss usually occurs in multilingual setups where some languages are preferred more than others; it can be by an individual, ethnic group, community or nation as a whole. Fasold (1990) suggests that multilingualism serves as an interactional resource for the multilingual speakers. This means people will be using more than one language. In that case one particular language may generally be used at home or with close friends, whereas another language may be used for commerce and trade, and even a third one for dealing with government agencies. It was a norm for English to be used mostly in official and formal business but now it has since changed because of the widespread use of social media platforms of communication. The unbalanced treatment of languages has been going on for a long time and if nothing better is done with regard to the formulation of policies that guard against linguistic imbalances in the foreseeable future, some will be brought into extinction. Despite the logical and empirical disclaimer given by different scholars, it is still reasonable to maintain that certain formal properties of language casually affect thought in many local and important ways.

Lower status given or associated with some indigenous languages drives speakers of the languages to develop an attitude towards them. Language attitudes are the feelings people have about their own language or the languages of others. Languages gain an upper or lower status through the policies that would have been given by the authorities or government. Currently the 2013 Constitution of Zimbabwe is the only document which stipulates on the equality and equity of all the 16 languages and prior to that the 1987 Education Act was the only document which showed how languages should be treated at schools. Not having a language policy which promoted all the languages even after Zimbabwe gained its independence in 1980 played a part in downgrading some languages whereas some gained dominance. To be declined the chance to use and practice one's language makes one to forget some of its pieces. States usually implement language policies as a result of pressure by indigenous language speakers who demand institutionalised language promotion not just for symbolic reasons but because they feel that adequate representation of their language in media, education and official communication will promote the development of the status and functionality of their language. It is claimed that all languages should be treated equally but the *de jure* status of Tshivenda/Xitsonga do not match the *de facto* function in the society and thus the speakers of the languages feel the pressure to shift to the dominant languages such as English so as not to be excluded from public life. Romaine (2007) notes that in showing preference for some languages, whether or not designated as official or as national, the state's decision benefits those for whom the chosen languages is a primary language, to the detriment or disadvantage of others who either have no or lower proficiency and are denied the benefit of using and identifying with their primary language.

The era of technology also mark the domination of English through its use in electronic gadgets. When tracing back to the introduction of industrialisation, English was used as the medium of instruction. As media gained power through the widespread use of television and radios, English was always on the upper hand of all other languages in the world. Krauss (1992:6) refers to television as 'cultural nerve gas' because it streams the majority language and culture into the homes of indigenous people and accelerates the rate at which they abandon their own languages and cultures. Technology in particular Internet facilities, for the most part, is not available in Indigenous languages, for example Google uses English. This again fuels the usage of English over indigenous languages. Though it was highlighted above that technology confines people to using the dominant language but when it comes to social media it was noted with great concern that people have all the autonomy to use the language of their choice yet still, English dominates the African native languages. It is therefore the thrust of this work to examine the usage of English, in informal setting through social networks, and its impacts on the indigenous languages, the culture and the identity of the native people affected. Factors that push people to abandon their own languages will be analysed.

The way languages are used reflects what people value and what they don't value. Language as a primary means of human communication is a powerful social force that does more than convey intended referential information. Language portrays personal, social and cultural characteristics of the speaker. For Melander (2003), depending on the particular listener, a speaker's accent, speech patterns, vocabulary, intonation etc. can serve as markers for evaluating that speaker's appearance, personality, social status and character, among other things. The language that we use entails some behaviour in us. In the African setup some words are not allowed to be used especially in a public forum or by kids for it is believed that they can influence bad behaviour in them: they were reprimanded for using such words. Swear words like 'piss off', 'damn it' and 'shit' are forbidden. Thus, the culture of a people finds reflection in the language employed.

Language choice results in a multilingual situation whereby one chooses to use a certain style or register for a special reason. Language choice can be taken for a careful selection of words, phrase, clause or sentence of another language within the speaker' linguistic repertoire. Coulmas (1997) explains that people make linguistic choices for various purposes. Individuals or groups choose words, registers, styles, and languages to suit their various needs concerning the communication of ideas, the association with and separation from others. David (2006) argues that language choice is triggered by factors such as social status, gender, educational attainment, ethnicity, age, occupation, rural and urban origin, speakers, topic, place, media and formality of situation. Qawar *et al* (2015) opine that the differences between communities such as power, size, wealth, prestige, and vitality are significant factors which often make speakers adjust their language choice patterns during their life time and / or from one generation to the next, along with the speaker' attitudes towards their languages. Meanwhile English is seen as more prestigious and as such some families believe that the use of Indigenous languages, at home, including with kids has been overtaken by time. Hoffman (2009:7) highlights that for many it is economically advantageous to learn the majority language and to teach it to their children, English will help their children to find jobs and be successful. In using English as the medium of communication, indigenous people will be adopting a number of western practices voluntarily and involuntarily, and ultimately they will be assimilated into a (neo-) imperial world.

The increasing prevalence of online social media or informal communication has lessened the burden and challenges of information dissemination as well as making communication to be cheap and fast but it has brought with it some disadvantages especially to indigenous languages. Indigenous languages in Zimbabwe were for a long time only relegated to the periphery of home usage which in a way hindered its growth with regard to terminology development. People run short of words to express ideas on the daily usage and thereby adapt to English. Usage of acronyms, abbreviation and shortenings are the order of the day on social media. Their usage is not a matter of concern at this point in time for there are other ways of word formulation in linguistics, a matter of worry is the domination of English terms. It cannot be claimed however that the option of using English instead of indigenous languages is all because lexicons in African native languages cannot meet the demand - most of the English equivalents are found in indigenous languages.

Romaine posits that many critics who have efforts to preserve endangered languages think in simplistic dichotomising fashion. Abandoning indigenous languages in favour of (neo-) imperial languages such as French and English means joining the modern world. In others words, some believe that using or sticking to indigenous languages means being backward and being uncivilised. For Trudger (2000) Indigenous languages and culture are dismissed as primitive and backward looking, an argument which is then used to justify their replacement by Western languages and culture as prerequisite to modernisation and progress. English in most instances is seen as a yardstick to measure intellectuality. For example, in Zimbabwe and most of the countries worldwide, English is a requirement for entrance to colleges, universities or even formal employment. Recently, because of high literacy and high rate of unemployment in Zimbabwe, English is also a requirement for manual jobs like sweeping, digging of trenches and this therefore, forces the populace to associate themselves with English. As the world becomes less biologically diverse, it is becoming linguistically and culturally less diverse as well, but the truth is there are prospects and development in diversity.

RIP (Rest in peace) which can be translated to mean *edelani nga mulalo/ wisa hi ku rhula*, and MHSRIP standing for "May Her/His Soul Rest in Peace" *muya wavho kha u edele nga mulalo / ingi moya wa yena u nga wisa hi ku rhula*" are the popular messages circulated on Facebook or WhatsApp in the event of the loss of life. Westerners, through Christianity, believe that one does not die but rest waiting the second coming of Jesus Christ for judgement and whoever passed on have no relation or communication with the living and have no power over the living. In the African perspective even after death, life continues in the living dead were the one who passed on has a role to play on the living. As such the saintly dead are well respected in Africa

English speakers use pronouns which show singularity even when referring to an elder person whereas in Tshivenda/Xitsonga the pronoun denotes plurality as honorary even referring to one person. In the use of pronouns in Tshivenda honorary ones are preferred or used. Thus will have *vhone/ vona* but it is noted that English *you* is regularly used in shortened form as *u*. Linguistically, it opened a room for the penetration of *inwi* which is singular and well accepted. Swear lexicons also exist in Indigenous languages but are considered to be taboo and not to be used regularly like the English usages.

There is quite a pool of commonly used English swear words that in the contemporary times have penetrated into the communication arena of the indigenous peoples. One of the most widely recognised swear word in English language is "Fuck". This, being the literal shortened version of "fornication under the consent of the king", is often used as a joke or when you are angry at someone else. The dominance of English has unwarily created a preoccupation of the indigenous people's minds with such foreign words that serve to undermine the survival and development of their indigenous languages. This is also the case with such words like "shit", a term that springs out from within, often when something unexpected comes up in your life. For example, if you forgot that you have a project that is due this week, you may say, "shit, I had totally forgotten about that!" This shift from indigenous words and phrases by the Vhavenda/Vatsonga people to English terms is one indication of the degree to which English has gained dominance over the indigenous languages in question.

Such supernumerary popular words and phrases are key in communication, and unavoidably and naturally evade and overlap linguistic boundaries with imperceptible easement. Speakers of indigenous languages often and unintentionally find themselves trapped in codeswitching by inserting within their communications such codes as would encompass, "Piss off", especially when they want someone to step away from their personal space. "Bastard" can also be used as a noun to describe someone who gives them an unpleasant experience. Literally, a bastard is an illegitimate child or mongrel. In some instances where someone may utter unreceptive or irritating words to somebody, responses such as "to hell" can be uttered back to ward off the speaker and to mechanically bar them from adding any such 'nonsense'. Such set-ups set pace for an English lead linguistic stratum whose speakers are their own enemies in subverting their own indigenous languages. Thus, the use of borrowed terminologies by the Vhavenda/Vatsonga is critical and instrumental in dismantling the integrity of their own languages.

Acronyms, Abbreviations and Shortenings in English Informalities and Transphonologies

Social network homophily is correlated with the use of English acronomy, abbreviation and shortening. Language expresses our social variables and our thinking. Eckeit (2008) *et al* has argued that the social meaning of linguistic variables depends crucially on the social and linguistics context in which they are deployed. In support of the hypothesis proposed by Edward Sapir and Benjamin Lee with regard to the relationship between language and culture, Wardhough (2002:219-220) reports that the structure of a language determines the way in which speakers of that language view the world or as a weaker view the structure does not determine the worldview but is still extremely influential in predisposing speakers of a language towards adapting their worldviews. Below is a list of some of the commonly used shorthand, acronyms or abbreviations:

Laugh out loud (u seela ntha) - (lol) In our African setup laughing out loudly is associated with not having good morals.
You only live once (hu tshiliwa luthihi)-(yolo). This encourages people to live a reckless life with the mentality that people live once and the belief that life is too short.
Missing in action – mia (u salela)
wud- what are you doing? (ni khou ita mini?/u endla yini?)
xem- shame (I khombo)
tbt- throwback Thursday -rhumela hi Ravumune)
lib- lying in bed (ndo edela/ndzi etlele)
hud- how are you doing? (hurini?/u njhani?)
omg-oh my God! (Mudzimu wanga/oho Xikwembu xanga!)

The low uptake of traditional culture by the young generation makes them to have a lot of autonomy which then yields to lack of respect for elders, loss of cultural values which are virtuous and of importance to the African society. Language is culture- specific, people often feel that an important part of their traditional culture and identity is also lost when language disappears. Languages of colonial conquest and dominant languages of nation states penetrate into, transform and undermine a minority community's ability to maintain its language, culture and identity in various ways. However, it is noteworthy that once the affected communities become aware of the erosive influence of the ostensibly civilising ventures of the foreign languages, and will be in a better position to claim their heritages and historicities and ultimately linguistic and cultural integrities (Chalande, 2006).

The Insidious Proliferation of English and the Loss of Identity among the Indigenous Peoples

Language is taken to be one of the key markers of 'ethnic' identity. Schimdt (2008) highlights that, in the European tradition, language has become a major maker of belonging to a particular 'ethnic' or national group. This therefore means that language is closely tied to identity. Schmidt (2008) goes on to say that identification of 'ethnic' minority groups includes many different markers of identity, of which language is important though not the only one. In addition Hoffman (2009:1) posits that language plays a large role in identity formation, and the loss of a language has significant consequences for its speakers. Language plays a major role in defining ourselves in relation to, and in contrast with others (Hoffman, 2009:20). The language one speaks defines one's identity in a major way and also binds one to others and creates a community of speakers.

Cultural Imperialism and the Inadvertent Espousal of English– Interrogating 'its' Ostensible Civilisation

Every major aspect of human culture is dependent on language for its transmission, thus if the language for that particular 'ethnic' group is no longer used, the cultural practices also cease to be observed or practised one way or the other. In support Hoffman (2009:3) states that endangered language communities also stand to lose valuable cultural practices. The disappearance of a language and its related culture almost always forms part of a wider process of social, cultural and political displacement where national culture and languages are in effect those of dominant 'ethnic' groups. In this regard English is still a dominant language in Zimbabwe and therefore it is forcing the disappearance of the African native languages together with its culture. The loss of language also causes the loss of other culturally significant practices that are dependent on the language. Oral histories are lost if no one can speak the language anymore. According to Thanaoulas (2001), language does not exist apart from culture, that is, from the socially inherited practices and beliefs that determine the texture of our lives. In as much as language is a key to the cultural past, it is also a key to the cultural present in its ability to express what is thought, believed, and understood by its members and in so doing losing it brings a lot of disadvantages and in a way people would have been robbed of their heritage.

Conclusion

There is no one single factor that can be pinpointed that will essentially save a language, but instead, a complex collection of factors are often held accountable. Elevating the prestige of a language is required and it can be achieved through use of the language in media and technology, official government recognition for the language, and increased economic status of its speakers. Although language is only one of many features (for example dressing, behaviour patterns, race, religion, nationality, occupation) that may mark identity, either individually or collectively, many regard languages as a benchmark for cultural diversity because virtually every major aspect of human culture ranging from kinship classification to religion is dependent on language for its transmission. Although there are some encouraging developments in the country with regard to the recognition of the once called 'marginalised', the absence of a language policy which clearly stipulates how they should be used or treated drags everything down. A more realistic way forward may reside not in trying to specify a particular policy but to establish fair background conditions under which members of different language communities can survive. Choosing to use one or more languages exclusively in public schools and administration services and activities offered by the government is tantamount to discrimination based on language.

References

Campbell, L. (1997) *The Sapir-Whorf Hypothesis*, Retrieved November 2017, http://Venus.va.com.au/suggestion/sapir.htm.

David, E. (2006) *The Relationship Between Language and Culture*, National Institute of Fitness and Sports in Kanoya International Exchange and Language Education, http://www2.lib.nifs-kac.jp/HPBU/annals/an46/46-11.pdf.

Eckert, P. (2008) *Variation and the Indexical Field, Journal of Sociolinguists* 12. 453-476

Fasold. R. (1990) *The Sociolinguist of Society*, Oxford, Blackwell.

Hoffman, (2009) *Endangered Languages, Linguistics and Culture: Researching and Reviving the Unami Language of the Lenape*, BA Thesis, Bryn Mawr College.

Krauss, M. (1992) *The World's Languages in Crisis*, Languages 68. 4-10.

Meander, L. (2003) *Language Attitudes: Evaluation Reaction to Spoken Languages*, Hagskolon, Dalarna.

Phillipson, R. (1992) *Linguistic Imperialism*, Oxford, Oxford University Press.

Qawar, H. A. and Boer, S.D. (2014) *Language Choice and Language Attitudes in a Multilingual Arab-Canadian Community: Quebec-Canada: A Sociolinguistic Study*, M.A. Thesis, Middle East University.

Epperson. R. (2009) *The New World Order*, https://archive.org/details/TheNewWorldOrder_342, accessed on 03/02/2018

Schmidt, U (2008) *Language Loss and the Ethnic Identity of Minorities*, European Centre for Minority Issues (ECMI), Denmark.

Thanasoulas, D. (2001) *Radical Pedagogy: The Importance of teaching Culture in the Foreign Language Classroom*. Retrieved 20 November 2017, http//radicalpedagogy.cap.org/content/issues

Wardhoug, H.R. (2001) *An Introduction to Sociolinguistics,* New York, Basil, Blackwell.

Chapter 12

Zimbabwean Youths and the Insecurities from "Bronco" Abuse

Nancy Mazuru

Introduction

Whilst the contemporary global era can be applauded for creating open and borderless economies that are discernible in the movement of people, goods, services and capital, the lopsided effects particularly on the developing world should be given due regard. While the operations of pharmaceutical companies in many parts of the world have eased accessibility of medicines, the extent to which people, especially those in the developing world, have benefited from this phenomenon needs to be scrutinised. This chapter examines the degree to which the availability of over-the-counter drugs, particularly Broncleer, popularly known as 'Bronco' has affected the lives of the youths in Zimbabwe. The chapter argues that although drug abuse is not a new phenomenon in Zimbabwe, the advent of Bronco and other over-the-counter drugs has heightened the insecurities for youths involved in substance abuse. The chapter argues that the smuggling of Broncleer, in Zimbabwe, which has led to its availability and accessibility has become an insecurity to the country. The chapter argues that Broncleer abuse has many social and economic ramifications on the youths themselves and the Zimbabwean society in general. Physical and psychological health problems, straining of household and national income to cater for the health costs of the drug addicts, suspension of education and other viable economic activities and delinquency are some of the visible socioeconomic repercussions of Broncleer abuse. The chapter further argues that strict measures should be put in place to curb the abuse of Broncleer and other substances in the country. Some of the measures include dealing with the problem of high unemployment through youth innovativeness, eradicating corruption, increasing awareness about the dangers of Broncleer abuse as well as other substances and introducing stiffer penalties on Broncleer smugglers and peddlers.

Methodology

The study that culminated into the present chapter was purely qualitative. The researcher conducted in-depth interviews with Ghetto youths from Mabvuku, Mbare and Budiriro in Harare, Mucheke A, in Masvingo, Sakubva in Mutare as well as students from different tertiary institutions in the country so as to have a deeper insight on why and how Broncleer is abused. Some adults in the aforementioned high density suburbs were also interviewed in order to get their perceptions on youth substance abuse, particularly Broncleer abuse as well as its effects at family and community level. The in-depth interviews were buttressed by secondary sources, particularly newspapers, academic journals, reports and books.

Overview on Drug Abuse

A drug is anything that modifies and influences the workings of the body system consumed by an individual in liquid, tablet, powder, and/or glue form (Beirne and Messerschmidt, 2006). Drug abuse refers to the chronic or habitual use of any chemical substance to alter states of body or mind for other than medically warranted purposes (Cherry *et al*, 2002). According to Horton *et al* (2012), drug abuse has a long history with humanity and has Native American roots which can be traced back to at least 200 AD. The global drug problem has three major themes which are clearly visible in many countries across the globe namely: concern about young people and drugs, concern about addiction and concern about the effects of the illegal production, trafficking and selling of drugs (Cherry *et al*, 2002). As in the West, the use of alcohol among young people has been increasing in developing countries and drug use has become more prevalent (Furlong, 2012). Drug trade is the third largest business in the world, next to petroleum and arm trade (Naqshbandi, 2012). Over the past 25 years the global illegal drug industry has grown to the point that it currently has annual revenues approaching $300 billion with a retail value of these substances exceeding that of the worldwide oil trade (Naqshbandi, 2012). The same author further states that an estimated 208 million people, or nearly 5% of the world's population between the ages of 15 and 64, consume illegal drugs. According to Dada *et al* (2015), the global misuse of prescription of over-the-counter pharmaceutical opioid analgesics, including those containing codeine, is an increasing public health issue. In Africa, Zimbabwe is not spared from countries experiencing this predicament. Substances being abused in Zimbabwe include, Broncleer, Cannabis, *Maragada* (chlorpromazine), Diazepam, *Musombodhiya* (an illicit alcohol brew composed of diluted ethanol or methanol), Steroids, *Zed* (an illegally brewed spirit smuggled into the country from Mozambique) and *Tegu-Tegu* (Chirisa, 2017). In Zimbabwe, the abuse of cough syrups, particularly Broncleer, is popular with youths of both sexes between the ages of 15 and 35 in urban areas (The Herald, 30 May 2015). The abuse of Broncleer by Zimbabwean youths validates Robertson's (1999) assertion that recently, youths have increased usage of over-the-counter medications for the purposes of getting "high". According to the Zimbabwe Republic Police (ZRP) report cited by Vunganai (2017), Harare has the highest number of drug abusers. However, this does not necessarily imply that other cities and towns are totally substance abuse free zones.

Bronco Saga

Broncleer is a cough syrup manufactured by Adcock Ingram Limited in South Africa (Chireka, 2015). It is used to temporarily treat cough, chest congestion and stuffy nose symptoms caused by the common cold, hay fever, or other breathing illnesses (Matambanadzo, 2014; Chipunza and Razemba, 2017). The drug is a bronchodilator which contains codeine and alcohol (Muchena and Makotamo, 2017). Codeine is also found in a range of other medications, including Myprodol and Mybulen, Benylin C, Syndol, AdcoDol, Tensodol, Sinutab C, and Sinumax Co, among other products (Mbanje, 2016). Due to the high alcohol content and codeine contained in Broncleer, many youths abuse it, taking large amounts, mostly 50ml to 100ml at once instead of the prescribed 10ml at a time for adults (Matambanadzo, 2014). Taking an overdose of Bronco makes the abusers to be easily intoxicated and they eventually become addicted to the drug. As a result of the rampant abuse of this drug, in 2014 the government of Zimbabwe banned the importation and selling of this syrup in country (Matambanadzo, 2014).

Though Broncleer has been banned in Zimbabwe, it is still very common among the youths and it is smuggled into the country via different ports of entry (Mbanje, 2016). Well-orchestrated smuggling syndicates originating from neighbouring South Africa and Botswana have fuelled the increase (The Herald, 30 May 2015). Investigations by The Herald showed that cross-border traders smuggle illicit drugs using haulage trucks and unscrupulous bus operators, mainly through Beitbridge Border Post (Chipunza and Razemba, 2017). For example, in January 2014, police arrested three suspected drug dealers aged 40, 30 and 21 in Southerton, Harare and seized Broncleer with an estimated street value of US$20 000 (Matambanadzo, 2014). The three suspects, one of them a truck driver, were arrested while offloading 111 boxes, each stashed with 100ml of Broncleer at a house in Southerton (Matambanadzo, 2014). In a similar occasion, in May 2015, two South Africa-based truck drivers were fined R15 000 (about USD $1 252) each for smuggling 797 boxes of Bronco into the country through the Beitbridge Border Post (The Herald, 30 May 2015). Each box contained 50 bottles (The Herald, 30 May 2015). In April 2017, two women were fined US$500 each for possession of Broncleer (Newsday, 2017). The duo were arrested inside the Beitbridge border post after they were searched and found each with 48 bottles of the banned cough syrup (Newsday, 2017).Therefore as the world is increasingly becoming a 'global village', it is more of a double edged sword in the sense that the increasing interactions between nations, for example through the movement of people, goods and services pose both benefits and costs to the nations involved. In the case of Broncleer smuggling and abuse, the author argues that the increasing connection and inter-dependence between countries have become an insecurity to nations as this has facilitated the smuggling and trafficking of drugs. According to Naqshbandi (2012), the geographical proximity has played a very vital role so far as the production, cultivation, trafficking and promotion of drug abuse in the world is concerned. In the same line of argument, UNDCP (1995) states that the global changes which have allowed people, goods and money to move from one country to another cheaply and easily have also had other consequences. Thus, while globalisation has improved the socio-economic wellbeing of people in other parts of the world, the opposite side of the same coin has produced detrimental side effects especially in the developing world. This therefore validates the assertion by UNDCP (1995) that the same macroeconomic environment which has facilitated the growth and development of global legitimate businesses has also provided the opportunity for drug producers and traffickers to organise themselves on a global scale, to produce in developing countries, to distribute and sell in all parts of the world, to move drug cartel members easily from country to country and to place and invest their drug profits in financial centres offering secrecy and attractive investment returns.

How Bronco Is Smuggling?

The cough syrupy is smuggled into the country using different methods. It may be mixed with groceries or repackaged into 20-litre containers and shipped into the country disguised as used cooking oil or oil and at times diesel (The Herald, 30 May 2015). In other circumstances, the syrup may be hidden underneath bed bases, sealed refrigerators or in secret compartments (The Herald, 30 May 2015). Sometimes the smugglers pay bribe to customs officials at the borders to facilitate the importation of this illegal cough mixture (The Herald, 30 May 2015). Investigations by The Herald revealed that Bronco is smuggled into the country disguised as transit cargo (The Herald, 30 May 2015). The cough syrup is usually sold and abused in high density suburbs and in Harare, such suburbs include Mabvuku, Kambuzuma, Mbare, Glen View, Mufakose, Warren Park and other high density suburbs (Chipunza and Razemba, 2017). Bronco is also common in Chitungwiza, a dormitory town located 30 km south-east of Harare city, as well as in Mukokoba high density suburb in Bulawayo (Musvipwa, 2015). Cities like Mutare, Gweru and Masvingo have also witnessed cases of Broncleer abuse.

Why Bronco Abuse?

Just like many other drugs, the abuse of Bronco has been perceived by many people including some of the abusers as a consequence of high unemployment rates coupled with economic hardships being faced by the country. Several writers like (Mutiso, 2012; Ibrahim, 2016; MacDonald and Pudney, 2000; Ayllon and Ferreira-Batista 2016) have also revealed the nexus between high unemployment rates among the youths and drug abuse. For example, in their study on the effects of drug abuse among the youths in Nigeria, Ibrahim *et al* (2016) found out that unemployment had more devastating effects on the youth to the extent that they took depressant in order to have peace of mind as the only alternative to escape from frustration and committing other offences such as robbery, theft among others. Similarly, in their study on illicit drug use, unemployment, and occupational attainment, MacDonald and Pudney (2000) also found out that drug abuse, particularly the use of opiates, cocaine and crack cocaine, is associated with an increased risk of unemployment, regardless of age or gender. In the same vein, Ayllon and Ferreira-Batista's (2016) study on the effects of the economic crisis on drug consumption of young individuals in Europe reveals that an increase of 1% in the regional unemployment rate was associated with an increase of nearly 0.7% of young people declaring to have consumed cannabis at any point in time. The problem of unemployment is not exceptional to Zimbabwe. Mpofu and Chimhenga (2016) aver that in Zimbabwe's urban areas, most of the youths are underemployed since the labour market is not offering competitive opportunities to the effect that the youths who are graduating from various colleges far outnumber the employment opportunities available on the market. Mago (2014) avers that urban youth unemployment creates socio-political and economic problems in urban societies. Mago (2014) further argues that socially, unemployment pushes young urban people to indulge in violence, drug abuse, prostitution and 'gangism'. Thus in Zimbabwe, high unemployment rate is one of the factors that have exacerbated substance abuse by young people with Bronco being the drug of the moment.

However, when looking at the relationship between unemployment and/economic crises and drug abuse, it is important to avoid focusing only on the drug abusers. A deep analysis on the abuse of Bronco in Zimbabwe reveals that the economic shambles facing the country combined with high unemployment rates have forced people to have the audacity to import and sell Bronco regardless of the consequences. Most of the studies on the relationship between unemployment and youth drug abuse have only focused on how unemployment can force the youth into substance abuse, paying little or no attention on how unemployment itself and poverty can actually force people to engage in drug dealing. In an interview conducted by the researcher on the 13th of December 2017, one woman in Mbare, Harare stated that:

I import and sell Broncleer and I am quite aware of the legal implications as well as the health effects of this drug on my clients. However, I have no choice because I am a widow and I am not employed, I need to take care of my three minor children. They need food, they need clothes, they need to go to school….you name it. So where am I supposed to get the money? Although I am a vender, you would find out that more often than not, we are at loggerheads with municipality police. They chase us from the streets and sometimes they confiscate our wares.

Concurring with the above sentiment, in another interview conducted by the researcher on the 15th of December 2017 in Budiriro, Harare, a certain man (not a peddler) asserted that:

It is common knowledge that the economic hardships in Zimbabwe are driving people to do incredible things. In most cases, the dealers are not to blame. They have families that need to be taken care of.

In a similar narrative, Newsday (6 April 2017) reported of two women aged 30 and 31 who testified in Beitbridge court that they were involved in the importation and selling of Bronco because they were single mothers and breadwinners for their families. Related to the above story, in October 2015, a 29 year old woman from Warren Park, Harare was fined US $300 after she was found in possession of 20 boxes of 50 bottles (Charumbira, 2015). In mitigation, the woman asked the court to be lenient with her saying she was a single parent with one child and two other minor dependants. This therefore shows that poverty and unemployment force people to indulge in illegal activities so as to provide food for their families. What is important to take into consideration is the age of the people involved in the selling of Bronco. Most of them are the working age group, an indication that unemployment is a factor in the Bronco saga in Zimbabwe.

However, while unemployment plays a role in the abuse of Bronco by Zimbabwean youths, a close analysis of this scenario reveals that it is not only the unemployed young people who abuse this drug but the generality of the youth. Mostly, groups of the youth who abuse Bronco include the ghetto youths, rank marshals, high school pupils, university and college students, Zim Dancehall musicians, among others. Thus, if Bronco can be abused by students and some of the employed youths, it therefore means that unemployment cannot be singled out as the only factor causing the misuse of this drug. In fact, it should be seen as a combination of factors. These factors are explained below.

Apart from high unemployment rates, the other issue is that unlike other hard drugs such as cocaine, crystal meth and heroin which have a high cost, and low market in Zimbabwe, Bronco is cheaper, with one bottle costing between US $3 and $5 (Matambanadzo, 2014; Mbanje 2016). Thus many of the Bronco abusers opt for this drug because of its affordability. Bronco has thus been regarded as a cheap new way of getting high (Musvipwa, 2015). The high alcohol content in it has seen many youths abusing it for high intoxication popularly known as *kusticker* in slang. In an interview conducted by the researcher on the 14th of December 2017, in Mabvuku, Harare, one of the youths stated that:

If you drink large amounts of Bronco, you become highly intoxicated to the effect that you become motionless physically and mentally. For example, if someone greets you or asks you a simple question, you cannot give an instant response, you may take 2 minutes to respond. *Unenge wakasticker* (You will be highly intoxicated).

Echoing similar sentiments, another youth stated that:

Bronco makes you highly intoxicated if you take large amounts of it, for example the whole bottle. You can sleep on open ground even if the weather is very hot or cold and you don't feel anything during that time.

Another factor that causes Bronco abuse stems from the fact that the drug is seen as easily accessible despite the fact that it has been banned. During interviews, most of the youths stated that Bronco is easily accessible because there is quite a number of dealers who are selling this illicit cough syrup. In an interview conducted by the researcher in Mabvuku, Harare on the 14th of December 2017, one young man stated:

There are many people, including women who are earning a lot from the selling of this drug. With the economic hardships that our country is facing, people are no longer afraid of engaging in illegal activities as long as they are getting something. Therefore it's easy for the youth to access this drug as many people are involved in its trading.

This goes in line with Musipwa's (2015) assertion that affordability, easy accessibility and high intoxication are the top three traits that are driving the increasing abuse of highly dangerous, intoxicating and illegal drugs in what is becoming the 'cheap' drug industry in Zimbabwe.

Closely related to the above, the penalty given to the Bronco dealers seem not to be deterrent enough to dissuade the culprits as well as would-be offenders from this act. In most of the cases, the perpetrators are simply fined or given short prison sentences. For example, the aforementioned cases of the culprits who were brought before the courts for smuggling Bronco (including two South Africa-based truck drivers, a woman from Warren Park and two women arrested at Beitbridge) reveal that they were fined R15 000, US $300 and US$500/ five months imprisonment respectively (The Herald, 30 May 2015, Charumbira 2015, Newsday 6 April 2017). In a related event, in December 2017, a 24-year old Murewa bus conductor was given a 20-day jail sentence or alternatively pay a $100 fine for smuggling 55 bottles of Broncleer from Namibia (Dlamini, 2017). Putting these penalties into consideration, it is clear that they are not stringent enough to daunt the Bronco smugglers and peddlers from this trade. Dealers who sell drugs like Marijuana are normally given a stiffer penalty as compared to those involved in the smuggling and selling of Bronco. For example, in August 2014, a 29 year old Mbare man was slapped with a four-year effective jail term for possessing 11kg of Marijuana (Laiton, 2014). Similarly, in January 2016, A 43-year-old Hurungwe woman was sentenced to 3 years in prison for possession of 7, 96 kgs of mbanje (Jena, 2016). Correspondingly, in November 2016, a 40-year-old Bulawayo man was sentenced to four years in prison after he was found in possession of Marijuana with a street value of $70 000 (Ncube, 2016). Thus, the light judgements given to Bronco peddlers, in a way, explains why this drug has flooded many high density suburbs in the country. The dealers know that if caught, they will be simply fined or given short prison services.

In addition to the above factors, high levels of corruption in Zimbabwe have also contributed to the flooding of Bronco in the country. Some of the respondents revealed that some Bronco peddlers bribe the police as well as customs officials when they are caught with the banned cough syrup. In the same line of view, Chireka (2016) asserts that had it not been the issue of corruption in Zimbabwe and neighbouring countries, it would not be easy for a banned medicine such as Broncleer to be smuggled in huge quantities into the country and end up being sold on the streets.

Apart from the above, the lifestyle portrayed by some Zim Dancehall (Zimbabwean music genre with roots in the Jamaican tradition of Reggae and Ragga genres) icons which glorifies the use of intoxicating drugs and substances is negatively influencing youth perceptions of drug abuse as being the 'in thing' (Musvipwa, 2015).

In the same vein, Langa (2014) asserts that youths in the ghetto end up resorting to musical genres that promote drug abuse. Zim Dancehall music has gained popularity among the youths especially the ghetto youths to such an extent that most of them try to imitate the lifestyle of these musicians including substance abuse, dressing and hairstyle.

In addition to that, some youths engage in Bronco abuse because of peer pressure since it has been perceived by many young people as the drug of the moment. In an interview conducted by the researcher on the 22nd of November 2017 in Masvingo, one university student stated that:

> Bronco is the drug of the moment. As a young person, I consume this drug because most of my peers are doing the same. I don't want to be the odd one out. If you don't do it, your friends may think that you are backward.

Thus, peer pressure has also a role to play in the abuse of Bronco by the youths. It therefore can be noted that the reasons behind Bronco abuse among Zimbabwean youths are quite multifaceted.

Considering most of the factors discussed above, it can be argued that the smuggling, peddling and abuse of bronco regardless of its negative consequences can be perceived in light of Nietzsche's philosophy of master-morality and slave-morality. For him master-morality values power, nobility, and independence whereas slave-morality values sympathy, kindness, and humility (Neitzsche 1907). Nietzsche thus criticises slave-morality for being the morality for the weak, a place of solace for the lazy ones and for encouraging people to live inauthentic life and deny obvious facts of nature as well as preventing the strong-willed from reaching their full potentialities (Neitzsche). He cherishes master-morality for qualities such as courage open mindedness and an accurate sense of worth (Neitzsche 1907). In the case of Bronco, the people who smuggle, sell and abuse this drug and other substances have their own perceptions different from those of the broad society. Due to reasons such as the need to bring food on the table, the need relieve stress, among others, Broncleer dealers and abusers don't see the act as evil as the general public does but as way of pursuing their self ends. Thus, Brocleer smuggling and peddling can be perceived to be a form of Neitzsche's master-morality values where people operate from a self-interest approach disregarding the insecurities arising from their actions. However, writers such as Sunday et al (2017) criticise these morals arguing that as a social being, man is naturally inclined to live in a community and operating from one's own selfish world leads to crisis

How Bronco Is Consumed

As mentioned earlier, Broncleer abusers exceed the recommended dose in order for them to be easily intoxicated. However, when taking this syrup, the drug abusers try to avoid contact with their teeth as this syrup may lead to quick and easy teeth decay (Musvipwa, 2015). Some of the respondents asserted that they widely open their mouth and pour the syrup down the tongue so that it flows downwards without getting into contact with their teeth. Bronco is sometimes mixed with other drugs like marijuana, Zed and mental health pills such as Chlorpromazine commonly known as Maragado among others, to increase the intoxication level (Musvipwa; 2015, The Standard, 16 June 2016). This corroborates the argument by Blachford and Crap (2003) that people who take codeine often abuse other drugs as well.

Socioeconomic Implications of Bronco Abuse

The consequences of substance use are serious, costly and extensive (Holleran and Jung, 2006). Just like many other drugs, Bronco has got many negative effects which range from economic to social implications. The most immediate effect of Bronco abuse is its addictive nature. Many youths who were interviewed revealed that it is very difficult to refrain from consuming Bronco once someone has started abusing it because it is highly addictive. This has been noted as the major reason why people who abuse it end up taking large amounts to the detriment of their physical and psychological health. In addition to causing addiction, Chireka (2015) asserts that Broncleer has codeine which can cause vomiting, constipation, drowsiness, dry mouth and confusion. Broncleer abuse affects the ability to pass stool properly as well as causing loss of appetite, thereby often giving the abusers a desire to eat sweet things like lollipops (Musvipwa, 2015). In addition to the above health problems, Chireka (2015) states that large doses which are taken by people who abuse this cough mixture can cause breathing problems, low blood pressure which result in circulatory failure and comma. The same writer also argues that Broncleer abuse may cause death if large doses are taken especially with other medication that affect the brain. World Drug Report (2014) states that globally, an estimated 183,000 drug-related deaths were reported in 2012. Given the health implications of Bronco abuse, it can be argued that pharmaceutical companies can also be seen as a double-edged sword in the sense that on one hand, they help people with medicine and on the other hand, they have become the 'gods' of drug dealers and abusers.

Broncleer abuse also affects the psychological health of the abusers. According to Holleran and Jung (2006), substance abuse has detrimental impacts on the mental health of the adolescents. It is estimated that half of all drug abusers and one third of alcohol abusers have had a mental disorder at some time, and 65 per cent of seriously mental ill persons have drug/alcohol problems (Kelly and Montfort, 2002). According to Chirisa (2017), abuse of drugs hijacks the dopamine (a pleasure neuro-transmitter in the brain) or activated pleasure centre in the brain. Chirisa (2017) further states that drugs cause an above normal release and increase of dopamine in this centre that causes a person to experience pleasure and look for more of the drug to experience that level of pleasure outside the natural pleasurable activities. However, dopamine at high levels causes psychotic symptoms; hallucination (hearing voices of people not there or seeing things not there) delusion, disorganisation and violent behaviour and this result in the user ending up in a psychiatric unit (Chirisa, 2017). A research by psychiatrist Rwafa cited by Tsiko (2017) on the prevalence of substance abuse on patients who were admitted to psychiatric units at Parirenyatwa and Harare Hospitals showed that there is high prevalence of substance use and a high burden of substance related psychiatric conditions in psychiatric units in Zimbabwe with emergence of some psychoactive substances such as cough syrups and illicit alcoholic beverages. Therefore, the abuse of Bronco and sometimes in conjunction with other drugs or substances is a threat to the health security of the youth in Zimbabwe.

In addition to the above, substance abuse affects work productivity and unemployment, incidences of violence, family deterioration, and academic and other problems among young people (Kumpeer, 1997). In an interview conducted by the researcher on 2 December 2017 in Sakubva, Mutare, one woman whose son is a Bronco addict stated that her son has been hospitalised on several occasions due to drug abuse related illness but he has not yet abstained from taking the cough syrup. This validates Kumpfer's (1998) assertion that substance abuse seriously affects the economic and social stability of communities, contributing to rising health care costs and to the increased costs of alcohol and drug abuse treatment. Kumpfer (1998) further states that reduced work productivity and unemployment are heavily correlated with substance abuse. In the same line of argument, Akpeninor (2013) avers that adolescents using alcohol and other drugs often disengage from school and community activities, depriving their peers and communities of the positive contributions they might otherwise have made. For example, in July 2015, police arrested 16 pupils from four schools in Bulawayo for conducting 'Vuzu' parties at a house in Cowdray Park were they abused drugs while engaging in sex orgies (Tshili, 2015). Police recovered bottles of Broncleer and other dangerous drugs as well as used condoms following a raid at the house (Tshili, 2015). In their (1989) study on drugs in the African-American community, Nobles and Goddard found out that substance abuse leads to an erosion of life chances, an erosion of family life, and the erosion of cultural traditions and sense of community life. Drug abuse is therefore a source of vulnerability in that it can lead to undesirable and negative consequences such as early termination of education, unemployment and even HIV/AIDS (United Nations, 2003). Adolescents are therefore more likely to be involved in risk-taking behaviours under the influence of substances (Holleran and Jung, 2006). Substance abuse hinders the youth from accomplishing important developmental tasks, performing expected duties, and building healthy relationships with others (Holleran and Jung, 2006).

Furthermore, Broncleer abuse just like other drugs/substances leads to violent behaviour and trigger misunderstandings. Most of the respondents who were interviewed asserted that people who abuse Bronco are often involved in conflict with their peers, parents, siblings, spouses as well as members of the public. Regarding domestic violence, scholars like Newman and Newman (2010) argue that alcohol and drugs contribute to domestic violence in the sense that they cloud one's judgement and rational thinking process and lower inhibitions and it may be used as an excuse to beat the intimate partner. For example in January 2018, a popular young Zim Dancehall musician is reported to have gone berserk and assaulted his wife with fists and iron bar while he was under the influence of drugs. This is in line with Akpeninor's (2013) assertion that drug and alcohol abuse may result in family crises and jeopardise many aspects of life, sometimes resulting in family dysfunction. All these ramifications of youth substance abuse if not curbed can escalate into national socioeconomic crises in the sense that the youth are a precious resource in as far as the present and future human capital of any country is concerned. According to Mou (2016), an increase in the number of physically and mental ill youths arising from drug abuse entails a reduction in the future working population of the nation. In the same line of argument, Ghodse (2008) argues that in the long term, the illicit drug industry causes major problems that eventually affect the economic development of the country concerned. As such, the earlier drug abuse is curtailed, the fewer the socioeconomic problems and the brighter the future of a country.

Given the diverse insecurities arising from the smuggling, selling and abuse of dangerous drugs like Broncleer, drug dealing as a whole should be perceived as wicked as the practice of sorcery and witchcraft. As noted by Nyabwari and Kagema (2014) witchcraft affects both communal and personal life because witches are regarded as opponents of the natural order of harmonious community life by causing illness, barrenness, accidents, sorrows, dangers, domestic and public aggression, and death among others. The same authors further argue that the practice of witchcraft negatively impacts the social, economic, political and spiritual development in Africa. From this view, Broncleer smuggling and selling can be seen as bad as witchcraft because of the negative economic and social effects they pose on individuals, families, communities and nation at large. While Broncleer peddlers do not force their clients to buy the drug nor involve the use of magic as under the practice of witchcraft, it should however be noted that the drug dealers and peddlers just like witches knowingly cause health problems, unnecessary deaths, family disputes as well as affecting the social and economic wellbeing of families and communities.

Way Forward

Having examined the causes and consequences of Broncleer abuse in Zimbabwe, it becomes important to consider measures that may help to curb this predicament. One important measure that should be employed is to deal with the issues of unemployment firmly. On one hand, the government should increase income generating activities for the youth so that they become occupied. On the other hand, the youth should be encouraged to be adventurous so that they become employment creators themselves rather than looking forward to be employed by other people. They should be urged to invent new ways of generating income thereby assisting in the reduction of unemployment. This will help them reduce stress emanating from thinking about how and where to get a job. When the youth are fully engaged in income generating activities, they will be busy most of the time to the effect that they will not think about drug abuse. Furthermore, reduction of unemployment also implies that even those involved in drug peddling will have a better option of earning a living. In addition to employment creation, corruption also need to be dealt with seriously. Reducing corruption minimises incidents where drug smugglers, dealers or abusers pay bribery to the police or customs officers. Parents also need to be conscientised about the importance of monitoring the behaviour changes of their children especially adolescents. This may assist them seek early intervention strategies to help their children before they become drug addicts. There is also need to conduct vigorous awareness campaigns consientising the young generation about the negative consequences of abusing Bronco. These awareness campaigns should extend to young musicians, for example Zim Dancehall musicians to make them aware of the influence they have on the lives of the young people. As such, young musicians should be encouraged to be good role models to the youth by disengaging from substance and drug abuse. Furthermore, stiffer penalties should be given to the Broncleer smugglers and peddlers to deter would-be offenders from partaking in the same trade.

Conclusion

This chapter has looked at substance abuse by Zimbabwean youths, paying attention to Broncleer abuse. Attention has been paid to the reasons behind the abuse of this cough syrup by the young people. Factors such as poverty and unemployment, corruption by the police and customs officers, peer pressure, the need to get "high", as well as the availability, accessibility and affordability of the drug have been identified as some of the major forces behind Bronco abuse dilemma in Zimbabwe. The study argues that the increased interactions between nations in the contemporary global era has become a double edged sword as it has facilitated the trafficking and smuggling of drugs between state frontiers. The chapter has noted that while pharmaceutical companies play an important role in providing people with medication, in the present day some of them have promoted drug dealers, thereby aggravating drug abuse crisis among the younger generation. Thus, the integration of the world in a global village should be likened to two sides of the same coin in which one side represents those benefiting and the other one represents those at disadvantage. The chapter notes that like many other drugs, the abuse of Broncleer by the youths poses a plethora of socio-economic quandaries such as physical and psychological health problems, violent behaviour which may lead to crimes, family dysfunction, straining of households and national income due to increased costs of alcohol and drug abuse treatment as well as early termination of education, among others. The chapter has therefore argued that the abuse of Broncleer together with other substances is a blow to the country's economic development. The study has recommended that the government should deal with the problem of

313

unemployment in order to curb its trickle-down effects on drug smuggling, peddling and abuse. Eradicating corruption, increasing the penalties on Broncleer dealers as well as increasing awareness campaigns on Broncleer abuse are other recommendations that have been suggested in this chapter to limit the socioeconomic problems emanating from Broncleer abuse.

References

Akpeninor, J.O. (2013) *Modern Concepts of security.* Bloomington: Author House.

Ayllon, S. and Ferreira-Batista, N. N. (2016) *The effects of the economic crisis on drug consumption of young individuals in Europe – Unemployment, drugs and attitudes among European youth.* University of Girona, NEGOTIATE working paper no. 4.2.

Beirne, P. and Messerschmidt, M. (2006) *Criminology.* Los Angeles: Roxbury Publishing Company.

Blachford, S. and Crap, K.M. (2003) *Drugs and Controlled Substances: Information for Students.* Michigan: Thomson/Gale.

Bulawayo24 News (18 January 2018), 'Soul Jah assaults wife Bounty Lisa' https://bulawayo24.com/index-id-entertainment-sc-music-byo-126040.html.

Charumbira, S. 'Woman fined for 'Bronco' worth $2, 500' In Newsday 23 October 2015, https://www.Newsday.co.zw/2015/10/woman-fined-for-bronco-worth-2-500/.

Cherry, A. L. *et al* (2002) *Substance Abuse: A Global View.* Westport: Greenwood Publishing Group.

Chipunza, P. and Razemba, F. (2017) 'Harare's drug abuse headache' In The Herald 6 March 2017, http://www.herald.co.zw/harares-drug-abuse-headache/.

Chireka, B. 'Let's talk about abuse of cough mixture Broncleer (Bronco)' In New Zimbabwe 19 September 2015, http://www.newzimbabwe.com/columns-24918-Dr+Chireka+Abuse+of+cough+mixture/columns.aspx.

Chirisa, S. 'Drug abuse, mental health matrix' In The Herald 9 February 2017, http://www.herald.co.zw/drug-abuse-mental-health-matrix/.

Crowe, A.H. (1998) *Drug Identification and Testing in the Juvenile Justice System: Summary.* Collingdale: DIANE Publishing.

Dada, S. *et al* (2015) 'Codeine misuse and dependence in South Africa: learning from substance abuse treatment admissions' In *SAMJ,* Vol 105 (9) pp. 776-779.

Dlamini, N. 'Bus conductor fined for smuggling Bronco' In Newsday 13 December 2017, https://www.Newsday.co.zw/2017/12/bus-conductor-fined-smuggling-bronco/.

Furlong, A. (2012) *Youth Studies: An Introduction.* New York: Routledge.

Ghodse, H. (2008) *International drug control into the 21st century.* Hampshire: Ashgate Publishing, Ltd.

Holleran, L. K. and Jung, S. (2006) *Screening substance use/abuse of middle and High school students in Franklin, C. et al, The school services source book: A guide for school-based professionals.* New York: Oxford University Press.

Horton, A. M. *et al* (2012) 'Psychopathology of pedpatric substance abuse' in Davis, A. S. (ed). *Psychopathology of Childhood and Adolescence: A Neuropsychological Approach.* New York: Springer Publishing Ltd.

Ibrahim, H. A. (2016) 'Effect of drug abuse among youth and its impact on *learning'* In *IOSR Journal of Pharmacy and Biological Sciences,* Volume 11 (1) PP 14-17.

Jena, N. 'Woman jailed over 8kg Mbaje' In Newsday 18 January 2016, https://www.Newsday.co.zw/2016/01/woman-jailed-over-8kg-mbanje/.

Kelly, K. and Montfort, L. (2002) 'Social Welfare policy in Arizona' In Smith, Z.A. *Politics and public policy in Arizona.* Westport: Praeger Publishers.

Kumpeer, K.L. (1997) *Drug abuse prevention: What works.* Collingdale: Diane Publishing.

Kumpfer, K.L. *et al* (1998) *Community Readiness for Drug Abuse Prevention: Issues, Tips and Tools,* Collingdale: Diane Publishing.

Laiton, C. 'Man jailed 5 years for possessing 11kg of mbanje' Newsday 16 August 2014,
https://www.Newsday.co.zw/2014/08/man-jailed-5-years-possessing-11kg-mbanje/.

Langa, V. '65% Zim youths suffer drug-induced mental problems' In Newsday 14 August 2014,
https://www.Newsday.co.zw/2014/08/65-zim-youths-suffer-drug-induced-mental-problems/.

MacDonald, Z. and Pudney, S. (2000) Illicit drug use, unemployment, and occupational attainment, Journal of Health Economics, Volume 19, PP.1089–1115.

Mago, S. (2014) 'Urban Youth Unemployment in Africa: Whither Socio-Economic Problems' In *Mediterranean Journal of Social Sciences,* Vol 5 (9) pp. 33-40.

Matambanadzo, P. (2014) 'Zim engages Bots over Broclee' In The Herald 14 January 2014, http://www.herald.co.zw/zim-engages-bots-over-Broncleer/.

Matambanadzo, P. (2014) 'City police bust bronco syndicate' The Herald 9 January 2014, http://www.herald.co.zw/city-police-bust-bronco-syndicate/.

Mbanje, P. (2016) 'Bronco' can't get you high any more' In The Standard, 26 June 2016,
https://www thestandard.co.zw/2016/06/26/bronco-cant-get-high-anymore/.

Mou, D. (2016) *National Security, Democracy, & Good Governance in Post-Military Rule Nigeria*, Volume One. Bloomington: AuthorHouse.

Mpofu, J and Chimhenga, S. (2016) 'Unemployment and Implications to Social and Political Conflict: Perspectives from Zimbabwe' in *Journal of Research & Method in Education*, Vol 6 (3), pp. 8-13.

Muchena, P. and Makotamo, J. (2017) 'Drug Misuse among High School candidates in Mutare Urban and Peri Manicaland Province' In *Zimbabwe, Journal of Research & Method in Education*, Vol 7 (3) pp. 63-72.

Musvipwa, R. (2015) 'Cheap, New ways of getting high' In Fair Planet, 10 December 2015 https://www.fairplanet.org/story/cheap-new-ways-of-getting-high/.

Mutiso, M.M. *et al* (2012) 'Factors contributing to drug abuse among the youth in Kenya: A Case of Bamburi Location' In *Elixir Soc. Sci* Vol 46, pp. 8259-8267.

Naqshbandi, M. M. (2012) 'Drug addiction and youth of Kashmir' *In International NGO Journal,* Vol. 7(5), pp. 84-90.

Nyabwari, B.G. and Kagema, D.N. (2014) 'The Impact of magic and witchcraft in the social, economic, political and spiritual life of African communities' In *International Journal of Humanities Social Sciences and Education (IJHSSE)* Vol 1(5).

Ncube, A. $70K 'Mbanje peddler jailed four years' In The Sunday News, 27 November 2016, http://www.sundaynews.co.zw/70k-mbanje-peddler-jailed-four-years/.

Neitzsche, F. (1907) *Beyond Good and Evil.* New York: Macmillan.

Newman. W.C. and Newman, E. (2010) *Domestic Violence: Causes and Cures and Anger Management,* Tacoma: Newman International LLC.

Newsday 6 April 2017, 'Two jailed 5 months for possession of Broncleer' https://www.Newsday.co.zw/2017/04/two-jailed-5-months-possession-Broncleer/.

Nobles, W.W. and Goddard, L. L. (1989) 'Drugs in the African-American community: A clear and present danger' In Dewart, J. *State of Black America – 1989.* New York: National Urban League.

Sunday, E.V. et al (2017) 'Implications of Friedrich Nietzsche's Master-Slave Morality in Inter-Personal Relationship' In *European Journal of Social Sciences,* Vol 55 (3) pp.262-274.

The Herald 30 May (2015), 'Bronco: Not what the doctor ordered' http://www.herald.co.zw/bronco-not-what-the-doctor-ordered/.

Tsiko, S. (2017) 'Mental illness and substance abuse, cause for concern' In The Chronicle, 20 April 2017, http://www.chronicle.co.zw/mental-illness-and-substance-abuse-cause-for-concern/.

UNDCP (1995), *The social impact of drug abuse, World Summit for Social Development.* Copenhagen, 6-12 March 1995.

Videbeck, S.L. (2010) *Psychiatric-mental Health Nursing*. Philadelphia*:* Lippincott Williams & Wilkins.

Vunganai, T. 'Drug abuse to blame for mental problems' In The Herald 21 January 2017 http://www.herald.co.zw/drug-abuse-to-blame-for-mental-health-problems/.

World Drug Report (2014) New York: United Nations.

United Nations, (2003) *Report on the World Social Situation 2003: Social Vulnerability, Sources and Challenges*. New York: United Nations.

Chapter 13

Democracy, Political Dynamics and (In-)security in the Global South: Hard Lessons for Africans

Misheck P. Chingozha & Munyaradzi Mawere

Introduction

This chapter seeks to explore the realism of democracy (particularly material and political democracy) in Africa, the threats of indoctrination imposed on the so-called less developed countries and the possibilities for growth and survival in the Emergent New World Order in which Africa has lost all its sovereignty, autonomy, ownership and control, possession and human essence. The chapter is meant to provoke efforts and stimulate creative discussions – whether out of agreement or disagreement – on the genuineness of democracy preached to Africa by the North. This provocation is necessitated by the fact that the majority of African States had to endure and grapple with wars of liberation that left many of their people maimed, dead or deprived and denied of their property. The wars were so protracted and pernicious but resilience and sacrifice forced the colonial robbers to the table. Ultimately, political independence was achieved and African states are now trying hard to reclaim their heritage – cultural, economic and political.

Democracy, in both the material and electoral senses, is what the Africans wanted to see prior to the bitter wars they fought, yet the colonial robbers were equally determined to repress, suppress and exploit the African people and their resources. This explains why Nelson Mandela was inspired to write the book *Long walk to freedom* published in 1994 for indeed it is such a long and tiring road to exonerate one-self from the bondage. Some African sons and daughters have, for instance, been brainwashed to the extent that they go to bed with (neo-)colonial robbers to satisfy their selfish ego. It has never been easy to unyoke Africa from the bondage of colonialism because the West is just determined to maintain the stranglehold. This can be equally confirmed by the fact that just before France conceded to African demands for political independence in the 1960s, it carefully orchestrated a plan to have its former colonies – the Communuate Financiere de l'Afrique (CFA countries) – in a system of compulsory solidarity. As Jabbar (2013) reminds us, this system obliged the 14 African states to put 65% of their foreign currency reserves into the French treasury plus another 20% in financial liabilities. What this means is that these 14 African states only have access to 15% of their own money. As if that is not enough, if these Francophone countries need more money, they have to borrow their own money from France at commercial rates. This has been the case since the 1960s (Siji Jabbar, Correspondent, The Herald, 2016). In view of this revelation, one wonders what democracy these people talk about when they themselves are perpetrators of such tilted practices. It also reminds Africans that the independence they desired was never to descend on a silver platter but called for a lot of patience, determination, resilience and sacrifice. The coming of independence was a result of enduring a lot of pain, torture, trauma and untold destruction of life and property.

At independence, Africa tried to reawaken its own democracy, going back to its roots. Unfortunately, Africa was hijacked in the process as the continent's unique democracy was never afforded any chance to exhibit itself to the world. The indigenous role of traditional institutions to resolve conflicts, foster peace, and promote equity and equality was never recognised. Africa's democracy thus, suffered abortion. It remained a stillbirth democracy that was never allowed to function naturally. It is out of this realisation that this chapter is born, with a view to interrogate the appropriateness of the North democracy which has been imposed on Africa as a 'perfect' universal template for global democracy. On the same note, the chapter, in view of the dynamics and politics associated with contemporary democracy, questions the place of and possibilities for rediscovering African democracy in global politics.

The cunnings of the Global North

The Global North has made sure that Africa remains on the hook. Sadly, as Africa tries to get away from the hook, the hook seems to be sinking even deeper into the belly of the continent. This has been necessitated by the cunning behaviour of the imperial countries of the North. Some decades after independence, France, for example, is said to have the first right to buy or reject any natural resources found in the land of the Francophone countries in the CFA zone (Jabbar 2013). This means that even if the African countries in the CFA zone can get better prices elsewhere, they cannot sell their resources to anybody until France says it doesn't need them. So is in the award of government contracts. See countries in the CFA zone in the map below:

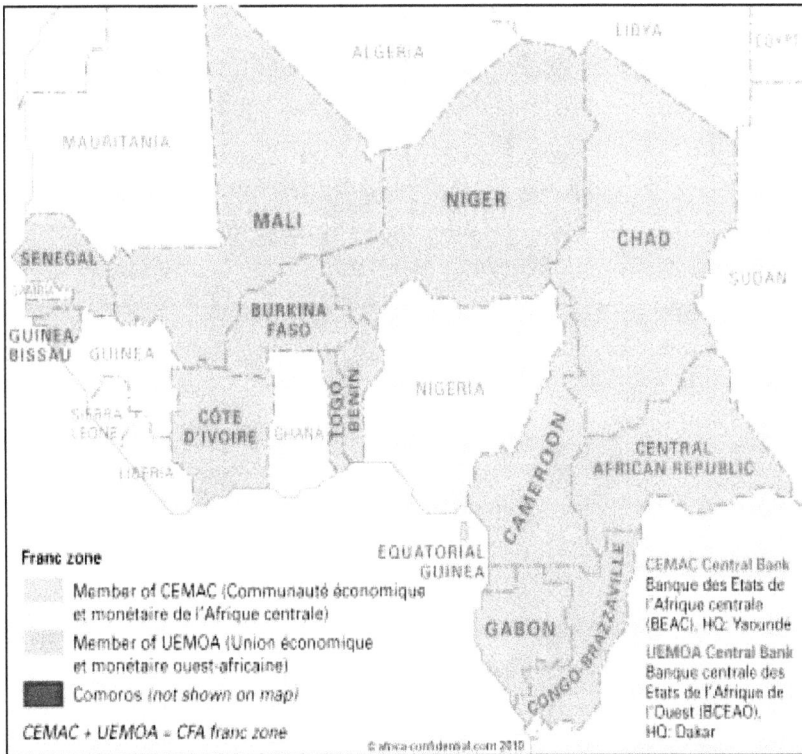

Map 1: CFA Zone countries
Source: https://thisafrica.me/author/sijijabbar.

As Jabbar further explicates, this also goes to confirm that if African countries can get better prices elsewhere, they cannot sell to anybody until France confirms that they are not interested. In the award of government contracts, it is actually said, the French companies must be considered first and only after that other companies will be considered. So the question is, when the Global North talks about democracy, which script will they be reading from, yet countries like America are watching but claim to be conscious about the plight of the vulnerable. If the truth be told, it can be said, that the African states are French taxpayers. Indeed, expressing the same feeling as Jabbar (Ibid), this is really sad and unfortunate for all Africans but more so for those in the CFA Zone.

One wonders if the African people across the continent have not always desired peace, harmony and prosperity! Sadly, that dream has remained elusive because the Euro-American block continues to interfere and meddle on the continent that has not been allowed to exercise its sovereignty and autonomy. Even more unfortunate is the fact that the love for peace by Africans has equally been misconstrued by some as docility. This is just surprising particularly when this comes from Africans who should be masters of their culture and politics. The desire for enduring peace has remained a pipe dream with the West and America maintaining heavy handedness as well as divide and rule in Africa. The West has made efforts since the partitioning of Africa in 1884 to ensure that they continue to wantonly reap the resources that Africa is endowed with. Talking of Britain, for example, Joseph Inikori's historic book, *Africans and the Industrial Revolution in England*, documents and clearly show how African consumers –free and enslaved – have over the years nurtured Britain's infant manufacturing industry. Worse still, it is on record that many dictators in Africa came to power through British covet action. Surprisingly, none of those in Britain who criticise African dictatorship and kleptocracy seem aware that Idi Amin came to power in Uganda through British covert action. On the same note, Nigeria's generals were supported and manipulated from 1960 onwards in support of Britain's oil interests (Drayton 2015). As alluded to above, the United States of America has also played big on the exploitation of Africa. Writing in view of the Congo, Ray (2000: 1) had this to say:

> Western multinational corporations' attempts to cash in on the wealth of Congo's resources have resulted in what many have called "Africa's first world war," claiming the lives of over 3 million people. The Democratic Republic of Congo (DRC) has been labelled "the richest patch of earth on the planet." The valuable abundance of minerals and resources in the DRC has made it the target of attacks from U.S.-supported neighbouring African countries Uganda and Rwanda. The DRC is mineral rich with millions of tons of diamonds, copper, cobalt, zinc, manganese, uranium, niobium, and tantalum also known as coltan. Coltan has become an increasingly valuable resource to American corporations. Coltan is used to make mobile phones, night vision goggles, fibre optics, and capacitators used to maintain the electrical charge in computer chips…The DRC holds 80% of the world's coltan reserves, more than 60% of the world's cobalt and is the world's largest supplier of high-grade copper. With these minerals playing a major part in maintaining US   military dominance and economic growth, minerals in the Congo are deemed vital US interests.

Ray (Ibid), further notes that:

> Historically, the U.S. government identified sources of materials in Third World countries, and then encouraged U.S. corporations to invest in and facilitate their production. Dating back to the mid-1960s, the U.S. government literally installed the dictatorship of Mobutu Sese Seko, which gave U.S. corporations access to the Congo's minerals for more than 30 years. However, over the years Mobutu began to limit access by Western corporations, and to control the distribution of resources. In 1998, U.S. military-trained leaders of Rwanda and Uganda invaded the mineral-rich areas of the Congo. The invaders installed illegal colonial-style governments which continue to receive millions of dollars in arms and military training from the United States.

We here add that the tragedy that befell Mugabe in November 2017 was a result of his lessons from the British, particularly on how to make the law serve a despotic private interest as well as how to govern without real popular consent. This attitude of the North has repeatedly threatened the security in Africa mainly in the false name of democracy, but some leaders in Africa have remained resolute, despite unrelenting international pressure and vilification. In fact, of late democracy has become the North's dangling carrot to catch the countries of Africa in the hook.

Democracy as a system of governance refers to the rule of a population by the whole population or the majority of its membership. This has been summarised in the widely accepted definition of Larry Diamond as a government of the people by the people and for the people. The power in this system of governance is vested in the people and to serve the people. This was the reason why the nationalists in Africa decided to take up arms and wage wars to dislodge the colonial robbers from the North. The liberation wars that the African nationalists fought were meant to untangle the vicious knot of oppression and exploitation so that sovereignty, harmony and peace are experienced by the indigenes who for very long had been subjects and objects of their colonial robbers, resulting in the expropriation of their heritage and resources such as land, which the former colonists (or their descendants) are still holding onto in the majority of African States. It is out of this realisation that the land redistribution, of course though with its own shortfalls, in Zimbabwe was executed. Sadly, it is land redistribution which actually made Zimbabwe, a former "darling" of the West after the concept of reconciliation of 1980, very unpopular in years that followed the year 2000 as the Fast Track Land Redistribution Programme takes its toll, dispossessing the "white" minority of the land.

However, like the Biblical story of Pharaoh who found it pretty hard to let go the children of Israel from Egypt where they were unkindly being treated, the West has never wanted to let go of Africans. This can be seen in numerous episodes in African history. Ken Flower, the Rhodesian Central Intelligence Chief, for instance, once acknowledged that it was necessary to operate a clandestine movement inside Mozambique as his forward intelligence eyes and ears against infiltration by Zimbabwean Nationalist Guerrillas (Utete 1979). It is clear that this would undoubtedly have the consequence of keeping the nationalists at bay and shatter all prospects for democracy including restoration of peace, law and order in Zimbabwe. Besides, this would be a gross divergence from ideal democracy and all its tenets.

Surprisingly, the gospel of democracy continues to be preached by the same people who manufactured (and continue to do) and instituted violence against others. One wonders if such is in fact what Western democracy entails! Is this what they mean by Western democracy, which they say Africa and the whole world should follow? If not the kind of democracy the imperial countries are preaching, why then is the case that these countries are known to always side with forces bent on perpetuating destabilisation in Africa in the name of democracy and rule of law. This attitude by the West and their friends in North America has repeatedly made it difficult for Africa to live in peace and showcase its own brand of democracy. Security in Africa has and continues to be threatened by the North's machinations which at times are so disguised as legitimate concerns, thereby hoodwinking the not so critical among the populace.

It does not seem like the North is ready to look at Africa as an equal partner in all life spheres including political, economic, cultural and social. That Africa is the second largest continent does not mean anything to the North who appear to suffer from the misapprehension that they are the superior race and would want to impose their biased and corrupted will on the Africans. It is every critical mind's question as to whether peace and security will ever be achieved in Africa with the glaring hatred of Africans exhibited at the highest and most influential institution such as the United Nation which in fact is controlled and used by the USA and other Western powers to advance their own agendas against Africa. In view of this backdrop, it remains clear that the future remains gloomy for Africa as long as no real action is taken to level the global political playground. America is actually working towards a situation in which it will be the ultimate ruler of the world. It is envisaging a one World Government, through the machinations of the UN which is pushing for global health, global economy, global politics, global civil service, global religion, global education, global law and so forth, all controlled by the US. A critical view at those efforts clearly indicate a skeweness against Africa as usual, and favouring the Euro-American block. This tramples upon the sovereignty, autonomy, human rights and potentials of the African people. This equally confirms that the UN is not a neutral player in this drama but advances the interests of the Americans and the Westerners. This can be seen from the deployments in Congo in 1961, when USA President J.F Kennedy tried to intervene directly in local politics and UN affairs (Melber 2011).

With such glaring attitude, the truth is there for all to see that the North still wants to re-colonise Africa so that they continue to loot and plunder their vast resources. Evidence of plunder is awash, in many African States. The Northern imperial countries have never been honest to Africa. The ascension to power of the Reagan Administration in 1981, for instance, actually legitimised direct African attacks and their presence in Southern Angola in the face of the UN Human Rights Charter of 1948 (https://en.wikipedia.org). This was hypocrisy at its highest confirming that the North cannot champion world peace since it does not have the legitimacy and democracy in their veins. The North pretends mightily which explains why America is said to have "permanent interests and not permanent friends". They have a record of interfering with the peace and security of sovereign States within Africa and even beyond. This is evidenced by the maps below which show military bases of the United States of America and France in Africa respectively:

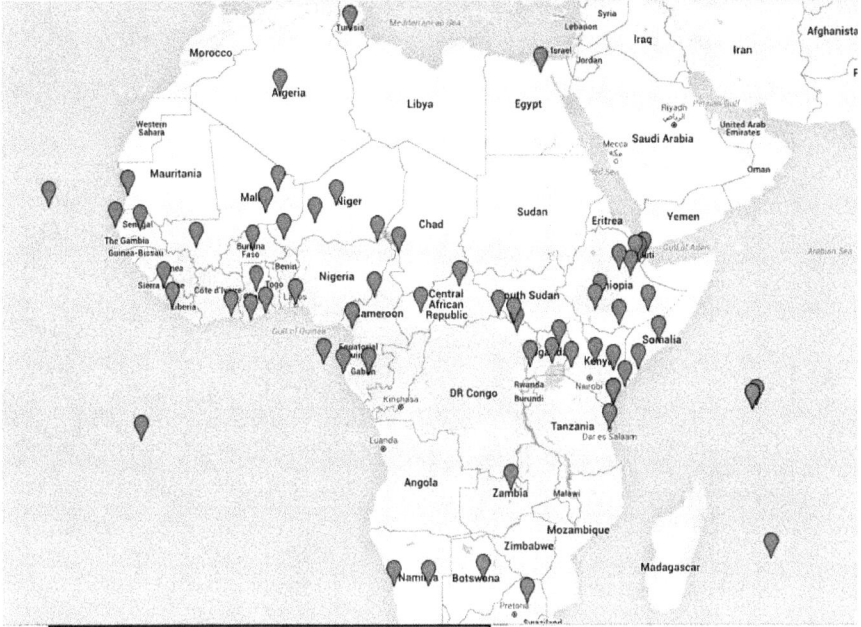

Map 2: US Military Bases in Africa
Source: africapublication.com

.

Map 3: France Military Bases in Africa
Source: africapublication.com

According to the Nigerian scholar, Toyin Falola, a professor of history at the University of Texas in Austin, USA, the United States of America has over 175 military bases **in** Africa (https://www.globalsecurity.org/military/facility/africom.htm). On the same note, France has over 3,000 troops spread across five countries in Africa — Mali, Mauritania, Burkina Faso, Niger and Chad — as part of Operation Burkhane. Based in Chad, the operation aims at disrupting potential militants threat across the Sahel region of the continent. The heavy military presence of the North in Africa leaves a lot to be said. This can be confirmed by the words of former UN Secretary General, Dag Hammerskjold, in 1960 when J. F. Kennedy was trying to put him under pressure in the Congo. He said "I do not intend to give away to any pressure be it from the East or the West: we shall sink or swim continue to follow the line you find in accordance with the UN Charter" (Melber, 2011: 5). In July 1985, the US Congress repealed the Clark amendment which had prohibited US aid to the Angolan rebels and UNITA immediately started receiving substantial financial and military assistance (www.netfind.com). Libya, through the UNSCR (1973), was mercilessly bombed by NATO, which only confirms the hypocrisy of West (https//en.m.wikipedia.org). The North thus, has a clear record of destabilizing destabilising the peace in the so-called developing world, which in itself is evil yet they continue to get away with it because of the military mighty they have. The developing world is in fact living at the mercy of the North. It is for this reason, among others that some critics argue that to bring democracy in Africa has never been a bed of roses. To this, Museveni (1992:118) avers:

> I feel pity for those Africans who do not see that sometimes to get over present day dilemmas, it may be necessary to live a life of self-denial in order to get to another stage of development.
>
> It, therefore, must be understood that the concept of democracy presupposes that it is about putting choices before an informed electorate.

The power dynamics in Africa have also caused a lot of uncertainties in Africa as can be seen in various conflicts across Africa. While Africa has been dealing with conflicts in varying approaches the position of the African Union and indeed the UN has been that, no coup is permissible. Following the military action in Zimbabwe in November 2017 the United Nations secretary General, Mr Antonio Gutervers, called for calm and preservation of human rights. (The Herald 17 November 2017). The military invention was defined as action far from being a coup though in reality it is a coup at its best, but indeed a "legitimised" coup. This comment actually come on heels of another comment by the SADC Organ on politics and defence and security Cooperation, which insisted on the setting of differences amicably. The whole World appears to have been interested and watching closely as Zimbabwe presented a unique discourse.

Why conflict has remained endemic in Africa?

Conflict is common everywhere in the world where people are habitat. However, with respect to Africa conflict has become endemic. Worse still, most of the conflicts in Africa have been disastrous as they are never resolved amicably. While in any conflict, the parties to the conflict are always reminded on the need to be calm, non-violent and to exercise restraint so that issues do not degenerate to levels that would persuade international forces to descend on the arena, this has never been the case in many countries in Africa. As such, most of Africa's conflicts are replete with misery and loss of lives. It is out of this realisation that the United Nations (UN) have always deployed peacekeepers in conflict zones to ensure that the generality of the people are not ultimately abused by the political players, or some criminal elements who may want to take advantage of the disturbances. The understanding has been that as much as differences may escalate, reason must prevail so that people do not end up engaging in heinous activities such as the 1994 genocide in Rwanda. In fact, the UN has always tried its best to ensure that leaders of conflicting groups and political parties must always engage their people to exercise restraint and avoid confrontational, strategies to addressing their problems. They have also ensured that the participation of a hidden hand, wherever there is one, must always be identified and screened so that the issues of concern or sticking points are deliberated on honestly by those who are directly affected by the issues. Sadly, the unexpected has always been the case, with rampant abuses, loss of lives, and wanton destruction of property witnessed in many conflict-torn countries in Africa such as Mozambique, Somalia and the DRC. This is abundantly the case because wherever there are resources the Global North does not easily let go their hold. This is why efforts since 1960 have failed to bring lasting peace and stability to the Congo (Democratic Republic of Congo, DRC). Talking of atrocities in the DRC, Montague and Berrigan (2001: 2) was apt to say:

> Nearly four million people dead in four years of war in the Democratic Republic of Congo (DRC), and the world remains silent in

the face of an abominable atrocity. The war in the DRC is not only significant because of its infamous status as the world's deadliest war; but also because of the active participation of an international contingent of multinational corporations, terrorist networks, arms brokers, and governments all clamouring for the legendary wealth of the Congo while exacerbating the war.

It should be reiterated that the major reason why conflicts in Africa have not been concluded easily enough relates to the aspect of resources that the North will be pursuing. As conflicts fail to be concluded, the North normally comes in as if they want to help addressing the challenges when in fact they would proceed to loot. The people become the ultimate victims as their resources are plundered in day light and lives of their beloved lost by day. In fact, "the locals are sacrificed on the altar of greed" (Melber 2011: 5). The sacrifice of the poor on the **altar of greed** has been so rampant in Africa as elsewhere in the Global South. This is the worst form of human rights abuse and disrespect of democracy that has to be guarded against by the international community at all costs. Every individual has a right to life, freedom and peaceful environment. A society devoid of this would find its members at pains to handle the hustles and calamities that descend on them with uncertainty and political discord. The people should be regarded first and foremost as individuals with rights and entitled to life before, they are viewed as political subjects. At whatever cost, the rights of individuals should never be trampled upon. Any such actions should be frowned at and dismissed with the contempt they deserve, especially when executed by the imperial powers that are historically known for abuse of their political power wherever there are benefits that would accrue to them. This can actually be inferred from the story around Dag Hammarskjold, who scholars say:

> even if his life would not have ended so untimely and tragically, Dag, Hammarskjold might not have been able to bring against all odds his mission to a successful end. Too much was at stake for the big powers and all of them had their vested particular interest guiding their own selfish agendas (Melber 2011: 6).

As has already been shown above, the imperial powers are known to play rugby politics over coated with ulterior motives about smaller States that might be endowed with resources of interest to these powers. This is further confirmed by the Secretary General of the United Nations, who before the UN Security Council on February 1961, characterised the Democratic Republic of Congo as a "happy 'hunting' ground for national interest" which required the UN's role as a 'roadblock' to such efforts (Ibid). While in view of the power dynamics that characterise conflicts in Africa the UN must present itself as an instrument for peaceful solutions to conflicts, more often than not, it (the UN) is seen to be supporting individual States such as Britain, France and the United States of America, among others who the chief funders of the UN. The 1973 UNSCR which granted NATO the power to bomb Libya is a case in point. This should never have been allowed to happen but the big powers were determined to exterminate this African leader. This was allowed by the UN to happen in spite of the standing Resolution 1514 of December 1960 popularly known as the 'Decolonisation Declaration', which clearly established that:

> [t]he subjection of peoples to alien subjugation, domination and exploitation constitutes a denial of fundamental human rights, is contrary to the Charter of the United Nations and is an impediment to the promotion of world peace and cooperation'; and that '[a]ll peoples have the right to self-determination; by virtue of that right they freely determine their political status and freely pursue their economic, social and cultural development' (United Nations 1960: 49).

The manner in which the Libyan leader was treated can be likened to how Dag, Hammarskjold was also treated in September, 1960, in which some powerful leaders such as those of the US demanded his resignation in which he responded:

> It is very easy to resign. It is not easy to stay on. It is very easy to bow to the wishes of a Big Power. It is another matter to resist. As is well known to all members of this Assembly, I have done so before on many occasions and in many directions. If it is the wish of those nations

who see in the Organisation their best protection in the present world, I shall now do so again (Melber 2011: 6-7).

What needs to be understood however is that those with nerves of steel are not so many. Not many have the audacity to stand in for the truth amid controversy consistent with Martin Luther King (jr) who once said 'the ultimate measure of a man is not when he is in comfort and convenience but when he is in controversy and challenges.' The vulnerable in varying communities thus look up to the United Nations for protection from the vagaries of insensitive big powers. However, the reality seems to be the opposite showing clearly the complexities associated with the African peoples' march towards freedom and national self-determination, especially against the backdrop that the Security Council is still dominated by the big five. "(USA, France, Russia, China, Britain). The manner in which Security Council operates also confirms the views of Malan (2011: 13) (in a letter to the Africans newspaper in Cape Town) in 1961 when this point was made abundantly clear:

> The selfishness that keenly accepts the work done by brown hands for your own comfort and/or enrichment, but does not grant the owner of those hands anything more than minimum privileges in life (for instance by the pay you regard as sufficient for his services)…The fact that we as whites think we have enough wisdom to regulate important   issues for non-whites without consulting them in any way, or by at most consoling them with a mere pretence of consultation (not even to mention proper representation in Government).

This remains true for many imperial countries whose people still feel being a superior race some more than half a century years after the Decolonisation Declaration Some "white" fellows hardly appreciate that all people in the world are equal before the law and should enjoy the same rights to life. A case in point is that of Januise Walus who killed Chris Hani of the now ruling African National Congress (ANC) who even after serving 20 years in jail has failed to show remorse for what he did. In an article published in *The Saturday Herald* of 18 November 2017, some decades after his heinous act,

Walus still showed no remorse for murdering the "black" nationalist, Chris Hani. He still rationalise his actions and insists that they were politically motivated. His ideas about communism still stand. Such examples are many. One wonders, for example, why there is the absence of a permanent representative in the Security Council of an African country yet it is the second largest Continent. This arrangement, as with many other racistic stories highlighted in this chapter, points at the tilt of power in favour of the North and lack of real democracy in global politics. The South remains subservient to the North and this does not appear like it will end soon (Saunders 2011), thus it can be argued that the rhetoric of democracy is still far from over.

In search of sustainable democracy for all

As Larry Diamond insists in his widely embraced conceptualisation, democracy should always be a government of the people by the people and for the people with at least the following four key elements: election (voting system), participation, respect of rule of law and upholding of human rights. This ideal understanding of democracy seems to be still far from being achieved at least in the North whose countries claim to be architects of democracy. This rot has extended to Africa. In Africa, democracy and the efficiency of running political affairs have equally been affected and influenced by individuals who would have captured the state, yet they are reactionaries and counter revolutionaries. This reverses the gains of the struggle that Africa fought in long years of suffering at the hands of the colonial monsters. Evidence of cruelty of the colonists throughout the South is abundant and the case of Charter in which people used to be slaughtered like sheep on the altar still stands today (The Sunday Mail, November, 19, 2017).

Yet, real democracy should neither be utopian nor selectively and blindly applied. There are always ideal democratic principles to be held by all global stakeholders for us to talk meaningfully of democracy, whether Western, African, Asian or American. These include but not limited to the following:

> ## Legitimate and voice
- Recognition of an individual's right to participate in decision making whether directly or via intermediaries that represents their interests or intentions.

> ## Direction
- The leadership and the public must share the same vision towards a desired/envisaged tomorrow.

> ## Performance
- The needs of the people must be met.
- Desired results must be achieved as a result of efficiency and effectiveness.

> ## Accountability
- All components of governance that is state, private sector, non-governmental sector must be accountable for all that they do, or say. In emphasizing this facet reference will be made to a statement made by Idi Amin, who once said "… freedom before speech I guarantee, but freedom after speech I cannot.' This confirms that citizens should be accountable for whatever actions are attributable to them.
- All citizens must never apportion blame for what they are accountable for.

> ## Fairness
- All citizens within a state ought to have the same opportunities. People should never be discriminated on the basis of colour, creed, religion or politics. This is actually consistent with section 9 of the constitution of Zimbabwe, which demands that all appointments ought to be on merit. When this is adopted all citizens will have the same opportunities.

The political dynamics in Africa, are just complex to the extent that some individuals devoid of ideological clarity, policy coherence can hijack the state system and programmes in pursuit of their selfish agenda. This is awash in Africa hence this call for progressive minds to remain on guard so that the ideals of the genuine leaders are not derailed by mischievous elements working as fronts of the West.

When democratic principles are not observed, democracy is interpreted as a long lie. Democracy ideally comes with free and fair elections or voting. However, these can be equally frowned at by political actors before, during and after the voting process as elections are often associated with vote rigging, intimidation and violence. Where democratic principles are respected peace will be observed. The manner Gbabgo of Cote D'Ivoire was treated by the army generals following the various allegations was just unfortunate. This is what democracy should avoid as constitutionalism carries the day. Armies should never be allowed to usurp power or interfere with civilian rule. This is because the role of the army should be to defend the nation when faced by external aggression (Sunday Mail, November 19, 2017).

Unfortunately, there are now so many cases in Africa of leaders who are motivated by the 'politics of eating' and would always try very hard to position themselves so that they line their pockets with corrupt money. This is actually shy of democratic principles and should never be tolerated in a truly democratic state. Governments in Africa as exposed by progressive citizens ought to be lean, clean, craft, competent and forward looking (The Herald Insight, November 29, 2017). Those that are corrupt within ranks and files of the government ought not only to be shown the exit but face the wrath of the law so that the electorate are led by a responsible team. The tendency of politicians to promote regionalism, nepotism, tribalism and indeed all other -isms should be abhorred. The economy should not be run on the basis of affection or familial relations. It is frowning at such ill malpractices that institutions will be in a position to attend to issues affecting their various communities.

The politics in Africa should as much as possible be influenced by the local needs and people as opposed to having those from outside defining how the affairs of the African State should be run. While this is noble, many of those from outside know pretty well that their involvement translate to their benefits in one way or another. This could actually explain why the hidden hand is always noted in virtually all conflicts in Africa. Not many seem to be guided by the principles of democracy that aptly recognize the autonomy and sovereignty of states. There is no state that ideally should be more equal than others. This however appears to be just in principles as the "Big Powers" of the North are on record for defining how Africans should deal with their affairs. The case of Libya is testimony to this. Any African leader who fails to abide by their ways is whipped into line.

At times the 'whipping into line game' is not so discrete while at times the North has outwardly shown it without any regrets. This could be seen in the sanctions against Zimbabwe, which up until now Euro-America deny and prefer to cosmetically define the sanctions as 'smart sanctions' or 'targeted sanctions' against Mugabe and a few around him and not the Zimbabwean government. The reality, however, is that the suffering of virtually all Zimbabweans as a result of the sanctions is visible even to the 'blind men'. The sanctions have so far caused untold suffering and deaths of many Zimbabweans, especially during the 2007/8 cholera outbreak. These deaths could have been avoided but the West who were fighting from the same corner with opposition political parties had really descended on the arena to squeeze the electorate through socio-economic suffering so that they would engage in an uprising. The leader of the Movement for Democratic Change, Mr Morgan Tsvangirai at one time was seen advocating for such punitive action.

During the 2007/8 socio-economic and political crises, the economy equally melted down, with one British official in a televised interview confirming that they really wanted the Zimbabwe economy 'to scream'. Indeed, it screamed and nearly grounded to a halt during the 2007/8 crisis. Inflation ballooned to the highest levels in living memory while unemployment swelled by day as many companies' closed shops. The participation of the West and the U.S in all this was so glaring, which seems to suggest that the Global North's definition of democracy is different from the Global South's definition of the same concept.

This attitude of the West has really affected security in Africa particularly Zimbabwe since 2000 when the former head of state of Zimbabwe, Comrade Mugabe led a campaign to repossess the farms previously owned by the colonial settlers to address the land imbalances perpetuated since the colonisation of Zimbabwe in 1890. This was never taken kindly by the former colonists (and their descendants), who viewed repossession of land by the Zimbabwean government as a violation of the commercial farmers' human rights. This remains the perception of the West and U.S on land repossession by the Zimbabwean government during the turn of the new millennium. The perception is in spite of the position of the current President of Zimbabwe, Comrade Mnangagwa as stressed in his inauguration speech appealing to the world to understand that the land reform was irreversible since it was the centre of the liberation struggle for independence by the indigenous Zimbabweans.

Democratic elections in Africa

The talk about democratic elections in Africa is so topical. Democratic elections are those that are declared by observer mission as free, fair and credible – and without spates of violence, intimidation and vote rigging. This has been viewed as very subjective by many political and social scientists. This is because there are times when observer missions within a certain state have come up with conflicting reports regarding the credibility of the elections.

The right to invite foreign observer mission rests with the country's plebiscite which means that there is no justification whatsoever for an observer mission to impose their will in a state that is not comfortable with their participation in the elections. It is on record that more often than not the European Union, Britain and America have always tried to impose themselves in Observer Missions in Africa especially in those countries where they have economic interests. This can be seen in the case of Zimbabwe (in its 2002 national elections) which was slapped with sanctions following the land redistribution programme of 2000. The idea in participating in such elections has always been to justify the continued sustenance of the sanctions because the elections would be described as unfair, marred with violence, spates of intimidation, vote rigging and therefore not credible.

The question that irks the minds of progressive citizens in the Global South is therefore: "Why the Global North should have the template that defines what amounts to fair, free and credible elections?" We argue in this chapter that such dominance of the West and the U.S should be challenged as undemocratic and oppressive because in a truly democratic environment people within the state should be given the space to decide on who should rule them and for how long. The misconception that the Americans' and Western way of doing things is the best way should be dismissed and thrown to the 20th century deep pool of African resistance. It is actually at times like this that Africa should stand with one unshaking and loud voice to denounce that attitude of the West that portrays America and the West as the pacesetters for the whole world to follow.

There are instances for example in Africa when the African Union, SADC, Caribbean and Pacific Countries have declared elections as credible yet the Western and American teams have gone on to discredit the same elections as long as their interests do not prevail. The West has been seen demonising African leaders whom the people would have voted into office. This is what confuses the critical minds because if people in Africa vote for their choices as suitable, one wonders what democracy is, and in whose eyes this democracy is defined, when the choice is disregarded by external forces such as the West.

Conclusion

This chapter has interrogated the concept of democracy and how it impacts on the security of states, especially those of the Global South. The evils of the emerged New World Order were also discussed. In this New World Order, the United Nations was presented as a front for the Euro-American world which takes every moment to advance the cause of the Global North. In view of this realisation, we have argued that the world should understand that no state is more important than the others. In a truly democratic world, all member states are implored to have respect and appreciation of one another without fear or favour. This would propagate unison, harmony, peace, and tranquillity which are the ideals that can surely make states scale to dizzy heights in all endeavours. All progressive citizens must be motivated by the need to be guided by the ethics that first and foremost, should characterise all positive thinking minds. The efforts of the Global North to regard Africa as second-class citizens therefore ought to be repelled and directed to the dustbin of oblivion.

References

Drayton, R. (20 August 2015) The wealth of the west was built on Africa's exploitation, T*he Guardian*, UK.

Jabbar, S. (24 Jan 2013) 'How France loots its former colonies', *Opinion-* African Identity. Available at: https://thisafrica.me/author/sijijabbar.

Malan, J. (2011) Foreword by the regular editor, *African Journal on Conflict Resolution, 11 (1): 11-14.*

Maphai, V. (Ed). (1994) *South Africa: The Challenge of change*, SAPES BOOKS, HARARE. Melber, H. 2011. Foreword by the guest editor, *African Journal on Conflict Resolution, 11 (1): 5-10.*

Montague, D. and Berrigan, F. (2001) The Business of War in the Democratic Republic of Congo: Who benefits? *Opinion*-Africa.

Museveni, Y. (1992) *What is Africa's problem?* NRM Publications, Kampala: Uganda.

Nhemachena, A. and Warikanda, T. V. (2017) *Mining Africa: Law, environment, society and politics in historical and multidisciplinary perspectives,* Langaa Publishers: Cameroon. Ray, E. (2000). U. S. 'Military and Corporate Recolonization of the Congo,' *Covert Action Quarterly,* USA.

Sachikonye, L. (Ed). (1995) *Democracy, Civil Society and the state: Social Movements in Southern Africa,* UNISA: South Africa.

SAPES BOOKS, HARARE Saunders, C. (2011) Hammarskjöld's visit to South Africa, *African Journal on Conflict Resolution, 11 (1): 15-34.*

Sichome, O. & Chikulo, B.C. (1996) *Democracy in Zambia: Challenges for the third Republic*, SAPES BOOKS, Harare.

UN General Assembly Resolution 1568 (XV) of 18 December 1960, quoted In: **Sellström, T.** (2011: 51) Hammarskjöld and apartheid South Africa: Mission unaccomplished, *African Journal on Conflict Resolution, 11 (1):* 35-64.

Utete, M. B. C. (1979) *The road to Zimbabwe: The Political Economy of settler Colonialism, National Liberation,* University Press, Washington DC.

The Saturday Herald November 18, 2017.

The Sunday Mail, November 19, 2017.

The Herald (21 November 2017)

The Herald Insight, November, 29, 2017.

https://zelalemkibref.files.

https://www.nesday.co.zw.

https://news.pindula.co.zw.

Chapter 14

The Role of Corporate Social Responsibility in Curbing Insecurity in Nigeria's Niger Delta Region

Chioma Elizabeth Abuba

Introduction

This chapter focuses on peace-building in Nigeria's oil rich but largely volatile Niger Delta region, through corporate social responsibility (CSR) initiatives by oil multinational companies (MNCs) in host communities. It seeks to investigate the contradictions inherent in CSR engagements in oil bearing communities and why there are still violent conflagrations in communities where oil MNCs have implemented some CSR programmes. Although the Niger Delta region has attracted a plethora of literature over the years, discourses on the role of CSR in curbing insecurity and promoting peace in region is only just emerging with more emphasis on micro-CSR measures which border on provision of physical infrastructure and a minimum level of social infrastructure such as schools and hospitals. The paper argues that CSR can only produce lasting results if the three major actors (oil MNCs, host communities and the state) cooperate to promote and sustain macro-CSR measures which address the issues of poverty, environmental sustainability, equitable distribution of resources and repressive regimes.

Nigeria has been on a long, tortuous journey to nation-building since its independence from Britain in October 1960. From military coups to different shades of dictatorships and a bitter thirty month civil war (1967-1970) which destroyed an estimated three million lives, the country has evidently survived but does not seem to have recovered. Insecurity, owing largely to unaddressed concerns for the needs of rural populations, has continued to shake the embers of the country's unity since the end of the war. Nigeria now has to contend with the Islamic terror group (the Boko Haram) in the north, secessionist clamours from the Indigenous People of Biafra (IPOB) in the east, the Niger Delta militants in the south, and a group of rampaging Fulani "herdsmen" who take pleasure in unleashing unimaginable terror on agricultural communities across the country. At no point since independence, has Nigeria been gripped by commotions on all front, as it is today. With oil accounting for over 98 percent of its total export earnings, 60 percent of gross government receipts and 37 percent of the Gross Domestic Product (GDP), the country is no more than a mono-mineral economy, a *rentier* state, dependent almost entirely on the vagaries of international oil prices.

The implication is that for the economy to remain viable, the government would have to secure the oil industry from possible threats which means putting down any action or reaction considered threatening to the continuous flow of oil from the Niger Delta Region. This phenomenon, in many cases, contradicts the needs and aspirations of the people of the area who live daily with the deleterious effects of oil exploration with minimal government intervention and little or no corporate social responsibility (CSR) programmes from multinational companies (MNCs) operating in their communities. As a result, the once pristine environment, rich in oil palm, mangrove forests, labyrinths of streams that empty into the Atlantic and limited arable lands for agriculture, has been rendered unconducive for human and aquatic existence and turned into a hotbed for militancy and violent clashes between local armed groups and government forces. This is what is referred to by observers, the media and writers as "the Niger Delta question."

Successive governments have deployed different approaches to curb local resistance in the Niger Delta, beginning with the Isaac Adaka Boro Revolt of 1966. These approaches have ranged from sweeping military invasions of resisting communities, to extrajudicial murders and even hanging of environmental rights activists, as the case of Ken Saro Wiwa and the Ogoni show. Brutal as they were, these measures did little to stop armed confrontations in the region. As military "pacification" failed, government resorted to financial compensation and some level of infrastructural development of the region. The result was the establishment of a number of interventionist platforms or what some writers have called "development bureaucracies" which have collectively proved ineffective in alleviating the suffering of the people and restoring peace and security to the area.

The multifaceted nature of the Niger Delta conflict has expectedly attracted a plethora of literature from scholars of diverse academic fields over the years. However, only a handful of these discourses focus specifically on the role of CSR in curbing insecurity in the Niger Delta Region. Among those which do, there appears to be a tendency to concentrate more on micro-CSR issues such as the building of schools, roads, hospitals, provision of water and electrification projects in host communities, among others. While these measures are vital as they cater for the immediate needs of the rural population, evidence is abound that they provide only temporary satisfaction among the host communities and have not served to end but perpetuate hostilities in the region. Broader CSR issues which border on corruption, equitable distribution of oil revenue and environmental sustainability are generally sidelined.

This study has been undertaken to investigate the failure of CSR to provide the much needed development, peace and security in the Niger Delta and to promote macro-CSR initiatives in oil bearing communities as a recipe for peace, security and sustainable development of the region. The aim is to develop a sustainable strategy for companies, the government and the people to tackle the resurgence of armed confrontations and other forms of conflict in oil producing communities. As Naanen and Tolani (2014: 15) aptly note, "there is need for a new sustainable development paradigm in the face of heightened insecurity and persistent poverty in the Niger Delta. Current government-centred approach through the creation of development bureaucracies such as the Niger Delta Development Commission (NDDC) has demonstrated conspicuous limitations."

According to Hindle (2008: 3), "CSR embodies basically four dimensions, namely, giving back to society, ethical business practices, commitment to environmental sustainability and ability to promote employee satisfaction." My focus in this chapter is on the first three dimensions. I argue that giving back to society entails far more than temporarily alleviating rural poverty through micro-CSR measures. It demands a broader perspective which involves a macro-CSR approach vital to investigating cases of bribery and corruption, persistent poverty, environmental degradation and human rights abuse.

Corporate Social Responsibility (CSR) and the Development of the Niger Delta: Definitions and Perceptions

Hennigfeld, Pohl and Tolhurst (2007: xxix) define corporate social responsibility as "undertaking business in an ethical way in order to achieve sustainable development, not only in economic terms but also in the social and environmental sphere." For Mead and Andrews (2009: 492), it refers to "strategies that sustain natural resources and the environment for the good of all in society." These definitions highlight an important element in corporate governance, which is the idea of sustainability – whether of local economies, peaceful working environment or the overall social capital of a company. Whether or not these will be achieved and how that will happen, depends largely on the perception of CSR by MNOCs and the content of the initiative when applied.

Corporate social responsibility is the major vanguard for corporate-community relations and a veritable element for peace-building and sustainable development in the Niger Delta Region as elsewhere where multinational companies genuinely operate. A sad reality, however, is that this vital concept has been consistently misinterpreted and sometimes disregarded especially by multinational oil companies (MNOCs) and the Nigerian government, over the years. During my oral interview sessions for this work, one of respondents, Chief Mgbigbi Osila Echu of Okerewa Community categorically stated that "when the Indorama-Eleme Petrochemicals Limited (IEPL) came, we watched them for a while and when we saw that they were ready to carry our people along, we decided to give them our support" (Oral interview with Chief Mgbigbi Osila Echu, Eleme community, Rivers State, Nigeria).

The concern highlighted by the chief clearly reveals the perceptions of the people of the Niger Delta about CSR and their expectations from MNOCs. It shows the condition on which the people's cooperation depends. 'Carrying the people along' as chief

Echu demanded entails much more than providing some level of physical and social infrastructure in communities that have been neglected by the leaders for several decades. It demands conscious efforts to investigate and address the factors fuelling rural poverty and continued conflict in these communities. As Idemudia (2010: 178) note: The categories used by community members in the Niger Delta to interpret and understand their relationship with oil MNCs are largely based on cultural values and traditional forms of relationships. Hence, oil MNCs are seen as members of host communities and should, like every other member of the community, instinctively take into consideration community concerns and treat them as priority. In contrast, the worldview of oil MNCs is shaped by a pure market logic driven in most cases, by profitability and the assumption that their role as corporate citizens is limited to the payment of taxes and that it is the responsibility of the government to ensure equitable distribution of oil wealth among the people.

In many instances, the perennial conflict in the Niger Delta stems from this difference in perception of CSR and the roles and responsibilities of the actors in the conflict. The Niger Delta conflict has taken a multidimensional nature and CSR has become part of a collective, multi-actor effort to create a more peaceful world for businesses and local populations, especially in emerging economies like Nigeria. Although the Niger Delta Region has attracted enormous CSR efforts from oil MNCs since the late 1990s, evidence on ground shows that the efforts made so far have not translated to visible improvement in the wellbeing of the people. Neither have they solved the conflict that has haunted the region for more than half a century. Increase in armed resistance and internal rivalry in the area thus call for a reconsideration of the methods of engagement with local communities deployed so far. Findings have shown that the problem is not necessarily a lack of CSR programmes in oil-bearing communities. Rather, conflict is triggered by the differences in perception of CSR by MNOCs and their host communities. This difference affects the content and structure of CSR engagements and most often translates to disappointment among community members, a feeling which easily translates to conflict between the parties.

CSR: Philanthropy or Corporate Responsibility?

Generally, CSR is viewed as philanthropy, volunteerism or social investment by MNOCs, the government and even scholars. This perception informs the nature of CSR engagement employed and the long run effect of such engagements in host communities. Interpreting CSR as a voluntary exercise grossly limits its scope and creates a huge gap between the people's expectations and the responses from MNOCs. One of the realities of global business which many MNOCs are trying hard to come to terms with, is that in most developing nations, oil companies have come to be seen as surrogate for the state. Writing about the role of multinational companies in development in Africa, Ghazvinian (2007: 31) notes and rightly too, that "in a region that political leaders had neglected and exploited for decades, locals understand well that the white men with the drills were their last, best hope for the development they had expected the oil wealth to bring."

It is crucial to note that CSR is not philanthropy. It is a binding responsibility and an integral culture of any responsible firm. CSR is not merely a voluntary support for host communities. It is a broad range programme which should form an indispensable part of the social capital of any company. Best practice CSR encapsulates three broad strategies. The first is to approach community development as a cross sector partnership with government, civil society and labour unions rather than philanthropy which only creates dependence and is open to corruption. The second strategy is to invest in improving governance and the third is to engage actively with social entrepreneurs and to support them financially.

Approaching community development as a cross sector partnership undoubtedly creates avenues for dialogue between the people, government and firms involved. It makes CSR a collective duty rather than complementary or voluntary support. No adequate CSR effort can be sustained when the scheme is viewed as mere philanthropy. According to Obi (2005: 81): Many of us have heard the saying, "the business of business is business," often used by managers of big business concerns to simplify the complexity of business management. This old model where the corporate managers

348

developed their plans solely on the basis of economic good, made the necessary arrangements with government and proceeded to implement, no longer works in civilized societies. In addition to creating wealth and jobs, corporations are now expected also to improve the living and social standards of the communities in which they live and work, and to protect the environment that provides the raw materials. Thus, corporations are compelled to accept societal realities, to expand their sphere of activity and their scope of responsibility. The distinct boundaries of the past are being destroyed as a result of growing awareness of interdependencies.

Sadly, however, there is yet no binding rule or constitutional framework for CSR practices in Nigeria. Companies are left to operate based on their own initiatives though sometimes, in concert with local communities. This situation does not encourage civic commitment on the part of MNOCs because the companies are not bound by any legal obligation to develop their operational areas. Although communities now insist on memorandum of understanding (MoU) as standard operating guideline for MNOCs but this also, has not yielded the expected result of peace and sustainable development in the region. It is crucial to note that CSR is now obligatory. It is unavoidable. Companies are not supposed to be compelled by law to carry out development projects in local communities which bear the direct consequences of their business activities. CSR is indispensable and should be a rule, not an exception.

MNOCs and Government-Centred Approaches to CRS Initiatives in the Niger Delta

Over the years, successive governments have taken steps to provide what they consider appropriate intervention for the protection of the Niger Delta environment and the development of the area. The first attempt came in 1961 with the creation of the Niger Delta Development Board (NDBD) by the Nnamdi Azikiwe and Abubakar Tafawa Balewa-led first indigenous government in Nigeria. The purpose was to tackle the developmental problems of the depressed areas of the Niger Delta Region. Charged with the duty of advising the Federal, Eastern and Mid-Western States governments with respect to the physical development of the Niger Delta, the major achievements of the NDBD was the clearing of seven creeks totalling about 171 kilometres between 1965 and 1966 and providing information for subsequent government interventions in the area (Aghalino 2009). The NDBD was hampered by bureaucratic bottlenecks and the Nigerian Civil War and thus could not achieve more than merely laying the foundation of future development boards. The Board was replaced with the Niger Delta Basin Development Authority (NDBDA) following the enactment of Decree No. 37 of 1976 by General Olusegun Obasanjo. The Decree established the NDBDA along with other River Basin Authorities in the country. The NDBDA was charged with developing agriculture in the Niger Delta, undertaking schemes for the development of land and water resources as well as improving the navigation of inland waterways to control flood and erosion.

Like its predecessor, the NDBDA accomplished very little in the end. Most of its plans remained on paper, crippled by poor funding from the government and gross mismanagement of the available funds. In 1981, the government approved the 1.5 percent Fund for the development of the Niger Delta. The disbursement of the Fund remained at the level of rhetoric until 1984 when the Allocation of Revenue Amendment Decree No. 36 was promulgated to ensure the disbursement of the Fund. This effort, too, was crippled by bureaucratic constraints and politicization of the Presidential Committee set up to administer the Fund. Government's response to the ineptitude of the Committee was the establishment, in 1992, of another such apparatus, this time called the Oil Minerals Producing Areas Development Commission (OMPADEC). According to Aghalino (2009: 181), "the Decree No. 23 of July 19, 1992 which established the OMPADEC raised the limit of the derivation fund to 3 percent of the Federation Account and outlined seven objectives for the Commission including to determine and identify, through the Commission and the respective oil mineral producing states, the actual oil producing areas and embark on the development of projects properly agreed upon with the local communities."

Four years after these fine pronouncements, OMPADEC collapsed; its Board was dissolved and the Commission went moribund, leaving a trail of unfinished projects littered in various communities of the Delta and several questions begging for answers. Reports indicate massive corruption, inequitable distribution of oil revenue and bureaucratic bottleneck as part of the reasons for the failure of the Commission (Aghalino 2009). Six years later, President Olusegun Obasanjo created yet another Commission apparently to continue from where OMPADEC left off. This time, it was called the Niger Delta Development Commission (NDDC), followed by the Ministry for Niger Delta Affairs established in 2009 by President Shehu Musa Yar'Adua.

Beginning from the 1990s, oil MNCs, following the fallout of the Ogoni Agitation, the indictment of Shell by the United Nations Environmental Project (UNEP) and the international outcry against gross abuse of human rights in the Niger Delta, were forced to start nibbling at CSR activities in some areas of the Delta. Chevron Nigeria Limited took the lead by adopting the Global Memorandum of Understanding (GMoU) in 2005 to cater for aspects of community development in its operational areas. The Shell Petroleum Development Company (SPDC) adopted the GMoU strategy for community engagement in 2006. According to Weli (2017: 4), "by 2016 Shell has remitted $29.8 billion to the federation account and another $1.2 billion to the NDDC." The NDDC records show also that Shell's Joint Venture made a total contribution to the Commission of about 166.5 million dollars between 2001 and 2005. The firm's community development spending averaged about 39 million dollars per annum between 2002 and 2006 (Naanen and Tolani 2014).

Similarly, Chevron's public records reveal that the company has spent more than $100 million on roughly 600 programmes that have provided scholarships, built new schools, medical facilities and housing; and supported agriculture development and infrastructure improvement in its host communities (*The Sun News*, 15 August 2017). Despite the widespread adoption of CSR in the Nigerian oil industry, violence in the region has increased both in intensity and in scale and oil MNCs continue to be held responsible for a range of infractions by local communities. This situation suggests that there are gaps in the quality of CSR initiatives aimed at changing the hostile attitude of local communities towards oil companies in the Niger Delta (Idemudia 2010).

For instance, the period between 1997 and 2006 were among the most turbulent in areas covered by Shell and Chevron in the Niger Delta, despite the volume of CSR interventions by the companies. Armed confrontations and militarization of the region increased by the day, as new militant groups continued to emerge. Rather than dissipate, the conflict took on a multi-dimensional nature, leaving writers and observers with the following questions: Why has the Niger conflict lingered? What factors fuel local discontent in oil bearing communities? What essentially is lacking in government's provisions to the people? Why has CSR not provided the much needed peace in the region?

Macro-CSR and Security in the Niger Delta: Challenges and Prospects

Macro-CSR includes the conscious involvement of the private sector in solving the social problems of members of host communities in order to create enabling environment for corporate-community engagement, peace and sustainable development in their operational areas. It means extending the frontiers of a company's social capital to include responsibilities that stretch beyond providing physical and social infrastructures, to addressing issues of corruption, equitable distribution of natural resources, weak government structures and repressive regimes. It is the solution to the top-down approach which characterizes government's relations with the people of the Niger Delta. A major source of conflict in the region is the gap in communication between the people and the government. MNOCs have generally followed government's pattern of deciding for, and not with the people in terms of development initiatives in local communities. This is because in many instances, the companies embark on development projects which do not address the crucial needs of the people but appear "appropriate" in the circumstance (Nzeadibe and Ajaero, 2015). More than any single factor, therefore, macro-CSR will help to bridge the existing gap in communication between MNOCs and their host communities through constant dialogue and concerted efforts to assess community perceptions through regular corporate-community workshops and research on community expectations.

More importantly, MNOCs are expected to expand the limits of their corporate investment in host communities and play far greater roles than just doing business. Macro-CSR provides the platform to address these challenges. In a country such as Nigeria with a mono-mineral economy, volatile political climate and an uneven socio-economic and political structure, the government is not often in touch with the people, especially those from the "minority" ethnic groups where incidentally, oil is located. The Niger Delta is a case in point. Although there have been visible efforts by government to provide some relief measures in the area as shown above, the efforts have yielded very little direct benefit to the people. As Ifidon (2013: 41) notes, "owing to the deterioration of physical infrastructure, incapacity to respond to new needs occasioned by demographic changes and pervasive insecurity among others, the promise of oil-driven industrialization and social stability in Nigeria has failed." In the face of biting poverty and intractable conflict especially in oil-bearing communities of the Niger Delta, private enterprises have a potentially vital role to play in supporting human-centred development as well as creating economic wealth, livelihood opportunities and support for social development activities needed to meet basic human needs (Nelson 2009).

More increasingly, therefore, MNOCs are expected to improve their CSR engagements in local communities and go beyond providing micro-CSR investments, to addressing issues of corruption, inequitable distribution of resources, weak political structures and abuse of human rights and privileges. CSR thus becomes an all-embracing approach to end rural poverty not only by providing educational facilities and infrastructure, but also looking into underlying causes of rural poverty which in most cases border on corruption among community representatives and their state and federal counterparts.

A major limitation of macro-CSR in Nigeria is lack of enabling environment for companies to undertake such programmes, due mainly to the inability of government to set minimum standards that oil companies are expected to conform to (Idemudia 2010). This raises the questions of legal frameworks for macro-CSR engagements and scope of operations. But as Jane Nelson notes, companies can develop mutually beneficial and transparent partnerships with other companies, civil society organizations and government bodies to address sensitive political and public policy issues especially those that affect local communities where they carry out their operations (Nelson 2009). One way this can be achieved is through collective action. Companies can act in concert with other companies and civil society organizations to advocate for transparency, equitable distribution of resources and environmental sustainability, among others. According to Nelson (2009: 38), "collective action can address activities such as advocacy for good governance and anti-corruption measures, negotiating peace and developing voluntary codes of corporate conduct." Bennette (2002: 410) affirms that "multinational corporations can actively engage in combating corruption in their areas of operation through dialogue with stakeholders and the people, demand for equitable distribution of company remittances and investigation of cases of mismanagement of local funds."

Finally, macro-CSR approach naturally engenders mutual cooperation between MNOCs and host communities. It brings the parties closer and creates the much needed peaceful atmosphere through cross-sector dialogue and broad-based communication. When a company goes beyond providing physical infrastructure in local communities and makes genuine effort to investigate the reasons for persistent poverty in such areas, such company is regarded as part of the community and accorded the full rights and liberties of corporate citizenship by the people. A good case is the Indorama Group and their host communities in Eleme, a sprawling oil-bearing town, seven kilometres from Port Harcourt, the Rivers State capital, Nigeria. The Indorama Group took over the defunct Eleme Petrochemicals Company Limited (EPCL) in August 2006 following the privatisation of the later. It did not take time before the new management realized that it had inherited a failed company in the heart of the Niger Delta with high expectations from the people in the midst of insecurity in the region.

The advent of Indorama in 2006 coincided with the period of heightened insecurity in the Niger Delta, following the incessant kidnap of foreign oil workers and attacks on oil facilities by militants. Indorama was not spared. In May 2007, twelve expatriates working for the company were kidnapped by militants in Port Harcourt. According to Chigbue (2008: 5), "it was a big blow to the company. Insecurity in the area was so pervasive that the company reportedly shut down its plants for some months." This situation did not discourage the new company. Rather, the Group started off by undertaking CSR programmes, targeting critical aspects of local livelihoods such as electricity, water, roads, schools and hospitals. Its first step was to identify and effectively undertake appropriate community development programmes in the area as part of its corporate social responsibility to the people. Using dialogue as a major tool, the company was able to secure the people's trust, a factor which availed it the tranquil working environment and set the stage for mutual cooperation between the parties. The company's Managing Director, Mr. Manish Mundra, affirmed that "indeed, we enjoy tremendous support and cooperation from our host communities and they form the first layer of our security system and peaceful operations." (*Indorama-Nigeria Impact*, 8 October 2015).

Beyond these micro-CSR activities, Indorama decided, in 2012, to integrate its host communities into the company by making them shareholders. Consequently, the company offered 7.5% of its 75% shares to members of host communities. The outcome has been tremendous. According to Achaziem (2012: 10), "by this acquisition of the shares the communities have become co-owners of the company and will earn dividends accruable from the shares yearly." More than any factor, the integration of the people of Eleme in Indorama has drastically improved security in the area, with tremendous improvement in the overall wellbeing of the people. This example justifies the view of Naanen and Tolani (2014: 167) that "communities should be made to have a sense of genuine stake-holding before they can be expected to protect oil facilities and promote the wellbeing of multinational companies operating in their areas."

Conclusion

Macro-CSR initiatives are veritable keys to peace and development in the Niger Delta. The longstanding conflict between companies operating in the Niger Delta and the people is not intractable. The road to peace, though not completely smooth, is largely embedded in improved and sustained CSR programmes in host communities. CSR programmes are an intrinsic part of a wholesome business environment especially the type prevalent in the oil industry with heavy machinery and sometimes unavoidable incidences of pollution. It therefore follows that such industries should necessarily be concerned about the wellbeing of the communities where they operate. CSR measures are undoubtedly expensive but they benefit the companies immensely, in the long run. As the example of Indorama and its host communities in Eleme shows, companies that exhibit this ethical behaviour benefit more; their facilities are largely safe from being tampered; they enjoy cordial relations with their staff and host communities and with these, a tranquil working environment. Incidences of kidnap or harassment of their personnel are reduced, if not forestalled. The companies also benefit from the skills and manpower of members of local communities who are often quite willing to offer their services or trained on the job, when encouraged.

Although this may be costly in terms of the financial requirement needed to offset CSR programmes, it makes financial sense because a company that is known to behave in this way often wins the goodwill of the people, and its bottom line profitability (Obi 2005). Macro-CSR is a recipe for the long sort sustainable development in the region and a pointer to the fact that in many instances, the violent conflagrations which had marred company-community relations were in the main, a result of unaddressed concerns in terms of the effects of oil production activities on the lives and livelihoods of the people and not necessarily because the people are prone to violence. What it connotes is that the Niger Delta debacle is indeed solvable.

What is required, however, is government's unalloyed support for CSR engagements in the form of providing concrete rules of engagement that meet international standards. It is also important to emphasize that the attitude of deciding for and not with the people in terms of making or implementing policies deemed relevant for the development of the Niger Delta should be changed completely. Dialogue, broad-based consultation and transparency are the basic elements that promote peace and sustainable development in the region. Militarizing the Niger Delta with the intention to spread fear and perhaps coerce the people to submission has obviously not yielded any positive benefits for the government. What such measures have done so far, is to create deep-rooted disdain for the state and inadvertently providing excuses for economic sabotage by angry youths of affected communities.

References

Aghalino, S.O. (2009) *Crude Oil Business in the Western Niger Delta, Nigeria: 1956 – 1995*, Enugu: Rhyce Kerex Publishers.

Aghalino, S.O. (2014) *Delta beyond Oil: A Quest for Sustainable Development.* Vol.1, Benin City, Mindex Publishing Company Ltd.

Aghalino, S.O. (2014) *Delta beyond Oil: A Quest for Sustainable Development.* Vol.2, Benin City, Mindex Publishing Company Ltd.

Aghalino, S.O. (ed.) (2014) *Delta beyond Oil: A Quest for Sustainable Development*, Benin: Mindex Publishing Co. Ltd.

Bennett, J. (2002) "Multinational corporations, social responsibility and conflict", *Journal of International Affairs*. 55, 2.

Chigbue, I. (2008) "Eleme petrochemicals: privatization's success story," *Indorama-Nigeria Impact*.

Ghazvinian, J. (2007) *Untapped: The Scramble for Africa's Oil*, Orlando: Harcourt Inc.

Hindle, Tim. (2008) *Guide to Management Ideas and Gurus*, London: The Economist.

Hennigfeld, J., Pohl, M., and Tolhurst, N. (2007) *Handbook on Corporate Social Responsibility.*

New York: Wiley.

Idemudia, U. "Corporate social responsibility and the Niger Delta conflict: issues and prospects," in Obi, C. and Rustad, A.S. (eds.) (2010) *Oil and Insurgency in the Niger Delta: Managing the Complex Politics of Petro Violence*, Sweden: Zed Books Ltd.

Ifeanyi, M.O. (2006) *Politics of Development and Underdevelopment*, Onitsha, Austino Press.

Ifidon, A.E. "Delta state beyond oil: anatomy, complexities and possibilities," in Aghalino, S.O. (ed.) (2014) *Delta beyond Oil: A Quest for Sustainable Development*, Vol.2, Benin City: Mindex Publishing Company Ltd.

Iroegbu, E. (2008) "Development initiatives for Eleme communities," *Indorama-Nigeria Impact*.

Kin, C. and Mauborgne R. (2005) *Blue Ocean Strategy: How to Create Uncontested Market Space and Make the Competition Irrelevant*, Boston, Harvard Business School Press.

Maier, K. (2000) *This House has Fallen: Nigeria in Crisis,* London: Penguin Books.

Mead, R. and Andrews, T. (2009) *International Management*, London: John Wiley and Sons.

Naanen, B. and Tolani, P. (2014) *Private Gain, Public Disaster, Social Context of Illegal Bunkering and Artisanal Refining in the Niger Delta*, Port Harcourt: Niger Delta Environment and Relief Fund (NIDEREF).

Nelson, J. (2000) *The Business of Peace: The Private Sector as Partner in Conflict Prevention and Resolution*, London: International Alert.

Nkwocha, J. (2015) "Indorama's 7.5% Shares Promotes Peace and Security in the State," *Indorama-Nigeria Impact*.

Nzeadibe, T.C., Ajaero, C.K., and Nwoke, M.B. (2015) "Rethinking corporate-community engagement in the petro-economy of the Niger Delta," *Singapore Journal of Tropical Geography* 36(3).

Obi, C. and Rustad, A.S. (eds) (2010) *Oil and Insurgency in the Niger Delta: Managing the Complex Politics of Petro Violence,* Sweden: Zed Books.

Obi, E. "Environmental justice and the quest for equitable and sustainable economic world order: reassessing the engagement of multinational corporations in the south-south of Nigeria," in

Wangbu, J. (ed.) (2005) *Niger Delta: Rich Region, Poor People.* Enugu: Snaap Press.

Ogbogbo, C. B. N. "Economic development in Delta State: moving beyond the frontiers of oil and gas," in Aghalino, S.O. (ed.) (2014) *Delta beyond Oil.* Vol.2, Benin City: Mindex Publishing Co. Ltd.

Ojakorotu, V. (ed.) (2009) *Contending Issues in the Niger Delta Crisis of Nigeria,* Florida: JAPSS Press Inc.

Oyovbaire S. (ed.) (2008) *Governance and Politics in Nigeria: The IBB and OBJ* Years, Ibadan: Spectrum Books Ltd.

Tamuno, T.N. (2011) *Oil Wars in the Niger Delta: 1849-2009,* Ibadan: Stirling-Horden Publishers.

Wangbu, J. (ed.) (2005) *Niger Delta: Rich Region, Poor People,* Enugu: Snaap Press.

Weli, I. (2017) "Shell pays $31 billion to federation account, NDDC," *The Sun News.*

Chapter 15

Should the West Keep on Playing God? Genetic Engineering, Bio-technological Insecurities and their Implications for Africa

Tapuwa Raymond Mubaya

Introduction

While it is generally acknowledged that the entire world has unequivocally and unanimously embraced technology in all its diversities as the developmental compass influencing and directing both the pace and the direction of people's lives on earth, very few people if any, have seriously and soberly thought about the perceived bio-technological insecurities and their implications for Africa. It is worth noting that the Global North has since the beginning of the so-called "New World Order," emerged as the leading pacesetter of scientific discoveries and bio-technological innovations. Unequivocally, it is evident that science and technology have made remarkable and tremendous progress particularly in the field of bio-technology (Amanze, 2005). Cognisant of the asymmetrical movement of knowledge which is always expected to flow from the North to the South, these scientifically propelled bio-technological inventions are generally expected to be embraced and adopted by especially developing economies such as those of Africa.

Evidently, the Global North is on record as being one of the privileged races to develop the technological ability to explore other habitable planets such as Mars and Venus. Nonetheless, such unparalleled achievements and breakthroughs are obviously remarkable and worth noting. Yet, in spite of these ever-increasing scientific machinations and advances, one wonders whether these celebrated technological innovations are genuine solutions to the current political and socio-economic ills confronting humanity or have hidden sinister ulterior motives which can only be noticed when the seemingly remarkable achievements are subjected to meticulous analysis and rational interrogation.

Suffice it to say that, for many unsuspecting people including scholars, a superficial glance at these highly celebrated scientific achievements would not reveal the negatives concealed and embedded in them. Rather, it is the positives and advantages of these bio-technological breakthroughs that more often than not, are cited as the basis for their pursuance. Notably, some of the bio-technological innovations, such as human cloning, besides raising a kernel of sceptical questions also ignite a host of spiritual controversies and quandaries of epic proportions across the globe. Resultantly, these bio-technological issues have spawned public discussion and heated ongoing debates. In fact, the advent of human cloning on the global scene has aroused as much controversy and debate in the twentieth and twenty-first centuries than any other scientific endeavour.

With the current insatiable scientific thirst and quest driving genetic engineering technology, many people are left confounded especially considering the undisclosed underlying motivations animating this bio-technology which is threatening to obliterate and dislodge the current set up of the various human societies populating the planet earth inclusive of Africa. Apart from that, people are also seriously questioning and interrogating the underlying motivations pushing scientists to try to intrude into affairs exclusive to God, the Creator and maker of mankind. This is in view of the standing observation that scientists from the Global North are perilously attempting to use their fallible mental faculties to "play God" through the human cloning discourses.

In light of the foregoing and the arbitrary support and investment rendered to this topical and adventurous bio-technological exercise by some countries from Europe and America, it comes as no surprise that the Global North's bio-technological gambit of human cloning has ignited a multitude of ethical and social insecurity issues which warrant a closer scrutiny and a thorough revisiting now than ever. It is worth reiterating that, issues to do with human cloning are currently being hotly debated in the corridors of science, in political circles, among religious communities, throughout academia, and

362

more broadly in the media and public spheres (Aldous, 1932). Amidst these unending debates, emerge conflicting ideas with some scholars openly supporting the idea while others are out rightly condemning and clamouring for a moratorium to human cloning.

What is worrying is the fact that since the conception of the idea, there is no common position regarding the issue. What exacerbates matters is the inability by scientists to fully convince the world about the logicality of genetically replicating human beings through cloning. It has since been generally noted that the move to clone human beings is a direct threat to the natural procreation process. In view of this observation, one then wonders whether bio-technology is not akin to "playing God." Besides, a multiplicity of critical questions associated with the discourses of human cloning have also been raised on various international forums but these have unfortunately fallen on deaf ears. I contend that this unrepentant, defiant and never dying spirit is pregnant in the mind-set of the Global North typical to "playing God" their Creator and maker.

Against this backdrop, the present chapter examines and interrogates the bio-technological dilemmas and concealed insecurities associated with the Global North's ploy to clone human beings, particularly from an African perspective. Indubitably, the bio-technology of cloning and its possible application to humans also elicits many complex questions that are difficult to answer with precision. Ultimately, mind boggling questions arise: 'What could be the future of the planet earth in a world dominated by bio-technology that is largely instigated and engineered from the Global North? What is the role of God in a world where human beings are zealous in assuming responsibilities characteristic of the Creator? What are the unforeseeable social insecurity consequences associated with human cloning, particularly from an African perspective? How far will humanity go in using technology to (re) produce human life? Which ethical dilemmas does human cloning present? The overarching question that arises from all this is: What insecurities are associated with genetic engineering and bio-technology in Africa? This critical question, among many others that shall be raised and addressed, makes this present chapter worth undertaking.

Meanwhile, the forthcoming section is an attempt to provide a working definition of the phrase human cloning.

Understanding Human Cloning

It is important to point out right from the onset that the term human cloning cannot be pinned down with precision under one rubric. This is largely because many scholars have approached the definition of this term from different angles. Confirming this, Klugman and Murray (1998) noted that the term "human cloning" has been used in many arenas, and with different meanings. Notably, one point of contention in the debates over human cloning has been the definition of the word "cloning" itself, with many advocates of certain forms of cloning seeking to circumvent debate through terminological obfuscation (Masahito Tachibana *et al*, 2013). Rather than using the word "cloning," advocates of cloning for biomedical research have sometimes preferred to use specific technical terms like "nuclear transplantation to produce stem cells,"(Stern and Doucleff, 2013) or to speak not of human cloning but of "therapeutic cloning" "cloning stem cells," (Ibid) or "cell reprogramming" (OHSU, 2013).

However, what is worth to note is that as a scientific and technical possibility, human cloning has emerged as an outgrowth of discoveries or innovations in developmental biology, genetics, assisted reproductive technologies, animal breeding, and, most recently, research on embryonic stem cells (TPCB, 2002). Historically, human reproductive cloning came to the public's attention when Dolly, a sheep, was cloned in Scotland in 1997 by a team of British scientists headed by Wilmut. The spread of these news around the world caused both excitement at the possibilities that cloning techniques could offer, as well as apprehension about the ethical, social and legal implications should human reproductive cloning become possible (Sanchez- Sweatman, 2000).

Now coming to the definition of the term human cloning, it is not a good practice to either appraise or critique a concept before first understanding what it means. As such, it is crucial to have an appreciation of what the term human cloning entails. Logically, to unpack the definition of the phrase human cloning, I will first explain the meaning of the term clone before unmasking the term human cloning. As rightly noted by Seidel (2007: 17), "definitions of terms should be considered carefully and cautiously because definitions can, at worst, be deliberately politically and emotionally misleading, and persuasive at best." Seidel went further arguing that etymologically the term "clone" is derived from the Greek word *klon*, which means "twig" (Ibid: 17). Derivatively, the meaning of the word "clone," in this sense, refers to the process of breaking a twig off from certain species of tree or plant and, when planted, a copy of the tree or plant will result (Ibid). From a biological perspective, the term "clone" is used to refer to a cell or organism that is genetically identical to another cell or organism from which it is derived (Amanze, 2005).

More so, another generally accepted definition of "clone" is to make a genetic copy or set of copies of an organism, that is, bisecting a mammalian embryo to form identical twins (Ibid). On another note, cloning can also be defined as the "fusion or insertion of a diploid nucleus into an egg (oocyte)" (Ibid: 17). It is important to note that this method of cloning is also known as Somatic Cell Nuclear Transfer (SCNT). Additionally, it is akin to asexual reproduction since there is no fertilisation involved. What this means is that in this type of cloning, reproduction takes place without sexual union, or without fertilisation or the union of the male and female gametes (Klugman and Murray, 1998). It is crucial to underline at this juncture that this was the cloning technology Wilmut and his colleagues at the Roslin Institute in Edinburgh used in order to clone Dolly (Ibid). From the foregoing, it emerged that the term cloning is a simple word with a lot of particular meanings. The common thread running through the various definitions is that cloning is the creation of an organism that is an exact genetic copy of another (see also Ching-Pou Shih, 2010).

Drawing from the above given definitions, it also came out clear that cloning is the process of making a genetically identical organism through non-sexual means. Unlike sexual reproduction in which a new organism is formed when the genetic material of the egg and sperm fuse, there is only a single parent in this cloning procedure (Akintola, 2014). Genetically, cloning refers to the process of making an identical copy of the deoxyribonucleic acid (DNA) of an organism. When applied to human beings, cloning is used to refer to the creation of a human being that is genetically identical to another, that is, a human being with the same exact features and characteristics.

It is worth noting that there are basically two types of cloning namely; Reproductive cloning and Therapeutic cloning (Akintola, 2014; Gurdon and Colman, 1999). On the one hand, Reproductive Cloning is the technique used to generate an animal that has the same genetic qualities, that is, the same nuclear DNA as another already existing animal. By and large, reproductive cloning is usually performed for the purpose of creating a duplicate copy of another organism (Harris, 2004; Amanze, 2005). It is accomplished using a process called somatic cell nuclear transfer. In somatic cell nuclear transfer, scientists extract the nucleus of a somatic cell, a cell which come from anywhere in the body, and insert it into an egg which has had its nucleus removed (Harris, 2004). The egg is stimulated, and it begins dividing and growing, developing into an embryo which can be implanted into a gestational surrogate and carried to term (Ibid).

On the other hand, therapeutic cloning which is also known as "embryo cloning" is a biomedical technique, which is intended to produce human embryos for use in research and then to develop a healthy copy of a sick person's tissue or organ for medical treatment and transplantation (Ching-Pou Shih, 2010). For example, it could theoretically be used to grow a replacement organ, to generate skin for a burnt victim, or to create nerve cells for someone suffering from brain damage or a neurological condition. Therapeutic cloning is similar to reproductive cloning, in which a copy of an organism is produced, but the two have very different end goals (Akintola, 2014). It is crucial to note that the goal of this technique is not to create a cloned animal or human being, but rather to harvest stem cells that can be used to study for human good and to treat disease (Ching-Pou Shih, 2010).

Let me hasten to point out that while it is theoretically possible to clone human beings technologically, so far there are no known incidents of a fully developed human being ever being cloned. Although there are rumours and possible suggestions of human cloning, the facticity of a cloned human has not been verified (Ayala, 2015; Amanze, 2005). The possibility of cloning human beings sprout out of the announcement of the birth of the first cloned mammal, Dolly the sheep in 1997 by Ian Wilmut and Keith Campbell of the Roslin Institute in Scotland (Ching-Pou, Shih 2010). With the introduction of Dolly, the international community has realised that the practice of human cloning will become real and possible in the future.

As underscored above, the idea of human cloning is moving from the realm of science fiction into the realm of real possibility (Ibid). Since Dolly, several other species of mammals, such as goats, mules, pigs, cows, cats, mice and rodents have also been successfully cloned around the world (Ibid). While it is acknowledged that the real dangers associated with human cloning are still in the making, it is noble that such transformative activities capable of changing the nature and traditional functioning of human society should be critically analysed using African theoretical lenses. This is largely because while the move currently appears to be distant to Africa, the move may turn out to be real any time soon given the pace at which bio-technology is progressing and developing.

Cognisant of the above, it is the contention of this chapter that the entire African continent must know the perceived implications and insecurities associated with human cloning well before the idea turns out to be real. This in recognition of the fact that there are some countries particularly in Africa such as South Africa which have since openly legalised the cloning of embryos (generally referred to as therapeutic cloning). Therapeutic cloning is whereby the cloned embryo is developed but never transferred into the female womb. This raises eyebrows as to whether this stance will be forever maintained especially considering the rate at which limitless changes are being witnessed in the field of bio-technology. In the ensuing section, I interrogate the idea why human cloning may be considered as the intrusion of mankind into affairs and realms exclusively reserved for none other than God the Creator.

Human Cloning as "Playing God"

"We should not play God before we have learned to be men, and as we learn to be men we will not want to play God" (Ramsey, 1970: 151).

Human cloning has attracted numerous problems across the spectrum of mankind (Genetic Centre, n. d). In recent years, with the rapid developments in science and medicine, there have been many controversies brewing around socio-medical issues. One such issue is that of human cloning (Ibid). It leads to a number of fundamental, yet powerful questions for instance, is it possible for man to play God? If so, is it correct and moral for man to play God? (Ibid). Notably, there have been a number of controversies over the past decades surrounding those who want to clone humans or those who have claimed to clone humans.

In pursuance of the above, in 1998 Dr. Richard Seed made the submission that he planned to set up human cloning clinics in 10 to 20 locations in the United States and 5 to 6 internationally to help infertile couples have children (Ching-Pou Shih, 2010). However, the mystics surrounding Dr. Seed's announcement tends to raise the argument that human cloning oversteps certain moral and ethical boundaries and may be regarded as a ploy to "play God," the Creator (Ibid). This is premised on the pretext that humans as fallible beings lack the authority to make certain decisions about the beginning or ending of life. Such decisions are instead only reserved to divine sovereignty (NBAC, 1998).

It is worth of note that the debate whether scientists are "playing God" has probably never been more real than now as it has always, more than any other bio-technological issue, opened up a cobweb of mixed feelings and opinions regarding the desirability and logicality of the move. Drawing from the words of Paul Ramsey quoted above, it has generally been noted that the attempt to clone human beings by scientists is tantamount to "playing God." That is, human beings are playing a role that is reserved exclusively for God. This is mainly because the creation of life, especially human life, is something that God alone has the right to control, and hence, that human efforts to attain that control represent a kind of dangerous arrogance and impiety (Antonucci *et. al.,* 2002).

Crucially important to note at this juncture is that, a critical reflection of the many various situations and contexts where human beings have been accused of "playing God" reveals that the phrase has been taken to have a broad range of meanings, including but not limited to the following: "Tinkering with nature, tampering with the basic structure of what it takes to be a human being, making decisions about the fate of our fellow human beings without proper authority, flirting with the unknown, genetic engineering, assuming a greater responsibility than one has the power or resources to assume, deciding when to end life, deciding when to begin a life, determining a person's destiny," among many others (Campbell, 1997: 15).

Used in the context of this chapter, "playing God" is the metaphor commonly used to denote to man's self-proclaimed ability to "sort of create human beings" through reproductive cloning. This move is strongly refuted by Christians across the divide who emphatically feel that scientists are trying to "play God." They base their argument on the premises that the role of changing the genetic composition of an organism is exclusively to God. They further argue that only God and God alone is the sole Creator, hence cloning human beings is tantamount to "playing God" (Ibid: 15).

The discussion above has aptly shown that term "playing God" is often used to show that human beings are overstepping their boundaries. The term further suggests that a clear demarcation exists between the roles of God and that of human beings. Apart from that, the term also carries the connotations that there are areas of life where God rules, where God is in charge, and where humans ought not enter (Verhey, 1995). In other words, the term evokes an omnipotent God who is the Creator of all and who commands all. The term also evokes the image of God as "God of the Gaps," that is, the God who is invoked when all else fails, or when we have exceeded our limits, our knowledge is at an end, and our powers frustrated. Thus, it is most clearly in the gaps that God rules, and it is in the gaps that God's power is most clearly evoked. Here, God reigns supreme, and, here, we cannot play God (Ibid).

Reasoning from the same framework, Ehlers (1999) postulates that when a human being is created through cloning, we have crossed the line from experimentation and legitimate scientific work to an activity with profound moral and social repercussions. The core notion of this argument is that humans must respect natural processes and desist from interfering into God's affairs (Dress, 2002). As noted by Tangwa (2004), human scientific and technological knowledge has advanced to the point where scientists and technologists are able to play real games with God.

Responding to the above cited accusations, scientists from the Global North make the counter claim that there is nothing wrong with their scientific proclivity of creating and authoring life. Extending the argument, these scientists even argue that they are authors in the same way God is an author. That is, they are putting themselves at equal footing with God. They further argue that human cloning is promising mankind a godlike powers to "create", to "re-create", or to design their own new humanity and immortality through such technologies as human cloning and human genetic engineering (Vatican's Mission to the United Nations, 2001). It is evident that human beings are moving away from being creatures to becoming creators in their own right. Now that I have discussed why human cloning may be construed as "playing God," the following section looks at the perceived negatives and insecurities associated with human cloning with a particular bias on Africans.

Exploring the Implications of Human Cloning to Africa

"Every scientific revolution brings with it a host of ethical and social questions. The so-called genetics revolution is no exception, giving rise to a broad international debate on how the undoubted benefits of progress in this area can be reconciled with certain core human values" (UNESCO, 2002a: 1).

In this section, I am going to present the insecurities and implications associated with human cloning from an African perspective. As alluded to in the vignette cited above, it is certainly true that like any other technological breakthrough introduced on the planet earth, genetic engineering as a technology and as a means of reproduction is not without its pros and cons (Amanze, 2005). Resultantly, the discourse on human cloning has been subjected to intensive public debates ever since the cloning of Dolly (Ching-Pou Shih, 2010). Arguably, beneath the topical, controversial and complicated debates about human cloning lie major questions about the relation between science and technology and the larger society (TPCB, 2002).

Honestly speaking, human cloning has serious negative effects on the moral, religious, and cultural values of the people of Africa. That being the case, there is need to carefully and cautiously tread a fine line between encouraging scientific progress while at the same time carefully considering the associated implications that go along with bio-technological advancements and developments such as human cloning. Nevertheless, some critical scholars are of the view that in the midst of the scientific enthusiasm and furore driving genetic engineering there has been almost no consideration for critical reflection for its insecurity implications to the people of Africa in particular.

This is in view of the observation that the people of Africa treat the family institution with high respect. Besides, they strongly cherish diversity, human dignity, the sanctity of life, family relations, parenthood, procreation and identity the very same principles and ideals that are being openly challenged and threatened by human cloning (see also Van den Berg, 2012). However, it must be pointed out that although most African societies cherish the family institution, feminists such as Helen Sullinger condemn the family institution on the basis that marriage constitutes slavery for women. In fact, they perceive marriage and motherhood as institutions of male domination. In light of this, Helen Sullinger thus argue:

> Marriage has existed for the benefit of men; and has been a legally sanctioned method of control over women. . . . We must work to destroy it. . . . The end of the institution of marriage is a necessary condition for the liberation of women. Therefore it is important for us to encourage women to leave their husbands and not to live

individually with men... All of history must be rewritten in terms of oppression of women (Buchanan, 2002: 42).

It is precisely because of the above noted reasons that feminists indirectly support the idea of human cloning. They base their argument on the pretext that human cloning frees women from male domination as well as from the stressful labour of pregnancy. It must be emphasised that this kind of thinking is unheard off in Africa where marriage is perceived as the bedrock of the family institution.

As alluded to above, it is worth pointing out that in the African continent as elsewhere, the family is highly considered as a prime social institution, and in some traditions, a divinely ordained institution for the bearing and nurturing of children (Akintola, 2014). In most societies African societies for instance, family ties and bonds are given utmost importance. In fact, the traditional idea of a family is looked at from a very orthodox point of view. An ideal family in an African set up is when two people get married, procreate and raise their own biological and genetic children in a shared community guided by social norms and values. It is almost always presumed that in Africa readiness for marriage is readiness for procreation; to get married is an opportunity to contribute freely, through procreation, to the survival of the lineage and society at large (Abasil n. d).

Contrarily, with the advancement of science and technology, there is no longer any requirement for sexual intimacy for reproduction. Those in favour of cloning further argue that humanoid robots can be used to quench human sexual needs since they are deemed to be more loving, romantic, docile and obedient. It must be noted that in Africa, marriage and procreation are intertwined and inseparable and that any form of sexual intimacy outside marriage is deemed immoral and unethical. Apart from that, sexual intimacy between a human being and an object is unacceptable in most African societies.

Furthermore, human cloning subverts the family. This is due to the fact that a clone by definition, does not have two parents since it derived from a single parent by asexual reproduction. Understood this way, cloning would license and enable people to produce children without any reference to sexuality ((McGee, n. d). In other

372

words, it would be possible to have a single parented child outside of the family unit. What this means is that in human reproductive cloning, the idea of procreation which is a natural Godly action that results in having a new life form is replaced with "making" in the laboratory without recourse to family or any conventional parent (Ibid). Thus, the responsibility of procreation shifts from the conjugal love to the technological laboratory. This obviously stands against human sexuality. Yet, humanity is incomplete without its sexuality. Confirming this, Demarco writes that:

> Fullness of both motherhood and fatherhood demands the unification of procreation and bodified conjugal love. As this unity is compromised or violated, the moral and spiritual meaning of motherhood and fatherhood are proportionally jeopardised (Demarco, 1980: 23).

From the above quote, it is evident that human reproductive cloning violates human sexuality from an African moral perspective. Although feminists and poststructuralists such as Michael Foucault condemn sexuality as oppressive and repressive, it has a profoundly public meaning particularly in Africa. It is important in the sense that it determines the relations between family members, shapes identities, creates attachments, and sets up responsibilities for the care and rearing of children (and the care of aging parents or other needy kin) (TPCB, 2002).

Furthermore, the most important reason of marriage especially from an African perspective is procreation and the orderly socialisation of the human offspring. Yet, human cloning is directly trying to dislodge and circumvent procreation. It is critical to note that in Africa marriage is the only socially sanctioned institution that permits adults to produce human species within the spiritual dictates and parameters of God (cf. Abikoye, 2000). Similarly, Mbiti (1969) [while commenting on the African way of marriage] noted that it is basically a tool for home building, community, national and world stability. Thus, any scientific theory and technological development that will attempt to destabilise and let alone dislodge the marriage institution would obviously be regarded as a misfit and an unwelcome move to Africa (see also Akintiola, 2014).

Assuming that human cloning is granted, what then would happen to this esteemed marriage institution? Anticipating that it is now possible for anybody that have the means to clone a replica of themselves; then marriage would be meaningless (Ibid). Yet, in Africa and even in many other societies in other regions of the globe, marriage is essential for an adult. In fact, it is marriage that bestows on someone a respectable position in African society. Precisely, a man/woman is regarded as a complete and responsible person in Africa when he is married and has children of his own (Ibid).

Contrarily, human reproductive cloning makes possible or rather permits children to come to the family through non-natural means. This raises the possibility that such children might encounter special problems in forming their identities or in forming relationships with other members of the family who were born through natural Godly means (Amanze, 2005). As a result, the sacred and cherished marriage relationship and the family institution of husband, wife and children would be severely undermined and disregarded. Put differently, cloning would circumvent God's natural laws, and thus be opposed to Biblical and natural principles of procreation (Ibid).

Apart from the various concerns regarding the cloned child as an individual, there are several concerns regarding the family, society and environment this child is introduced into. Will the cloned child be given the same treatment as other children? Without having any emotional attachments to the parental world, can they be integrated into the human society? (Zzman, n. d). Is it possible for a mother to have a normal mother-daughter relationship with her cloned child, especially if they are genetically identical? What would be the consequences of the father-daughter relationship if the mother and daughter were genetically identical? (CEJA, 1998). It was once said by a famous philosopher, "cloning shows itself to be a major violation of our given nature as embodied, gendered, and engendering beings-and of the social relations built on this natural ground" (Kass, 1998: 13). Familial relationships help define who we are as individuals, and to a great extent are the bedrock upon which society is based. The other implication of human cloning to Africa is that it would undermine identity. According to Lemaire (1977: 81):

> The advent of human cloning has the potential to initiate an identity crisis. A cloned human being, if brought into the world, could threaten society's traditional theories about the self and reveal an intrinsic insecurity within traditional conceptions of human identity. Should a clone come into being, he or she would closely resemble, or look exactly like, another human being. In a very real sense, the clone appears as the pseudo-self, an "other" whose inherent correlation to the self is so strong that the boundaries between self and other can no longer be delineated.

As Gilman concludes, despite demarking ourselves from the other, in truth "we know we are not different" (Ferguson, 1999: 240). Vidal, in The Ethics of Genetic Engineering, gets to the point in her statement that "the most important consideration of all is that human beings have their own identity; cloning impacts directly on this basic requirement for being a person" (Vidal, 1998: 109). Clones literally replicate another person, and so cannot be said to possess an essential identity of their own.

Furthermore, the ability to create multiple clones of the same human being represents a dilution and disintegration of a stable sense of an integral, original self. Traditional notions of the uniqueness of the human being would be directly challenged by the emergence of these pseudo-selves. As Freud asserts: "there is a doubling, dividing and interchanging of the self" (Freud, 2001: 940). Freud's ideas invite comparison with the human clone. Humans would be literally challenged to look themselves in the eye and ask the question: if you are me, then who am I? In this instance traditionally-born human beings could find their previously fixed notions of identity and selfhood threatened by the emergence of a new pseudo-self.

Against this backdrop, one would seriously consider the place of a cloned person in an African context. Some of the pertinent questions that quickly come to the mind are: What family tree would such a person claim? Is he/she going to claim the same lineage with the cell owners or donors if at all it is possible to identify the donor?

(Akintola, 2014). Is he/she going to claim the same ethnic identity with the donor? These are some of the critical questions that need to be seriously considered in view of human cloning (Ibid).

Although it is acknowledged that African heritages are under siege from hybridisation and culture cross fertilisation, Africans still place high regard on family inheritance in the sense that there is no African person that does not have an inheritance. Now the question is: is he going to share in the family inheritance of the donor? Will the other family members regard him as a human being or part of the family? (Ibid). These are some of the mind boggling question that are inevitably raised by the issue of human cloning. It goes without saying that a cloned person does not belong to any community in Africa. This is mainly because the community gives each person belongingness and cultural identity for self-fulfilment and social security (Ibid).

In view of the preceding discussion, a cloned person cannot share anything in collective honour because in the first instance he/she is never referred to as a human being. In other words, he/she does not fit into any African culture because he/she would have come into being through a process that is alien to African conception of reproduction (Ibid). "A man without lineage is a man without citizenship, without identity, and therefore without allies..; or as the Kongo put it, a man outside his clan is like a grasshopper which has lost its wings" (Davidson, 1969: 55).

On the one hand, human cloning technology would foster an understanding of children and of people in general, as objects that can be designed and manufactured to possess some specific characteristics. It is no different to buying any other commodity or merchandise in an ordinary market (Akintola, 2014). As such, human cloning technology would foster an understanding of children and of people in general, as objects that can be designed and manufactured to possess some specific characteristics. As alluded to above, it is no different than buying any other commodity or merchandise in an ordinary market (Ching- Pou Shih, 2010). On the other hand, human cloning would destroy the value of death since death has its own role to play in the African society. It is vital to note that with the cloning of persons the dead can always be replaced thereby causing social problems for those who believed in ancestral practice and the existence of ancestral spirits (Akintola, 2014). The Africans conceive the cosmos as consisting of two distinct but inseparable realms-the visible world of the living and the spiritual and invisible domain of the ancestors, gods and spirits (Henry *et al.,* 2003). Notably, the two realms are closely connected in the sense that the inhabitants of spiritual and invisible regularly involved themselves in human affairs.

Drawing from the discussion above, it is worth noting that a typical African community was not just perceived as a geographical entity with clearly defined boundaries and with a web of horizontal networks of kinship relationships (Ibid). Instead, it was also seen as a transcendental continuum, which stretched back into the past to include the dead, represented by the ancestors, and at the same time anticipated the future world of the yet unborn. These three elements: the dead, the living and the unborn always featured prominently in African traditional discourses on life. Therefore, death was not seen as the end of life. It was a means of crossing to the other side (Babatunde Lawal, 1977). So any attempt or any invention that will erase this belief from African minds would be unwelcome.

From the foregoing, it is the contention of this chapter that human cloning is a weird science meant to destabilise peace and security in Africa. What is the motive of technologically producing identical people? This will create a society consisting of many similar people albeit of different ages. This will also culminate into a monotonous society devoid of diversity. Apart from that, it seems unheard off that humans would want to consider the idea of taking life into their own hands, rather than letting things happen naturally. Besides, the process of cloning carries many dangers throughout society including loss of identity, theft control issues, and attempts to create a superior race.

Notably, one argument against cloning is that it makes personal identification much more difficult. Suppose someone committed a murder and multiple witnesses saw him do it. Well, suppose the description of the murderer matches that of the dozens of clones. How can the particular clone be identified if they all look the same and all deny committing the murder or knowing who did it? Thus, with cloning the correct identification of suspected criminals is highly problematic.

Conclusion

It is worth noting that the issue of human cloning has since its advent generated heated debates and still continues to attract the attention of scholars especially considering the manner in which the Global North is dicing with bio-technology both on the earth and in extra-terrestrials. Recent developments in genetic engineering show that human cloning, in spite of immense technical difficulties and the profound ethical and anthropological objections to it, is more than a hypothesis and is gradually becoming a possibility.

It has been further noted that the culmination of human cloning into reality would obviously create serious numerous problems ranging from loss of identity, subversion of the family, threats to diversity, reduction of human beings to objects and commodities, threats to marriage, procreation and sexuality, among many other social vices. Besides, human cloning would severely affect the conceptualisation of personhood.

In conclusion, it has been demonstrated that human cloning technology engages not only religious, cultural, social, and moral challenges, but also ethical and legal issues, as well as human and fundamental rights concerns; in particular, liberty of procreation, right to health, and freedom of thought and scientific inquiry? (Mahnoush, 2006). In general, there is nothing wrong with technology, as such. In itself, it is morally neutral, neither right nor wrong. It is an important non-moral value, connected with human ingenuity and achievements. But, the uses to which any technology is put, is a moral issue (Tangwa, 2004).

References

Abasili, A. I. (n. d). 'Seeing Tamar through the prism of an African woman: A contextual reading of Genesis 38,' Biblical Studies Department, K.U. Leuven.

Abikoye, J. S. (2000). 'Sex and Family Life Education,' Unpublished Physical and Health Education, College of Education Oro.

Akintola, L. (2014). 'Human Cloning: An African Perspective,' *International Journal of Humanities and Cultural Studies* (IJHCS), 1 (2): 1-10.

Amanze, S. O. (2005). 'Technologised Parenthood: An Ethical Implication of Human Reproductive,' Cloning, Master's Thesis in Applied Ethics, Linköping University.

Antonucci, *et. al.* (2002). 'Playing God/Perfect Children Communities of Colour and Genetics Policy Project: A report for the Communities of Colour and Genetic Policy Project,' http://www.sph.umich.edu/genpolicy/current/reports/playing_god.pdf).

Ayala, F. J. (2015). 'Cloning humans? Biological, Ethical, and Social Considerations,' Proceedings of the National Academy of Sciences of the United States of America, 112 (29): 8879-8886.

Babatunde, L. (1997). 'The Living Dead: Art and Immortality among the Yoruba of Nigeria,' *Africa*, 47 (1): 51-63.

Buchanan, P. J. (2002). *The Death of the West,* New York, St Martin's Press.

Campbell, C. (1997). 'Religious Perspectives on Human Cloning, Cloning Human Beings:' Report and Recommendations of the National Bioethics Advisory.

Ching-Pou Shih. (2010). 'Moral and Legal Issues concerning contemporary Human Cloning Technologies: Quest for Regulatory Consensus in the International Community to safeguard Rights and Liberties essential to Future Humanity,' Unpublished PhD Thesis, Golden Gate University.

Council on Ethical and Judicial Affairs (CEJA). (1998). 'Opinion: Genetic Testing of Children,' Code of Medical Ethics: Current Opinions and Annotations, Chicago.

Demarco, D. (1980). 'In my Mother's Womb: the Catholic Church's Defence of Natural Life,' Manussas, Virginia: Trinity Communications.

Drees, W. B. (2002). 'Playing God? Yes! Religion in the Light of Technology,' *ZYGON*, 37 (2): 643-654.

Drewal, H. J. (2003). 'The Yoruba World,' In: Gikandi, S (ed.), *Death and the King's Horseman: Authoritative Text Backgrounds and Context Criticism,* New York.

Ehlers, V. J. (1999). 'The Case against Human Cloning,' *Hofstra Law Review*, 27 (3): 524-532.

Ferguson, C. (1999). 'Dr. McGrath's Disease: Radical Pathology in Patrick McGrath's Neo-Gothicism,' *Spectral Readings: Towards a Gothic Geography*, Basingstoke: Macmillan.

Freud, S. (2001). 'The Uncanny,' *The Norton Anthology of Theory and Criticism*, New York; London: Norton.

Genetic Centre. (n. d). The University of Utah. Available at:http://learn.genetics.utah.edu/content/tech/cloning/whatiscloning/

Gyekye, K. (1984). 'The Akan concept of a Person,' In: Wright, R (ed.), *African Philosophy: An Introduction* (pp. 199–211), Lanham, MD: University Press of America.

Gogarty, B. (2003). 'What Exactly Is An Exact Copy? And Why It Matters When Trying To Ban Human Reproductive Cloning in Australia,' *Journals of Medical Ethics*, 29 (2): 84-89.

Gurdon, J. B. (1999). 'The Future of Cloning,' In: *Nature*, 402 (4): 743-746.

Kass, L. R. 'The Wisdom of Repugnance,' In: Kass, L. R, Leon, R and James, W (eds,). (1998). *The Ethics of Human Cloning*, Washington, D.C.

Kluman, C. M and Murray, T. H. (1998). 'Cloning, Historical Ethics,' In: Humber, J and Almeder, R. F. (eds.), *Human Cloning*, New Jersey: Humana Press.

Lemaire, A. (1977). *Jacques Lacan*, London: Routledge and Kegan Paul.

Masahito Tachibana *et al.*, (2013). "Human Embryonic Stem Cells Derived by Somatic Cell Nuclear Transfer," (June 6, 2013): 1228 – 1238, http://dx.doi.org/10.1016/j.cell.2013.05.006.

McGee, G. (n. d). 'Human Cloning will Redefine Families,' *The Ethics of Human Cloning*, Greenhaven Press.

National Bioethics Advisory Commission (NBAC). (1998). 'Religious Perspectives,' In: Nussbaum, M. C and Sustein, C. R. *Clones and Clones: Facts and Fantasies about Human Cloning*, W.W Norton and Company.

OHSU. (2013). Oregon Health and Science research team successfully converts human skin cells into embryonic stem cells" (press release), May 15, 2013, http://www.ohsu.edu/xd/about/news_events/news/2013/05-15ohsuresearchteamsucce.cfm.

Ramsey, P. (1970). *Fabricated Man: The Ethics of Genetic Control*, New Haven and London, Yale University Press.

Sanchez-Sweatman, L. R. (2000). 'Bioethics, Reproductive Cloning and Human Health: An Ethical, International, and Nursing Perspective,' *International Nursing Review*, 47 (1): 28-37.

Stein, R and Doucleff, M. (2013). "Scientists Clone Human Embryos to Make Stem Cells," National Public Radio, May 15, 2013, http://npr.org/blogs/health/2013/05/15/183916891/scientist sclonehumanembryostomakestemcells.

Tangwa, G. B. (2004). *Bioethics, Biotechnology and Culture: A Voice from the Margins*, Blackwell Publishing Ltd.

Ted, P. (2001). 'Embryonic Stem Cells and the Theology of Dignity,' In: Lebacqz, K and Zoloth, L (eds). *The Human Embryonic Stem Cell Debate, Science, Ethics, and Public Policy*, Massachusetts Institute of Technology Press.

The Presidential Council on Bioethics (TPCB). (2002). *Human Cloning and Human Dignity: An Ethical Inquiry*, Washington D. C.

UNESCO. (2002a). 'Human Genetic Data: Preliminary Study of the IBC on their Collection, Processing, Storage and Use,' Paris.

Van den Berg, M. E. S. (2012). 'Human Reproductive Cloning and Biotechnology: Rational, Ethical and Public Concerns,' *Koers-Bulletin for Christian Scholarship*, 77 (2): 412-421.

Verhey, A. D. (1995). 'Playing God and Invoking a Perspective,' 20 Journal of Medical Philosophy, 20 (3): 347-64.

Vidal, M. (1998). 'Cloning: Technical Reality and Ethical Evaluation,' *The Ethics of Genetic Engineering*, London: SCM Press.

381

Wiredu, K. (2009). 'An oral philosophy of Personhood: Comments on Philosophy and Orality,' *Research in African Literatures*, 40(1): 8–18.

Zzaman, K. (n. d). *Human Cloning and its Social Impacts,* Ground Report, Available at: http://groundreport.com/human-cloning-and-its-social-impacts/.

Chapter 16

Freedom to Become Insecure? Vulnerabilities from the Emergent Digital Media in Zimbabwe

Last Alfandika; Gift Gwindingwe & Golden Maunganidze

Introduction

The advent of new technologies in communication has brought opportunities and challenges for traditional or old media (Garrison, 1996). It has revolutionised the dynamics of journalism practice (Pavlik, 2001) as anyone can now be involved in the production and consumption of content. Indeed, it has increased the public's chances of accessing news and engaging with news content anywhere in the globe, thus, making digital media a valuable tool for information dissemination across rural and urban dissections. The emergency of social media marked a communications revolution (Harper, 2010). It can be described as a shift from traditional media that had also revolutionized oramedia. Undeniably, social media has enhanced freedom of expression, media freedom and access to information the world over and Zimbabwe in particular. The responsibility of gate keepers has drastically been reduced as information dissemination and access has become almost free. Transparency; honesty, equality and the voice of the voiceless have become visible and/or audible in this digital age.

The question of whether digital media, especially social media, are benign or malignant has been a cause for concern in both academic and industrial enquiries but has received no conclusive response from a Zimbabwean perspective. In an endeavour to plug this gap, this chapter discusses specific issues aligned to benevolence and malevolence of emergent digital media focusing on social media platforms such as the YouTube, Facebook, WhatsApp and Twitter. Habermas' concepts of the *transformation* of the public sphere as developed by Fraser (1990) is re-casted in a discussion which hopes to demonstrate how freedom of expression and access to information occupy a central position in Zimbabwean media democratisation process yet poses critical threats and insecurity among the people and the nation at large. Using Habermas' lenses, this study anticipates to explain the rationale behind the celebration of social media after a long struggle against media oppression. However, gleaming on the downside of the information revolution, this chapter engages the French intellectual Jean Baudrillard's understanding of social media in the post-modern era as lenses to forge an understanding of emergent insecurities and threats embedded within the social media revolution. Furthermore, the chapter discusses social, cultural, political and economic threats in Zimbabwe. The emerging insecurities reproduced by social media have become a threat to social fibre, leading to "tribal" wars and "ethnic" divisions and national insecurity.

The social media as a public sphere: an enhancement of the freedom of expression and access to information.

Social media sites are web based services that allow the people to build a public or semi- public profile within bounded system (Amedie, 2015). It encompasses several users usually called friends which share some common connections. Social media enable the building of personal relationships, sharing of common, and other interests. This chapter focuses on Facebook, WhatsApp, Twitter, and YouTube basically because they are among common social media that are in use in Zimbabwe. Indeed, social media has become one of the most important vectors for freedom of expression while at the same time posing some threats and insecurities within the modern communication system. Ironically, the weaknesses with social media are conversely their strengths. For instance, they encourage interaction among users, thus increasing freedom of expression and access to information yet on the other hand, this freedom of expression and access to information also open gaps to expression of "tribal" and "ethnic" hatred, intimidation and harassment, degradation and humiliation of other persons, races and "tribes", threats to national security and are catalytic to personal insecurity, health, crime and other several threats that may be posed. These fears and insecurities range from, culture threat to "tribal" wars and ethnic divisions, exploitation of the grassroots to enhance global capitalism and danger to national security among others.

The emergence of the digital media platforms was not only a celebration of the birth of democratic fissures emerging to operate alongside traditional media institutions such as the print and broadcasting media. It also saw the emergence of a media puzzle where the ethical red lines were crossed but with no punitive measures being meted onto the 'professional offenders' maybe because of the absence of legal pathways to reach the pervasive offenders. Moyo (2015) exposes the ultimate dilemma that citizen journalism faces as a result of the emergent digital media and he calls the puzzle an 'ethical maze'. He juxtaposes the two conflicting ethical considerations that one faces in pursuit of citizen journalism: the De-ontological ethics and the Teleological ethics (Moyo, 2015). The area of contestation becomes duty in pursuance of journalism. Human beings as moral agents have to weigh between call of duty and personal ego. That is where the nexus between freedom and insecurity can be located.

Journalism guided by policy is professional. Now with the emergence of digital media platforms, editorial policies became irrelevant and outbursts of freedom unlimited overrode ethical considerations. In the absence of professional ethics, there is nothing to guide professionals, neither will there be anything to constrain the thoughts and feelings of individuals (Hicks, 2004). The ultimate consequence is that individuals will be free to do or say whatever they feel like (ibid). This is contrary to traditional news outlets which were guided by editorial policies. How then, do the contradictions between the De-ontological and the Teleological ethics theories pose a challenge?

The de-ontological ethics stipulates that people are duty bound and would remain faithful to duties of informing and educating. Truth should be told and justices defended; evil must be exposed and perpetrators named and shamed. The de-ontological ethics demands that duty takes precedence over all other considerations which include one's personal happiness and pleasures (Moyo, 2015). This concludes that the utilitarian concerns of self-interest and community happiness are of lesser centrality. The question that needs to be answered now is: Is this ethical consideration feasible to adhere to, considering that the advent of the Internet has 'democratised journalism as a social and professional practice'? (Moyo, 2015:04).With the emergence of digital media platforms, there has been a marked 'shift from traditional outlets to digital news sources', and journalism as a profession has become independent (Harper, 2010:01). It is this shift from a policy driven profession to an independent profession that should gnaw the brains of media scholars.

The teleological ethics are consequentialist in nature, argues Moyo (2015). All that matters in teleological ethics is that which brings forth happiness and pleasures to the majority and, as Moyo puts it, 'one's duty and rights are subordinated to what maximises the collective' goodwill of the generality (ibid). Naturally, people are excited or ecstatic about the super real (post-modernist thinking) where the true/false and the real/imaginative lines are blurred. The question that becomes central now is: does this teleological ethics theory save right with the deontological ethics theory in journalistic practice where the informational role (truth) and the educational role (morality) are to be performed? More so, how do social media conflate the ethical theories to strike a journalistic equilibrium? Does not this puzzle expose social media as risky? There is need to look at the emerging digital media as a double edged sword. This kind of analysis draws upon, on one side, the application of the Public Sphere theory as elaborated by Nancy Fraser (1990) and on the other side, the Postmodernist theory as espoused by Baudrillard.

Fraser's approach on the Harbermasian public sphere is not an excoriation of the whole theory but a conceptual rebuilding of it. In this rebuilt concept, we find analogous and contradictory features in our trying to draw extensions of the public sphere concept to critically look at whether the emergent digital media ushered in freedom to liberate speech and expression or they also brought fears of insecurity amongst citizenry.

Whereas the liberal public sphere is considered as 'a body of private persons assembled to discuss matters of public concern or common interest' (Fraser, 1990:54), the emergence of digital media platforms decongested these assemblies, thereby assuring enhanced freedom to individuals or 'private persons'. Transmission of issues of concern through digital media platforms to hold the state accountable is no longer through '*legally guaranteed*[1] free speech, free press and free assembly'. There is no legal space to monitor users of digital media platforms and so free speech and free press are no longer bound by such things as editorial policy. We shall take this to mean enhanced opportunity to the 'weaker publics' to converge virtually to express their concerns. However, note should be taken that in the Southern context of the geopolitical landscape, there still remains the weaker of the weaker publics in form of the poor rural people who are excluded through poverty, inaccessibility to Information Communication Technologies (ICT) and illiteracy. So in as much as we applaud the freedom ushered in by the digital media, we should take cognisance of the limitations that still weaken the conclusion that the public sphere is all encompassing. Of course the point that remains undisputed is that those that have access engage in 'unrestricted rational discourse of public interest' (Fraser, 1990:59).

The bourgeois public sphere rationalised 'political domination' through legal guarantees in which issues of 'private interest were to be inadmissible' and therefore the issue of 'unrestricted rational discussion' (Fraser, 1990:59) becomes a fallacy of inclusion amongst the citizenry. Now with the emergence of the digital media platforms, teleological ethics seem to override de-ontological ethics. The anonymity that is associated with digital media platforms leaves every citizen a potential generator of news or information with no ethical and /or restrictive strings attached. Digital media has therefore demonopolised hegemonic tendencies in news, content and cultural production as the elitists would always prescribe what should be produced for and consumed by the public. At least, as Harper (2010) puts it, 'people do not want to be fed with information' but they also want to partake in the production and sharing of it.

Social media has ensured a forward shift in the concept of the public sphere. Media organisations ceased to be in charge and people took control (Harper, 2010). But, there is a point of interest to note

---

[1] Own emphasis

in this shift: when media organisations relinquish or shed part of their roles to the general citizenry, ethics are also relegated to inconsequential; when people are in charge, there is more democratic space created even though it is not without misgivings as shall be explained later.

The digital media platforms have also proved to be breakaway counter publics in many ways. Fraser cites Geoff Eley (1987) who envisages the public sphere (in stratified societies) as 'the structured setting where cultural and ideological contest or negotiation among a variety of publics takes place'. The emerging digital media platforms have deconstructed such a structural societal segmentation and freed the citizenry from dangers of 'discursive assimilation'. In the Habermasian framework, the subordinates 'were less likely to find the right voice or words to express their thought'…and 'more likely to… keep their wants inchoate' (Fraser, 1990:66). Now Li and Bernoff (2008) argue that digital media has given impetus to individuals to find their right voices and they have pushed the idea of 'news media to morph' despite the fact that the industry has desired the twist or not.

Habermasian geanacologies are not adequate to address issues of threats and insecurities advanced by emerging social media in Zimbabwe. They address more the freedoms brought about by the digital media platforms than they enlighten on the darker side of these platforms. Therefore, the works of Jean Baudrillard, a French intellectual and a post-modernist critique are essential in discussing the impending dangers of the emergent digital media. A major argument advanced here is that the new media has created a new world which is not real but a simulation of the real, effectively eroding the notion that media mirrors the society.

The oxymoron of freedom in the emerging digital media: an encounter with Jean Baudrillard's hyperreal and simulacra concepts

Whilst the emergent digital media have brought with them applausive optimism amongst the generality, the societal demands for social order, rationality and undisputable structural formations that are characteristic of every society may face the risk of being threatened by the 'social media revolution' (Harper, 2010). A revolution overhauls the existing structures. The de-ontological ethics that seemed to be guiding the journalistic profession and information flow stands threatened by the teleological ethics that characterize the Information Society. The pessimistic mode grips the society, especially the older order and this brings us to the post-modernist thinking where the world seems likely to come to a halt because nothing is real anymore.

Vulnerability refers to susceptibility or being weak. Thus vulnerabilities of the emergent digital media are their weaknesses: the tendency of becoming susceptible in the era of information super highway. So in the celebrative euphoria of the digital media and all the pseudo freedoms that go along with the emergence of digital media, it is our contention that the pessimism foreshadowed by the digital media can better be explained within the post-modernist frame.

One of the biggest threats that come along with the digital media is the 'subversion of the media code, (Baudrillard and Maclean, 1985) leading to information rapture defying censorship or gatekeeping. Traditionally, gatekeeping saved several advantages such as controlling dissemination of sensitive issues with the upshot of handling moral panics in society. Now the advent of digital media 'no longer permits us to isolate reality or human nature as a fundamental variable' (Baudrillard and Maclean, 1985:3) and the 'public's confidence has reached its lowest' ebb as a result of the pervasive nature of social media (Harper, 2010:1). The absence of the media code and the resultant loss of public confidence has collapsed the boundaries of the virtual and the real.

With the emergence of digital media, media organisations appear to have relinquished their roles and individuals have seemingly taken over responsibility (Harper, 2010) because people want to be in charge of their information. This is super real as it points to lawlessness, structureless society and the result is information rapture. Many bloggers' publications are opinion-oriented rather than first-coverage news oriented (Holtz, 2009) threatening investigative journalism due to lack of meticulousness in its work. This is akin to deprofessionalised and deinstitutionalised journalistic practices that have weakened the media code (Moyo, 2014, 2015 and Allan, 2013).

An insightful analysis reveals a likelihood of pitfalls of the much applauded freedom or democracy that the digital media is purported to bring considering that Moyo (2015) and Allan (2013) raise the argument that citizen journalism is associated or linked to the narratives of the ordinary people and social crises as well as the 'socially and historically contingent', (Moyo, 2015:4). If the narratives are of the ordinary and contingent, the unordinary become sceptical and lose confidence in the product. News uptake becomes contentious.

The postmodernist concern with digital media is its excessive provision of information leading to information overload and confusion (Baudrillard and Maclean, 1985:5). The ultimate scenario is that 'the space of the representable' is cluttered up by the 'hyperinformation' (Baudrillard and Maclean, ibid). Moyo (2015:7) weighs in in exposing the susceptibility of digital media especially as an agent of cluttering up the space of the representable:

> As an amateurish, accidental reporter whose personal naivety and technological obsession override his/her respect for integrity and privacy for others, a citizen journalist becomes a threat… a danger to security or a catalyst to insecurity that stems from his/her freedom.

It is the freedom that lies uncontrollable in a technologically obsessed naïve and accidental reporter that pose a challenge in the information super highway era. In the previous section, we applauded the public sphere as advancing rational debate but Moyo's (2015) argument here leaves one questioning the 'rationality' of the alternative public sphere or counter publics (in particular digital media platforms) in view of the uncodified freedom that it renders, measured against the corruption and confusion that it brews which all lead to insecurity.

Baudrillard (1972) sees digital media as a 'subversive strategy'. This is analogous to the idea that citizen journalism seeks to 'wrestle journalism from the publishing monopolies and recast it to serve the public good, free speech and politics of life and not death' and so citizen journalism as a rhizome is not singular but plural and is a diverse web of citizen news, cultures and practices (Moyo, 2015:5). Postmodernism is "an activist strategy against the coalition of reason and power" (Hicks, 2004:13). But, the questions that need to be answered are imbedded in Fish's (1982:180) argument for deconstruction when he claims that it 'relieves me of the obligation to be right...and demands only that I am interesting': What will become of a society that is not bound by morality? Is it tenable to balance the De-ontological and the Teleological ethics in journalism? We are therefore, in view of these questions, persuaded to go along Baudrillard's argument of collapsed boundaries and distorted reality. He calls it hyperreality that results from social media platforms.

Signs, images and models that circulate are no longer representations of the things they actually are supposed to represent. Reality in this world has actually been replaced with signs and symbols. In actual fact, reality has disappeared from the face of this world which is now composed of simulations of reality. Social media rise above the modern era into the postmodern era where reality is not attainable but simulations. Social media discourses decentre the self, making it difficult for public sphere conception to remain relevant as a normative concept for evaluating social media practise (Dahlberg, 2001). In social media, the concept of reality is disrupted and there is multiplication of pure representation (Simulacra) leading to a state of hyperreality. In this state, binary oppositions such as (real/unreal, subject/object etc.) crash and a "simulacra world" a world of copies without origins, where reality and what is original is illusory comes alive. Participants in this world have no reference. The world is no longer in touch with reality. Instead, it is hooked into a simulation of reality which is essentially poignant for social media. The real things have been replaced by new reality. Simulacra describes that copies of things have become so detached from the original, or at times the original is non-existent at all, hence they are just copies without originals.

Relevant to this issue is the fact that social media creates situations in which people or online friends do not directly communicate with each other but interact with a hyperreal space, a space were models, images, and symbols no longer represent things they should be representing. In these spaces, there are overwhelming symbols of communication creating and interpreting confusion and failure. Streams of updates, fascinating entertainment on social media overwhelm us. Indeed, they become our reality and we lose focus and fail to connect with reality. Traces are rubbed and in the thick of entertainment and postings, humanity is exposed and subjected to several threats and insecurities (Moyo, 2015).

In a country like Zimbabwe that is characterised by more than two decades of political polarisation, is the deconstruction argument by Fish (1982) marketable in the field of journalism? One thinks of the polarity that was a wedge between the ruling ZANU-PF and the opposition MDC (which later became MDC-T); the recent polarity within ZANU-PF between the Emmerson Mnangagwa-led Lacoste faction and the Grace Mugabe-led G40 faction; polarity between the ruling ZANU-PF party and the civic organisations such as Tajamuka; ThisFlag# etc! The analysis stage in this chapter will look at how the digital media exposed the vulnerabilities, threats and insecurities and with what effects.

Vulnerabilities of the grassroots at the hands of global capitalism

Social media breakdown boundaries and blur the distinction between consumer and producer, creating prosumers (Jenkins, 2006). The ordinary, the grassroots, celebrate activities belonging to either sphere, regardless of time and space (Tofler, 1980). However, a new type of capitalism different from capitalist systems that are more focused on either production or consumption has emerged alongside the digital media. Social media as part of digital revolution, potentially exacerbates existing social inequalities (Schiller, 2000). A new form of exploitation towards unpaid labour and offering products at no cost has emerged. The 'prosumer' is forced to pay for accessing the product they are giving at no cost, supporting exploitative nature of cyber capitalism. Thus, global capitalism is now rooted in the grassroots, supporting ideological and cultural competition, taking the little they have for survival but leaving them celebrating cultural imperialism notwithstanding the vulnerabilities that it creates.

Putting digital divide on a blind spot, the digital media enable ordinary people to engage in information and cultural production and dissemination while minimising barriers to ordinary people participation. In Africa, cell phones are common and ubiquitously used for interpersonal communication (Berger, 2009:13). Receiving and sending content using the cell phone has become relatively easy as most cell phones are equipped with capacities such as Wi-Fi access, the ability to receive digital broadcasts, and even built-in miniaturised data projectors (ibid). This has enabled networked communities to share information through voice, videos, and text as digital platforms converge. The emerging digital Media Entertainment and Information (MEI) offerings are the main drivers of smartphone, tablet and other connected device adoption. To some extent, this has influenced changing relationships with many other elements of daily life, such as health, consumer products and mobility, creating "hyper-connectivities" among imagined communities, affecting how people interact as well as impacting on cultures of the societies. However, on the other hand, even as technology turn out to be more affordable and internet access seems increasingly ubiquitous and efficient, a "digital divide" between the rich and the poor remains. The rich and the educated are still more likely than others to have good access to digital resources.

Methodology

The study engages online ethnography to review messages sent on Facebook, WhatsApp, YouTube and Twitter platforms. The idea of carrying out online ethnography on the Facebook, WhatsApp, YouTube and Twitter is because a lot of information circulates on these online news platforms with little gatekeeping. Therefore, it is appropriate to examine these social media platforms so as to understand the level of emergent insecurities and threats to individual lives and the nation at large.

Online ethnography is a computer mediated study of communities and culture. Here we examine patterns of communication and social relationships accomplished through language in online community groups. This method enables us to examine and understand the threats posed by emergent social media usually celebrated as media freedom. For the purpose of the study, we will examine the Facebook pages, WhatsApp groups, YouTube and Twitter handles for a duration of six (6) months, that is, between June 1, 2017 and December 30, 2017. This is a period in which social media use was heightened in Zimbabwe due mainly to factional politics within the ruling party ZANU PF. The ZANU-PF succession debate degenerated into fearsome, life and nation threatening battle putting the nation under siege. The battle ultimately led to the demise of Robert Mugabe and the rise of incumbent president Emmerson Dambudzo Mnangagwa[2].We now provide a description of how the online presences of the emerging social media produced insecurities and the analysis of the content of the online platforms as described above.

Freedom of expression: Online "tribal" wars and "ethnic" divisions in Zimbabwe

As social media creates situations in which people or online friends do not directly communicate with each other but interact with a hyperreal space, a space were models, images, and symbols no longer represent things they should be representing, "tribal" wars are fought in text, graphics, and voice over social media with no restrictions or legal instruments to limit the extent of the vitriol. The tension between the "ethnic" groups have spilled over into social media where language use is not regulated and calls for "tribal"

---

[2] Robert Mugabe is a former president of the Republic of Zimbabwe who resigned on 21 November 2017 after leading the nation as Prime Minister from 1980 to 1987 and as Executive president from 1987 to November 2017. EmmersonDambudzoMnangagwa is a long serving member of ZANU-PF from independence to present. He took over the reigns of ZANU-PF and government in dramatic circumstances after he was fired by Mugabe but re-instated by the army after two weeks.

attacks go unabated. Although the tension between the *Shona*[3] and the *Ndebeles*[4] is not a recent phenomenon, it has been intensified by the availability of the pervasive social media accessed by anyone with a gadget capable of accessing internet. It is in these situations where social media wars manifest in physical battles which include wars of words, fights and hooliganism. Although social media has been instrumental in creating the Habermasian public sphere, it fuels divisions along "tribal" and "ethnic" grounds. Facebook pages where Ndebeles and Shona square off are created and insults are hurled at each other without restrictions. The massacre of the Ndebele people in Zimbabwe during the *Gukurahundi*[5] era is still an open wound on Zimbabwean conscience. Zimbabweans are entrenched in genocidal "tribalism", which is a result of tragic decades of political manipulation by political leadership to incite hatred in order to control and retain power and social media is now being used to play a crucial role to influence divisions. The same applies to other platforms such as YouTube and WhatsApp where memes stereotyping some "tribes" and "ethnic" groups are circulated. Overtones of caricature, derision and ridicule flood social media platforms solely because digital media platforms offer anonymity. Identities are hidden and accountability is difficult to trace.

Of recent note in Zimbabwe, there has been an outcry on social media platforms such as Facebook, WhatsApp, YouTube, Twitter and others over the '*Mukaranga*[6]'jibe. This insult was clearly targeted at people who hail from Masvingo province. The online "tribal"

---

[3] The Shona are a predominant tribal group in Zimbabwe that geographically occupies the Northern, Eastern and Central parts of Zimbabwe.

[4] The Ndebele are a significantly large ethnic group that occupies the Southern region of Zimbabwe, covering Bulawayo, Matebeleland South, Matebeleland North and part of Midlands provinces.

[5] Gukurahundi is a satirical term employed soon after Zimbabwe's independence to suppress a seemingly Ndebele uprisings against a Mugabe-led government. The term means chuff, and so it meant whipping off the chuff. The Joshua Nkomo-led ZIPRA units were labeled dissidents and so were chuff in a legitimate government.

[6] Karanga is a Shona dialect that predominantly occupies the Southern part of Zimbabwe in Masvingo province.

insult transformed into non-digital spaces resulting in fights among people. Some people believed that the Masvingo memes were not a free value affair but were linked with national politics. Coincidentally, it was during the same period when the then Vice President Emmerson Mnangagwa, considered a *Karanga*, was being accused by the *ZANU PF G-40* faction as harbouring ambitions to take over from president Robert Gabriel Mugabe. Using social media, some people began to create memes and jokes mocking, belittling and insulting the people from Masvingo and there was a clear chance that it could be someone driving a political agenda. There was a publication that carried a news item about a physical fight between teens in Chivhu over the *Masvingo/Mukaranga* jibes[7]. "Ethnic" purgative is a result of ingrained hatred of other "tribes" and is usually politically motivated. The 1994 genocide of the Tutsis in Rwanda should have jolted us out of this idyllic stupor[8]. The *weMasvingo* jokes evoked hatred and fights among people in different social circles. A series of jokes which portray the people from Masvingo as dull, redundant and ostracised from current affairs are derogatory and have led to brawls, hatred and fights among people. The digital media platforms have therefore become sites for hegemonic contestations between and within nation states. We are left convinced that the *Masvingo/Mukaranga* jibes circulated on Social media were politically axiological considering that Emmerson Dambudzo Mnangagwa, a contender in the race to succeed Robert Mugabe, also hails from the *Karanga* "ethnic" group in Midlands[9]. Also, of interest in this scenario is the passion with which social media jibes were taken by the Grace Mugabe-led G40[10] faction as evidenced by Grace's public reactions at Youth Interface Rallies.

---

[7] August 2017 edition of TellZim News published a story where two teens from Chivhu fought over the Masvingo/Karanga jibes.

[8] Two films: Sometimes in April and Hotel Rwanda portray horrendous tribal genocides in Rwanda in 1994.

[9] History has it that EmmersonMnangagwa is originally from Masvingo province, Chivi District though he relocated to Midlands Province.

[10] Grace Mugabe is the wife of Robert Mugabe. G40 means Generation 40 which simply implied ZANU-PF insiders who wanted

A meme circulating on WhatsApp platform attacking the Karanga people from Masvingo

Popular culture which thrives on innocuous things such as jokes, rumours, cartoons, popular music etc aptly drives home the ideological struggles that Zimbabwe witnessed via social media platforms, (Willems, 2010). The digital media platforms become cultural sites of ideological struggles and representations. Popular songs were enacted to graphical representations to enhance the ethnic fights on social media in Zimbabwe in jostling for succession and Mugabe's attention.

Social media and emergent insecurities: a critical examination of social media as a threat to national security in Zimbabwe

Social media has far reaching social and security implications for the people of Zimbabwe, the government and its national security agencies such as the military and the state security. Social media

the party to be led by youngsters. It is a ZANU-PF faction that fronted Grace Mugabe in the succession battle within the ruling party.

present challenges to national security to a great extent (Cuman, 2012). While in such countries as Syria, Tunisia and Egypt, social media was used to mobilise, share opinion and influence change, in Zimbabwe, social media has been at the fore-front of several actions which may be described as security threats. These security threats may range from causing unnecessary shortages of basic commodities and cash, the recent polarity within ZANU-PF between the Emmerson Mnangagwa-led Lacoste[11] faction and the Grace Mugabe-led G40 faction, leading to the vicious circle that saw the sacking of the Vice President (Emmerson Mnangagwa) and his subsequent re-engagement as the new president under the protection of the military and the fall of Mugabes and the G40 cabal. To a great extent, social media played a crucial role as it was at the centre of the brawl, disseminating information through text, voice, videos, and pictures.

Rumour and misinformation occupy an important place in destabilising the state security. Although it has not been established whether the rumour was peddled by the enemies of the state or by ordinary citizens, what has been established is that rumours affected economic operations as panic buying and cash hoarding syndrome crept in. Based on its ubiquity and its pervasiveness, online prosumers began to create and circulate statements which caused panic and alarm among the people of Zimbabwe. For instance, statements announcing looming shortages of basic commodities and cash resulted in panic buying and hoarding of cash. The ultimate caused artificial shortages of basic commodities and cash, denting the people's confidence in the banking sector and the government in power. Long queues resurfaced at banks as some people would sleep over in bank queues. What vexes here is that the message does not have a clear origin and there is no one who can be responsible for its distribution regardless of the extent of its damage. Furthermore, there is no legal instrument to deal with such behaviour and an infringement ultra vires the constitution of Zimbabwe. Usually, such messages are copies without origin and they spread quickly as they are referred from one media platform to another, creating what

---

[11] Lacoste is another faction within ZANU-PF wa led by EmmersonMnangagwa. It rivaled G40 in the succession battle.

Baudrillard referred to as "simulacra' (Baudrillard, 1972). Indeed, it is an attack on the national economy, hence it's a security issue. On the other hand, it can be viewed also a political agenda, a threat to the incumbent government designed for regime change agenda.

On the same note, in the period stretching from June 1, 2017 to December 30, 2017, Facebook pages, WhatsApp and Twitter discussions were awash with political fights within the governing party, ZANU PF, jeopardising national security. The succession wars within the ruling party degenerated into factionalism within both the party and the government. Social media as an open form of communication took a central position in these wars most of the time, fuelling feuds among party members. Social media created situations in which people or online friends did not directly communicate with each other but where engaged in interaction within a hyperreal space, a space were new models, images, and symbols are not real but clearly designed to cause anger, pain, alarm, and despondence among the factions of the same political party. For instance, refashioned graphics indicating the 'infamous' vice president holding a cup inscribed 'I AM THE BOSS' would be circulated on social media inviting vitriol from Grace Mugabe denouncing an unfounded and unrealistic social media graphic. At times graphics would be circulated showing both Mnangagwa and Grace Mugabe sternly looking at each other. The fact that these issues were then referred to during political rallies indicates that social media effects were playing a central role in the feud. The Gramscian concept of 'incorporation' where digital media platforms as sites of ideological contestations facilitate co-option of debased things such as social media jokes and jibes by the ruling elite to use them as ammunition in political factional wars becomes central in this debate. Grace Mugabe would be heard at Youth Interface Rallies (organized at the behest of G40 faction) referring to some of these social media messages.

The use of social media as new communication platforms by some government officials in Zimbabwe introduced a serious conflation of private and national security concern. YouTube, Facebook, Twitter, and WhatsApp platforms were at the centre of distribution of the messages around the country and its diaspora. For instance, Grace Mugabe rallies dubbed "meet the people" to oust the then Vice President Dr Joyce Mujuru were all distributed on YouTube while updates were being done through WhatsApp and Twitter platforms copying each other and at times exaggerating through emphasis on words or graphics and voice, taking advantage of social media ability to distribute messages through voice, picture and video and written format. Social media has become the new and effective channels of propaganda distribution in Zimbabwe. Instead of treating them as alternative to traditional media, social media are being used to support the traditional media such as the press and the broadcasting media in Zimbabwe. On social media, old media such as recorded radio programmes and the traditional press are being distributed to reach wider audience. For instance, TellZim News lead stories are firstly featured on social media such as WhatsApp and then redistributed to other social media channels such as Twitter, Facebook and YouTube. Also, links are being provided on WhatsApp platforms to redirect readers to other platforms for more news or detailed information. At the end of the day, people are overwhelmed with information whose origin and authenticity they are not quite sure of, making that information simulacra as it is its own origin. This renders the digital media susceptible and uncertain. Uncertainty obtains because the 'space of the representable' is cluttered up by the 'hyperinformation'(Baudrillard and Maclean, 1985:5). It is important to note that in that thick of confusion and uncertainty, some information which pose threat to individuals and national security at large is distributed as the war to outwit each other intensifies. The factional fights within ZANU PF based on factional lines allegedly led by Professor Jonathan Moyo and Emmerson Mnangagwa as they tried to outwit each other were centred on social media. The fight ended up posing a serious national threat, as the Vice President was later dismissed although he later came back to take over the presidium, leaving Professor Jonathan Moyo without option but to seek refuge elsewhere.

The then Minister of Higher and Tertiary Education Professor Jonathan Moyo began his assault on Mnangagwa through Twitter and YouTube platforms. These copies would then be redistributed through the WhatsApp and Facebook channels. For instance, he attacked Emmerson Mnangagwa, describing him as not presidential material in a video distributed through social media. At this occasion, he, with reckless wanton, attacked a very senior government official, subjecting the nation to security threats.

In a presentation titled, " *Whither the Nationalist Project in Zimbabwe*[12]" distributed on YouTube and other social media channels, the office of the Vice President and his person was embarrassed, ridiculed and derided, posing yet another national security concern as the military joined in warning the minister's behaviour as reckless and a threat to national security. It is common

---

[12] Jonathan Moyo's public lecture at SAPES in June 2017.

sense that when a top government official of the Vice President's statue is attacked and exposed, and has become insecure, the whole nation is also insecure (Amedie, 2015). Attacking the Vice President on social media, advancing serous allegations is an attack on the state itself.

Successionists who are a minority in the Party but who are very vocal and are now openly backing Vice President Mnangagwa to succeed President Mugabe … they see the Vice President as the Party's Presidential Candidate in 2018…, you then must now come to terms with the so-called Lacoste or Team Lacoste which is presenting itself in general and its candidate, VP Mnangagwa in particular, as a shoo-in. ….And if you go to the braais (where they have their braais) because these are masters of whispers you will find them quiet excited saying "*TapindaTapinda*" (we are in) [laughter], …Then they say "*MudharaAchauya*" (the big man is coming) [laughter]…This is because the Team and its leader, in my assessment, have no sense or regard for the importance of collective belonging or having a view of national unity (which is inclusive) which is fundamental to the Nationalist Project, which was fundamental before independence and remains fundamental even today. If people start saying "*ndechedu ichi*" (its ours) who are you, you were not there. It's a problem… Of greater concern to me about the threat to order and stability posed by the so-called Team Lacoste and its leader are the issues contained in a document dubbed "Blue Ocean" that started circulating in 2015 and in an interview that Vice President Mnangagwa gave to an elite British Magazine the New Statesman last year entitled, "The Last Days of Robert Mugabe". These two documents tell a very sad story about a sinister programme of capturing state institutions and targeting individuals for extrajudicial attacks in ways that betray the Nationalist Project in as much as they threaten order and stability in the country…; the notion peddled by the so-called Team Lacoste that its leader is the only one who is above or senior to everyone else below President Mugabe is false, … It is false and that falsehood should now be engaged and stated. There are others, that are senior to the leader of the so-called Team Lacoste in the Party. One of them …is Dr Sydney Sekeramayi. (*extract from Jonathan Moyo presentation at SAPES Trust*)

'Blue Ocean' is yet another politibro-leaked video and was found on YouTube attacking the person and the office of the Vice President on social media. It is a 72-minute video presentation reportedly made by Professor Jonathan Moyo to the Zanu-PF Politburo on the 19th of June, 2017 and found itself on YouTube, WhatsApp, Facebook and virtually some social media platforms. In the presentation, Jonathan Moyo alleges that Vice President Emmerson Mnangagwa and his loyalists are aiming to succeed President Mugabe through a number of evil schemes. Some of the schemes were so intense and posed a threat to national security.

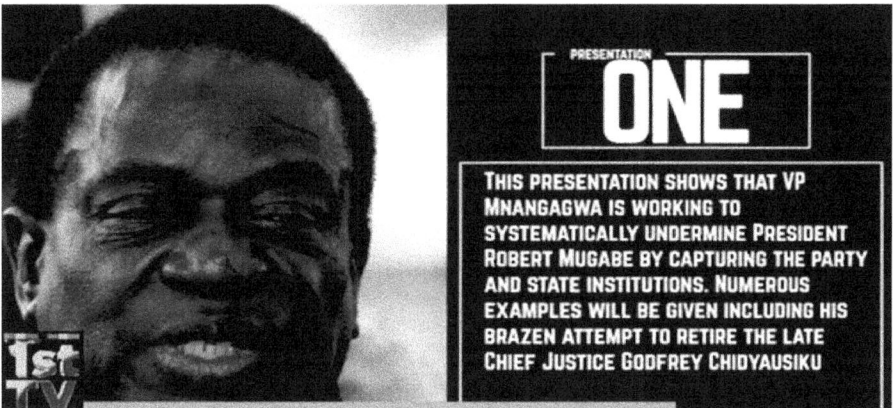

Adapted from 1ˢᵗ TV (A presentation by Minister Jonathan Moyo to the politibro)

The document had been leaked and was found on YouTube. It was supposed to be a presentation to the cabinet on the alleged illicit dealings of the then Vice President Emmerson Mnangagwa but it found its own way on social media, raising tension among ZANU PF supporters. These issues have a strong bearing on the nature of national security as warned by the military. The challenge comes when such information found its way on virtual public platforms especially when it is alleged to have been advanced by the Minister of State. Indeed, while no one can confirm the truth or falsehood of these documents, the million dollar question is: why should such high profile matters be discussed on open platforms such as the unsanctioned social media? Some would suggest that it was a propaganda campaign to oust the Vice President from office and replace him with Grace Mugabe, a suggestion which was later confirmed by the sacking of the Vice President and the endorsement of Grace Mugabe as the candidate for the then vacant position of the Vice President. The vulnerability caused by the use of social media among the generality of Zimbabwean people, the politicians and the government at large gradually became a real threat to national security, resulting in a classic military intervention. The intervention was classic as it was never precedented anywhere in the world. While some classified it as a military coup, others believed that it was just an operation to restore order after a series of disorders in both the party and the government. Whether it was a military coup or an operation to restore order, social media played a central role to advance factional fights, anger, panic, pandemonium and reactions in both the ruling party ZANU PF and the government. While one cannot blame the availability of social media based on the recklessness of its users, it is also pertinent to advance that its availability and capability can pose some national threats and insecurity especially when it is used recklessly.

As reality fall and social media rise, new signs, images, voices and models circulate, purporting to represent some institutional authorities, causing confusion among the online media consumers and the nation in general. Social media enables the unlawful use of national army logo and colours by anyone due to their availability online. As a result, messages purporting to be coming from the military headquarters began to circulate on WhatsApp and copied to other social media platforms instructing Zimbabweans to stop public protests with immediate effect. What was vexing was the timing of the message. The message circulated in the wake of the Vice President sacking and as ZANU PF prepared for its 10th and the last of "Youth Interface" rallies. What irked most was that this was the message circulated at the height of political tension with the factionalism battle at its peak. The message threw the public into panic mode as they suspected military intervention in ZANU PF factional battles and any intervention of military nature in political situation is always unpredictable. The message created discomfort in ZANU PF and in the country at large as people were not sure of the action the army was about to take.

The Zimbabwe National Army (ZNA) stepped in to dispel the rumours adding that all its notices are signed to show authenticity. ZNA urged local people to disregard such a message circulating on social media platforms claiming that the ZNA has recommended the suspension of all demonstrations due to heightened political clashes in the ruling Zanu PF party and opposition parties. In a statement signed by the Army Public Relations Director, Lieutenant Alphios Makotore, the army said:

> The ZNA would like to categorically state that it does not communicate its activities and or intentions through social media. The social media article must therefore be discarded and dismissed with the contempt it so deserves. The ZNA noted that the unsigned statement circulating on social media did not originate from the ZNA. (*The Herald* *5 October 2017*)

This statement was issued to diffuse malicious statements aimed at disturbing peace and stability in the country by circulating such inflammatory contents on social media. These statements were created by imposters masquerading as ZDF members and enhanced by the availability of the untraceable social media authors.

The crisis of social media use could not be easily contained in Zimbabwe as events continued unfolding causing panic among the general public, politicians and government employees as each day had a new message on social media. As the former President Robert Mugabe got older with each day, ZANU PF succession battles and factional fights intensified and were picked up by social media. They became exaggerated and reduced into graphical presentations, further exacerbating anger and responses. The hyperbolic elements in the social media communications are the ones that create the super-real, thereby blurring the real and the imaginary. The battle took a dramatic twist as Vice President Mnangagwa was allegedly said to have consumed poisoned ice cream from Gushungo Dairies at a rally in Gwanda and was flown by a helicopter for treatment at a medical facility in Gweru, and then to South Africa. Although no authentic media mentioned that he ate poison-laced ice cream, social media intensified the feud by putting claims that the Vice President had eaten poison-laced ice cream from Gushungo Dairies and memes began circulating on social media. Incidentally, Gushungo Dairies had given people ice cream at the rally and is owned by the then first (Mugabe) family which was already fighting the Vice President. The connection of these events did not spare the Vice President (VP) and his sympathisers, dividing the nation. This further intensified the animosity between the Vice President and the first family as social media refuelled the issue by insisting that VP Mnangagwa had consumed poisoned ice cream from Gushungo Dairies, a company owned by the then first family. Further comic posts were circulating on social media and the following is one example:

*Tichauya ne ice cream tione mukagara nemufaro ipapo (*We will bring ice cream and see if you do not panic*) (posted Tellzim WhatsApp group by Wakurawarerwa on 16 august 2017)*

On social media, ice cream was recreated to be a weapon rather a tan delicacy. This irritated the first family especially the then first lady Dr Grace Mugabe who intensified the campaign for the fall of Vice President Mnangagwa.

Given the above scenarios that obtained in Zimbabwe on digital media platforms and their translation onto real political platforms such as Youth Interface Rallies, we are persuaded to call unedited, raw and unowned news/information that circulate on digital media platforms 'news litter' and the digital media platforms 'media dustbins'. However, it is the power of social media to court consumers to consume the 'news litter' that should not go unchecked in the academic circles. Zimbabwe has witnessed the ZANU-PF elites rummaging the 'media dustbins' in search of 'news litter' to both attack perceived foes and to enhance their potential in succeeding Robert Mugabe at the helm of ZANU-PF and government. At the end of it all, we should not be surprised to realise that the much-celebrated 'media scent' (freedom of speech and expression) does not take long before it gets stale and smelly (posing threats and uncertainties, panic and confusion). The oxymoronic nature of social media is realised at two planes: they can cause mayhem, panic and pandemonium if not well-handled and yet they can stand as neutral counter publics that do not budge to influence from the ruling elite. We also note positively the potential of social media to pose as public platforms where battle of wits can be fought on virtual spaces as experienced in Zimbabwe between June 2017 and November 2017 when Emmerson Mnangagwa (representing team Lacoste) and Jonathan Moyo (representing G40) undressed each other.

Another observation out of this discussion is one that is advanced by Sardar and van Loon (1999) who argue that sometimes there is a mathematical line between high and low culture. We herein take digital media platforms as popular culture artefacts if we are to go by Raymond Williams' explanation of popular culture wherein he says that it is that culture that has popular demand. Now with the rate at which digital media platforms court and win users, it suffices to say that they belong to that category of popular culture. The irony, as demonstrated in the above discussion, is in the ruling elite gesture of also dabbling in the same pool with the masses.

A pen is mightier than a sword: regulating the social media in Zimbabwe

Realising the nature of insecurities and threats paused by social media, the state began to warn the public against what they called abuse of social media. The Postal and Telecommunications Regulatory Authority of Zimbabwe (POTRAZ) issued a warning against abuse of social media:

> Together with all the telecommunications service providers in Zimbabwe have noted with concern, the gross irresponsible use of social media and telecommunication services made through our infrastructure and communication platforms over the past few days….We are therefore warning members of the public that from the date of this notice, any person caught in possession of, generating, sharing or passing on abusive, threatening, subversive or offensive telecommunication messages, including WhatsApp or any other social media messages that may be deemed to cause despondency, incite

violence, threaten citizens and cause unrest, will be arrested and dealt with accordingly in the national interest (POTRAZ 2017).

Having realised that "A pen is mightier than a sword", the state intensified its effort to legislate the use of cyber-space including the social media. In the last days of President Mugabe's rule, a new ministry was established. In a stance emphasising how serious the state was in dealing with Cyber-threats, a new ministry headed by Hon Patrick Chinamasa, the *Ministry of Cyber Security, Threat Detection and Mitigation,* was established. This was viewed by cyber enthusiasts as a direct attack on their freedom of expression as given by the Constitution of Zimbabwe and enhanced by the social media. As a result, they began to register their disgruntlement through circulating memes on various social media websites mocking the new minister, equating his new cabinet post to *the National WhatsApp Group Administrator.*

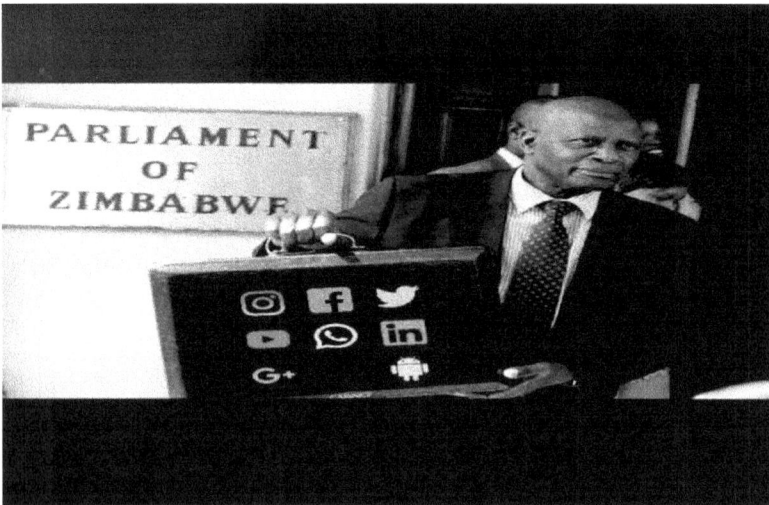

A meme showing Honourable Patrick Chinamasa holding a briefcase emblazoned with social media signage signalling the dawn of a new fight against social media by the state.

The stance taken by the state to regulate social media is neither good nor bad, it depends on the rationale behind regulation and how the law will be applied. The significance of democratised communication as a core element essential in democracy does not, however, leave out the possibility of the same democratised communications platforms being abused to the detriment of national security and other emerging threats and insecurities. For instance, in South Africa, the media is alleged to have been used to perpetuate racism during apartheid and xenophobia in the post-apartheid era. In Rwanda, it was used to spread hatred that led to the 1994 genocide. Hence, while jealously guarding against infringement on freedom of expression, there should be duties and responsibility on the beneficiaries of the democratised communication. Media regulation has taken a centre stage in the global world as the struggle for balancing effective media regulation and democratic rights to freedom of expression proves to be hard and unattainable (Sarpong, cited in Akpojivi and Fosu, 2013). Social Media regulation can be justified when it is done in the "public interest".

`Public interest' refers to the extent to which the public sphere values are clearly identified and articulated and is likely to be key to whether meaningful objectives can be established for the regulatory regime (Feintuck and Varney, 2006). However, public interest can be essential to the longer-term welfare of society and its members (McQuail, 2010). Public interest originates from the will of the people. It is what the majority wants (Iosifidis; 2013; 24). Furthering this argument, Iosifidis (2013) advanced that Public interest should be decided by absolute standard of value regardless of what citizens want. It embodies the power of the people and emphasises that the public interests override the interests of the individuals to create a common value. In this case, public interest is considered a 'common good' which presupposes that the society benefits in the long run by adopting the principles that are accepted by the entire public. The use of social media in Zimbabwe during the last few months of 2017 does not represent 'Public interest', calling for regulation of social media to enforce responsible posting and desist from incitement of violence, advocacy of hatred or hate speech, malicious injury to a person's reputation or dignity among others and causing national insecurity. Indeed, regulation must be done in protection of public order and support for instruments of government and justice. In addition, it must protect individual and sectional rights and interests that might be trampled by unrestricted use of public means of communication. It also must promote access, freedom to communicate, diversity and universal provision as well as securing communicative and cultural ends chosen by the people (McQuail 2010).

Conclusion

Social media have been very active in Zimbabwe, triggering wide celebration on freedom of expression and access to information considered under siege since 2000 when the government passed Access to Information and Protection of Privacy Act (AIPPA). However, what has come to reality as soon as the celebratory mode died down are the glaring vulnerabilities being caused by cyber space-induced freedoms. Indeed, a new culture has emerged, one that is impervious to the old forms of resistance and one that is impenetrable by theories rooted in traditional metaphysical assumptions. Culture is now dominated by simulations: objects and discourses which have no firm origin, no referent, no ground or foundation (Baudrillard, 1972).While these simulations are fascinating and have become centres of alternative media or a public sphere, it is hardly noticed that these alternative media for dissent are emergent insecurities and threats which do not warrant celebration but pretermit.

References

Amedie. J. (2015) *The impact of social media on society. Advanced writing: Pop culture intersections.*

Barret, T. (1977) *Modernism and Postmodernism: An Overview with Art Examples*, in Suggs, M. and Hutchens, J. (1977) *Art Education: Content and Practice in a Postmodern Era*, Washington, DC:NAEA.

Baudrillard, J. and Maclean, M. (1985) *The Masses: The Implosion of the Social in the Media*, New Literary History, Vol 16, No. 3, 577-589.

Burger, G. (2009) *The changing media ecosystem: what African media leaders need to know; Doing Digital Media in Africa Prospects*, Konrad-Adenauer-Stiftung, Johannesburg, South Africa.

Cuman, K. (2012) *the role of social media in international relations. Arab revolution of 2011.*

Dahlberg, L. (2001). *The Habermasian Public Sphere encounters cyber-reality* [online]. 2001. Vol. 3, no. 8, p. 83–96.
[Accessed 22 December 2017]. Retrieved from:
http://www.dlib.si/details/URN:NBN:SI:DOC-QW0PMVBC.

Fraser, N. (1990) *Rethinking the Public Sphere: A Contribution to the Critique of Actually Existing Democracy*, Duke University Press.

Fraser, N. (1992) '*Rethinking the Public Sphere: A Contribution to the Critique of Actually Existing Democracy.*' In Calhoun, C. (Ed.) *Habermas and the Public Sphere.* Cambridge: Massachusetts, MIT Press. pp 109-142.

Feintucky, M. ad Varney, M. (2006) *Media regulation, public interest and law*, Edinburg University Press.

Garrison, B. (1996) *Successful Strategies for Computer-Assisted Reporting*, New Jersey: Lawrence Erlbaum Associates.

Giddens, A. (1984) *The Constitution of Society. Outline of the Theory of Structuration.* Cambridge, Polity Press.

Gordon, R. (2009) '*Social Media: The Grown Shifts*'. Nieman Reports. Nieman Foundation for Journalism at Harvard, Fall 2009.

Harper, R. A. (2010) '*The Social Media Revolution: Exploring the Impact on Journalism and News Media Organisations*' Inquiries Journal/Student Pulse, 2(03).

Hicks, S.R.C. (2004) *Explaining Postmodernism: Scepticism and Socialism from Rousseau to Foucault*, Scholarly Publishing: Arizona.

Holtz, S. (2000) '*The Continuing Need for Professional Journalism*'. *A shell of my Formal Self*, Accredited Business Communicator, 18 May 2009.

Li, C. and Bernoff, J. (2008) *Groundswell: Winning in a World Transformed by Social Technologies*, Boston: Harvard Business Press.

Moyo, L. (2015) *Digital age as Ethical Maze: Citizen Journalism Ethics during Crises in Zimbabwe and South Africa*, African Journalism Studies, 36:4, 125-144,DOI:10.1080/23743670.1119494.

McQuail, D. (2010) *Why Regulate the Media?*, Leicester, University.

Nsude and Onwe E. C (2017) *Social Media and Security challenges in Nigeria: The way forward*, World Applied Sciences Journal 35 (6).

Pavlik,J. (2001). *Journalism and the new media.* New York: Columbia.

Sardar, Z. and van Loon, B. (1999) *Introducing Cultural Studies*, Icon Books Ltd: Cambridge.

Schiller, D. (1999). *Digital capitalism: networking the global market system.* Cambridge, Mass, MIT Press.

www.ingramcontent.com/pod-product-compliance
Lightning Source LLC
Chambersburg PA
CBHW060019030426
42334CB00019B/2104